Microsoft SQL Server 2012 Integration Services: An Expert Cookbook

Over 80 expert recipes to design, create, and deploy
SSIS packages

Reza Rad

Pedro Perfeito

BIRMINGHAM - MUMBAI

Microsoft SQL Server 2012 Integration Services: An Expert Cookbook

Copyright © 2012 Packt Publishing

All rights reserved. No part of this book may be reproduced, stored in a retrieval system, or transmitted in any form or by any means, without the prior written permission of the publisher, except in the case of brief quotations embedded in critical articles or reviews.

Every effort has been made in the preparation of this book to ensure the accuracy of the information presented. However, the information contained in this book is sold without warranty, either express or implied. Neither the authors, nor Packt Publishing, and its dealers and distributors will be held liable for any damages caused or alleged to be caused directly or indirectly by this book.

Packt Publishing has endeavored to provide trademark information about all of the companies and products mentioned in this book by the appropriate use of capitals. However, Packt Publishing cannot guarantee the accuracy of this information.

First published: May 2012

Production Reference: 1140512

Published by Packt Publishing Ltd.
Livery Place
35 Livery Street
Birmingham B3 2PB, UK.

ISBN 978-1-84968-524-5

www.packtpub.com

Cover Image by Artie Ng (artherng@yahoo.com.au)

Credits

Authors

Reza Rad

Pedro Perfeito

Reviewers

Phil Brammer

Brenner Grudka Lira

April L. Rains

Rafael Salas

Milla Smirnova

Acquisition Editor

Rukshana Khambatta

Lead Technical Editors

Kedar Bhat

Meeta Rajani

Technical Editors

Joyslita D'Souza

Manasi Poonthottam

Aaron Rosario

Project Coordinator

Leena Purkait

Proofreaders

Mario Cecere

Chris Smith

Indexer

Monica Ajmera Mehta

Graphics

Valentina D'silva

Manu Joseph

Production Coordinator

Aparna Bhagat

Cover Work

Aparna Bhagat

Foreword

Data Transformation Services (DTS) was Microsoft's first entrance into the world of advanced data transformation and task-oriented tools, allowing users to rapidly move data from one point to another, or to perform common tasks such as FTPing files from one server to another. New to SQL Server 2000, this tool was the foundation for many developers' toolkits. The UI was easy to use and understand, precedence constraints could be applied between tasks ensuring business rules were maintained, and custom code could be added to perform advanced tasks not found in the boxed feature set. DTS is still the bar against which many measure SQL Server Integration Services.

SQL Server Integration Services (SSIS), introduced in SQL Server 2005 and largely unchanged through SQL Server 2008 R2, was a rewrite of both the toolset and the paradigm by which developers were used to thinking as compared to the relatively easy-to-use DTS. SSIS has its strengths in separating the work surface of a DTS package into distinct parts, the Control Flow and the Data Flow. The Control Flow is designed to direct the "flow" of the package, ensure dependencies are met before executing a downstream task, perform looping operations over a varied list of sources, execute SQL statements, and so on. A Data Flow Task is designed to move data from one source to another, transforming data along the way. The separation allows for greater flexibility in developing a package by limiting the scope of what a developer can edit at once, and by allowing specific tasks to be copied and subsequently reused.

SSIS is not without its list of negatives, however. Through SQL Server 2008 R2, an SSIS package was a single entity, which could be executed in any number of places from within Business Intelligence Developer Studio, from the filesystem, or on a SQL Server instance. In a shop that has a large number of packages deployed, it was extremely difficult to manage all of the packages and track all of the activities that the packages were doing. This meant that developers were forced to write their own logging solutions to capture data such as row counts, start and end times, audit information, and any other pertinent information necessary to support the package. SSIS also has a steep learning curve, which many developers find very hard to overcome.

SQL Server 2012 introduces some very welcome additions to the existing SSIS product. The most welcome addition, and the one I am most excited about, is the inclusion of a true server-side component to SSIS. Choosing to deploy packages to the server will allow developers and administrators to finally get ease of deployment, and capture the most often requested information about the execution of packages. This server component, called the SSIS Catalog, and its new project deployment model allow administrators to override logging levels, set input parameters, and view built-in reports in an easy-to-use presentation format. In the new project deployment model, the project build process creates a `.ispac` file, which can be shared with any person doing the physical deployment of the project. The file includes all of the packages in the project, any shared project-level connections, and other metadata pertaining to the project. Double-clicking on the file will start the deployment wizard. Very easy.

Some other changes found in SQL Server 2012 SSIS are a revamped design surface helping to meet accessibility requirements, full undo/redo capability, a removed limit of 4,000 characters on expressions, ability to change variable scopes, and so on.

This book will walk you through, step-by-step, each major feature of SSIS in SQL Server 2012, and how to use them. Pedro and Reza have given contextual examples where possible, and you will be able to download and implement them yourself to help you follow along each recipe. If you are an experienced SSIS developer or you are new to the product, this book will be an often-referenced resource in your bookshelf. Pedro and Reza have put together a great reference book that I know you'll enjoy.

Phil Brammer
Microsoft MVP – SQL Server

About the Authors

Reza Rad is an author, trainer, speaker, and consultant. He has a BSc in Computer Engineering; he has more than 10 years' experience in programming and development mostly on Microsoft technologies. He received the Microsoft Most Valuable Professional (MVP) award in SQL Server in 2011 and 2012 for his dedication in Microsoft BI and specially SSIS. He has been working on the Microsoft BI suite for more than six years. He is an SSIS/MSBI/.NET Trainer and also software and BI Consultant at some companies and institutes. His articles on different aspects of technologies, specially on SSIS, can be found on his blog `http://www.rad.pasfu.com`.

He was the co-author of *SQL Server MVP Deep Dives Volume 2*. He is one of the active members on online technical forums such as MSDN and Experts-Exchange. He is a Microsoft Certified Professional (MCP); Microsoft Certified Technology Specialist (MCTS) and Microsoft Certified IT Professional (MCITP) in Business Intelligence (BI). His e-mail address is `a.raad.g@gmail.com`.

I would like to thank my wife who has been a wonderful supporter in writing this book; she encouraged me a lot to complete this book, she was a light during my difficult moments.

I would also like to thank my parents and sister, who were my teachers for many years of my life.

I would like to thank Pedro, my good friend who helped a lot in writing this book. He did a good job in completing this book in his busy hours with full-time job and teaching.

Pedro Perfeito was born in 1977 in Portugal and currently works as a BI Senior Consultant and Developer at Novabase. He's also an invited teacher in master and short-master BI degrees at IUL-ISCTE (Lisbon) and at Universidade Portucalense (UPT-Porto) respectively. He received the Microsoft award Microsoft Most Valuable Professional (MVP) in 2010, 2011, and 2012 for all his dedication and contribution in helping theoretical and practical issues in the various BI communities. He is also the co-author of *SQL Server MVP Deep Dives Volume 2*. He has several Microsoft certifications including MCP, MCSD, MCTS-Web, MCTS-BI, and MCITP-BI. He also has worldwide certifications in the area of BI provided by TDWI/CBIP (The Data Warehouse Institute, http://www.tdwi.org). He's currently preparing for his PhD degree on BI. For further details you can visit his personal blog at http://www.pedrocgd.blogspot.com or even contact him directly at pperfeito@hotmail.com.

I would like to express my gratitude to all teams at Packt who trusted me—a Portuguese author—and helped me complete this book. I would like to thank my friend and co-author of this book Reza Rad because without him this book would not have been possible.

I have furthermore to thank Barbara Chambel for all the support she gave me since the first moment at Novabase, to Luis Ferreira (Project Manager at Banco de Portugal) and Simão Fernandes (ex-student and colleague at Novabase) for all hints and complaints from the previous SSIS version (you both know which ones I mean!) and for all my Master BI students from Universidade Portucalense (Oporto) and from ISCTE-IUL (Lisbon) who have directly and indirectly motivated me in this challenge.

I am deeply indebted to Dr. Maria José Trigueiros for all the encouragement to go inside this amazing world of Business Intelligence and make my dream come true. She's not physically with us but she will be remembered for ever.

Especially, I would like to give my special thanks to my family and my girlfriend Joana whose patient love helped me to complete this work!

Thanks to all who I haven't mentioned here and who believed in me, even more than myself.

About the Reviewers

Phil Brammer, a fifth year Microsoft MVP in SQL Server, has over 12 years' data warehousing experience in various technologies from reporting through ETL to database administration. He has worked with SSIS since 2007 and he continues to play an active role in the SSIS community via online resources as well as his technical blog site, SSISTalk.com. He has contributed to SQL Saturdays, SQL PASS Summits, and the first volume of the *SQL Server MVP Deep Dives* book.

Most recently he has taken on the role of a full-time operational DBA managing over 120 database instances in the health-care insurance industry. He is an avid golfer and loves spending time with his wife and two children.

Brenner Grudka Lira joined NeuroTech as a Data Analyst in 2012. He has a Bachelor's degree in Computer Science from the Catholic University of Pernambuco in Recife, Brazil. He also has experience in building and modeling Data Warehouses and has knowledge of Oracle Warehouse Builder, SQL Server Integration Services, SAP Business Objects, and Oracle Business Intelligence Standard Edition One. Today, he is dedicated to the study of Business Intelligence with focus on the ETL process and Risk Management in Financial Operations.

April L. Rains has 13 years of experience building Business Intelligence, Web, and Windows applications using Microsoft tools and platforms. Working in the transportation and logistics industry for many years provided numerous opportunities for ETL, EAI, and trading partner EDI using both SSIS and BizTalk. She has a wide range of hands-on experience in multiple roles across the application lifecycle. You can e-mail her at april@aprilrains.com or contact her through her website at www.aprilrains.com.

I would like to thank my son Kieran who provides amazing and never-ending inspiration to me.

Rafael Salas is a Data Warehousing and Business Intelligence professional with more than a decade of experience in many industries and Fortune 500 companies. He provides technical leadership and helps organizations to improve performance through Business Intelligence strategies and solutions. His credentials include a Bachelor's degree in Computer Sciences, a Master's degree in Business and Technology, and a number of industry certifications. He has been recognized as Microsoft Most Valuable Professional (MVP) since 2007 and is a published author, blogger, and frequent speaker at conferences and technology community events. His specialties include architecture, Data Warehouse appliances, data integration, data quality, OLAP databases, and Dimensional Modeling. You can find more about him on his blog at www.rafael-salas.com.

Milla Smirnova is a Data Architect, DBA, and BI specialist. She possesses over 10 years of experience in Information Technology; most of those years of experience are in SQL Server Administration and Development. As her involvement with Business Intelligence technologies increased drastically within the last few years so has her passion for ETL design, development, and optimization utilizing SSIS.

I would like to thank my wonderful husband Larry for all his help and support. I would like to thank Maria and Nikolay as well.

I would also like to thank everyone at Packt Publishing for their encouragement and guidance.

www.PacktPub.com

Support files, eBooks, discount offers and more

You might want to visit www.PacktPub.com for support files and downloads related to your book.

Did you know that Packt offers eBook versions of every book published, with PDF and ePub files available? You can upgrade to the eBook version at www.PacktPub.com and as a print book customer, you are entitled to a discount on the eBook copy. Get in touch with us at service@packtpub.com for more details.

At www.PacktPub.com, you can also read a collection of free technical articles, sign up for a range of free newsletters and receive exclusive discounts and offers on Packt books and eBooks.

http://PacktLib.PacktPub.com

Do you need instant solutions to your IT questions? PacktLib is Packt's online digital book library. Here, you can access, read and search across Packt's entire library of books.

Why Subscribe?

- Fully searchable across every book published by Packt
- Copy and paste, print and bookmark content
- On demand and accessible via web browser

Free Access for Packt account holders

If you have an account with Packt at www.PacktPub.com, you can use this to access PacktLib today and view nine entirely free books. Simply use your login credentials for immediate access.

Instant Updates on New Packt Books

Get notified! Find out when new books are published by following @PacktEnterprise on Twitter, or the *Packt Enterprise* Facebook page.

Table of Contents

Preface

Microsoft SQL Server 2012 Integration Services: An Expert Cookbook is a complete guide for everyone, from a novice to a professional in Integration Services 2012. SQL Server Integration Services is an ETL tool, which stands for Extract Transform and Load. There is a need for a data transfer system in all operational systems these days, and SSIS is one of the best data transfer tools. In this book, all aspects of SSIS 2012 are discussed with lots of real-world scenarios to help readers to understand usage of SSIS in every environment.

What this book covers

Chapter 1, Getting Started with SQL Server Integration Services, provides an overview of the ETL concepts and ETL terminologies, why ETL is needed in the technology world, and what problems ETL will solve. Then an overview of SSIS as an ETL tool is provided to help readers to get an overall view of the other parts of the book.

Chapter 2, Control Flow Tasks, explores all Control Flow Tasks with real-world samples of each Task. The reader will learn what each Task stands for, what is its usage, real-world scenarios, and the new tasks available in SSIS 2012.

Chapter 3, Data Flow Task Part 1—Extract and Load, explains the data sources and data destinations under the Data Flow Task. Data Flow Task is the most functional part of SSIS, to which an SSIS Developer probably dedicates most time.

Chapter 4, Data Flow Task Part 2—Transformations, explores the transformations used to apply data quality and business rules that are essential to prepare data loaded into destinations. Data Flow Task provides an easy way to transform source data into the form needed by its destination in several different ways.

Chapter 5, Data Flow Task Part 3—Advanced Transformation, briefly discusses Advanced Transformations. In real-world scenarios, different data sources don't provide the same structure, so there is a need to unify them in a unique structure. There are some transformations in SSIS Data Flow Task that use complex ways to apply such changes on data stream. We call them Advanced Transformations.

Chapter 6, Variables, Expressions, and Dynamism in SSIS, describes how SSIS works with dynamism with the aid of expressions, what are the limitations of some tasks in dynamism, and what are the alternative solutions. SSIS as an executable unit needs to have a structure for declaring in-memory variables and store some data in memory to pass between Tasks through the execution phase. Besides the variables, there is a built-in statement language in SSIS components and Tasks to do many operations such as data conversion, data splitting based on a condition, or creating text filenames based on date. In this chapter, readers will learn how to work with variables and expressions in many scenarios. Dynamism is the most powerful aspect of an ETL tool in data transfer operations.

Chapter 7, Containers and Precedence Constraints, explains three types of containers and precedence constraint in the SSIS Control Flow, which help developers to control the flow of task execution. All of these containers and the precedence constraints are covered in this chapter with real-world samples.

Chapter 8, Scripting, explains the powerful aspect of SSIS: scripting—developers can use scripting whenever other tasks or transformations can't help them to fulfill their requirements. There are two places for scripting in SSIS the—Script Task in Control Flow and Script Component in Data Flow. Scripting in both of these components will be covered in this chapter with samples.

Chapter 9, Deployment, describes how to deploy the developed packages and projects to a production environment, discussing different methods of deployment with the pros and cons of each way in real-world scenarios.

Chapter 10, Debugging, Troubleshooting, and Migrating Packages to 2012, explains the ability of SSIS to debug and troubleshoot like all robust systems. Developers need to know how to face problems in Control Flow or Data Flow, how to handle errors in Data Flow Task, and troubleshoot them. Debugging and troubleshooting have two sides in SSIS—Control Flow and Data Flow. This chapter describes both sides with appropriate examples. Also, this chapter has two recipes on migrating packages from the previous versions to 2012.

Chapter 11, Event Handling and Logging, explores all aspects of event handlers in SSIS besides logging in custom or built-in modes. SSIS provides a set of handlers for events on executable objects of Control Flow, which helps developers to handle these events and design appropriate operations on them. These event handlers also help developers to do some custom logging in their packages. There is a built-in logging feature in SSIS which can be used in general logging scenarios.

Chapter 12, Execution, covers different methods of package execution, and the properties and settings that can be configured at the time of execution.

Chapter 13, Restartability and Robustness, covers all these aspects of SSIS: SSIS has the structure to get input parameters from other applications. On the other hand, Packages can operate in a restartable mode. They can store their state at the time of failure and continue execution from that state next time. They are also capable of running Tasks in packages as a transaction.

Chapter 14, Programming SSIS, explains library classes for creating package and tasks, configuring them, deployment of a package, and running the package. Integration Services provide a set of .NET library classes and methods to do all parts of SSIS lifecycle operations from .NET programming.

Chapter 15, Performance Boost in SSIS, covers recommendations and best practices for raising the performance of packages and Data Flow. As an advanced part of each tool, there are some tips to raise the performance; they are described in this chapter.

What you need for this book

You need to have Microsoft SQL Server 2012 Business Intelligence Edition for running all recipes of this book.

Visual Studio 2010 is also needed for *Chapter 14, Programming SSIS*, which is about creating SQL Server Integration Services packages programmatically; so if you want to read and practice all the recipes in this book it is necessary to have Microsoft Visual Studio 2010.

Who this book is for

If you are a SQL database administrator or developer looking to explore all the aspects of SSIS and need to use SSIS in the data transfer parts of systems, then this is the best guide for you. Basic understanding of working with SQL Server Integration Services is required.

Conventions

In this book, you will find a number of styles of text that distinguish between different kinds of information. Here are some examples of these styles, and an explanation of their meaning.

Code words in text are shown as follows: "This Data Flow reads some customer data (first name and last name) from an Excel file, applies some common transformations and inserts the data into an SQL table named `SalesLT.Customer`."

A block of code is set as follows:

```
<title>The First Book</title>
<title>Becoming Somebody</title>
<title>The Poet's First Poem</title>
```

When we wish to draw your attention to a particular part of a code block, the relevant lines or items are set in bold:

```
<xsd:element name="genre"    type="xsd:string"/>
<xsd:element name="price"
  type="xsd:float" minOccurs="0" maxOccurs="unbounded" />
<xsd:element name="pub_date"
  type="xsd:date" minOccurs="0" maxOccurs="unbounded" />
<xsd:element name="review"   type="xsd:string"/>
```

Any command-line input or output is written as follows:

```
x "C:\SSIS\Ch02_ControlFlowTasks\R03_FTP Task\LocalFolder\files.7z"
```

New terms and **important words** are shown in bold. Words that you see on the screen, in menus or dialog boxes for example, appear in the text like this: "If any error occurs while executing the process, the error can be stored into a variable with the **StandardErrorVaraible** option".

Warnings or important notes appear in a box like this.

Tips and tricks appear like this.

Reader feedback

Feedback from our readers is always welcome. Let us know what you think about this book—what you liked or may have disliked. Reader feedback is important for us to develop titles that you really get the most out of.

To send us general feedback, simply send an e-mail to feedback@packtpub.com, and mention the book title via the subject of your message.

If there is a topic that you have expertise in and you are interested in either writing or contributing to a book, see our author guide on www.packtpub.com/authors.

Customer support

Now that you are the proud owner of a Packt book, we have a number of things to help you to get the most from your purchase.

Downloading the example code

You can download the example code files for all Packt books you have purchased from your account at `http://www.PacktPub.com`. If you purchased this book elsewhere, you can visit `http://www.PacktPub.com/support` and register to have the files e-mailed directly to you.

Errata

Although we have taken every care to ensure the accuracy of our content, mistakes do happen. If you find a mistake in one of our books—maybe a mistake in the text or the code—we would be grateful if you would report this to us. By doing so, you can save other readers from frustration and help us improve subsequent versions of this book. If you find any errata, please report them by visiting `http://www.packtpub.com/support`, selecting your book, clicking on the **errata submission form** link, and entering the details of your errata. Once your errata are verified, your submission will be accepted and the errata will be uploaded on our website, or added to any list of existing errata, under the Errata section of that title. Any existing errata can be viewed by selecting your title from `http://www.packtpub.com/support`.

Piracy

Piracy of copyright material on the Internet is an ongoing problem across all media. At Packt, we take the protection of our copyright and licenses very seriously. If you come across any illegal copies of our works, in any form, on the Internet, please provide us with the location address or website name immediately so that we can pursue a remedy.

Please contact us at `copyright@packtpub.com` with a link to the suspected pirated material.

We appreciate your help in protecting our authors, and our ability to bring you valuable content.

Questions

You can contact us at `questions@packtpub.com` if you are having a problem with any aspect of the book, and we will do our best to address it.

1

Getting Started with SQL Server Integration Services

by Reza Rad and Pedro Perfeito

In this chapter, we will cover the following topics:

- ▶ Import and Export Wizard: First experience with SQL Server Integration Services (SSIS)
- ▶ Getting started with SSDT
- ▶ Creating the first SSIS package
- ▶ Getting familiar with Data Flow Task
- ▶ SSIS 2012 versus previous versions in Developer Experience

Introduction

As technology evolves, it is always necessary to integrate data between different systems. The integration component is increasingly gaining importance, especially the component responsible for data quality as well as the cleaning rules applied between source and destination databases. Different vendors have their own integration tools and components, and Microsoft with its SSIS tool is recognized as one of the leaders in this field.

SSIS can be used to perform a broad range of data integration tasks, and the most common scenarios are applied to Data Warehousing. The known term associated with Data Warehousing is the **Extract Transform and Load** (**ETL**) that is responsible for the extraction of data from several sources, their cleansing, customization, and loading into a central repository (for example, to a Data Warehouse, Data Mart, Hub, and so on). SSIS is also used in other scenarios, for example data migration and data consolidation. **Data Migration** is the one-time movement of data between databases and computer systems, and is needed when changes occur or when we upgrade our systems. **Data Consolidation** combines and integrates data from disparate systems and assumes high importance in a business environment with increasing acquisitions and mergers. The following diagram adapted from TDWI (www.tdwi.org) helps clarify the different scenarios where SSIS could be used:

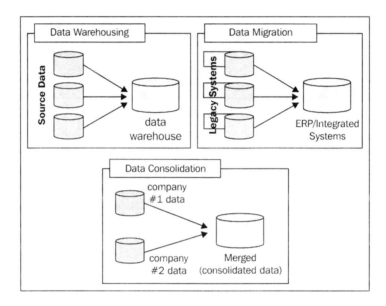

New business challenges are driving organizations to adopt data integration projects. Some of these challenges are:

 ▶ Increasing demand for real-time information reporting and analysis

 ▶ Large volumes of data spread along the entire organization

 ▶ The need to comply with regulations, which often require to continuously track all changes to data and not just the net result of those changes

Although SSIS is an amazing tool for data integration, the same work can be done manually in almost all cases. As you can imagine, performing data integration tasks manually could be hard to maintain in terms of code, hard to scale properly, and would require more time to implement. From our perspective, since we have SSIS, there is no real reason to do it manually. The cost of ownership is not a problem either, because SSIS is included with SQL Server licenses that most organizations have already acquired.

In this chapter you will learn how to work with SSIS, how to create packages for data transfer, and you'll perform some simple operations with SSIS Package. At the end, we will highlight several improvements which are included in this new version.

 As we will cover many recipes in this book, it is advisable to have **Adventure Works SQL 2012 sample database** installed.

Import and Export Wizard: First experience with SSIS

The Import and Export Wizard will be our first stop at SSIS. This wizard provides a simple ETL and is easy to use for basic data transfer operations. With this wizard you can choose a source, a destination, and map columns with few constraints on data transfer options. We will take a brief look at this wizard in our first experience with SSIS.

Getting ready

Install SQL Server 2012. SQL Server 2012 comes with three editions: Standard, Business Intelligence, and Enterprise. The Business Intelligence edition covers all requirements for this book that you'll need to install. With this edition you will have all SQL Server Integration Services features.

For many recipes in this book, you need to have the `AdventureWorks2012` and `AdventureWorksLT2012` sample databases installed. Information about installing these databases can be found in the book introduction.

To install sample databases, first download the database files from `http://msftdbprodsamples.codeplex.com` and then open SSMS to execute this statement (download `AdventureWorks2012` Data File and `AdventureWorksLT2012_Data`):

```
"" CREATE DATABASE AdventureWorks2012 ON (FILENAME = '<drive>:\<file
path>\AdventureWorks2012_Data.mdf') FOR ATTACH_REBUILD_LOG ;""
CREATE DATABASE AdventureWorksLT2012 ON (FILENAME = '<drive>:\<file
path>\AdventureWorksLT2012_Data.mdf') FOR ATTACH_REBUILD_LOG ;
```

Note that you should replace the path of the file here with the path of the file downloaded on your machine.

Create a new database in SQL Server. Open **SQL Server Management Studio** (**SSMS**) from **Start Menu | Microsoft SQL Server 2012 | SQL Server Management Studio**. In the SSMS, connect to local computer instance and create a new database. Name this database as `PacktPub_SSISbook`.

Note that you should run SSMS as administrator, to do this just right click on SQL Server Management Studio from path above and right click on it and choose Run as Administrator.

How to do it...

1. Open the Import and Export Wizard; there are three ways you could do it:

   - In the **Run** window, enter `DtsWizard`.

   - Open the wizard from the following address: **Start Menu | All Programs | Microsoft SQL Server 2012 | Import and Export Data**.

   - In SSMS, right-click on any database and then under **Tasks**, select *Import Data or Export Data*.

2. At the first step in the Import and Export Wizard, a welcome page will appear. Click on **Next** to enter the **Choose a Data Source** step, in this step you should choose where the **Data Source** comes from. The **Data Source** can be any source; from an Oracle database or SQL Server to any other database, flat files (such as `.txt` and `.csv`) or even Excel files, the range of source and destinations is based on data providers installed on the machine. For this sample, leave the **Data Source** option as its default option which is *SQL Server Native Client 11.0*.

3. We want to export two tables from the `AdventureWorks2012` database to another database. Therefore, leave the **Server name** as *(local)* or a single dot (.) or if you have a named instance you could use `.\<Instance-Name>`, and in the **Authentication** section leave the **Authentication Type** as *Windows Authentication*. This option will use your Windows account for connecting to the database, so obviously the Windows account should have read access to the underlying database.

4. In the Database drop-down box, select *AdventureWorks2012* from the list. Then click on **Next** and go to the next step.

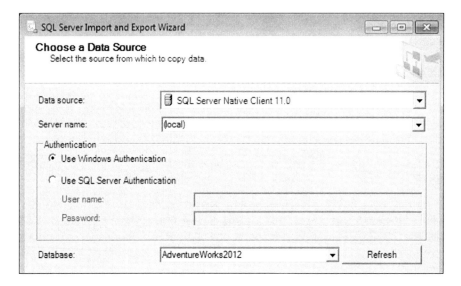

5. The next step is required to choose a **Destination**, therefore, provide the connection details of the data's destination (types of destinations can differ from databases to flat files). For this sample leave the destination as default value which is *SQL Server Native Client 11.0.*

6. Set the **Server Name** to *(local)* or dot (.) to connect default instance of current machine. Set the **Authentication** as *Windows Authentication*. Select *R1.1* in the **Database** drop-down list. Then click on **Next** to follow the wizard's steps.

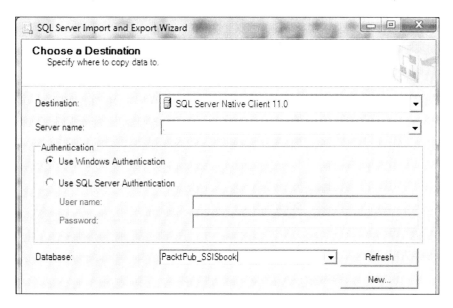

7. In the **Specify Table Copy or Query** step you can choose between selecting a table or view name for a source database or writing a query to fetch data from a source. For this example, choose the **Copy data from one or more tables or views** option.

8. Next, a list of tables and views from the source database will appear. For this example, select *HumanResource.Department*, *Person.Address*, and *Production. Product*. Then click on **Next**.

9. The **Save and Run Package** step is next; it provides the ability to save all the settings and configurations that you've set for an SSIS Package. We are going to save this package to see what the SSIS Package looks like. There are a lot of concepts and options associated with saving SSIS Packages which will be discussed in upcoming chapters, so don't worry about some terminologies here, all of them will be explored later. Check the **Save SSIS Package** option and click on the **Next** button.

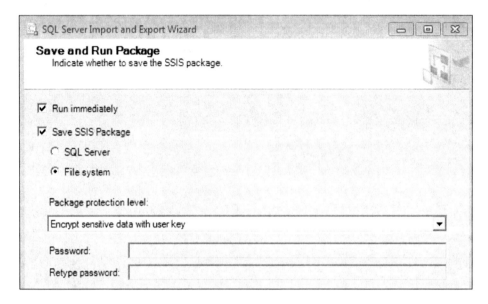

10. In the next step which is the **Save SSIS Package** dialog, type the name as R01_ImportExportWizard, and choose a location for the package file. Then click on **Next**.

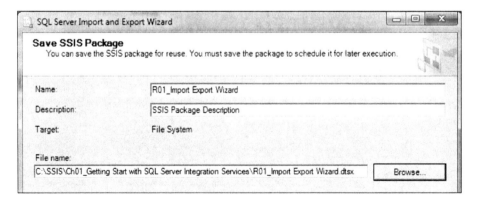

11. Now a summary of all settings that you've done appears here; after reviewing the summary click on **Finish**.

12. After clicking on the **Finish** button, the Import and Export Wizard will show up and we can see all the messages generated during the package's execution. The number of rows copied are displayed, or any other information such as the number of rows transferred, validated, and any other actions.

13. Open and see the execution's report by clicking on the **Report** button.

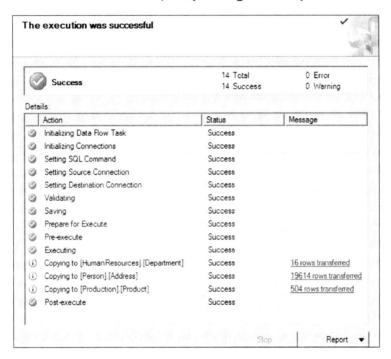

14. Close the Wizard and open SSMS to check the destination database, you can see transferred tables there with data.

How it works...

In this recipe, we created the first SSIS Package with the Import and Export Wizard, this simple scenario exports some tables from the `AdventureWorks` database to an empty database. In the last few steps, we saved the whole data transfer scenario to an SSIS Package on a file system that we'll be able to open with **SQL Server Data Tools** (**SSDT**) in later recipes.

With the Import and Export Wizard you can import or export data from a source to a destination, this is the most simplistic ETL scenario. In the **Select a Data Source** step you perform the **Extract** part of ETL and fetch data from SQL server database (data source). The second step, which was the **Destination Select**, was configured during the **Load** part of ETL. **Load** indicates where data should be exported; we export data to a SQL Server database. In this first example scenario we don't have any specific **Transform** stage. We will see this part of the ETL later, during the *Data Flow* chapters of this book.

When you choose table(s) from the `AdventureWorks` database in the **Select Source Tables or Views** section, tables that don't already exist in the destination database will first be created.

After matching the columns and metadata, data will be transferred and a summary of all logs will show what happened during execution.

We saved this package to the file system; we can also save packages to an SQL Server. The difference between the different storage options for SSIS Packages with their pros and cons will be explored later in *Deployment* chapters.

There's more...

As you've seen so far, the Import and Export Wizard is a simple way to transfer data that covers our most basic requirements. But in real-world scenarios, you need some additional features, which we'll now discuss.

Mapping columns

In the **Select Source Tables and Views** step, when you select a table or view to transfer, an **Edit Mappings** button will be enabled. Note that you need to select a row in order to enable this button.

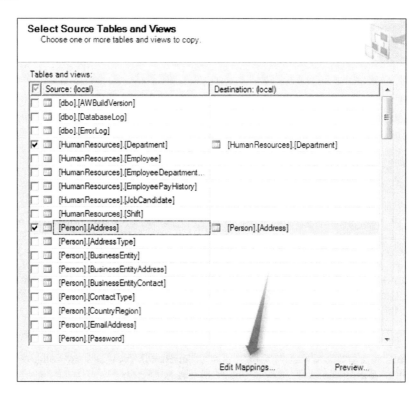

When you click on **Edit Mappings**, the **Column Mappings** window will appear. As you see, there are some options here for mapping **Source** and **Destination** columns.

When the destination table doesn't exist in the destination database, the **Create Destination Table** step will flag it. This means that the missing table will be created in the destination database; you can click on the **Edit SQL** button to see what the exact create table statement is; you can change the script as you want here.

When the destination table already exists in the destination database, the **Delete Rows** and **Append Rows** options in **Destination Table** will be selectable. You can select between deleting rows in a destination table before data transfer or appending new rows to existing records with these options.

The **Drop and re-create destination table** option will be selectable when the destination table already exists. Another important option is **Enable identity insert**, which should be checked if you load data into an IDENTITY column. The last part of the **Column Mappings** window is the **Mappings** section, which shows **Source** and **Destination** columns, as well as some additional column information. By default, all columns with the same name in **Source** and **Destination** will be mapped automatically. However, if the column names are different you should select columns by selecting the correct column name in the drop-down box. If you want to remove a column from data transfer you can simply choose the **<ignore>** option.

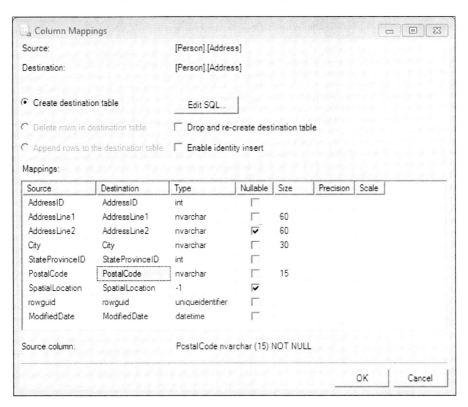

Configure transfer settings for multiple tables

In real-world scenarios, you need to configure transfer settings for all tables at once. Select multiple rows in the **Select Source Tables or Views Wizard** step by holding the *Ctrl* key and clicking on every row that you need, and then click on the **Edit Mappings** button. The **Transfer Settings** dialog box will open; all configurations that you set here will be applied to all selected tables.

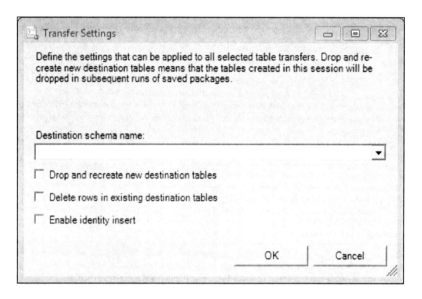

In the **Destination schema name** you can choose a schema name from the destination database and use this schema for all selected tables. You can also type a schema name there; if that schema doesn't exist in the destination database it will be created and all tables will be created under this new schema. The **Drop and recreate new destination tables** option will be applied to all new tables, and the **Delete rows in existing destination tables** option will be applied to all existing tables. **Enable identity insert** is also applicable to all tables that have **Identity** columns.

Mapping data types

Data types which are automatically mapped through the **Column Mappings** window of the Import and Export Wizard are defined in XML files based on source and destination type. A list of all these XML files is available here:

```
<system drive>:\Program Files\Microsoft SQL Server\110\DTS\
MappingFiles
```

There is a mapping file for each source or destination, and details of data type mappings can be found there. The next screenshot shows a portion of the `MSSql8toOracle8` mapping file:

```xml
<?xml version="1.0" encoding="utf-8" ?>
- <dtm:DataTypeMappings
    xmlns:dtm="http://www.microsoft.com/SqlServer/Dts/DataTypeMapping.xsd"
    xmlns:xsi="http://www.w3.org/2001/XMLSchema-instance"
    SourceType="SQLOLEDB;SQLNCLI*" MinSourceVersion="*" MaxSourceVersion="*"
    DestinationType="MSDAORA;OraOLEDB.Oracle;System.Data.OracleClient.OracleConnection"
    MinDestinationVersion="08.*" MaxDestinationVersion="*">
    <!-- smallint -->
- <dtm:DataTypeMapping>
  - <dtm:SourceDataType>
      <dtm:DataTypeName>smallint</dtm:DataTypeName>
    </dtm:SourceDataType>
  - <dtm:DestinationDataType>
    - <dtm:SimpleType>
        <dtm:DataTypeName>INTEGER</dtm:DataTypeName>
      </dtm:SimpleType>
    </dtm:DestinationDataType>
  </dtm:DataTypeMapping>
</dtm:DataTypeMapping>
```

Querying the source database

If you need the ability to provide a custom query to read data from the source table(s), you can choose to write a query in order to specify the data to be transferred, and in the next step write the query to fulfill your requirements. You can also open a query from a file.

See also

▸ *Creating the first SSIS Package*

▸ *Getting familiar with Data Flow Task*

Getting started with SSDT

This recipe is an overview of **SQL Server Data Tools** (**SSDT**), where a user will spend most of his/her time while developing and maintaining SSIS projects.

This version is based on Visual Studio 2010, and the whole structure that supports the process of developing such projects has been significantly improved. Working with SSDT is not only easier for advanced users who require more flexibility, but also for beginners who can enjoy some new and interesting user interfaces to help them take their first steps with SSDT. Previous versions of SSIS used **Business Intelligence Development Studio (BIDS)** as their development environment.

How to do it...

Open **SQL Server Data Tools** (**SSDT**) through the shortcut placed under Microsoft SQL Server 2012 or Open Microsoft Visual Studio 2010 under the Microsoft Visual Studio 2010 Start menu folders.

Once SSDT is open, a start page will be seen by default. The **Start Page** window contains useful information about the SSDT environment such as recently opened projects, links to create or open an existing project, and is also a useful area with several resources and the latest news to help stay up to date about several Microsoft platforms such as Windows, Web, Cloud, and so on.

Now that SSDT is already opened, let's create a new SSIS project from the **Start Page** window in order to understand the basic steps as well as the remaining windows placed in the SSIS project example.

1. Click on **New Project...** and a Windows dialog will appear.

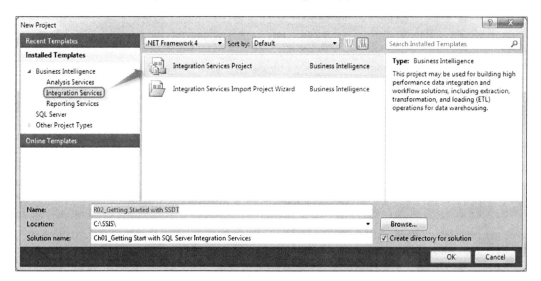

2. Under **Installed Templates**, expand **Business Intelligence** and click on **Integration Services**. In the center pane, select **Integration Services Project**.

3. Name the project as R02_Getting Started with SSDT. Name the solution as Ch01_Getting Start with SQL Server Integration Services in c:\SSIS and click on **OK**. An empty SSIS project will be created using the Project Deployment Model approach (default) with an empty package included.

4. In the **Solution Explorer** pane, right-click on the **SSIS Package** folder, and choose *Add Existing Package.*

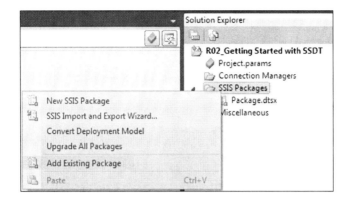

5. In the **Add Copy of Existing Package** dialog box, set **Package location** to *File System* and choose the package path from the file that you saved in the previous recipe from this address: `C:\SSIS\Ch01\Ch01R01_ImportExportWizard.dtsx`.

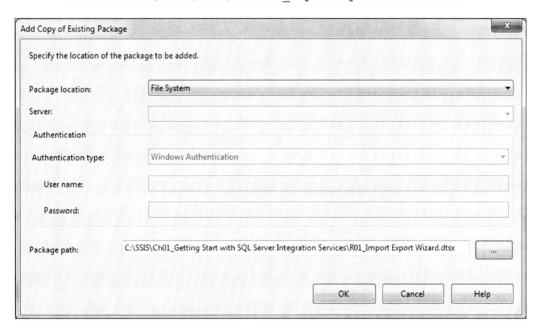

6. The new package will be added under the SSIS `Packages` folder, double-click on the package name in Solution Explorer to open it in Package Designer.

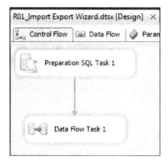

7. Double-click on **Preparation SQL Task 1** and the **Execute SQL Task Editor** dialog will open. Verify the **SQL Statement** property with a click on the ellipsis button in front of **SQL Statement**, and then close the editor.

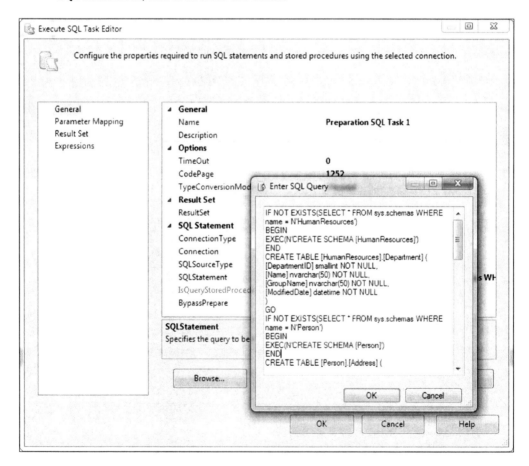

8. Double-click on **Data Flow Task 1**, and you will be redirected to the **Data Flow** tab, there are three source or destination combinations in **Data Flow**.

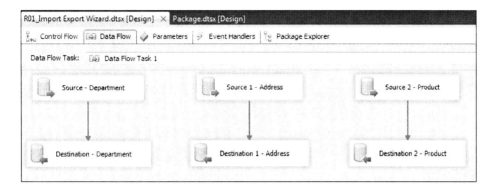

9. Double-click on the **Source-Department** component and the **OLE DB Source Editor** will open, verify the table name there.

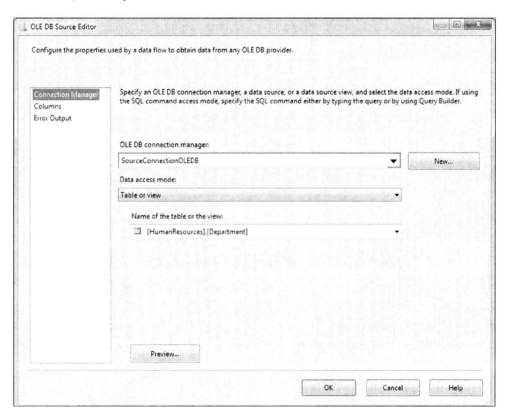

10. Double-click on **Destination-Department**, and in the **OLE DB Destination Editor**, verify the connection and table name.

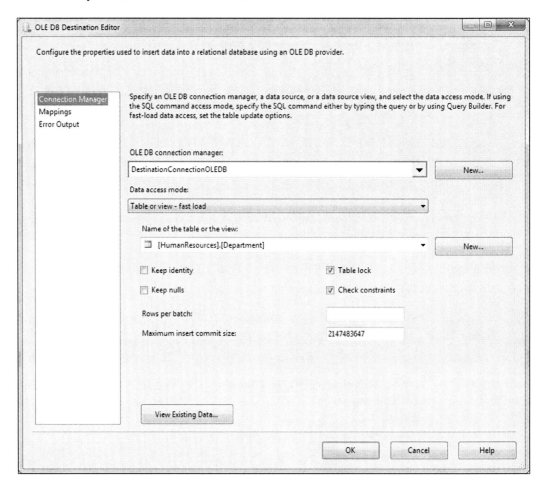

The next recipe will explain the process of creating a new SSIS Package in more detail, and for that reason this recipe will focus on how we could get more value from SSDT to make the development and maintenance easier and faster.

How it works...

Now that the SSDT is open with an empty package, let's describe some of the windows that you should be familiar with, as shown in the next screenshot:

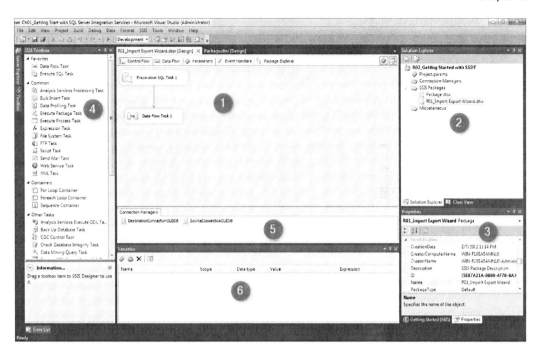

By default, SSDT creates a new and empty SSIS Package named `package.dtsx`. A **package** is a collection of SSIS objects including connection managers, tasks and components.

▶ **Package design area (1)**

Control Flow is the most important tab; it's where a developer "explains" to SSIS what the package will do. The remaining tabs such as **Data Flow** (see recipe), **Parameters** (see *Chapter 11, Event Handling and Logging*), **Event Handlers** (see *Chapter 10, Debugging, Troubleshooting, and Migrating Packages to 2012*), the **Package Explorer** and **Progress** bar (available just at runtime) are also important and will be described in later recipes.

▶ **Solution Explorer (2)**

The Solution Explorer section contains projects and their files.

Each project consists of Project Parameters, Connection Managers, SSIS Packages, and the Miscellaneous folder.

Project Parameters are parameters which are public for all packages in the project. We will discuss parameters in later chapters.

The Connection Managers folder in the Solution Explorer consists of shared connection managers which are shared between all packages in a project.

All SSIS Packages will be listed under the SSIS Packages folder.

The Miscellaneous folder can consist of any other files that are relevant to projects and packages, files such as documentation files, screenshots, and so on.

▸ **Properties panel (3)**

In this panel, it's possible to read and edit the properties of each selected object in the Design area or Solution Explorer.

▸ **SSIS Toolbox (4)**

In the SSIS Package, there are tasks and components which will be available depending on the tab selected in the Package design area. When the tab selected is **Control Flow**, the SSIS Toolbox will be grouped into four areas. The groups of tasks are the **Favorites**, **Common**, **Containers**, and **Other Tasks**. With these tasks, it's possible to control and inform SSIS about what should be done during execution. An interesting tip is that you can add tasks to the **Favorites** area anytime you like by right-clicking on each task and selecting **Move to Favorites**.

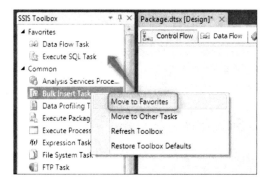

Note that the SSIS Toolbox is completely different on the **Data Flow** tab; we will talk about it in later recipes.

▸ **Connection Managers (5)**

Connection Managers are connections from the SSIS Package's components to source or destination data providers. There are different types of connection managers, some of them which are much in use are OLE DB Connection manager, Flat File Connection Manager and so on.

Each connection manager can be used in one or more components in the SSIS Package to work with underlying data provider. Some data providers require the installation of special drivers to have connections to their data source.

Each connection manager which is relevant to the current package will be listed in the Connection Manager's pane. Some connections are bold, these are referenced from a shared project's connection manager.

We will discuss more about connections in the next recipes.

▶ **Variables Pane (6)**

Each task in SSIS Package can send information to other tasks and it is possible by resorting to Variables. Package variables, their data types, their scope, and other properties exist in this pane, which will be described in greater detail in later chapters.

Creating the first SSIS Package

After understanding the SSDT environment, you will be able to make your first SSIS Package. Depending on the Data Integration project's complexity, it's always recommended to think carefully while selecting tasks and components to apply, as well as the order in which to execute them.

In this recipe, the first package created will read the number of records in an Adventure Works Microsoft Sample table and store it inside the SSIS Package.

Getting ready

You can reuse the recipe created in the previous section (adding a new package to it), or start from scratch as explained in the following steps:

1. Open **SQL Server Data Tools** (SSDT).
2. Click on **New Project...** and a Windows dialog will appear.
3. Click on the **Business Intelligence Projects** tab and under the **Installed Templates** section, select **Integration Services Project**.
4. Provide a name and location for the SSIS project and an empty structure as well as a package will be created.
5. In the **Solution Explorer**, select the empty *package.dtsx* and rename it to: `P01_FirstSSISPackage.dtsx`.

How to do it...

Now that the SSIS project is created, ensure that the empty package created by default is open and follow these steps:

1. Create an OLEDB Connection to the Adventure Works Microsoft sample database at the package level. (As already mentioned, if you create this connection in the Solution Explorer window, the connection will be created at the project level and will be automatically included inside all the existent packages).

2. In the **Configure OLE DB Connection Manager** Editor, select **New...** to create a new connection. If the connection already exists in the **Data Connections** list then select it here.

 Ensure that the **Control Flow** tab is selected in the Package Designer area.

3. Drag-and-drop **Execute SQL Task** from **SSIS Toolbox** and place into the control flow design surface.

4. Double-click to edit **Execute SQL Task** or right-click and click on the **Edit** option.

5. Set the **Connection** property of the task to the connection created in step two.

6. Set the **Result set** to *Single row*.

7. Add the SQL Statement: SELECT COUNT(*) AS NR_ROWS FROM SalesLT. Customer to get the number of records from the Customer table.

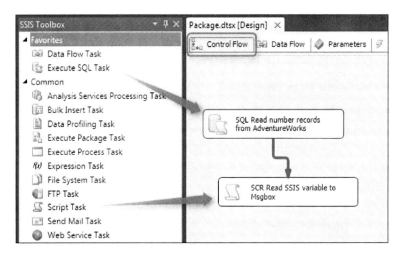

8. Drag-and-drop **Script Task** from **SSIS Toolbox** and place into the Package Designer area and edit it by double-clicking on it.

9. Create a new variable to store the value provided by the previous task and add a message box inside the script (the script task is explained more clearly in *Chapter 11, Event Handling and Logging*) as follows:

```
MsgBox (Dts.Variables(0).Value, MsgBoxStyle.Information)
```

10. Run the package by pressing *F5*.

How it works...

This recipe created a basic SSIS Package that included the most used tasks among SSIS projects: the **Execute SQL Task**, to communicate with a database through SQL queries and the **Script Task** that allows us to create some custom "work" when other tasks fall short. Naturally, it is too early to go into details with these two tasks, but this way it's possible to have an initial look at these common tasks.

Getting familiar with Data Flow Task

While the **Control Flow** tab under the Package Designer is where the main workflow of the package is manipulated, the **Data Flow** tab introduced in this recipe is the place where data is transformed and moved between a source and destination. The **Data Flow** tab under the Package Designer is used to create or edit such transformations and movements for each **Data Flow** task which is placed in the **Control Flow** tab.

Getting ready

It's possible to have several Data Flows in the Control Flow, but the order of execution for those Data Flows should be planned carefully. To be familiar with the Data Flow task, this recipe introduces a simple but very common scenario of incorporating the content of an Excel file into a database, a SQL Server database for example.

1. Open **SQL Server Data Tools** (SSDT).
2. Create a new project and provide a name and location for it.
3. Open the empty `package.dtsx` created by default and rename it to `P01_DataFlowTask.dtsx`.

How to do it...

Imagine a case where SSIS needs to periodically integrate data produced by an external system, and this data needs to be prepared to fit the destination requirements such as schema and data values exactly. To accomplish this task, we need to read data from an Excel worksheet, perform data conversions, verify whether data already exists at the destination, and finally insert into an SQL table at the destination.

1. In the Package Designer select the **Control Flow** tab.
2. Drag-and-drop a **Data Flow** task from the **SSIS Toolbox** to **Control Flow**.
3. Open **Data Flow** for editing by double-clicking under the task or just right-click and select **Edit**.

4. Make sure that the **Data Flow** tab is selected in the Package Designer. At this step **Data Flow** is naturally empty.

5. Because we need to read some data from an Excel file, simply drag-and-drop the **Excel Source** component (under the **Data Sources** group) from **SSIS Toolbox** and place it into the Package Designer area. Note that **SSIS Toolbox** has different content listed; it has components in spite of tasks that exist when the **Control Flow** is selected in the Package Designer.

6. Double-click on the **Excel Source** component and click on the **New** button to create a connection to the source Excel file.

7. Set the Excel file's path to `C:\SSIS\Ch01_Getting Start with SSIS\FILES\R04_NewCustomers.xlsx` and click on **OK**.

8. In the **Excel Source Editor**, set the name of the Excel sheet to `Sheet1$`.

9. Select the **Columns** tab and choose the columns **Firstname** and **Lastname**, which will be used along the data flow.

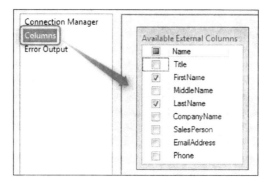

10. Click on **OK** to finish editing **Excel Source**.

11. Drag-and-drop **Data Conversion** from **SSIS Toolbox** to the Package Designer.

12. Select the column's **FirstName** and **LastName**, and change the **Length** for each to 50 characters.

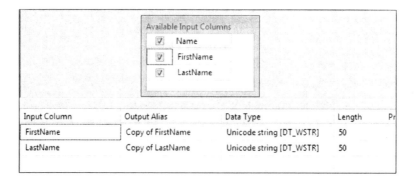

13. Drag-and-drop the **Lookup** component from **SSIS Toolbox** into the Package Designer.

14. Maintain all the properties with default values and create a connection to an SQL destination database (`AdventureWorksLT`).

15. In the list to select table or view, select the destination table *'SalesLT'.'Customer'*.

16. Map the source converted columns **Copy of FirstName** and **Copy of LastName** to the destination SQL columns.

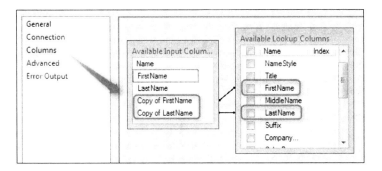

17. Click on **OK** to finish editing the lookup.

18. Drag-and-drop the **OLE DB Destination** component from **SSIS Toolbox** into the Package Designer in order to load data into SQL.

19. Link the output **No Match Rows** from **Lookup** to insert into destination only those records that don't yet exist at the destination.

20. Edit the destination component and set the SQL connection and also the destination table; maintain all the default values for the remaining controls.

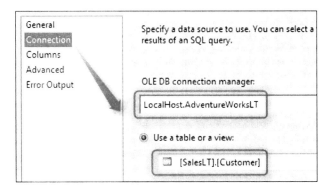

21. Click on **OK** to finish editing the **OLE DB Destination** component.

22. Run the package by pressing *F5*.

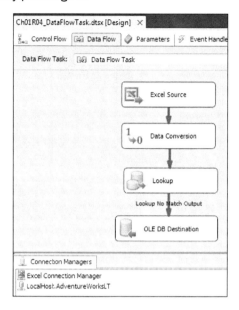

How it works...

This Data Flow reads some customer data (first name and last name) from an Excel file, applies some common transformations and inserts the data into an SQL table named SalesLT.Customer. Some transformations are usually applied to make source data fit the destination's requirements. In this example, data is converted and we verified whether the current data in the incoming rows already exists at the destination (the purpose is to avoid data duplication).

Detailed descriptions about each source (**Transformation** and **Destination**) used in this example will be explored in later chapters. In this recipe, we just need an overview of **Data Flow**.

SSIS 2012 versus previous versions in Developer Experience

This book aims at the new version of SSIS, which is SSIS 2012. There are a bunch of changes in SSIS 2012, this recipe covers some of the differences between SSIS 2012 and previous versions. The SSIS 2012 changes aren't limited to SSDT and design changes alone, there are also many changes while interacting with outside packages and package deployment, as well as new tasks and transformations; all of which we will explore in different recipes of this book in appropriate case scenarios. For this recipe, differences in SSDT as compared to previous versions are highlighted.

Getting ready

As this recipe compares the two versions, having SSIS 2012 and SSIS 2008 installed can be useful. SSIS 2012 is required but 2008 is optional (will help in comparison).

How to do it...

1. Create a **New SSIS Project**.

2. The first difference you'll notice in SSIS 2012 is that the SSDT is Visual Studio 2010 with a lot of improvements in the Editor. Earlier versions of SSIS work with previous versions of Visual Studio. SSIS 2008 worked with Visual Studio 2008, and SSIS 2005 worked with Visual Studio 2005.

3. When a new Package is created, the SSIS Toolbox is shown in the SSDT. As you would notice in the SSIS Toolbox, there are some categories that differ from the previous SSIS 2008 version. The previous version had only three sections: **Control Flow Items**, **Maintenance Plan Tasks**, and **General**. In SSDT 2010, sections are organized as: **Favorites**, **Common**, **Containers**, and **Other Tasks**. **Favorites** contain tasks that can be moved in here by right-clicking on items and then clicking on **Move to Favorites**. **Common** consists of a list of tasks that is among the most useful tasks. **Containers** have their own section in this version of SSDT, and all other tasks are placed in the **Other Tasks** section.

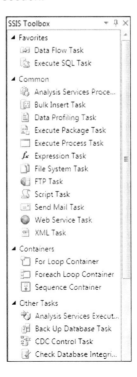

4. A quick description of each task or container is available under the **SSIS Toolbox**, as you can see in the following screenshot:

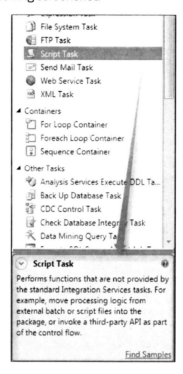

5. There are two icons for switching between the **Toolbox** pane and the **Variables** pane in Package Designer.

6. There is a scroll bar magnifier on the **Control Flow** tab which adds the ability to magnify a view of Control Flow, you can also choose auto fit.

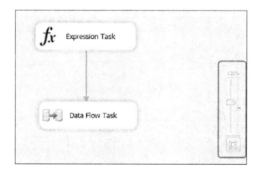

7. There is a new tab in the SSDT 2012 Package Designer named **Parameters**; we will discuss this Parameters tab in later chapters.

8. There is also an **Undo** icon; SSIS 2008 and 2005 suffered from the lack of undo operations, but in SSDT 2012 you can undo operations with *Ctrl + Z* or by clicking on the undo icon.

9. In the **Solution Explorer**, create a new **Project Level** connection. This is a shared connection which can be seen in all packages' connection manager's pane within the project.

10. Right-click on the blank **Control Flow** area and select **Getting Started**; you will see the new **Getting Started** pane on the right-hand side at the bottom of SSDT, which shows some help and links as seen in the following screenshot:

11. Drag-and-drop a **Script Task** from toolbox to control flow, and double-click on Script Task. In the **Script Task Editor**, in the **Script Language** property, you can select between *Visual C# 2010* and *Visual Basic 2010* both of which are under the .NET 4.0 Framework. We will explore all details about scripting SSIS in later chapters.

12. Go to the **Data Flow** tab, you will see this sentence: **No Data flow task has been added to this package. Click here to add a new data flow task**. Just click on the link and a new empty data flow will be created.

13. Notice that there are two new options **Source** and **Destination** in the **SSIS Toolbox** which can be found under the **Favorites** sections **Source Assistant** and **Destination Assistant**. With these assistants you can simply select a data source or destination as you want with a single assistant component.

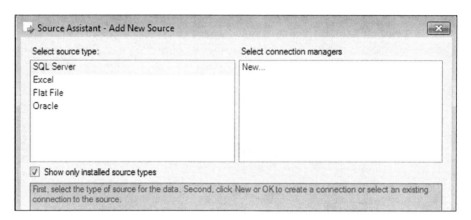

How it works...

We had already reviewed some changes to SSDT Design in the **Control Flow** and **Data Flow** tab areas. There are lots of other changes such as better annotations, grouping components in data flow, and many other improvements in the UI which we will explore with the many examples in this book in later recipes.

On the other hand, there are some major changes like new tasks and transformations, like Expression Task, CDC Control Task, Data Flow Components, and DQS Cleansing transformation which we will explore in appropriate chapters.

There are major changes in the deployment of packages and working with packages from outside and package execution, which will be explored in package deployment chapters later on.

2
Control Flow Tasks

by Reza Rad and Pedro Perfeito

In this chapter, we will cover the following topics:

- Executing T-SQL commands: Execute SQL Task
- Handling file and folder operations: File System Task
- Sending and receiving files through FTP: FTP Task
- Executing other packages: Execute Package Task
- Running external applications: Execute Process Task
- Reading data from web methods: Web Service Task
- Transforming, validating, and querying XML: XML Task
- Profiling table statistics: Data Profiling Task
- Batch insertion of data into a database: Bulk Insert Task
- Querying system information: WMI Data Reader Task
- Querying system events: WMI Event Watcher Task
- Transferring SQL server objects: DBMS Tasks

Introduction

There are many components that made SSIS a powerful tool for data integration. The objects in SSIS known as **Tasks** can be found under the **Control Flow** tab in the **SSIS Toolbox** and they are usually referred to as **Tasks** or **Control Flow Tasks**. The Control Flow Tasks consist of a wide variety of operations, from a simple File System Task that moves files, to XML Tasks such as XSLT or XPath that work with XML data in different ways.

Control Flow Tasks are categorized into sections; re-organizing them is simple (refer to *Getting started with SSDT* recipe in *Chapter 1, Getting Started with SQL Server Integration Services*). Each task has an editor; which is a graphical user interface that is useful for SSIS Developers. Some of the most important properties of a Task can be configured in its editor.

A good SSIS Developer should be familiar with the use of all Control Flow Tasks and use them in appropriate situations. In this chapter you will see an example of each Control Flow Task with their most useful "real-world" applications.

Executing T-SQL commands: Execute SQL Task

One of the most useful tasks in SSIS is the **Execute SQL Task**. This task can be used for executing every T-SQL command on an underlying database. Underlying databases can vary because there is a wide variety of connection managers that have SQL Task support. In this recipe, we will see some of the most useful scenarios such as the execution of T-SQL commands and fetching results, or passing input and output parameters.

How to do it...

1. Open SSTD and create a new Integration Services Project type at the following location: `C:\SSIS\Ch02_Control Flow Tasks\` and name the project `R01_Execute SQL Task`.

2. Rename the package as `P01_SingleRowResultSet.dtsx`.

3. From the SSIS menu select **Variables**; the **Variables** pane will appear. Create a new variable with the **Name** RowCount and **Data type** *Int32* at the package **Scope**.

4. In the empty package's **Control Flow** tab, drag-and-drop a **Execute SQL Task** from the toolbox under **Favorites** into the **Control Flow**.

5. Double-click on **Execute SQL Task**; the **Execute SQL Task Editor** will open. Name the task `SQL_StaticSelectCommand`.

6. In the **Connection** property under the **SQL Statement** section, create a new **OLE DB Connection**, and in the new **OLE DB Connection Manager**, set the server name as (**.**) for the default instance and . *InstanceName* for named instances (for example: *ServerName\InstanceName*). In the **Select or enter a database name** option choose *AdventureWorks2012*. Test the connection and confirm it. Click on the **OK** button to return back to the **Execute SQL Task Editor**.

7. In the **SQLStatement** option enter the following select query:

   ```
   select Count(*) as Cnt from Person.Person
   ```

8. In the **General** tab of the **Execute SQL Task Editor**, set the **ResultSet** property to *Single row*.

9. Confirm all configurations in the **General** tab of the SQL_StaticSelectCommand editor as shown in the following screenshot:

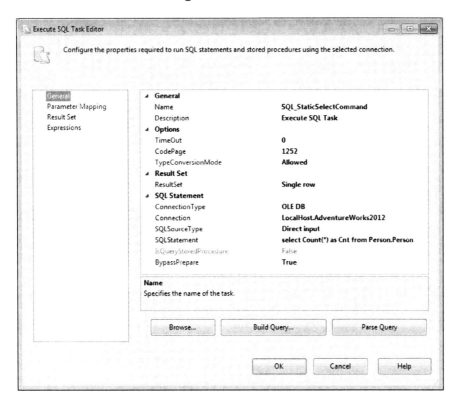

10. In the **Result Set** tab of the **Execute SQL Task Editor**, click on the **Add** button. Set **Result Name** as *Cnt* and set **Variable Name** as *User::RowCount*.

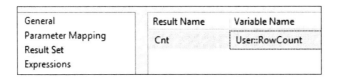

11. Click on **OK**, and close the **Execute SQL Task Editor**. Add a **Script Task** from the **SSIS Toolbox** into the **Control Flow** right after the **SQL_StaticSelectCommand**, and connect the green arrow from **SQL_StaticSelectCommand** to the script task.

12. Double-click on the **Script** task to open its editor and in the **Script** tab, in the **ReadOnlyVariables** property, write the user variable name as User::RowCount.

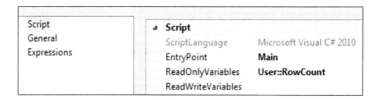

13. Click on **Edit Script**. In the new Script Editor, within the Main method, add a line for MessageBox as follows:

```
public void Main()
    {
      MessageBox.Show(
        Dts.Variables["User::RowCount"].Value.ToString()
      );
      Dts.TaskResult = (int)ScriptResults.Success;
    }
```

14. Run the package by pressing *F5* and check your record count in the message box.

15. Right-click on the SSIS packages folder in **Solution Explorer** and then click on **Add New Package**; name this package as P02_WorkingWithParameters.

16. At the package **Scope**, create a new variable of type *String*. Name it IssueName and set its default value as *Engine Malfunctioned*. Add another variable of type *DateTime*, and name it Date. Confirm the default value as current date.

17. Drag-and-drop a new Execute SQL Task into Control Flow and name it SQL_ParametrizedCommand.

18. Double-click on **Execute SQL task**, and in the editor, set a connection to **AdventureWorks2012** and write the following command in the **SQL Statement** property:

```
INSERT INTO [Production].[ScrapReason]
          ([Name],[ModifiedDate])
     VALUES (?,?)
```

19. Go to **Parameter Mapping** and click on the **Add** button. Set the **Variable Name** as User::IssueName, **Data Type** as *NVARCHAR*, and **Parameter Name** as 0. Then add another row with the variable name as User::Date, data type as *DATE* and parameter name as 1.

General	Variable Name	Direction	Data Type	Parameter Name	Parameter Size
Parameter Mapping	User::IssueName	Input	NVARCHAR	0	-1
Result Set	User::Date	Input	DATE	1	-1
Expressions					

20. Click on **OK** and close the Execute SQL Task. Right-click on the **SQL_ParameterizedCommand** Task and choose *Execute Task*. After running the task check the ScrapReason table in **AdventureWorks2012**.

21. Confirm the newly inserted row as follows: Open SSMS, under **Databases** expand **AdventureWorks2012**, under **Tables** right-click on **ScrapReason** and then click on **Select top 1000 rows**. You can find your new rows there.

How it works...

In this recipe, we used an Execute SQL Task to run T-SQL commands on an SQL Server database. First of all, a connection manager should be selected to an underlying database; the connection has a wide range of types that are supported by SSIS such as OLE DB, ADO.NET, and Excel. Differences between these connection types will be discussed in later chapters.

The SQL statement is where the T-SQL Command took place; the command can vary based on underlying databases. For example, if an underlying database is SQL Server 2005 and higher, functions such as row_number() can be used. If the underlying database is an Oracle DB then built-in functions for Oracle can be used.

T-SQL Commands in the Execute SQL Task can return a result, and the result is definable in the **General** tab's **ResultSet** property, which can be *None*, *Single row*, *Full result set*, or *XML*. *None* means that the T-SQL Command generates no result, *Single row* is used when a single record of data is returned by T-SQL Command; the *Full result set* and *XML* options will be discussed in later chapters and recipes.

When we set the **ResultSet** property as *Single row,* we should define where the resultant columns will be stored. The **Result Set** tab of the Execute SQL Task Editor is where you map result names, which are exactly the same as column names in the output for T-SQL Commands and package variables. Note that if the T-SQL Command returns columns with no specified name, we should set an alias name for that column in order to access them. Look at Step 6 for example.

It is obvious that T-SQL Commands should be parameterized and that they can read input parameters from package variables or fetch output parameters into variables. The Execute SQL Task provides this feature with parameter markers in T-SQL Command. The parameter marker is a placeholder for parameter value. In the previous example, we used a question mark (?) as a parameter marker; the question mark is a parameter marker for the *OLE DB Connection* type. Each connection type has its own parameter marker. Here's a list of parameter markers for all connection types:

Connection type	Parameter marker	Parameter name	Example SQL command
ADO	?	Param1, Param2, ...	SELECT FirstName, LastName, Title FROM Person.Contact WHERE ContactID = ?
ADO.NET	@<parameter name>	@<parameter name>	SELECT FirstName, LastName, Title FROM Person.Contact WHERE ContactID = @parmContactID
ODBC	?	1, 2, 3, ...	SELECT FirstName, LastName, Title FROM Person.Contact WHERE ContactID = ?
EXCEL and OLE DB	?	0, 1, 2, 3, ...	SELECT FirstName, LastName, Title FROM Person.Contact WHERE ContactID = ?

The details in this table were obtained from: `http://msdn.microsoft.com/en-us/library/cc280502%28v=SQL.110%29.aspx`.

Besides adding parameter markers in the SQL Statement property, the mapping of parameters with package variables should be defined in the **Parameter Mapping** tab of the Execute SQL Task Editor. In this tab, for each variable or parameter mapping, a row will be added. There are some properties here; **Direction** is for choosing between input and output for input and output parameters if we want to use them inside a stored procedure. **Parameter Name** is the next important property, which should be selected based on connection type. You can see different parameter names for the different connection types listed in the previous table.

We can run stored procedures on an underlying database with execute commands in SQL (statements such as `exec dbo.CalculateSalarySP ? , ?` for example). However, there is an another option named **IsQueryStoredProcedure** for ADO.NET and ADO connection managers. When this property is `True`, the SQL statement should be the name of the stored procedure, such as, `CalculateSalary`. The following table shows how we can set up an Execute SQL Task to run stored procedures:

Connection type	EXEC syntax
EXCEL and OLEDB	EXEC uspGetBillOfMaterials ?, ?
ODBC	{call uspGetBillOfMaterials(?, ?)}
	For more information about ODBC call syntax, see the topic *Procedure Parameters* in the ODBC Programmer's Reference in the MSDN Library.
ADO	If IsQueryStoredProcedure is set to False, EXEC uspGetBillOfMaterials ?, ?
	If IsQueryStoredProcedure is set to True, uspGetBillOfMaterials
ADO.NET	If IsQueryStoredProcedure is set to False, EXEC uspGetBillOfMaterials @ StartProductID, @CheckDate
	If IsQueryStoredProcedure is set to True, uspGetBillOfMaterials

The details in this table were obtained from: `http://msdn.microsoft.com/en-us/library/cc280502%28v=SQL.110%29.aspx`.

There's more...

We used Execute SQL Tasks with two types of SQL statements, one statement with no result set, and another one with a single row result set. In real-world scenarios we have to run queries that have different result sets.

Full result set

If the SQL statement returns multiple rows, then we can't use a *Single row* result set; in this case we should set the *ResultSet* property of the **General** tab to *Full result set*. Also, in the **Result Set** tab, an object type variable should be mapped to result name `0`.

After running the Execute SQL Task, the object type variable will have all records of the result set and we can loop through records and perform appropriate operations. We will cover object type variables, loop structures, and real-world scenarios for *Full result set* in later chapters.

XML result set

There are some cases where we need to get XML results from a T-SQL query. This is where the XML result set comes into play in Execute SQL Tasks. One of the most useful scenarios is a T-SQL query that uses the `For XML` clause to return data as XML.

We will bring a sample of this type of result set during this chapter's *Transforming, validating, and querying XML: XML Task* recipe.

All types of result sets and mapping output to variables are described in the following table:

Result set type	Data type of variable	Type of object
Single row	Any type that is compatible with the type column in the result set.	Not applicable.
Full result set	Object	If the task uses a native connection manager, including the ADO, OLE DB, Excel, and ODBC connection managers, the returned object is an ADO Recordset.
		If the task uses a managed connection manager, such as the ADO.NET connection manager, then the returned object is a System.Data.DataSet.
XML	String	String
XML	Object	If the task uses a native connection manager, including the ADO, OLE DB, Excel, and ODBC connection managers, the returned object is an MSXML6.IXMLDOMDocument.
		If the task uses a managed connection manager, such as the ADO.NET connection manager, the returned object is a System.Xml.XmlDocument.

The details in this table were obtained from: `http://technet.microsoft.com/en-us/library/cc280492.aspx`.

BypassPrepare

The **BypassPrepare** option is in the **General** tab of the **Execute SQL Task Editor**. This option is only available with OLE DB Connection types, and provides Prepared Execution.

Prepared Execution is a way to reduce time for parsing and compiling an SQL statement. In this way, the `SQLPrepare` function will first parse and compile the SQL statement into an execution plan, and then use the `SQLExecute` function to run the execution plan. So combining `SQLPrepare` and `SQLExecute` provides a way to get rid of the parsing and compiling overhead of SQL statements that will be run many times.

This option is `True` by default. For more information about Prepared Execution, look up: `http://msdn.microsoft.com/en-us/library/ms131667(v=SQL.110).aspx`.

See also

- *Transforming, validating, and querying XML: XML Task*
- *Foreach loop container: looping through the result set of a database query* recipe in *Chapter 7, Containers and Precedence Constraints*

Handling file and folder operations: File System Task

Although systems have evolved greatly in terms of technology, communications, and security, data access to source systems is often achieved through flat files. The people responsible for "Operational Systems" (OS) do not like applications that they don't fully understand pulling unknown volumes of data at unknown times from their systems. Even when someone tries to change this, they always get the same reaction: "I'm not letting you alter my system with something I don't know!" They prefer to stay in control and make data sources available in flat files on some 'staging area', in spite of directly opening the OS 'doors'. Therefore, reading text files and subsequent treatment, is a widely used practice mainly in a Data Warehousing scenario known as the **PUSH model**. In this approach, the OS starts data extraction to an external repository (usually known as a staging area) that will be accessed by an ETL Process.

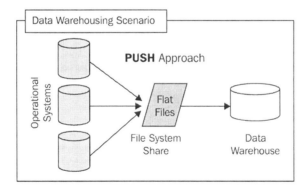

To handle these file and folder operations, SSIS provides the File System Task. This task performs file operations available under the `System.IO.File` .NET class listed here:

- Copy directory—Copies a folder from one location to another.
- Copy file—Copies a file from one location to another.

> Create directory—Creates a folder at a specified location.

> Delete directory—Deletes a folder at a specified location.

> Delete directory content—Deletes all files and folders in a folder.

> Delete file—Deletes a file at a specified location.

> Move directory—Moves a folder from one location to another.

> Move file—Moves a file from one location to another.

> Rename file—Renames a file at a specified location

Getting ready

To make use of this recipe, the flat file `R02_SampleTextFile02.txt` and the folder `Processed Files` should exist at the following file system location:

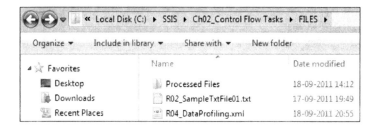

How to do it...

Consider the scenario where SSIS periodically needs to look in a specific share (file system) for a flat file produced by the Operational System (OS) that contains data to be integrated in a central repository. It is therefore necessary to read data from the flat file under a specific share folder and, if the task succeeds, then the source file should be renamed and moved to the `Processed Files` folder. The most important steps are described below here:

1. Open SQL Server Data Tools (SSDT) and create a new SSIS project.

2. Provide a name and a location for the SSIS project and proceed.

3. Select the package created by default and rename it to `P01_FileSystem.dtsx`.

4. To make the package flexible for future changes, create SSIS variables for source, destination and the filename values. In the **Variables** panel, click on the **Add variable** button to create the following variables:

   ❑ `uvSourceFolder` as *String* data type with the flat file source path: `C:\SSIS\Ch02_Control Flow Tasks\FILES`

   ❑ `uvDestinationFolder` as *String* data type with the flat file destination path: `C:\SSIS\Ch02_Control Flow Tasks\FILES\Processed Files`

❑ uvFilename as *String* data type with the flat file source name:
R02_SampleTxtFile01

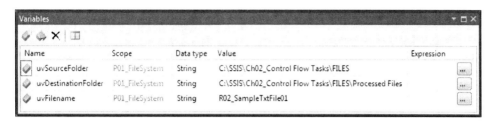

5. Add a Data Flow to Control Flow in order to read data and make a simple transformation.

6. From the SSIS Toolbox, drag-and-drop a **Flat File Excel Source** component to the designer and edit it.

7. Create a new connection **cmFlatFile** that points to the flat file source **R02_SampleTxtFile01.txt**.

8. From the SSIS Toolbox, drag-and-drop a **Derived Column** to apply a concatenation of the first name with the last name (use the following expression: `Firstname + " " + Lastname`).

9. To view the data flowing in the pipeline, add a **Union All** component (this component should be replaced with a destination component).

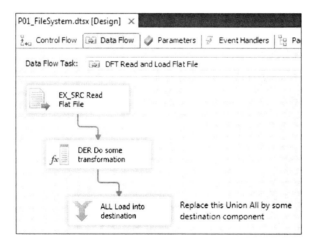

10. The package is ready to read data from the source. It's now necessary to move and rename the source file. Back in the Control Flow designer, drag-and-drop a **File System Task** to move the file to a new location. Add a precedence constraint between the Data Flow and this component and use the following steps to edit it:

    ❏ In the **Operation** drop-down, select *Move File*.

    ❏ In the **Source Connection** properties select the connection *cmFlatFile* in the **SourceConnection** drop-down created previously.

    ❏ In the **Destination Connection** properties, set **IsDestinationPathVariable** to *True* and select the user variable *uvDestinationFolder* in the **DestinationConnection** drop-down with destination folder path.

11. Press the **OK** button to finalize and link the Data Flow Task to this task through the green output row.

12. Execute the package by pressing *F5* and if successful, take a look at the file system location to confirm if the file was moved to . . . \Processed Files.

13. Drag-and-drop another **File System Task** to rename the file moved in the previous step.

14. In the **Operation** drop-down, select *Rename File*.

15. In the **Source Connection** properties select *New Connection* in the **SourceConnection** drop-down , and set this connection to the renamed file created before. Rename the newly created connection as cmProcessedFile.

16. In the **Destination Connection** properties select *DestinationConnection* in the drop-down **New Connection**, and set this connection to the renamed file created before. Rename the newly created connection as cmRenamedFile.

17. Press the **OK** button to finalize and link the previous File System task to this task through the green output row.

18. In the connection manager of the package, select **cmRenamedFile**, go to the **Properties** panel, and press **Expressions** to dynamically construct the connection.

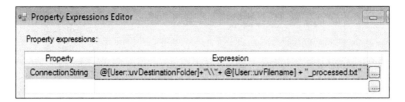

19. Manually move the file R02_SampleTxtFile01.txt moved during the previous execution to the . . . \Processed Files directory, its original location.

20. Execute the package again by pressing *F5* and if successful, take a look at the file system location to confirm whether the file was renamed and moved to `...\Processed Files`.

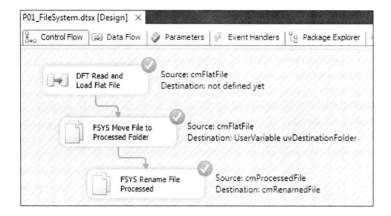

21. If the package is executed again, an error will fire because the source file does not exist anymore (the file was renamed and moved to a different location).

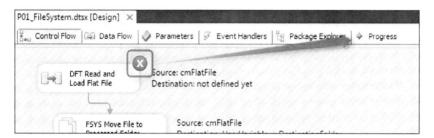

22. Make use of the logs generated by SSIS under the **Progress** tab for each package execution and see several types of log entries that will provide more accurate information about each execution.

There's more...

This recipe could need several improvements. If there is a need to iterate over a series of files or directories, the File System Task can be placed within a loop such as a `Foreach` loop. As a consequence, and because the filename changes, the package connections must be passed dynamically through SSIS expressions. It is suggested that you include a task to verify if each file that will be executed in each loop interaction exists in the file system location as configured in the package.

Sending and receiving files through FTP: FTP Task

The FTP Task gives us the ability to send files from a local system to a remote host or retrieve them from a remote host to a local system. There are other types of operations such as creating a remote folder or local folder. This task is very handy because FTP is in use between many companies for sharing their data. A company may export all its data into some CSV files, ZIP them and put them on an FTP address, and another company may need to get those files from FTP. The FTP Task also provides a way to work with multiple files.

How to do it...

1. Create new Integration Services project and name it `R03_FTP Task`.
2. In the package Control Flow, drag-and-drop an FTP Task and name it `FTP_ReceiveFiles`.
3. Double-click on **FTP_ReceiveFiles** to open the **FTP Task Editor**.
4. In the **General** tab of the **FTP Connection** property, create a new FTP Connection Manager. In the **FTP Connection Manager Editor** dialog window, type `ftp.microsoft.com` in **Server Name**. Leave all other options as default. Click on **Test Connection** and watch for the successful connection message.

5. Go to the **File Transfer** tab; set the **Operation** to *Receive Files*. In the **Remote path** enter /MISC/*.txt. Also, for the local path, create new file connection and set a local folder to store downloaded file there. In this example we use the following address: C:\SSIS\Ch02_Control Flow Tasks\R03_FTP Task\LocalFolder.

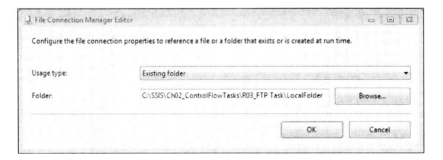

6. The **File Transfer** tab should appear similar to the next screenshot after all the configurations are set.

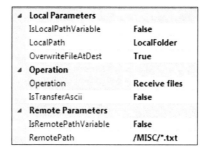

⊿ **Local Parameters**	
IsLocalPathVariable	False
LocalPath	LocalFolder
OverwriteFileAtDest	True
⊿ **Operation**	
Operation	Receive files
IsTransferAscii	False
⊿ **Remote Parameters**	
IsRemotePathVariable	False
RemotePath	/MISC/*.txt

7. Run the package, and after successful execution check the destination folder; the downloaded files can be seen there. There are some text files downloaded here, we will use this list of files in the *Running external applications: Execute Process Task* recipe also.

How it works...

The FTP Task is for the transfer of files through FTP from local to remote or the reverse. To work with the FTP Task, we first need to create an FTP connection manager.

When creating the FTP connection manager, server name and port can be defined. Credentials for connections to the FTP Server are also configurable. For this sample we used `ftp.microsoft.com` with anonymous access without any password. The FTP connection timeout can be defined; the default value is 60 seconds.

Operations in the **File Transfer** tab define what operation should be done in the FTP Task; these are the operations available, and their usage should be clear:

- ▶ Send files
- ▶ Receive files
- ▶ Create local directory
- ▶ Create remote directory
- ▶ Remove local directory
- ▶ Remove remote directory
- ▶ Delete local files
- ▶ Delete remote files

When the **Operation** is selected as *Receive files*, both the local and the remote path should be defined. With *Receive files* we can download files from a remote FTP address to a local path. In this recipe we want to download all text files from the MISC folder under `ftp.microsoft.com`, so we write the remote path with a Mask to fetch only those files with a .txt extension (under `/MSIC/*.txt`).

The **OverwriteFileAtDest** option will provide an overwrite option for the local destination folder defined in the **localPath** property.

We can choose *Receive files* or *Send files* to download or upload a single file; we just need to address the exact file by its remote or local path.

There's more...

There are some advanced options in the FTP Task and FTP Connection Manager that can be used in some scenarios; we will take a look at them in this section.

FTP Connection Manager's advanced options

- ▶ **Use Passive Mode**
    - ❑ There is an option in FTP Connection Manager to choose between Passive or Active mode for connection type. In the Active mode, the server initiates the connection, but in Passive mode the client initiates the connection. By default, FTP Connections are in Active mode.

- ▶ **Chunk Size**
    - ❑ Maximum number of bytes for each FTP Connection read/write operation, default value is 1KB.

- ▶ **Retries**
    - ❑ Defines the number of times to retry a connection. A value of 0 means an endless retry cycle.

File Connection Manager

In operations that work with local paths, we can create a File Connection Manager for a specified file or folder. This is an easy-to-use type of connection that can create a file or directory and use an existing file or directory.

All of these options will be defined in the **FileUsageType** property.

Value	Description
0	File Connection Manager uses an existing file.
1	File Connection Manager creates a file.
2	File Connection Manager uses an existing folder.
3	File Connection Manager creates a folder.

The file connection manager is one of the most useful connection managers, it's useful in many tasks such as the File System Task, XML Task, and so on.

Working with variables

The FTP Task gives us the ability to set a local and remote path dynamically from package variables.

The **IsLocalPathVariable** and **IsRemotePathVariable** properties define whether the local or remote path comes from a variable or not. The **LocalVariable** and **RemoteVariable** properties can contain the package variables which contain the path for the local or remote address.

Executing other packages: Execute Package Task

The Execute Package Task executes another package (known as the child) from the current package (known as the parent). This parent-child approach is fundamental:

▸ When the project needs to be developed by more than one person (it's easier when you delegate tasks to each team member).

▸ While breaking down complex package workflow (also reusing parts of packages).

▸ To have a more organized project, reducing the risk of failures and their impact when a specific or small subset of the project must be updated or refined.

It's not recommended to try to do all your work inside one package; the project should be divided into several components that can work together and be called by a parent package.

This recipe demonstrates the logic inherent to an Extract, Transform, and Load (ETL) project. ETL is a project that, by nature, is divided into three stages: the first stage is responsible for extracting data from sources, the second stage is responsible for the application of several transformations such as data quality and business rules, and the last stage is responsible for loading the transformed source data into the destination.

Getting ready

Let's follow these steps to get ready:

1. Open SQL Server Data Tools (SSDT) and create a new SSIS project.
2. Provide a name and a location for the SSIS project and proceed.
3. Select the package created by default and rename it to `P01_Master.dtsx`.

How to do it...

Consider a scenario where SSIS needs to periodically execute an ETL process. Because the most common and efficient approach is to split the process into several stages, this recipe will have one parent package called **Master** and three new **Child** packages, one for each ETL stage.

Therefore, it is necessary to add three **Execute Package Tasks** to the Control Flow for, one each stage described before. Even knowing that we could have more packages at each stage, it's not intended to create more complexity.

1. Add three new packages to the SSIS project created for this recipe. In the **Solution Explorer**, under the **SSIS Packages** folder, select **New SSIS Package**. Repeat this step twice and rename each package to: `P02_Child01_Extract.dtsx`, `P03_Child02_Transform.dtsx`, and `P04_Child03_Load.dtsx`.

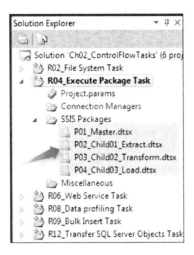

2. For each child package, add a **Script Task** to the Control Flow designer displaying a message box with the package name.

3. Rename the script task to `SCR PackageName Message` and open it for editing.

4. In the **Script** tab, select the system variable `System::PackageName` from the **ReadOnlyVariable** property's drop-down box,. This variable is used inside the Script Editor to display a message with it's respective value.

5. Press the **Edit Script...** button and add the following line the to `Main()` procedure:

```
Public Sub Main()
    '
    ' Add your code here
    '
    MsgBox(Dts.Variables("System::PackageName").Value, MsgBoxStyle.Information, "Message Information")
    Dts.TaskResult = ScriptResults.Success
End Sub
```

6. Close the script task and go to the master package `P01_Master.dtsx`.

7. In the master package, drag-and-drop three **Execute Package Task** instances, one for each child package, from the **SSIS Toolbox** to the **Control Flow** designer; they will be called from here.

8. Select and edit the first **Execute Package Task**. In the **Package** tab, select the *PackageNameFromProjectReference* property and choose the child package to be called within this task. Repeat this step for the two remaining child packages.

9. Execute the package by pressing *F5* or through **Debug menu | Debug | Start Debugging**. During execution, the various packages will be called in the sequence indicated on the master, and a message with the package name will be displayed.

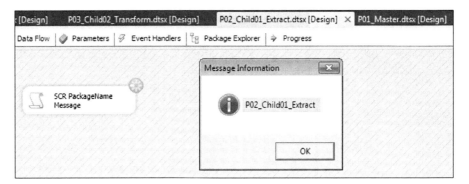

The final appearance of the master package P01_Master.dtsx is supposed to be similar to the following screenshot:

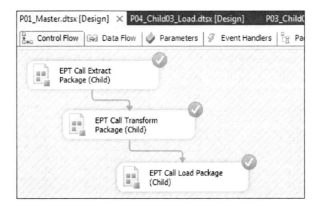

How it works...

The previous steps explain a simple and basic scenario for the Parent-Child approach. Naturally, more requirements could arise in real-world situations, and for that reason some configuration details need to be highlighted here.

- **Project reference versus external reference**

  In this new version, the **Execute Package Task** has a new and useful property called *ReferenceType*. There are two types associated with this property: **External Reference** and **Project Reference**. When **External Reference** is selected, the task will be will switched back into the previous SSIS version's 2008R2 style of working with SQL Server and available File System package locations. When **Project Reference** is selected, it's allowed to choose another package from the current project. This last type is a new feature that uses the project deployment model scenario. We will explore the new project deployment model during the chapter on SSIS deployment later in this book.

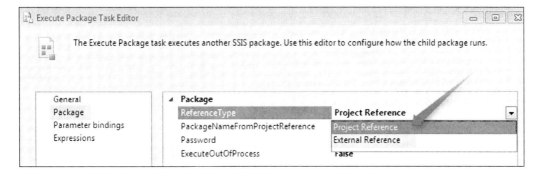

- **Execute processes out-of-process versus in-process**

  There are two possibilities to execute the called child package: out-of-process or in-process. This functionality can be changed with the *ExecuteOutOfProcess* property, which is used to specify whether child package runs in the process of the parent package or in a separate process.

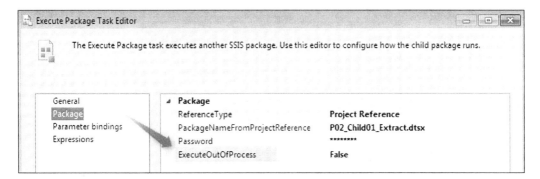

When a child package is executed out-of-process, it results in a new process being started in which the package is executed. When this recipe is executed with the *ExecuteOutOfProcess* property set to True, multiple instances of dtshost.exe running in **Windows Task Manager** will be created and remain "alive", using up resources.

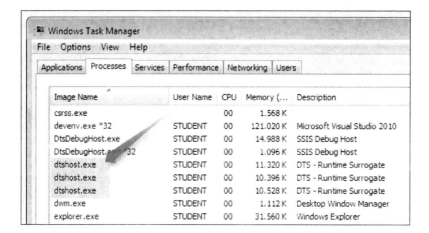

There's more...

It's often necessary to pass some data between the parent and child packages. An example could be the "run ID report" of the entire process that child packages must know to accomplish a specific integration task. If the project deployment mode is used, it's possible to create parameters to share important information between packages.

1. Create a variable in the parent package (in this recipe the master package P01_Master.dtsx):

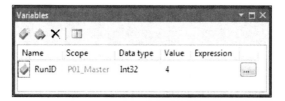

2. Create a parameter **childRunID**, which receives the value provided by the parent package. The name of this variable is used in the parent package; set both the **Sensitive** and **Required** properties to False in the child **Parameters** tab. The **Sensitive** property should be True when the parameter value must be encrypted (stored in SSIS catalog and shown in the package as NULL) while the **Required** property should be True when a value should be assigned before package execution.

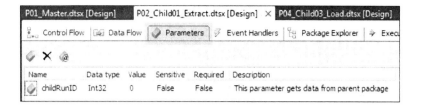

3. Now that the variable in the parent package and the parameter in the child package are created, we just need to bind them. Under the parent package (master) select and edit each **Execute Package Task**. At the **Parameter bindings** tab set the **Child package parameter** to *childRunID* and in **Binding parameter or variable** set the parent variable to *User::RunID*.

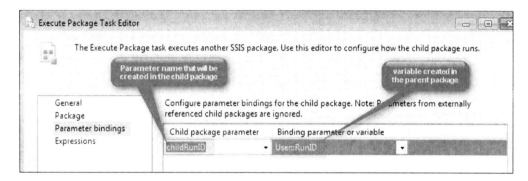

4. The easiest way to test whether the variable value is passing between parent and child is to create a script task, as we did in the *How to do it...* section of this recipe.

Advanced options for executing external packages

There are some options for when we want to execute a package that will be explored during the Deployment chapter later in this book.

Running external applications: Execute Process Task

One of the handiest tasks in SSIS Control Flow is the Execute Process Task. With this task we can run any other application that has an executable file. The only thing to consider is that the executable file should be run in silent mode because SSIS isn't made for interaction with users. In this recipe, we compress and decompress some files within this task with the help of 7-Zip.

Getting ready

1. Complete and finish the *Sending and receiving files through FTP: FTP Task* recipe and use the downloaded text files as input for this recipe. Those files should be at `C:\SSIS\Ch02_Control Flow Tasks\R03_FTP Task\LocalFolder`.

2. Download and install 7-Zip from `http://www.7zip.com`.

3. Create a new empty directory for extracted files here: `C:\SSIS\Ch02_Control Flow Tasks\R05_ExecuteProcessTask\ExtractedFiles`.

How to do it...

1. Create a new Integration Services project in BIDS and name the project `R05_ExecuteProcessTask`.

2. Drag-and-drop an Execute Process Task from the **SSIS Toolbox** to **Control Flow**.

3. Name the task `EPR_Compress` and double-click to open the **Execute Process Task Editor**.

4. Go to the **Process** tab. In the **Executable** property select the `7z.exe` file from the installed directory; the address should look like this: `C:\Program Files\7-Zip\7z.exe`.

5. Set the **Working Directory** to the path for text files that should be compressed; for our recipe the path is to text files from Recipe 2.3 here: `C:\SSIS\Ch02_ControlFlowTasks\R03_FTP Task\LocalFolder`.

6. In the **Arguments** property write a command line switch and commands for `7z`, as follows:

    ```
    a -t7z files.7z *.txt
    ```

7. Confirm all your configurations with the following screenshot:

⊿ Process	
RequiresFullFileName	True
Executable	C:\Program Files\7-Zip\7z.exe
Arguments	a -t7z files.7z *.txt
WorkingDirectory	C:\SSIS\Ch02_ControlFlowTasks\R03_FTP Task\LocalFolder
StandardInputVariable	
StandardOutputVariable	
StandardErrorVariable	
FailTaskIfReturnCodeIsNotSuccessValue	True
SuccessValue	0
TimeOut	0
TerminateProcessAfterTimeOut	True
WindowStyle	Normal

8. Drag-and-drop another **Execute Process Task** after the first one, name this one `EPR_Decompress`, and connect the green arrow from `EPR_Compress` to `EPR_Decompress`.

9. Double-click on **EPR_Decompress**, go to the **Process** tab and set the executable to the `7z.exe` file path: `C:\Program Files\7-Zip\7z.exe`.

10. Set the **WorkingDirectory** with the address of the folder to extract your files to; in this example it would be: `C:\SSIS\Ch02_Control Flow Tasks\R05_ExecuteProcessTask\ExtractedFiles`.

11. Set the **Arguments** with an unzip command and switches as follows:

    ```
    x "C:\SSIS\Ch02_Control Flow Tasks\R03_FTP Task\LocalFolder\
    files.7z"
    ```

12. Confirm that your **Process** tab in `EPR_Decompress` matches with the following screenshot:

⊿ **Process**	
RequiresFullFileName	**True**
Executable	C:\Program Files\7-Zip\7z.exe
Arguments	x "C:\SSIS\Ch02_ControlFlowTasks\R03_FTP Task\LocalFolder\files.7z"
WorkingDirectory	C:\SSIS\Ch02_ControlFlowTasks\R05_Execute Process Task\ExtractedFiles
StandardInputVariable	
StandardOutputVariable	
StandardErrorVariable	
FailTaskIfReturnCodeIsNotSuccessValue	**True**
SuccessValue	0
TimeOut	0
TerminateProcessAfterTimeOut	True
WindowStyle	**Normal**

13. Run the package. `EPR_Compress` will create a zipped file named `files.7z` from all the text files at the specified path and then `EPR_Decompress` will extract the content from `files.7z` into another folder.

How it works...

With the Execute SQL Task we can run every executable file in control flow. We can also pass arguments and define a working directory for the executable file.

In this recipe we used two Execute Process tasks. The first one, `EPR_Compress`, will archive all text files from `C:\SSIS\Ch02_Control Flow Tasks\R03_FTP Task\LocalFolder` into `files.7z`. For this recipe we use the application 7-Zip which is free and open source.

The **Executable** property in **Execute Process Task** should contain the address of the executable file, which is the address of the `7z.exe` file in our recipe. **Arguments** are commands and switches that should be provided for the command-line executions. In this recipe, we first compress files with the `a` command argument, which is a command for archiving files in 7-Zip. Then with the `x` command we extract data from the compressed file.

All of the switches and command-line arguments for 7-Zip can be seen here: `http://www.dotnetperls.com/7-zip-examples`.

Working Directory defines where the addresses in the command line will work; if we do not provide full address, the address will be searched for under the working directory.

We can choose to pass input to the executable from a variable, and we should use **StandardInputVariable**.

We can also store the output of an executable in a variable with **StandardOutputVariable**. If any error occurs while executing the process, the error can be stored into a variable with the **StandardErrorVaraible** option.

WindowStyle defines how the dialog window of an executable should appear; it is useless when applications are executing on the server.

SuccessValue will define the interpretation of the retuned code of executable file. Its default value is zero, and this means that an executable will be considered as failed if it returns a value other than zero. We can change this behavior by changing the **SuccessValue** option. Obviously, different executables return different values as their successful feedback.

Reading data from web methods: Web Service Task

Web services are in wide use nowadays as a method to interact between systems in a cross-platform environment. As web services work with XML and serialize their outputs in the XML format and also get their inputs in the XML format, they are widely used as a standard way to interconnect systems together. There are lots of benefits of using web services, but discussing all of them is beyond the scope of our book.

This recipe demonstrates the use of the Web Service Task using a free web service chosen from among several alternatives on the Internet. This web service is very simple and returns the cities from a specific country:

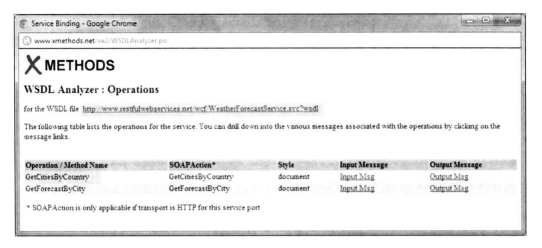

How to do it...

Consider a scenario where SSIS periodically needs to get data from an external source that provides data through a web service.

The WSDL file lists the methods that the web service offers, the input parameters that the methods require, and the responses that the methods return.

1. Create a connection to the free web service found on the Internet. This HTTP connection manager can point to a website or to a **Web Service Description Language** (**WSDL**) file as follows:

   ❑ In the **Connection Manager** right-click to add a **New Connection**.

   ❑ In the **Connection Manager**, click on the **HTTP** type and press **Add**.

   ❑ In the **Server URL** add the location for the WSDL: `http://www.restfulwebservices.net/wcf/WeatherForecastService.svc?wsdl`

   ❑ Press the **Test Connection** button and if the test of the HTTP connection succeeds, press **OK** to finish.

2. Create one SSIS variable (**user::uvCountry**) to pass the country parameter for the web service method that will use it as an input parameter (give the default value: *Italy*).

3. Add a Web Service Task from the SSIS Toolbox to the Control Flow designer and open it for editing.

4. In the **General** tab, under the **HttpConnection** property drop-down select the *HTTP* connection that we created earlier.

5. In the **WSDLFile** property, select the absolute path of the WSDL file that is required by SSIS to "understand" the web service. By default this file is created empty by SSIS in the defined location. For example: `C:\SSIS\Ch02_Control Flow Tasks\FILES\R06_CitiesFromCountry.wsdl`.

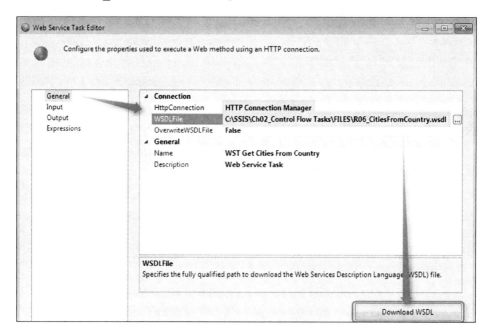

6. Because the WSDL file is needed locally, press the **Download WSDL** button to update the `R06_CitiesFromCountry.wsdl` file. If the test is successful then a message box will appear.

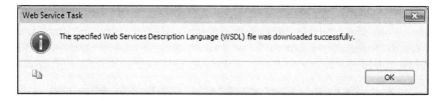

7. In the **Input** tab, in the **Service** property drop-down, select the service provided *WeatherForecastService*.

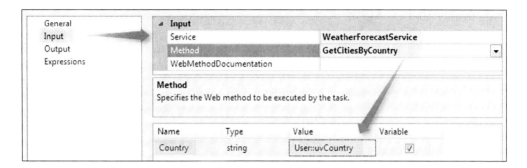

8. In the **Output** tab, set the output connection to an XML file where data provided by the web service will be stored.

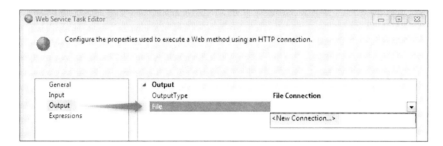

9. Set the **Usage Type** to *Create file* and set the file system location for the `R06_Result.xml` file.

10. Execute the package by pressing *F5*, or through **Debug menu | Debug | Start Debugging**. Open the `R06_Result.xml` file and analyze the output provided by the web service called from the package.

How it works...

The SSIS Web Service Task is handy when data comes from another company or application through web services. **Web services** are a platform-independent way to connect systems together. In this recipe we read some data from a forecast web service and save the results into an output file.

Transforming, validating, and querying XML: XML Task

XML is a universal format for data on different platforms, and there are lots of companies that work with XML data and send and receive data through systems as XML files. There are some operations which can be done with XML data: validating XML files over XSD or DTD files, transforming XML data with XSLT, querying data from XML with XPath, and other operations that are supported in many applications and programming languages nowadays.

The SSIS XML Task is a powerful task that provides a few of these operations on XML data. In this recipe, we fetch data from a table as XML, validate it on an XSD file, and then transform it with XSLT.

Getting ready

1   Save the contents of books.xml and books.xsd from this address into physical files: http://msdn.microsoft.com/en-us/library/ms762258(v=VS.85).aspx.

2. Create a new empty file at this address: C:\SSIS\Ch02_Control Flow Tasks\ R07_XML Task\Files\xslt_result.xml.

How to do it...

1. Create a new SSIS project and name it R07_XML Task.

2. Create a new variable of type *String* in package scope; name it IsValid.

3. Drag-and-drop an **XML Task** from the **SSIS Toolbox** into the **Control Flow**.

4. Double-click on the **XML Task** and open the XML Task Editor.

5. In the **General** tab set **Operation** as *Validate*.

6. Set **SourceType** as *File connection*, and create a new file connection manager for the books.xml file in the **Source** property.

7. Set **SaveOperationResult** as *True*.

8. In the **OperationResult** section, set **DestinationType** as *Variable*, and set **Destination** as *User::IsValid* and **OverwriteDestination** as *True*.

9. Set **SecondOperandType** as *File connection* and create a new file connection manager for books.xsd in the **SecondOperand** property.

10. Verify whether the **ValidationType** is *XSD*, and verify whether your settings match those of the following screenshot:

⊿ Input	
OperationType	**Validate**
SourceType	**File connection**
Source	**Books.xml**
⊿ Output	
SaveOperationResult	**True**
⊿ OperationResult	
DestinationType	**Variable**
Destination	**User::IsValid**
OverwriteDestination	**True**
⊿ Second Operand	
SecondOperandType	**File connection**
SecondOperand	**Books.xsd**
⊿ Validation Options	
ValidationType	**XSD**
FailOnValidationFail	**False**

11. Click on **OK** and close the XML Task.

12. Add a **Script Task** from the **SSIS Toolbox** into the **Control Flow** right after the XML Task and double-click on it, type `User::IsValid` in the **ReadOnlyVariables** property, then click on **Edit script** and write a line of code for `MessageBox` as shown next in the script's `Main()` method:

```
public void Main()
    {
            MessageBox.Show(
                string.Format("Validation Result: {0}",
                Dts.Variables["User::IsValid"].Value));
        Dts.TaskResult = (int)ScriptResults.Success;
    }
```

13. Run the package and check the message box value; you will see **Validation Result: false**.

14. Create a new package and perform all steps from **2** to **12** again for this new package, this time change the **SecondOperand** file connection to point to the `books_new.xsd` file. A copy of the file can be found in this book's code bundle.

Downloading the example code

You can download the example code files for all Packt books you have purchased from your account at `http://www.packtpub.com`. If you purchased this book elsewhere, you can visit `http://www.packtpub.com/support` and register to have the files e-mailed directly to you.

15. Run the package again, and this time you will get **Validation Result: true**.

16. Create a new package and name it P03_XSLT.

17. Drag-and-drop an **XML Task** from the **SSIS Toolbox** into the **Control Flow**. Double-click on the **XML Task** and open the XML Task Editor.

18. Set the **OperationType** as *XSLT*.

19. Set **SourceType** as *File Connection* and create a connection to books.xml in the **Source** property.

20. Set the **SecondOperandType** as *File connection* and create a file connection to the books.xslt file in **SecondOperand** property.

21. Set the **SaveOperationResult** as True. Under **OperationResult**, set the **DestinationType** as *File connection* and create a file connection to xslt_result. xml under the **Destination** property; set the **OverwriteDestination** as *True*.

22. Verify all configurations with the following screenshot:

▲ **Input**	
OperationType	**XSLT**
SourceType	**File connection**
Source	**Books.xml**
▲ **Output**	
SaveOperationResult	**True**
▲ OperationResult	
DestinationType	**File Connection**
Destination	**xslt_result.xml**
OverwriteDestination	**True**
▲ **Second Operand**	
SecondOperandType	**File connection**
SecondOperand	**books.xslt**

23. Close the XML Task and run the package. After running the package, check the xslt_result.xml file content. You should see a transformed version of the data from books.xml in a new style.

How it works...

XML Task provides extensive operations for XML data. To choose what to do with XML Task we should set the **OperationType** property.

For the first thirteen steps of this recipe we used XML Task for validating XML data against an XSD structure file. For this example, we set the **OperationType** as *Validate*. Validate will check the validity of XML data against XSD or DTD structure files.

As XML is a standard way to store data and is widely used across applications and programming languages, there is a need to define syntax for the XML data. When we store data in an SQL Server table, we should obey rules defined at the time of designing the table that define the structure of the table.

We can create a file for the syntax and structure of XML data. The XML structure can be defined in three ways: DTD, XDR, and XSD. Each of these ways has its own format for defining the structure. An explanation of the difference between them is beyond the scope of this book; you can read more about these types and how to use their validation methods in .NET languages at `http://support.microsoft.com/kb/307379`.

The SSIS XML Task supports only DTD and XSD for validation. We can choose validation type by the **ValidationType** property in the XML Task Editor's **General** tab.

We can also configure the XML Task to fail if validation against the schema file (DTD or XSD file) fails. For this we should set **FailOnValidationFail** to *True*. This option is false by default.

Each Operation in the XML Task needs two operands; in the first twelve parts of our recipe we used Validate, which needs two operands; the first operand is the XML data and the second operand is its schema.

We set **Source** as the `books.xml` file connection, which fetches XML data from the `books.xml` file, the first operand in the XML Task.

We set the second operand as a file connection pointing to the XSD file `books.xsd`.

Both the source and the second operand can be *File connection*, *Variable*, or *Direct input*.

The result of the XML Task in each operation is different, but in all cases the result can be saved somewhere. In this example, we used a *String* variable named `IsValid` for storing the result of the XML Task. We also set properties that store XML results in the **Output** section of the XML Task Editor's **General** tab.

After describing the different options in XML Task Editor, it's time to describe how XML will be validated against the XSD. Let's take a look at XML data first. The `books.xml` file's data looks similar to the following:

```
<?xml version="1.0"?>
<x:books xmlns:x="urn:books"
      xmlns:xsi="http://www.w3.org/2001/XMLSchema-instance"
      xsi:schemaLocation="urn:books books.xsd">
  <book id="bk001">
    <author>Hightower, Kim</author>
    <title>The First Book</title>
    <genre>Fiction</genre>
    <price>44.95</price>
    <pub_date>2000-10-01</pub_date>
```

```
        <review>An amazing story of nothing.</review>
    </book>

    <book id="bk003">
      <author>Nagata, Suanne</author>
      <title>Becoming Somebody</title>
      <genre>Biography</genre>
      <review>A masterpiece of the fine art of gossiping.</review>
    </book>

    <book id="bk002">
      <author>Oberg, Bruce</author>
      <title>The Poet's First Poem</title>
      <genre>Poem</genre>
      <price>24.95</price>
      <review>The least poetic poems of the decade.</review>
    </book>

  </x:books>
```

The XML data contains multiple book elements and each book element has some sub-elements such as author, title, genre, price, pub_date, and review. Describing the structure of XML is beyond the scope of this book; you can read more about XML at `http://www.w3schools.com/xml/default.asp`.

The schema for this XML is in the `books.xsd` file, and the schema looks like:

```
<xsd:schema xmlns:xsd="http://www.w3.org/2001/XMLSchema"
            targetNamespace="urn:books"
            xmlns:bks="urn:books">

  <xsd:element name="books" type="bks:BooksForm"/>

  <xsd:complexType name="BooksForm">
    <xsd:sequence>
      <xsd:element name="book"
            type="bks:BookForm"
            minOccurs="0"
            maxOccurs="unbounded"/>
    </xsd:sequence>
  </xsd:complexType>

  <xsd:complexType name="BookForm">
    <xsd:sequence>
      <xsd:element name="author"    type="xsd:string"/>
```

```
        <xsd:element name="title"     type="xsd:string"/>
        <xsd:element name="genre"     type="xsd:string"/>
        <xsd:element name="price"     type="xsd:float" />
        <xsd:element name="pub_date" type="xsd:date" />
        <xsd:element name="review"    type="xsd:string"/>
      </xsd:sequence>
      <xsd:attribute name="id"    type="xsd:string"/>
    </xsd:complexType>
  </xsd:schema>
```

As you can see in the XSD, schema information is described. Each book element consists of a complex data type, which contains author, title, genre, price, pub_date, and review sub-elements, and the data type of each element is defined in the `type` attribute.

Note that when `minOccurs` isn't defined in an element, that element will be considered as required. This means that all the above elements should exist for each book element, and if one of these sub-elements are missing, the validation against this XSD will return *False*. This is why the `IsValid` variable had a *False* value in step **13**.

We change the XSD in step **14** and created a new XSD file named `books_new.xsd`. Schema information for this file appears as follows:

```
<xsd:schema xmlns:xsd="http://www.w3.org/2001/XMLSchema"
            targetNamespace="urn:books"
            xmlns:bks="urn:books">

  <xsd:element name="books" type="bks:BooksForm"/>

  <xsd:complexType name="BooksForm">
    <xsd:sequence>
      <xsd:element name="book"
            type="bks:BookForm"
            minOccurs="0"
            maxOccurs="unbounded"/>
    </xsd:sequence>
  </xsd:complexType>

  <xsd:complexType name="BookForm">
    <xsd:sequence>
      <xsd:element name="author"    type="xsd:string"/>
      <xsd:element name="title"     type="xsd:string"/>
      <xsd:element name="genre"     type="xsd:string"/>
      <xsd:element name="price"
        type="xsd:float" minOccurs="0" maxOccurs="unbounded" />
      <xsd:element name="pub_date"
```

```
            type="xsd:date" minOccurs="0" maxOccurs="unbounded" />
      <xsd:element name="review"   type="xsd:string"/>
    </xsd:sequence>
    <xsd:attribute name="id"   type="xsd:string"/>
  </xsd:complexType>
</xsd:schema>
```

In this new schema file notice the bold part for the `price` and `pub_date` sub-elements. We defined the `minOccurs` as 0; this means that `price` and `pub_date` are optional elements and omitting these sub-elements will not cause the XML to fail on validation. This was the reason why the `IsValid` variable was *True* in step **15**.

From step **16** we started another example of an XML Task with the XSLT Operation.

XSLT stands for **eXtensible Stylesheet Language Transformation**. XSLT is a common stylesheet language, which provides a way to transform existing XML data to a new style. This operation is a very useful way to decrease the complexity of XML data. If we try to read complex XML data with XML Source (which will be explored during the Data Flow chapters), we will get weird results, and the XML Source sometimes won't resolve complex XML data structures. This is where the XML Task with the XSLT Operation comes into play. With simple XSLT we can transform existing XML to simpler XML data.

In this example, our `books.xml` file is simple enough and there is no need to change it. However, assume that we want to fetch just the author and title parts from the XML and have them as attributes instead of sub-elements.

So we create XSLT code to do this transformation, the XLST in our example looks like:

```
<?xml version='1.0' ?>
<xsl:stylesheet version="1.0"
  xmlns:xsl="http://www.w3.org/1999/XSL/Transform"
  xmlns:x="urn:books"
      xmlns:xsi="http://www.w3.org/2001/XMLSchema-instance"
      xsi:schemaLocation="urn:books books.xsd">
  <xsl:output method="xml" indent="yes" version="2.0"
    encoding="UTF-8" />
  <xsl:template match="/">
    <xsl:element name="x:books">
      <xsl:for-each select="x:books/book">
        <xsl:element name="book">
          <xsl:attribute name="author">
            <xsl:value-of select="./author"/>
          </xsl:attribute>
          <xsl:attribute name="title">
            <xsl:value-of select="./title"/>
```

```
        </xsl:attribute>
      </xsl:element>
    </xsl:for-each>
  </xsl:element>
 </xsl:template>
</xsl:stylesheet>
```

Details of XSLT syntax and language are beyond the scope of this book; you can start learning more about XSLT from `http://www.w3schools.com/xsl/default.asp`.

The result of applying this XSLT on the `books.xml` data (which is already stored in `xslt_result.xml`) looks like:

```
<?xml version="1.0" encoding="utf-8"?>
<x:books xmlns:x="urn:books">
  <book author="Hightower, Kim" title="The First Book" />
  <book author="Nagata, Suanne" title="Becoming Somebody" />
  <book author="Oberg, Bruce" title="The Poet's First Poem" />
</x:books>
```

Each book is separated in an element and the author and title sub-elements are transformed to attributes in the new XML data structure.

There's more...

There are more Operations that XML Task provides us with to work with XML data; we're going to explore those operations in this section of the chapter.

XPath

XPath is a query language for XML. We can fetch data from XML with XPath queries. The syntax and structure of XPath queries can be found here: `http://www.w3schools.com/xpath/default.asp`.

Assume that we want to fetch the title from all nodes and create new file with only title nodes. So let's try to do this with these steps:

1. Drag-and-drop a new **XML Task** from the **SSIS Toolbox** into the **Control Flow**, and in the XML Editor, set the **Operation** as *XPath*.

2. Set the source as a *File connection* to `books.xml`.

3. Set **SecondOperandType** as *Direct input*, and set **SecondOperand** as *x:books/book/title*.

4. In **Namespaces** add an item with a prefix as *x*, and URI as *urn:books*.

5. Set **XPathOperation** as *Node list*.

6. Set **Output** properties to save output to the `xpath_result.txt` file.

7. Confirm all your configurations with this screenshot:

◢ **Input**	
OperationType	**XPATH**
SourceType	**File connection**
Source	**Books.xml**
◢ **Output**	
SaveOperationResult	**True**
◢ OperationResult	
DestinationType	**File Connection**
Destination	**xpath_result.txt**
OverwriteDestination	**True**
◢ **Second Operand**	
SecondOperandType	**Direct input**
SecondOperand	**x:books/book/title**
◢ **XPath Options**	
Namespaces	**(Collection)**
PutResultInOneNode	**False**
XPathOperation	**Node list**

8. Run the package and check the `xpath_result.txt` file for results; they should looks like this:

```
<title>The First Book</title>
<title>Becoming Somebody</title>
<title>The Poet's First Poem</title>
```

Merge

With the Merge operation we can merge two XML files, the first XML file will be set in **Source**, and the second file will be set in **SecondOperand**. The XML Task will merge the content from the second XML file into the first XML file.

Diff

This operation will compare the first XML file with the second file and generate a **Diffgram** document with differences between two input XML files.

In the Diff operation we can choose some options, such as ignore comments, namespaces, prefixes, and other pretty clear options that don't need further explanation.

Patch

Patch will apply the result of a Diffgram document (which is the result of a Diff operation on two XML documents), and create a parent XML document that contains the content of the Diffgram document.

More explanation about Diffgram can be found here: `http://msdn.microsoft.com/en-us/library/aa302295.aspx`.

See also

▶ *Importing XML data with XML Source* in *Chapter 3, Data Flow Task Part 1—Extract and Load*

Profiling table statistics: Data Profiling Task

Data Profiling is an increasingly used task, and as such, it's necessary to understand the data extracted from sources in detail and also to reduce problems with the data's quality during the data integration process. In an ETL scenario, this data profiling should be done before the ETL process accesses the source system directly, or if that's not possible, then after the Extract stage where there usually isn't any transformation on data applied. If the data profile is not known, the risk of problems during later stages (Transform and Load) will significantly increase.

When source data is profiled using this task, the output could be a column null ratio, column lengths and values distribution, column pattern, and also the candidate columns for being keys. The output of this analysis generates XML reports that can be saved to a file or an SSIS variable.

The results gathered by the Data Profiling Task are very useful for tuning a database.

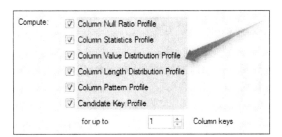

Getting ready

To get ready for this recipe, use the following steps:

1. Open SQL Server Business Intelligence Development Studio (BIDS) and create a new SSIS project.

2. Provide a name and a location for the SSIS project and proceed.

3. Select the package created by default and rename it to `P01_ProfileCustomers.dtsx`.

How to do it...

Consider a scenario where it's required to make a pre-analysis report or profile of the data that needs to be extracted from sources. This analysis is required to view the data quality level in order to reduce problems during the ETL process.

1. In the connection manager panel, create a **New ADO.NET connection** that points to the **AdventureWorksLT2012** database sample.

2. If the connection doesn't exist, press the **New** button to configure a new one. Rename the connection created to cmAdventureWorksLT.

3. Add a **Data Profiling Task** to the **Control Flow** for profiling the customers' data in the Adventure Works sample.

4. Open the task for editing.

5. Press the **Quick Profile...** button to use default configurations.

6. In the **ADO.NET connection** property, select the connection created in the previous step.

7. In the **Table or View**, select the table [SalesLT].[Customer] to be profiled under this task.

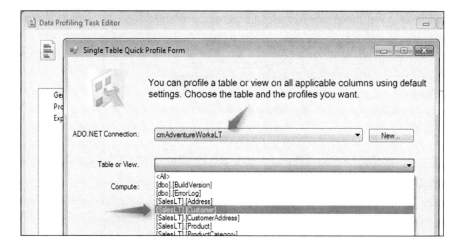

8. Press the **OK** button and take a look at the details of each profile request under the **Profile Requests** tab. Each profile type or request has its own properties that can be changed to fit each project's requirements.

9. Now the profile request is created, it's necessary to configure where the output will be placed. In the **General** tab, under **Destination** set the property **DestinationType** to *FileConnection* and the property **Destination** to *New File Connection*.

10. In the **File Connection Manager Editor** pop-up, set the **Usage type** property to *Create file* and in the **File** property set the name of the XML file that will store the output provided by the task.

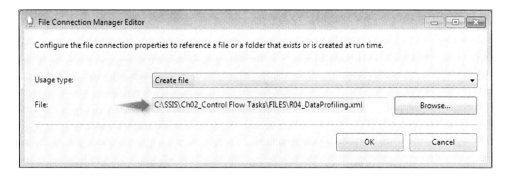

11. Execute the package by pressing *F5*. If the execution succeeds, the report will be generated in the XML file defined previously.

12. There are two options to view the report generated: the **Open Profile Viewer...** option in the **Data Profiling Task Editor** or the shortcut under **Start Menu | All Programs | Microsoft SQL Server 2012 | Integration Services | Data Profile Viewer**.

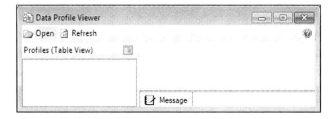

13. In the **Data Profile Viewer** press **Open**, locate the XML created before, and open it.

14. The extensive results for each column could be analyzed in detail by selecting the table and profile type on the left-hand side panel and selecting each column in the right-hand side panel.

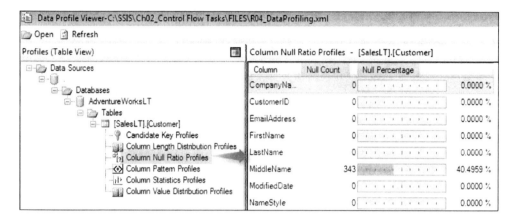

How it works...

The previous steps explain a simple and basic scenario for profiling source data that will be extracted, transformed, and loaded during the ETL process. Basically, to apply this task, it's necessary to identify the tables and columns that may cause quality problems, select which profile type is applied to each one, and finalize executing the package that will generate the output report in an XML file.

There's more...

The Kimball Group created an **SQL Server Reporting Services** (**SSRS**) project to apply data profiling analyzes under SQL Server Databases. Check out the project at http://www.kimballgroup.com.

Batch insertion of data into a database: Bulk Insert Task

Bulk Insert is used in scenarios where a large volume of data should be quickly inserted into a destination database. There are several ways to deal with this under SSIS but the difference will be in the speed of inserting such volumes of data into a database. This approach is used to ensure speed while copying data or performing transformations while the data is moving.

Some constraints should be considered before using this approach:

▸   Data must be transferred from a text file to an SQL Server table or view.

▸ The destination must be a table or view in an SQL Server database.

▸ Only members of the `sysadmin` fixed server role can execute a package with this task.

Getting ready

Make sure that the database created exclusively for this book is available in the SQL Server Management Studio (SSMS). For more information about this database, refer to the chapter's introduction.

In this recipe the `Customers` table from the `PacktPub` database sample will be required to store each value supplied from the flat file.

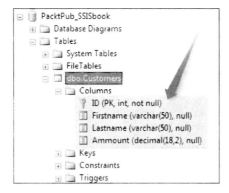

To get ready for this recipe, use the following steps:

1. Open SQL Server Management Studio (SSMS) and execute the SQL Statement included in the file `C:\SSIS\Ch02_Control Flow Tasks\Files\R09_ ScriptCreateTable.sql`.

2. Open SQL Server Business Intelligence Development Studio (BIDS) and create a new SSIS project.

3. Provide a name and a location for the SSIS project and proceed.

4. Select the package created by default and rename it to `P01_BulkLoad.dtsx`.

How to do it...

Consider the scenario where SSIS periodically needs to import a large volume of data into a central repository. This import should be as fast as possible and based in a flat file produced by an Operational System (OS).

1. As mentioned earlier, it's necessary that the source connection be a flat file. Therefore, and before configuring the main task, a flat file connection should be created.

2. On the connection manager's panel, right-click and select **New Flat File Connection**.

3. Browse for the flat file R09_SampleTxtFile01.txt, go to the **Columns** tab, maintain all the properties as default, and press **OK**.

4. Add a **Bulk Insert Task** to the **Control Flow** for bulk insertion of the source data.

5. Open the task for editing.

6. At the **Connection** tab task editor, select the **File** property's drop-down box and then select the flat file **Connection** created in the previous step that points to the source.

7. Select the value that sets the destination table Customers to the PacktPub database sample in the **DestinationTable** drop-down box.

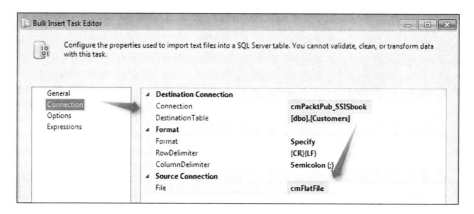

8. To ignore the first row in the flat file that corresponds to the header, change the **FirstRow** property from **1** to **2**.

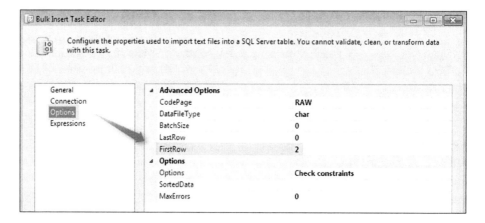

9. Execute the package by pressing *F5*. If the execution succeeds, the new data in the database `PacktPub_SSISbook` should now exist.

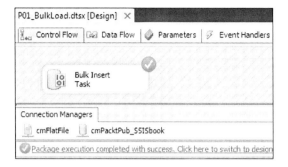

How it works...

Bulk Insert provides a method to insert records from a flat file into a database in batch mode. The number of rows in each batch, the start line number and end line number, the columns delimiter, the row delimiters, and some other options are configurable.

The Bulk Insert Task uses the built-in Bulk Insert SQL Server operation.

In the Destination Connection, we made a connection to an underlying database and table for the Bulk Insert operation. The Source Connection that points to a flat file is just needed to create the file connection manager; this is different from the flat file connection manager, which will be discussed in the next chapter.

Format defines how the source file is structured. There are two ways to provide the format, and our first option is **Specify**. When **Specify** is selected at the **Format** drop-down property, it's possible to specify the **RowDelimiter** and **ColumnDelimiter** exactly.

RowDelimiter defines how rows are separated in the source file (by default, this value is `{CR}` `{LF}`, which means a new line, but it's possible to specify any character or combination of characters here as delimiter). **ColumnDelimiter** defines how columns are separated. Common column delimiters are comma (**,**) semicolon (**;**) or vertical line (**|**), but we can define any other set of character(s) as **ColumnDelimiter**.

When *Use File* is selected at the **Format** drop-down box, another property will appear and it's possible to insert the physical address of a format file. The format file is a syntax file that's useful when it's required to load data into SQL Server with Bulk Insert mode. For more information about what the format file looks like and how to create a format file, check out `http://msdn.microsoft.com/en-us/library/ms178129.aspx`.

The format file is extremely useful when it's necessary to define data structures in a flat file in more advanced ways than a simple row or column delimiter. With a format file, it's possible to define each column in data flow, its data type, and some other advanced options.

Querying system information: WMI Data Reader Task

WMI stands for **Windows Management Instrumentation** and this Task provides easy access to information form the management objects of Windows-based operating systems. For example: the number of hard drivers, CPU usage statistics, a list of running processes, and any other information can be fetched with WMI. We use a language named WQL to fetch information from WMI, which is a query language for WMI.

As WMI provides extensive access to management information for our system and the operating system, SSIS provides two tasks for WMI. In this recipe, we take a look at the WMI Data Reader Task and read the running processes' information and load its data into a file.

Getting ready

Create an empty destination file at this address: `C:\SSIS\Ch02_Control Flow Tasks\R10_WMI Data Reader Task\Files\RunningProcesses.txt`.

How to do it...

1. Create a **New SSIS Project** and name it `R10_WMI Data Reader Task`.

2. Drag-and-drop a **WMI Data Reader Task** from the **SSIS Toolbox**'s other tasks section into the **Control Flow**.

3. Double-click on the WMI Data Reader Task and go to the **WMI Options** tab.

4. Click on **WMI Connection** and create a new **WMI Connection**. In the WMI Connection Editor, check the **Use Windows Authentication** option, and then **Test** the connection to confirm it.

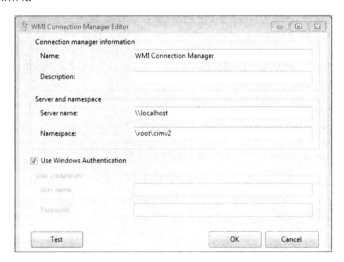

5. Click on **OK** and return back to the **WMI Options** tab; write the following statement in **WmiQuerySource**:

```
select * from Win32_Process
```

6. Set **OverwriteDestination** as *Overwrite destination*.

7. In the **Destination** property create a new file connection manager and point it to an existing file at this address : `C:\SSIS\Ch02_Control Flow Tasks\R10_WMI Data Reader Task\Files\RunningProcesses.txt` (we create this file in the *Getting ready* phase of this recipe).

▲ WMI Options	
WmiConnection	WMI Connection Manager
WqlQuerySourceType	Direct input
WqlQuerySource	select * from Win32_Process
OutputType	Data table
OverwriteDestination	Overwrite destination
DestinationType	File connection
Destination	RunningProcesses.txt

8. Click on **OK**, close the WMI Data Reader Task Editor, and execute the package. After running the package check the `RunningProcesses.txt` file, and verify that the list of all running processes exists there with comma-separated values.

```
Caption, CommandLine, CreationClassName, CreationDate, CSCre
System Idle Process, , Win32_Process, , Win32_ComputerSystem
System, , Win32_Process, 20110913203501.781250+270, Win32_Co
smss.exe, \SystemRoot\System32\smss.exe, Win32_Process, 2011
csrss.exe, %SystemRoot%\system32\csrss.exe ObjectDirectory=\
wininit.exe, wininit.exe, Win32_Process, 20110913203512.3437
csrss.exe, %SystemRoot%\system32\csrss.exe ObjectDirectory=\
services.exe, C:\windows\system32\services.exe, Win32_Proces
lsass.exe, C:\windows\system32\lsass.exe, Win32_Process, 201
lsm.exe, C:\windows\system32\lsm.exe, Win32_Process, 2011091
winlogon.exe, winlogon.exe, Win32_Process, 20110913203513.48
svchost.exe, C:\windows\system32\svchost.exe -k DcomLaunch,
svchost.exe, C:\windows\system32\svchost.exe -k RPCSS, Win32
```

How it works...

The WMI Data Reader Task provides a way to read management object information through WQL statements. In this recipe, we read a list of running processes and their related information.

For working with WMI Tasks in SSIS we need to create a WMI connection manager. A WMI connection manager has two important properties: **Server name** and **Namespace**. **Server name** means the name of a computer that WQL should run under and from which it should read data from. **Server name** starts with double back slashes (\\ ) and then the computer's name. The default value for this property is \\localhost, which indicates the current system.

Namespace should be the namespace for that WMI Class under which queries will execute. WMI Classes are divided into namespaces; reading Hard Drive information would use `\root\cimv2 namespace` for example, but for some information from IIS the `\root\WebAdministration` namespace would be more useful.

A list of WMI Classes and Namespaces is available at `http://msdn.microsoft.com/en-us/library/aa394554(v=VS.85).aspx`.

Another important option in WMI Connection Editor is the **Authentication** information. As the WMI is under administrative privilege it needs an administrative account to execute. If we provide an account that doesn't have the appropriate privileges, we'll get an error during the execution of WMI Tasks.

After setting up a WMI Connection Manager, it's time to specify the WQL query for WMI. WQL has a simple syntax for querying WMI Classes. In this recipe we used the following query:
`Select * from Win32_Process`

To better understand the syntax of WQL and for more information about it check out `http://msdn.microsoft.com/en-us/library/aa394606(v=VS.85).aspx`.

The WMI Query can be provided from different sources; WQL can come from a file in which case the **WqlSourceQueryType** should be *File connection* and a connection to the file should be created in **WqlSourceQuery**. WQL can also come from a variable or can be fetched directly. In this recipe we set **WqlSourceQueryType** as *Direct input* and provided a query directly in **WqlSourceQuery**.

The output of the executed WQL can be in different formats; *Data table*, *Property name and value*, and *Property value*. In *Data table* the output will be in the shape of a data table with column headers and data rows. In *Property name and value* all output consists of property names and their equivalent values; it is the same for the *Property value* option, but this time without a name. In this recipe we used *Data table* for the **OutputType** property.

The output of the executed WQL can be appended to an existing result, or be overwritten on an existing result, or you can also choose to keep an existing result and deny new results from overwriting it. These options are available in the **OverwriteDestination** property.

DestinationType can be a package variable or a file connection. In this recipe we used a file connection and created a file connection manager to an existing file. For more information about the file connection manager, look up Recipe 2.3, *Sending and receiving files through FTP: FTP Task*.

One of the most common scenarios with **WMI Data Reader Task** is reading system information at the time of running a package for logging and troubleshooting purposes.

There's more...

Both WMI Data Reader Task and WMI Event Watcher Task in SSIS Control Flow are based on WMI and having tools to work with WMI would be very useful to test and check the results of WMI queries and find appropriate WMI Classes before implementing them in SSIS. In this part of the chapter, we introduce such a tool for WMI.

WMI code creator—a useful tool for WMI

Microsoft provides a simple and light application for WMI test and code generation. This light tool can be downloaded from `http://www.microsoft.com/download/en/details.aspx?displaylang=en&id=8572`.

After installing this application, you can choose a namespace, a WMI Class, and then select the properties that you want to fetch; the WMI code for C# and VB can be created and results can then be seen in a command-prompt window.

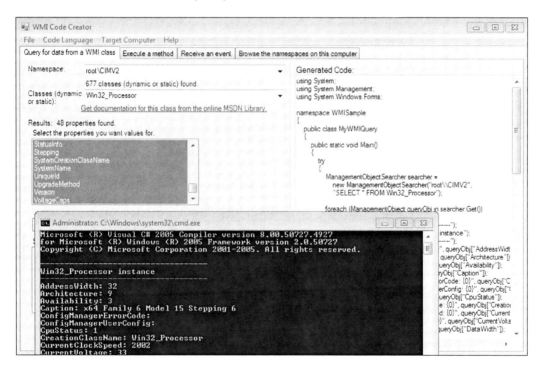

Using this tool for testing and finding appropriate WMI namespaces and classes will be helpful.

See also

▸ *Querying system events: WMI Event Watcher Task.*

Querying system events: WMI Event Watcher Task

In the previous recipe, one of the most common scenarios was reading system information from WMI. SSIS provides another WMI Task named **WMI Event Watcher Task**, which is more useful than the Data Reader Task. WMI Event Watcher Task provides a way to watch for a WMI event. This awesome feature will make the SSIS package very powerful. As WMI provides extensive information for the management of objects, interaction with this information as events will be very useful. Scenarios such as watching a folder for new files or watching CPU for 50 percent usage are some of the most common scenarios that can be accomplished with this task.

In this recipe we will watch a folder for new files, and if a new file comes into the folder, we will raise a message box after the WMI Event Watcher Task.

Getting ready

Create an empty directory for watching at this address: `C:\SSIS\Ch02_Control Flow Tasks\R11_WMI Event Watcher Task\Files`.

How to do it...

1. Create a New SSIS Project and name it `R11_WMI Event Watcher Task`.

2. Drag-and-drop a WMI Event Watcher Task from **SSIS Toolbox**, other tasks section, into the **Control Flow**.

3. Double-click on **WMI Event Watcher Task** and go to the **WMI Options** tab.

4. Click on **WMI Connection** and create a new WMI Connection. In the WMI Connection Editor, check the **Use Windows Authentication** option, and then **Test** the connection and confirm it.

5. Click on **OK** and return back to **WMI Options** tab. Write this statement in **WmiQuerySource**:

```
SELECT * FROM __instancecreationevent WITHIN 60 WHERE
TargetInstance ISA 'Cim_DirectoryContainsFile' AND TargetInstance.
GroupComponent='Win32_Directory.Name="C:\\\\SSIS\\\\Ch02_
ControlFlowTasks\\\\R11_WMI Event Watcher Task\\\\Files"'
```

6. Click on **OK** and close the WMI Event Watcher Task Editor.

◢ WMI Options	
WmiConnection	**WMI Connection Manager**
WqlQuerySourceType	**Direct input**
WqlQuerySource	**SELECT * FROM _instancecreationevent WITHIN 60 WHERE**
ActionAtEvent	**Log the event and fire the SSIS event**
AfterEvent	**Return with success**
ActionAtTimeout	**Log the time-out and fire the SSIS event**
AfterTimeout	**Return with failure**
NumberOfEvents	**1**
Timeout	**0**

7. Add a Script Task after the WMI Event Watcher Task and connect a green arrow from the WMI Event Watcher Task to the Script Task. In the Script Task go to **Edit script** and add a line to display a message box for **File Found** as follows:

```
public void Main()
    {
            MessageBox.Show("New File Detected!");
       Dts.TaskResult = (int)ScriptResults.Success;
    }
```

8. Save your script, click on **OK**, and close the Script Task Editor.

9. Run the package. In the **Progress** tab you will see that package execution will wait on the WMI Event Watcher Task; then copy an image file from `C:\Users\Public\Pictures\Sample Pictures` into the watching folder (`C:\SSIS\Ch02_ControlFlowTasks\R11_WMI Event Watcher Task\Files`) and after less than 60 seconds, we will see in the WMI Event Watcher Task that it completes its progress and the `MessageBox` comes up.

How it works...

As described in the previous recipe, WMI provides a way to work with Management objects. The previous recipe was about how to read system information through WMI Data Reader Task. However, the use of WMI isn't limited to reading data. We can use system events by means of WMI Event Watcher Task.

The WMI Event Watcher Task provides a way to use a WQL query for watching a WMI event, and notify other tasks if the event occurrs or not. There are many scenarios for using WMI Event Watcher Tasks; one of the most common scenarios is to watch a folder for new incoming files and then do appropriate operations such as data flow tasks.

In this recipe we watch a folder at the address `C:\SSIS\Ch02_ControlFlowTasks\R11_WMI Event Watcher Task\Files`, and if a new file appears we display a message box.

The WMI Event Watcher Task uses a WMI Connection Manager like the WMI Data Reader Task. For more information about WMI Connection Manager refer to the previous recipe for the WMI Data Reader Task.

WqlSourceQuery consists of a WQL query for watching the event. As we described in the previous recipe, you can use WMI Code Creator to find events that you want. In this recipe we want to watch a folder, so we use a WQL query that fetches data from the `__instancecreationevent` WMI Class and finds appropriate information. We watch the folder within 60 second intervals. So when a new file appears, WMI Event Watcher Task will catch it in less than a minute.

The **ActionAtEvent** property defines how SSIS behaves when a WMI event occurs; the default behavior is that SSIS will log the event (a log entry can be seen in the **Progress** tab of SSDT) and an SSIS event will fire. With this SSIS event, Control Flow catches events and performs appropriate operations. You can set this property to just log events as well.

We can choose what action should be performed after the WMI event. The `AfterEvent` property is set to return *True* by default. This means that whenever the event is triggered, WMI Event Watcher Task will succeed and the control flow goes to the task after this task. We can choose to return *False*, or watch for the event again.

The SSIS Package will wait for the WMI event to be triggered, and this may cause a halt in package execution if the event never fires. Hence, a `Timeout` property can be defined here. The default value of `Timeout` is zero and means that no timeout is set for this task. You can specify any number (in seconds) as a timeout.

As the `Timeout` property is set for this task, an action at the timeout can be chosen on the **ActionAtTimeout** property; **AfterTimeout** can also be defined similar to **AfterEvent**.

There are times when we need to catch an event if a specified number of events occur. For example, we want to watch for new files in a folder, but we will begin the process after three new files are created; so we set the `NumberOfEvents` to 3.

Transferring SQL server objects: DBMS Tasks

Transferring SQL database objects and data between databases is often needed in the real-world. For example, some scenarios could be the creation of the database environment along with multiple environments such as development, testing, and production; and for example, to create temporary tables to assist the ETL process.

This recipe demonstrates how we can simply transfer all database objects and data between the Adventure Works case sample and a new and empty database created for this recipe.

Getting ready

To get ready for this recipe, use the following steps:

1. Open SQL Server Management Studio (SSMS) and connect to SQL Server.
2. Create a temporary and empty database to which to transfer SQL objects from **AdventureWorksLT2012** database.
3. Under Database Folder, press **New Database...**.
4. Provide a name for the new database (`AdventureWorksLT2012_DEV`) and keep the remaining properties as default.
5. Open SQL Server Business Intelligence Development Studio (BIDS) and create a new SSIS project.
6. Provide a name and a location for the SSIS project and proceed.
7. Select the package created by default and rename it to: `P01_TransferSQLObjects.dtsx`.

The task used in this recipe is the **Transfer SQL Server Objects Task** and has a very intuitive layout to rapidly transfer objects such as **Tables, Views, Stored Procedures, User Defined Functions,** and **User Defined Data Types** between databases. This task makes use of the SQL Server Management Objects (SMO), which is nothing more than a collection of objects that are designed for programming all aspects of managing Microsoft SQL Server. Given next a is list of the most important steps that should be followed to use this task:

1. Create a new SMO connection to the SQL server that has the source database and also the new database created before. If these databases are located on different servers, another connection must be created.

2. In the **Connection Manager** right-click to add a **New Connection**.

3. In the **Add SSIS Connection Manager** pop-up that opens, search for the *SMOServer* connection type in the list and click on the **Add...** button.

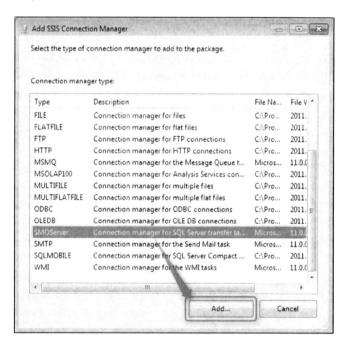

4. In the **SMO Connection Manager Editor** add the server name to the **Server name** property.

5. Test the connection and if successful press **OK**.

6. Add a **Transfer SQL Server Objects Task** to the **Control Flow** in order to transfer SQL objects and data between two databases.

7. From the SSIS Toolbox, drag-and-drop a **Transfer SQL Server Objects Task** to the designer and open it for editing.

8. In the **Connection** group under **Objects** tab, select the source and destination connection and database.

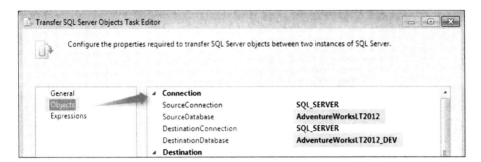

9. Once the connections are established the destination scenario should be configured. Highlighted in the picture below are the most common used properties of this task.

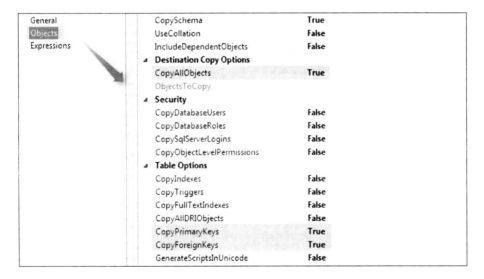

10. Set the **CopyAllObjects**, **CopyPrimaryKeys**, and **CopyForeignKeys** parameters as *True* and maintain the remaining properties as default.

11. Close the editor by pressing the **OK** button.

12. Execute the package pressing *F5*. If the execution is successful, the new database `AdventureWorksLT_DEV` should have all the objects created.

13. Edit the task again and change its configurations. This time, insert data into the destination.

14. Execute the package again by pressing *F5*. If the execution is successful, the new database `AdventureWorksLT_DEV` should also have data.

How it works...

There are lots of scenarios where we need to transfer objects such as database tables, views, stored procedures, functions, data, logins, and other SQL Server Objects between two databases. SSIS provides a set of Transfer Tasks to provide all this functionality between two SQL Servers:

▶ Transfer Database Task

▶ Transfer Error Messages Task

▶ Transfer Jobs Task

▶ Transfer Master Stored Procedures Task

▶ Transfer Logins Task

3

Data Flow Task Part 1—Extract and Load

by Reza Rad and Pedro Perfeito

In this chapter, we will cover:

- Working with database connections in Data Flow
- Working with flat files in Data Flow
- Passing data between packages—Raw Source and Destination
- Importing XML data with XML Source
- Loading data into memory—Recordset Destination
- Extracting and loading Excel data
- Change Data Capture

Introduction

Extract and Load are two main parts of an ETL (Extract, Transform, and Load). In this chapter, we will cover Extract and Load. Transform will be covered in the next two chapters.

SSIS Data Flow Task provides all the three parts of an ETL. Extract means fetching data from sources. Data Flow Task has some sources which are responsible for extracting data. Load means exporting data into destination. Data Flow Task provides bunches of Destination which helps you to perform the Load part of the ETL.

SSIS Data Flow Sources contains the following sources:

- OLE DB Source
- ADO.NET Source
- ODBC Source
- Excel Source
- Flat File Source
- Raw File Source
- XML Source
- CDC Source

And Data Flow Destinations consists of the following destinations:

- ADO.NET Destination
- Data Reader Destination
- Excel Destination
- Flat File Destination
- OLE DB Destination
- Raw File Destination
- Recordset Destination
- SQL Server Compact Destination
- SQL Server Destination

In this chapter, all of these sources and destinations will be covered. Two new components, Source and Destination Assistant, which have been added in SSIS 2012 will also be explained.

Working with database connections in Data Flow

In this recipe, we will explore the OLE DB Source and Destination, ADO.NET Source and Destination, and SQL Server Destination. These are the most common components used to move data from sources to destinations.

All the database connections provide a way to connect to the underlying database which can range from DB2 database to Oracle and MS SQL Server databases. For some of the databases we may need to install the Data Provider, but after installing the Data Provider we can use sources/destinations to connect to the underlying database.

In this recipe, different database sources and destinations will be explored and their pros and cons in different scenarios will be considered.

In this recipe, we will create a table in the MySQL database and transfer its data into SQL Server database table.

Getting ready

1. To install MySQL on Windows, you need to download WampServer which is available at `http://www.wampserver.com/en/download.php`. Install the WampServer once the download is completed.

2. After installing WampServer, if it doesn't start, it may be because Port 80 is busy with IIS. Click on the WampServer icon in systray, and under **Apache** select **httpd.conf**. In the opened file, replace **Listen 80** with **Listen 8083** and **ServerName localhost:80** with **ServerName localhost:8083**.

3. Click on the WampServer icon in systray. Then click **Apache | Service | Start/ Resume Service** as shown in the following screenshot:

4. After starting the Service you will see a green icon of the WampServer in systray.

5. Now, open IE and browse to `http://localhost:8083/phpmyadmin`.

6. Create a database and name it `PacktPub_SSISbook`. Then, go to the **import** tab, and select the `MySQLScript.sql` file from the source code provided for the book at the following address: `Ch03_Data Flow Task-Part 1-Extract and Load\R01_DatabaseConnections\Files\MySQLScript.sql`, or run the following script:

```
CREATE TABLE IF NOT EXISTS `user` (
  `ID` int(11) NOT NULL AUTO_INCREMENT,
  `FirstName` varchar(50) NOT NULL,
  `LastName` varchar(50) NOT NULL,
  PRIMARY KEY (`ID`)
) ENGINE=InnoDB  DEFAULT CHARSET=latin1 AUTO_INCREMENT=3 ;

INSERT INTO `user` (`ID`, `FirstName`, `LastName`) VALUES
(1, 'Reza', 'Rad'),
(2, 'Pedro', 'Perfeito');
```

7. You will see a table named `User`, and when you browse you will see the following data rows:

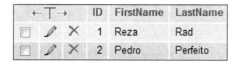

8. Download the latest MySQL connector available at `http://dev.mysql.com/downloads/connector/net/` and install it on your machine.

How to do it...

1. Open **SSDT**, create a new Project of type **Integration Services** and name it `R01_DatabaseConnections`.

2. Drag-and-drop a Data Flow Task from the SSIS Toolbox to the **Control Flow** empty area, double-click on it, and you will be redirected to **Data Flow** tab.

3. Drag-and-drop an ADO.NET Source from the SSIS Toolbox, under other sources into the **Data Flow** tab's empty area, and double-click on it.

4. In the **ADO.NET connection manager** section, click on the **New** button.

5. In the **Connection Manager Editor**, click on the drop-down list next to **Provider**, and under **.Net Providers** choose **MySQL Data Provider** as shown in the following screenshot:

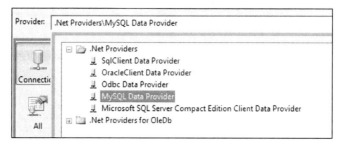

6. Set **Server name** as *localhost*, set **User name** as *root*, and leave **Password** blank, check the **Save my password** checkbox, and select *PacktPub_SSISbook* from the databases drop-down list.

7. Click on **Test Connection**, and confirm the successful connection.

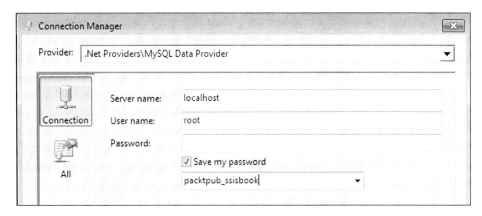

8. Click on **OK**, and return back to ADO.NET Source. Set **Data access mode** to _SQL Command_.

9. In the **SQL command text** text area type the following T-SQL query:

```
select * from user
```

10. Click the **Preview** button to see a preview of data rows in the `mysql` table.

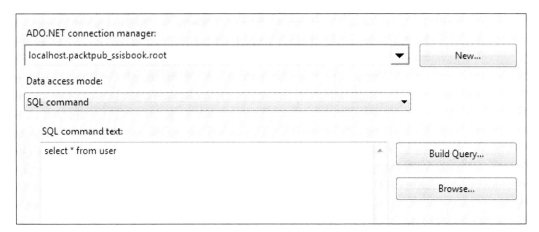

11. Click on **OK**, and close ADO.NET Source.

12. Drag-and-drop an **OLE DB Destination** from the **SSIS Toolbox**, under other sources. Double-click on **OLE DB Destination**.

13. In the **OLE DB Destination Editor**, create a new **Connection Manager**. In the **Connection Manager Editor**, set **Server name** to `local` or a single dot (`.`) and then set the authentication. In this recipe, we use Windows authentication. Select `PacktPub_SSISbook` from the databases list. Test the connection and verify it.

14. Click on **OK**, close the OLE DB connection manager editor and return back to OLE DB Source Editor. Set the **Data access mode** to *Table or view*. Click on the **New** button which is besides the **Name of the table or the view** drop-down list. Change the table name in the **Create Table** script from `[OLE DB Destination]` to `[User]` as shown in the following screenshot:

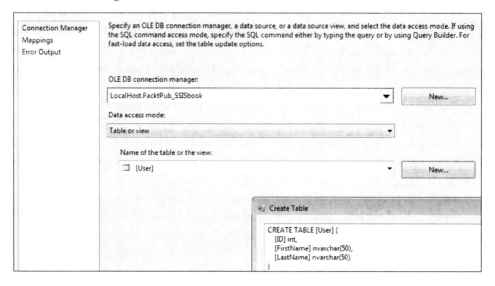

15. Go to the **Mappings** tab and verify the source and destination columns mappings.

16. Click on **OK**, close the OLE DB Destination, and run the package. Two rows will be transferred successfully to the SQL Server database table.

How it works...

Two different types of the most common database connection providers in SSIS are used in this recipe. We fetch the data from MySQL database with ADO.NET Source, and export data to SQL Server database with OLE DB Destination.

ADO.NET Source

ADO.NET Connection is a common way to connect to databases that do not have an OLE DB Connection. In this recipe, we used the ODBC connection for MySQL with an ADO.NET Source.

The first step in using ADO.NET Source or Destination is to create an ADO.NET connection manager. Connection Managers in SSIS provides a connection to the underlying database or data provider.

In this recipe, we used MySQL .NET connector to fetch data from MySQL database with ADO.NET source. There is another way to connect MySQL which is based on ODBC connectors. You can download the appropriate ODBC connector from mysql website and then create an ODBC connection. An ODBC connection to MySQL database can created with the connection string **"Driver={MySQL ODBC 5.1 Driver};server=localhost;uid=root;database=PacktPub_SSISbook"**. This string will use MySQL ODBC Driver version 5.1 which we downloaded and installed earlier and use `localhost` as the server name which will connect to MySQL database server on the local machine. `uid` defines a user to connect to the underlying database. The root user is the default user and is similar to `sa` in SQL Server database engine. By default, the root user has no password and that is the reason we do not have the password part mentioned in the connection string. The last part of the connection string is the database name.

If you have a DSN for connecting a database such as Foxpro and you want to connect to this database from SSIS, you just need to create an ADO.NET connection manager, and in the **Data source specification** section, choose *Use user or system data source name* and then you can choose that DSN from the list of system DSN.

Access mode in the ADO.NET Source determines how to read data, we can choose between the **Table or view** and **SQL Command**. Table or view will allow us to select a table or view from the source database and select all the columns from that table or view. But if we need to customize our source, write a complex query, or join some tables with the SQL Command we can choose the second option.

The **Build Query** button in the ADO.NET Source Editor provides a simple GUI for generating queries. You are probably familiar with its interface, you can add tables, choose fields as you want, define where conditions, and so on.

When the **Data access mode** is set to *SQL command*, a **Browse** button will appear. This button provides a way to select a file containing an SQL command as the source query.

The **Columns** tab in ADO.NET or other types of sources in SSIS Data Flow Task will show a list of all the columns that are fetched from the table or view name or sql command. We can change the name of output columns simply by clicking on the **Output Column** for the appropriate field and typing in that field as shown in the following screenshot:

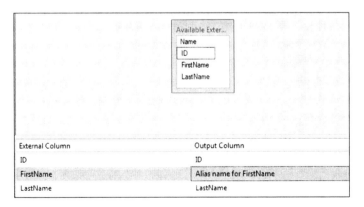

OLE DB Destination

OLE DB Connection provides a way to connect many databases. Using OLE DB Connection provides much faster access to underlying data than legacy ODBC connection providers. So try to use ODBC connections only if you cannot find any appropriate OLE DB connection provider for the underlying database. Fortunately SQL Server has an OLE DB Provider and we could use OLE DB Source when we want to fetch data from SQL Server databases.

We need an OLE DB Connection Manager to work with the OLE DB Source or Destination. The first step in the creation of an OLE DB Connection manager is to set the Provider. By default, the Provider is set to **SQL Server Native Client 11.0**. This provider has best performance to read SQL Server data than other providers. There are many OLE DB Providers for different database engines such as Oracle and Access as shown in the following screenshot:

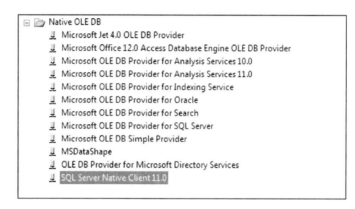

In the OLE DB connection manager there are important parts in the **Connection** tab. The server name should be the name of a database server or SQL Server Instance. A single dot or local represents the current system's default instance. Authentication is required for granting access to the underlying database. There are two types of authentication for SQL Server databases, that is, SQL Server authentication and Windows authentication. SQL Server authentication uses SQL Server login and password, and Windows authentication uses Windows accounts for SQL Server database connection. As our sample database is located under the default instance of an SQL Server which exists on our current machine, we used Windows authentication. The database name will obviously be the name of the underlying database which we are trying to connect to.

In OLE DB Destination, there is a `Data access mode` property. There are more options for data access in the OLE DB Source or Destination than in the ADO.NET Source or Destination. The access mode in OLE DB Destination is divided into the following options:

- A table or view. You can specify an existing table or view, or you can create a new table.
- A table or view using Fast Load options. You can specify an existing table or create a new table.

▶ A table or view specified in a variable.

▶ A table or view specified in a variable using fast load options.

▶ The results of an SQL statement.

Table or view option and Table or view from Variable (Without fast load postfix) loads data into the destination table row by row. We will discuss fast load option in the *There's more...* section later in this recipe.

When we choose the Table or View name as the **Data access mode**, we should select the table or view from the drop-down list. We could also generate a new table by clicking on the **new** button which is besides the drop-down list. This feature helps us to create a destination table with the structure of incoming columns, and generates it based on the incoming column names and data types. In this recipe, we create a `User` table in SQL Server database with this feature.

Lastly, in the OLE DB Destination Editor, similar to many other destination editors, there is a **Mappings** tab. In the **Mappings** tab all the input columns will be mapped to available destination columns. SSIS will map columns automatically if the names of columns are the same. If not, you will have to map them manually. For mapping columns you can click on the input columns and drag-and-drop them to the available destination column or you can map them with the grid below. You can remove any mapping by deleting that line of mapping directly.

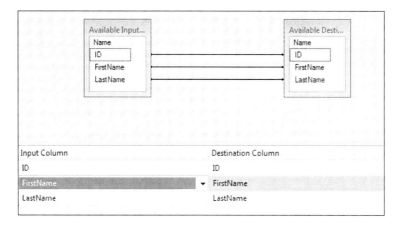

There's more...

There are many advanced features of Database Connections, Sources, and Destination. We will discuss them one by one in this section.

Connect to ODBC data providers

If you have worked with legacy databases you may have some ODBC defined in the **Control Panel | Administrative Tools | Data Sources (ODBC)**. You can use these defined DSN to create an ADO.NET Connection. In the ADO.NET connection manager's editor, in the **Data source specification** section, choose **Use user or system data source name**. A list of defined DSNs in the system will be explored as shown in the following screenshot. Select the appropriate DSN from the drop-down list.

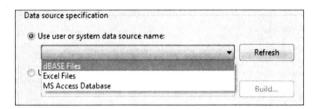

Exploring All properties of connection managers

There are many properties in ADO.NET or OLE DB connection managers. We can find these properties in the Connection Manager editor's **All** Tab.

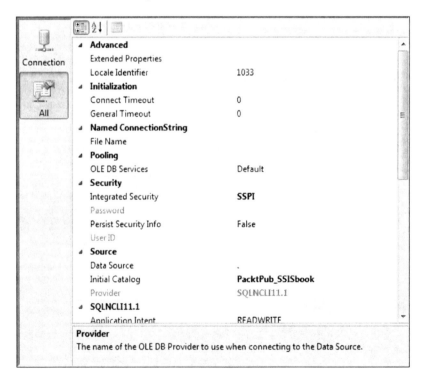

The **All** tab of OLE DB Connection Manager is shown in the previous screenshot. The properties have a wide range from basic settings to advanced options. Basic settings such as **Data Source** and Advanced options such as **Connect Timeout** and other options can be set here.

We will discuss these parameters later in this book.

Advanced Editor

The default editor of many Sources and Destinations is a basic editor that provides the ability to change few properties. But there is an Advanced Editor which provides a complete access to all settings in the Source or Destination.

The Advanced Editor can be reached by simply right-clicking on the source or destination and choosing **Advanced Editor**.

The Advanced Editor contains four tabs:

- **Connection Managers**
- **Component Properties**
- **Column Mappings**
- **Input and Output properties**

One of the most common scenarios of using Advanced Editor is changing the data type of output columns from the Source. We will explore different parts of Advanced Editors in different sources and destinations in the later chapters of this book.

Source and Destination Assistant

In the SSIS 2012 there are two new components in the Data Flow Toolbox—Source and Destination Assistant. These components provide a simple way to access sources or destinations. They provide a wizard such as the source and destination.

To work with these components we just need to drag-and-drop them in Data Flow. An **Add New Source** dialog box will appear. In this dialog box we can choose the source or destination as we want. There are a set of connection types in this dialog box. You should have some of these providers installed on your machine in order to use them.

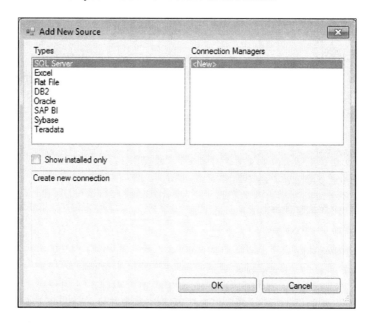

Shared Connection Manager

SSIS 2012 provides a way to create a shared connection manager and use it in all packages. To create a shared connection manager simply right-click on the **Connection Managers** folder in the **Solution Explorer** and choose **New Connection Manager**.

In the **Add SSIS Connection Manager** dialog box, select the appropriate type and create a connection.

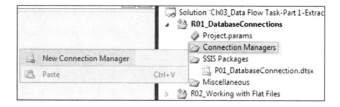

After creating the shared connection manager, you can simply see it in the package's **Connection Manager** pane in a bold font.

SQL Server Destination

There is another Destination for database connections in the SSIS Data Flow Toolbox named SQL Server Destination. This destination provides a high performance way to extract data into the SQL Server databases.

This Destination has a big limitation; we can use it only if the destination SQL Server database is on the same system that the SSIS package runs on.

We will discuss this destination later in this book.

Fast Load option

In the OLE DB Destination, when we choose the **Data access mode** to one of the options with a Fast Load prefix, there will be some advanced options to consider. The Fast Load option provides a way to load data into a destination table in batch operation and will obviously be much faster than the ordinary load.

The options without Fast Load postfix in the Data access mode will insert the data row by row, commit each row, and then go to next row. But the options with Fast Load will load a number of rows and commit them in a batch. The number of rows can be defined in the **Rows per batch** property or the size of data in each batch can be set in the **Maximum insert commit size**.

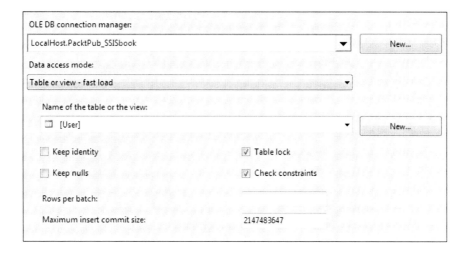

There are some options when Fast Load is selected. They are as follows:

▸ Keep identity values from the imported data file or use unique values assigned by SQL Server

▸ Retain a null value during the bulk load operation

▸ Check constraints on the target table or view during the bulk import operation

▸ Acquire a table-level lock for the duration of the bulk load operation

▸ Specify the number of rows in the batch and the commit size

One of the side effects of using Fast Load is that if one of the rows in the data stream fails while loading into the destination table then the whole batch will fail.

Querying source data dynamically

There are a lot of times when we need to query the source database dynamically and fetch data from a source based on some `where` conditions. OLE DB Source provides a way to parameterize the source query. We will discuss this feature in *Chapter 6, Variables, Expressions, and Dynamism in SSIS*.

See also

▸ *Data Flow best practices in Extract and Load* recipe in *Chapter 15, Performance Boost in SSIS*

▸ *Dynamic data transfer with different data structures* recipe in *Chapter 6, Variables, Expressions, and Dynamism in SSIS*

Working with flat files in Data Flow

In this recipe, we will demonstrate the use of the Flat File Source component that is often used in data integration projects. As explained in *Chapter 2, Control Flow Tasks* for security reasons, the Operational Systems (OS) owners usually prefer to push data to an external location in spite of providing direct access to the OS.

Data quality problems exist in conventional databases such as SQL Server, Oracle, DB2, and so on. It's possible to imagine the quality problems that could arise when dealing with flat files, the construction of these files could generate several problems because the external system that will read each record in this file (for example, the *Extract* step of the ETL process) needs to know how to split the record into columns and rows. The Row delimiter is required in order to split each row whereas the Column delimiter is required to split each column from each row. But in many cases, the Column delimiter can appear in the column content that will make an error arise. These scenarios will be described in this recipe.

Getting ready

To get ready for this recipe, use the following steps:

1. Open the **SQL Server Data Tools (SSDT)** and create a new SSIS project.
2. Provide a name and a location for the SSIS project and proceed.
3. Select the package created by default and rename it to `P01_FlatFileSource.dtsx`.

How to do it...

Consider the scenario where SSIS periodically needs to get data from a flat file to load it into a central repository. This recipe will begin using a simple flat file with four columns delimited by the ";" character and row delimited by "{CR}{LF}".

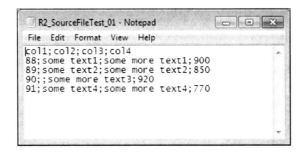

1. Add a **Data Flow** to the **Control Flow** and open it.

2. Create a Flat File Connection that points to the sample file included in the recipe.

3. Right-click the **Connection Manager** and select **New Flat File Connection...**.

4. Add a name to the connection manager property and locate the sample file `R2_SourceFileTest_01.txt` by clicking on the **Browse...** button.

5. The encoding will be recognized automatically by SSIS, but if not change it in the **Code page** property.

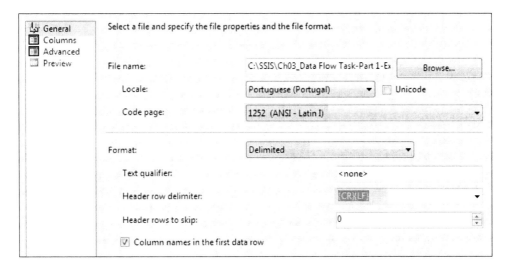

6. SSIS will also detect the flat file default values associated with this connection like the row and column delimiters.

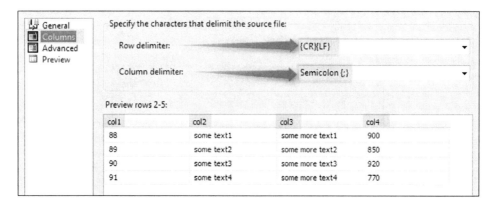

7. Drag-and-drop the **Flat File Source** component from the **SSIS Toolbox | Other Destinations** to the **Data Flow** design area.

8. Open the component for the purpose of editing.

9. The connection created in the previous step will be automatically assigned to the source component. It is required to assume the empty values from the source as NULL, tick the checkbox **Retain null values from the source as null values in the data flow**.

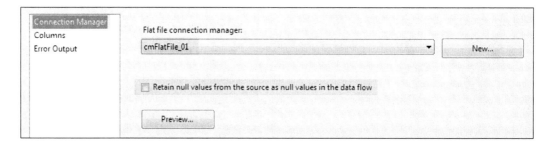

10. Add a **Union All** component for seeing data moving in the pipeline and link the source to it. Under the row that links the two components enable the data viewer.

11. Select the arrow that links the source to the destination components and activate the option **Enable Data Viewer** in order to visualize the data moving and to better understand it.

12. Press *F5* to execute the package. (Take a look at the **NULL** cell after ticking the **Retain null values from the source as null values in the data flow** checkbox).

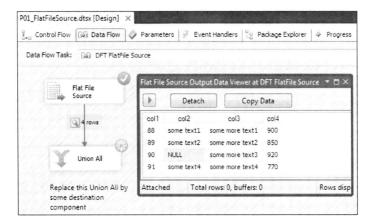

How it works...

The previous steps explain the configuration of a Flat File Source for a simple scenario with each row having four columns delimited by "`;`". Now imagine the case where the Column delimiter character "`;`" is used in the content of a column. How will SSIS split the columns?

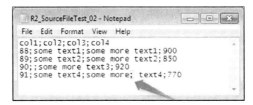

The problem is that SSIS ignores the last part of the record as can be seen in the following screenshot:

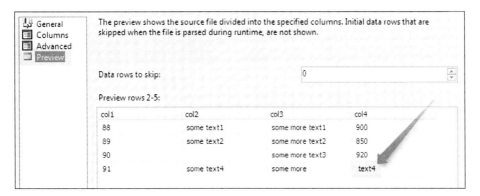

The solution for these kind of issues is to include the text qualifier between the entire columns as shown in the following screenshot:

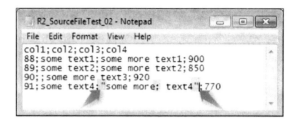

If this qualifier exists, insert " into the **Text qualifier** property of the Flat File Source as shown in the following screenshot:

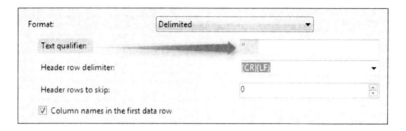

In this approach, SSIS ignores the " ; " character, it is just a normal character in a normal text column.

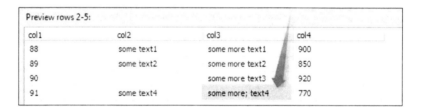

Passing data between packages—Raw Source and Destination

Staging is a very familiar terminology when working on Data Integration and ETL Tools. Staging in simple words means a space for storing data temporarily. In between the ETL steps, there are many times where staging plays an important role for data transfer and ETL cannot be implemented without staging.

The Raw Files format provided by SSIS is a binary format especially for SSIS which stores data in a binary format with special headings related to SSIS metadata. This binary format provides the fastest way to read and access data compared to other staging areas. Raw Source and Destination provides a way to read data from Raw File and Store data there respectively.

In this recipe, we will load data from a source into a Raw File for the purpose of staging. Suppose that this staging Raw File is used after some Control Flow Tasks or after some hours, then we use the Raw File as the source and extract its data to a destination.

How to do it...

1. Create a new **Integration Services** project and name it R03_RAW.

2. In the package **Control Flow** drag-and-drop a **Data Flow** Task into the Raw File and name it DFT_Load into Raw File.

3. Double-click on this Data Flow Task. In the **Data Flow** tab, add an OLE DB Source, and set the **Connection Manager** to AdventureWorks2012 database.

4. Select the table [Person].[Person] in **Table or view name** in the **OLE DB Source Editor**. Then click on **OK** and close the OLE DB Source Editor.

5. Drag-and-drop a Raw File Destination from the **SSIS Toolbox** under other destinations.

6. Double-click on the Raw File Destination, in the Raw File Destination Editor; verify that **File name** is selected as the **Access mode**.

7. Set the **File name** to C:\SSIS\Ch03_Data Flow Task-Part 1-Extract and Load\Files\rawfile.

8. Verify that **Create Always** is selected as the **Write option**.

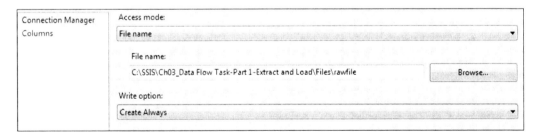

9. Go to the **Columns** tab, check only the following three columns: **BusinessEntityID**, **FirstName**, and **LastName**.

10. Click on **OK** and close the Raw File Destination Editor. Verify the schema of Data Flow for DFT_Load into the Raw File. It should be similar to the following screenshot:

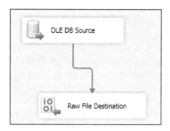

11. Go back to the **Control Flow**, add another Data Flow Task from the Raw File, and name this one as DFT_Extract.

12. Double-click on this Data Flow Task, and you will be redirected to **Data Flow** tab.

13. Drag-and-drop a Raw File Source from the SSIS Toolbox under the other sources into the **Data Flow**.

14. Double-click on Raw File Source, and in the Raw File Source, verify the **Access mode** to be **File name**.

15. Set the **File name** to C:\SSIS\Ch03_Data Flow Task-Part 1-Extract and Load\Files\rawfile.

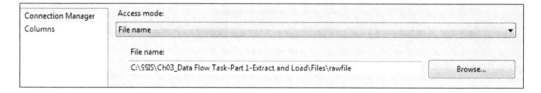

16. Click on **OK**, and close the Raw File Source.

17. Drag-and-drop a SQL Server Destination from the SSIS Toolbox under other destinations into the Data Flow Task right after the Raw File Source.

18. Double-click on SQL Server Destination, and the SQL Server Destination Editor will show up.

19. Create a new **Connection Manager** to `PacktPub_SSISbook` database. Then, click on the **New** button next to the **Use a table or view** drop-down, and rename `[OLE DB Destination]` to `[Person]` in the **Create Table** script as shown in the following screenshot:

20. Go to the **Mappings** tab and verify all mappings.

21. Close the SQL Server Destination Editor, and verify the Data Flow schema of `DFT_Extract` from the Raw File as shown in the following screenshot:

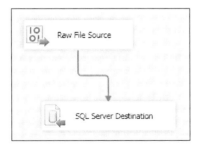

22. Go back to the **Control Flow**; connect the first Data Flow Task to the second one.

23. Run the package, and check the `Person` table in the `PacktPub_SSISbook` database, you will see records of data there.

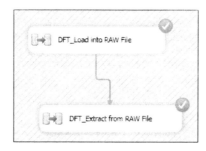

How it works...

In this recipe, we used a Raw File as the staging area. Real-world samples of Raw File Usages probably fill data into the Raw File and return back to this file after some control flow tasks, or after some hours in another scheduled package on the server.

In the first Data Flow Task, **DFT_Load into Raw File**, we fetched data from the OLE DB Source, and filled it in a Raw File Destination. Raw File Destination has some properties which will be described in the following section.

Raw File Destination

Access mode defines the path of the Raw File. It can be directly addressed by choosing the **File name** option, and the address will be filled in the **File name** textbox. The path can also be accessed from variable, by choosing **File name from variable**, and then choosing **variable** as the source.

The **Write option** determines how the Raw File will be written. We can choose between **Append**, **Create always**, **Create once**, and **Truncate and append**. The following table shows how each option behaves:

Option	Description
Append	Appends data to an existing file. The metadata of the appended data must match the file format.
Create always	Always creates a new file.
Create once	Creates a new file. If the file exists, the component fails.
Truncate and append	Truncates an existing file and then writes the data to the file. The metadata of the appended data must match the file format.

The table reference is available at `http://msdn.microsoft.com/en-us/library/ms141661.aspx`.

Raw File Source

Access mode is a property similar to Raw File Destination setting and we can choose between addressing the Raw File directly or from a variable.

There's more...

Raise performance with Raw Files

Raw Files as we mentioned earlier are binary files, and they don't need any coding or character rules of other staging areas conditions. Both of these aspects will make Raw files a very good place for staging data. We can also use Raw Files for cross-data flow or cross-package data posting.

Working with Raw Files is very easy and you can configure them a bit more with **Write option**.

Importing XML data with XML Source

XML is a global and platform-independent method to transfer data as we mentioned earlier. In the previous chapter, we used Web Service Task to fetch results of a web method into an XML file; also we tried to change the style of the XML data with XML Task. One of the most useful scenarios with XML data is to import the data into a database. We can do this with the help of XML Source.

XML Source provides a way to read data from the xml file based on the XSD schema file. XML Source can read simple flattened xml data or more complex data with hierarchical structure. In this recipe, we will import `books.xml` data into SQL Server database table.

Getting ready

Save contents of `books.xml` and `books.xsd` from this address into physical files: `http://msdn.microsoft.com/en-us/library/ms762258(v=VS.85).aspx`.

How to do it...

1. Create a new **Integration Services** project in BIDS, and name the project as `R04_XML Source`.
2. Add a **Data Flow Task** in the **Control Flow**, and double-click on it.
3. In the **Data Flow** tab, drag-and-drop the XML Source from the SSIS Toolbox under other sources.

4. Double-click on the XML Source, and in the XML Source Editor, verify if the **Data access mode** is set to *XML file location*.

5. In the **XML location** section, click on **Browse...** and select the books.xml file.

6. In the **XSD location** section, click on **Browse...** and select the books.xsd file.

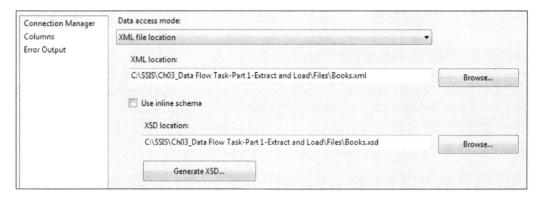

7. Go to the **Columns** tab, you will probably get a warning message. The message contains some lines similar to the following lines:

    Warning at {567DF984-7041-49EC-B472-BD389DB560F4} [XML Source [1629]]: No maximum length was specified for the XML Source.Outputs[book].Columns[id] with external data type System.String. The SSIS Data Flow Task data type "DT_ WSTR" with a length of 255 will be used.

8. Don't worry about this message; this message is just because the maximum length of columns wasn't set in the XSD file. Just click on **OK**, and leave this warning. This has no impact on our recipe, if XSD has the Length property for the element then this warning won't show up.

9. In the **Columns** tab verify **columns of data** fetched from the XML Source.

10. Click **OK**, and close the XML Source Editor.

11. Drag-and-drop an OLE DB Destination from the SSIS Toolbox under other destinations into the **Data Flow** tab, right after the XML Source.

12. Click on the XML Source, and drag the green line outgoing from this source to the OLE DB Destination.

13. Double-click on the OLE DB Destination, and OLE DB Destination Editor will show up.

14. Create a new OLE DB Connection Manager, in the **Connection Manager** Editor, verify if the **Provider** is set to *Native OLE DB\SQL Server Native Client 11.0*.

15. Set the server name as a single dot (.), and then choose **authentication mode**. In this recipe, we use Windows Authentication to make things simpler.

16. In the **Connection to database** section select the PacktPub_SSISbook database from the drop-down box, test the connection, and confirm it to be ok.

17. Go back to OLE DB Destination. Click the **New...** button besides the **Name of the table or the view** drop-down box. The **Create Table** dialog box will appear, change the name of the table from [OLE DB Destination] to [Book] and click on **OK**.

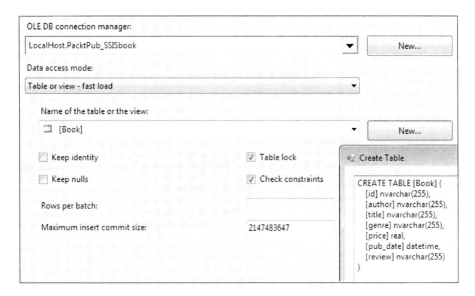

18. Go to the **Mapping** tab and verify that all the columns are mapped correctly together.

19. Click on **OK** to close the OLE DB Destination and run the package.

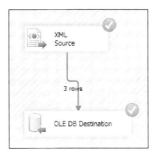

20. Open **SSMS**, under the PacktPub_SSISbook database, under Tables. Right-click on the Book table and choose **select Top 1000 rows**. After showing up content rows of table there will be three rows imported from the books.xml file as shown in the following screenshot:

id	author	title	genre	price	pub_date	review
bk001	Hightower, Kim	The First Book	Fiction	44.95	2000-10-01 00:00:00.000	An amazing story of nothing.
bk003	Nagata, Suanne	Becoming Somebody	Biography	NULL	NULL	A masterpiece of the fine art of gossiping.
bk002	Oberg, Bruce	The Poet's First Poem	Poem	24.95	NULL	The least poetic poems of the decade.

How it works...

In this recipe, we will read the book's information from an XML file and load it into the SQL Server database. XML Source reads the xml data provided by the XSD schema.

XML Source Editor has some options which will be discussed here; the first option is Data access mode. Data access mode determines where the XML data comes from. We can choose between:

- **XML file location**
- **XML file from variable**
- **XML data from variable**

In this recipe, we will use the first one and set the XML location to the path of the file. We can choose other options if our xml file path exists in a package variable.

Use Inline Schema should be set if the schema of an xml file exists in the xml data itself. In our recipe, the xsd file is another file so we didn't check this option.

We took a look at XSD in the *XML Task* recipe of the previous chapter. The address of the XSD file can be set in the XSD file location box.

Usually we will get the XSD file from the vendor who provides xml data, but if we have no XSD Schema file for the input xml data then SSIS XML Source itself can generate an XSD based on current data in the xml file. For using this feature we can click on **Generate XSD...** button. A **Save as** dialog box will appear to choose the path of the XSD file. Note that XML Source cannot generate XSD for complex xml files, in such cases you should generate the XSD yourself or simplify the xml data with the XML Task before feeding it in the Data Flow xml source.

The columns in the XML Source will be fetched based on metadata in XSD Schema; the XSD should contain column names, data types, maximum length, and so on. If the XSD schema misses some of these parts we will probably get an error or warning related to the metadata information about xml structure.

There's more...

XML data isn't always as simple as our recipe's sample data. Actually in many real-world scenarios XML files are complex.

Hierarchical XML data

One of the most useful scenarios of XML Source is to read hierarchical data from xml and fill it into Master-slave database tables. In these cases, the XML Source will generate multiple outputs based on sequence tags in XSD file and the outputs are related together with ids. In such scenarios, a single xml file may have more than one output to appropriate destination tables.

For example, we used the R4_XMLSource.xml file which contains books information and their chapters in the following way:

```
<Books>
  <Book ISBN="1849685245">
    <Title>Microsoft SQL Server Denali Integration Services Denali:
      An Expert Handbook</Title>
    <PublishDate>January 2012</PublishDate>
    <Chapters>
      <Chapter>
        <index>1</index>
          <Title>Getting Start with SQL Server Integration
            Services</Title>
      </Chapter>
      <Chapter>
        <index>2</index>
        <Title>Control Flow Tasks</Title>
      </Chapter>
```

The XML Source based on XSD is auto-generated, and it will solve these data into three outputs:

- ▶ Book
- ▶ Chapters
- ▶ Chapter

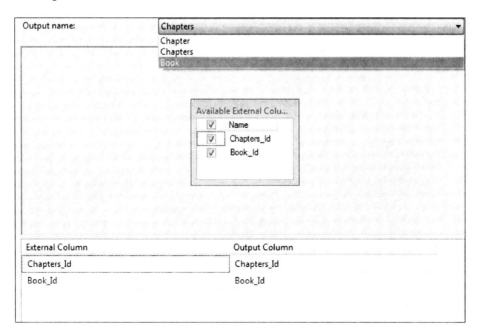

Loading data into memory—Recordset Destination

In this recipe, the use of the **Recordset Destination** component is demonstrated. Although not often used, it could help to fix specific real-world issues. This destination component does not save data to an external data source. Instead, it saves data into a memory ADO recordset through a SSIS object data type variable. This data is stored temporarily during the package execution and prepared inside a Data Flow. In other words, data is extracted and transformed along the Data Flow and inserted into the memory through the Recordset Destination which is to be used in another Data Flow or event in the Control Flow. Usually this component is used in conjunction with the Foreach loop task located in the Control Flow to loop through each record and act on each. This component follows the same logic of the remaining destination components that gets it metadata at design time from the source. Therefore, it is not possible to create it at runtime.

Getting ready

To get ready for this recipe, use the following steps:

1. Open the **SQL Server Data Tools (SSDT)** and create a new SSIS project.
2. Provide a name and a location for the SSIS project and proceed.
3. Select the package created by default and rename it to
   P01_RecordsetDestination.dtsx.

How to do it...

Consider the scenario where SSIS periodically needs to read customer data and for each record it needs to dispatch some marketing information about new products or services, or even alert the customer to a missed payment by SMS or e-mail. Therefore, after reading each customer data (extracting) and deciding what should be done with each customer (transformation), a task should be executed. A task such as Web service or Send Mail tasks can be called to execute a specific action related to each record/customer.

1. Add a **Data Flow** to the **Control Flow** and open it.

2. Create a **Flat File Connection** that points to the sample file included in the recipe.

3. Right-click on the **Connection Manager** and select **New Flat File Connection...**.

4. Click on the **Browse...** button and locate the sample flat file `R05_CustomerData.txt`.

5. The properties of the file such as encoding and delimiters are automatically detected by SSIS. (In this recipe, the **Column delimiter** is _Tab_.)

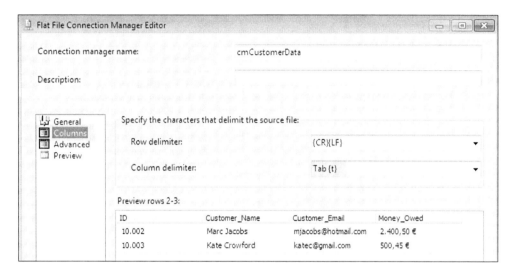

6. Drag-and-drop **Flat File Source** component from **SSIS Toolbox | Other Sources** to the **Data Flow** design area.

7. Open the component for the purpose of editing.

8. The connection created in the previous step will be automatically assigned to the source component. If not, select it from the respective drop-down.

9. Drag-and-drop the **Recordset Destination** component from **SSIS Toolbox | Other Destinations** to the **Data Flow** design area.

10. Link this component to the previous through the green output of the first.

11. In the **SSIS Variables** panel, create a new SSIS variable of the type `Object` to store data supplied from the Flat File Source.

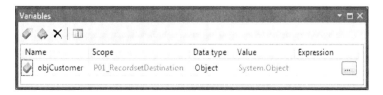

12. Open the Recordset Destination component for the purpose of editing.

13. In the **VariableName** under the **Custom Properties** group, select the SSIS variable created previously.

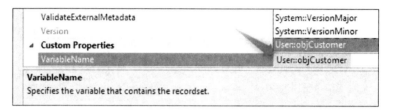

14. Select the columns in the pipeline that needs to be included in the memory, ticking the checkbox associated to each one as shown in the following screenshot:

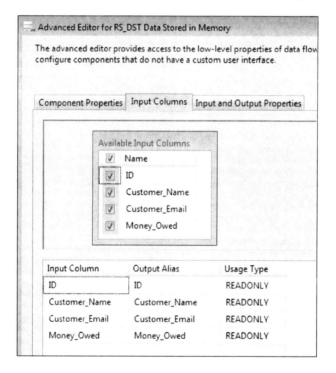

15. Execute the package by pressing *F5*.

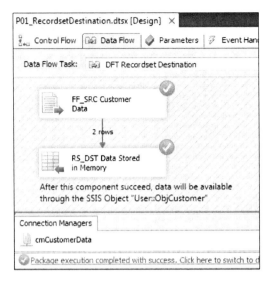

How it works...

The previous steps explain how to read some customer data from a flat file and save it to the memory. Before saving the data into memory, some transformations can be applied such as sorting, filtering, applying business rules, and other transformations. For example, if the money owed from the customer is less than 1.000€, the contact to the customer is done by e-mail, but if the amount owed is more than 1.000€, then the contact will be done by SMS to make sure that the customer will be alerted. Another scenario where this component is usually used is when it is required to read several files from a filesystem and a list of those files are saved into memory and combined with a `Foreach` loop to read each file at a time.

Extracting and loading Excel data

In this recipe, the use of Excel components to extract and load Excel data is demonstrated. As referred in the previous recipes, for security reasons, systems prefer to work with flat files, but people prefer work in Excel. Even if they have an application to use, they always end up exporting data to Excel. For that reason, there are hundreds of Excel files spread in all organizations. Even though with poor data quality initiatives, these files have important data to integrate and to be analyzed by end users, mainly decision makers. For that reason, the Excel Source and Destination components are often used in SSIS projects.

An Excel sample file is shown in the following screenshot:

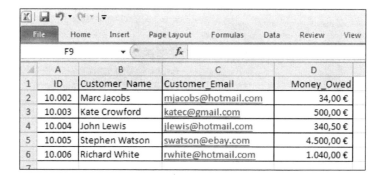

Getting ready

To get ready for this recipe, use the following steps:

1. Open **SQL Server Data Tools (SSDT)** and create a new SSIS project.
2. Provide a name and a location for the SSIS project and proceed.
3. Select the package created by default and rename it to `P01_WorkWithExcel.dtsx`.

How to do it...

In this recipe, a simple example package that extracts data from an Excel worksheet and loads the same data into another worksheet of the same file is created.

1. Add a **Data Flow** to the **Control Flow** and open it.
2. Create an Excel File connection that points to the sample file included in this recipe.
3. In the **Connection Manager** right-click and click on **New Connection...**.
4. In the **Connection manager type** list, select **Excel** type and click on the **Add...** button.
5. Click on the **Browse...** button and locate the sample Excel file `R06_CustomerData.xlsx`.
6. Drag-and-drop the **Excel Source** component from **SSIS Toolbox | Other Sources** to the **Data Flow** design area.
7. Open the component for the purpose of editing.
8. The connection created in the previous step will be automatically assigned to the source component. If not, select it from the respective drop-down.

9. In the **Data access mode** property, select **Table or view**. (Other options could be applied and are explained in the next section.)

10. In the **Name of the Excel sheet**, select the first worksheet **Sheet1$**.

11. The **Error Output** tab redirect rows to a destination in case of errors in conversions.

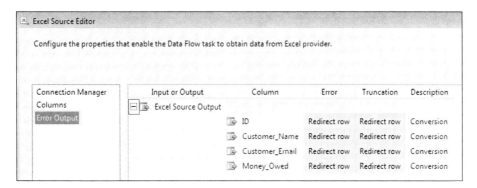

12. Drag-and-drop the **Union All** component from **SSIS Toolbox | Common** to the **Data Flow** design area.

13. Link this component to the previous through the red output of the first.

14. Drag-and-drop the **Excel Destination** component from **SSIS Toolbox | Other Destination** to the **Data Flow** design area.

15. Link this component to the previous through the green output of the first.

16. Open the **Excel Destination** component for the purpose of editing, and go to the **Mappings** tab to ensure the input columns in the pipeline are mapped to the destination columns.

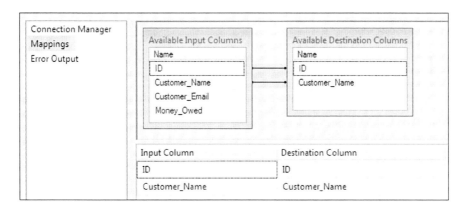

17. Click on the **OK** button to finish this component configuration.

18. Execute the package pressing *F5*.

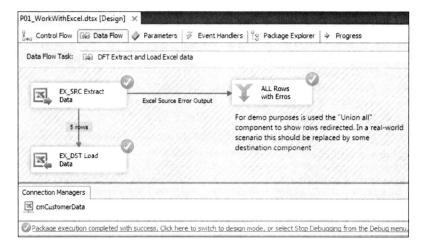

How it works...

The previous steps explain how to read some customer data from an Excel file worksheet and insert it in another worksheet of the same Excel file. The example is simple enough to show some key points to consider when using Excel in the scope of an SSIS package. These key points are described in the following section and are referred to the data access modes and how Excel deals with data types and errors.

Data access

The Excel Source extracts data from worksheets or ranges in Excel workbooks and provides four different data access modes:

- ▸ A table or view.
- ▸ A table or view specified in a variable.
- ▸ The results of an SQL command. The query can be a parameterized query.
- ▸ The results of an SQL command stored in a variable.

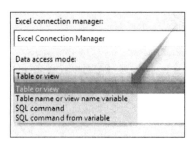

The Excel worksheet [Sheet1$] works similar to an SQL table. For that reason, for creating an access mode with a SQL command, it is just required to add a sentence as usual in SQL. In this recipe, we will replace the worksheet with the following statement:

```
SELECT ID, Customer_Name, Customer_Email, Money_Owed
FROM [Sheet1$]
```

The previous statement can also be improved using parameters as described in the following screenshot:

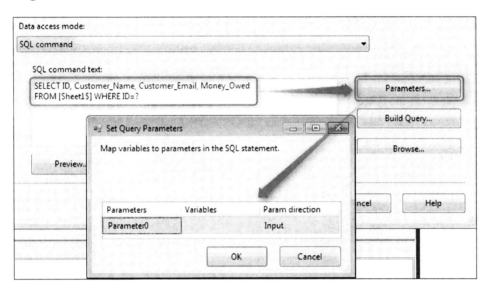

It can also be improved by using the SQL statement from a SSIS variable, in spite of including it inside the Excel component.

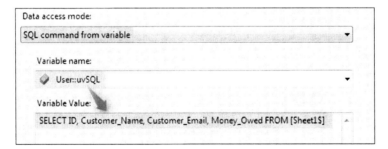

Data types

Excel recognizes only a limited set of data types. This limitation usually generates a large amount of issues when working with Excel. When a specific column in the source is a numeric then Excel considers a double type (DT_R8). Another common example is when a column is a string that is recognized by Excel driver as a Unicode string (`nvarchar`) with 255 characters length.

- ▸ **Numeric**: double-precision float (DT_R8)
- ▸ **Currency**: currency (DT_CY)
- ▸ **Boolean**: Boolean (DT_BOOL)
- ▸ **Date/time**: Datetime (DT_DATE)
- ▸ **String**: Unicode string, length 255 (DT_WSTR)
- ▸ **Memo**: Unicode text stream (DT_NTEXT)

To overcome this Excel limitation, it's suggested for some columns to set the **External Columns** (columns from the source) as strings with big length and in the **Output Columns** set them as the correct data type. If some column in a row is not of the desired format, this row is redirected to another output (**Error Output**) as shown in the following screenshot:

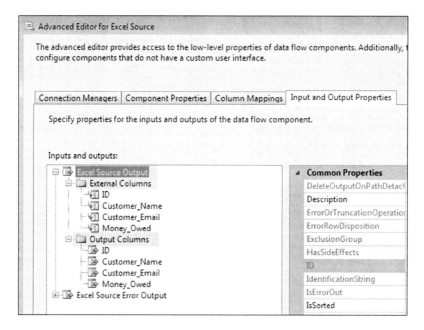

Whenever possible, columns should be converted in the source. Converting columns during the pipeline execution should be the last option.

Change Data Capture

An important concern, when dealing with data integration, is to detect which data has changed since the last time we accessed the source data location. It's required to avoid affecting source system operations and to make the process of reading data from a source location faster. It's better to get just the changed data, than extracting all the data.

Change Data Capture (CDC) feature was included in SQL 2008 version. It provides the possibility to detect change in data in a database. CDC seems to be one of the most powerful approaches as compared to the other known approaches such as audit columns, timed extracts, database log scraping, check sums, and others, CDC has low impact (does not require any changes into the main tables), low overhead (runs asynchronously, unlike the triggers used in the audit columns approach (the most often used approach)), is also easy to use.

In spite of using the `Datetime` field to get the data change ranges, CDC uses a unique and sequence identifier, known as **log sequence number (LSN)**, to get a range of data in a specific period of time.

Getting ready

To get ready for this recipe, use the following steps:

1. Open **SQL Server Data Tools (SSDT)** and create a new SSIS project.
2. Provide a name and location for the SSIS project.
3. Select the package created by default and rename it to:
   `P01_IncrementalLoad.dtsx`.

How to do it...

To enable CDC some important steps must be considered. They are as follows:

1. Enable CDC on database and respective table(s).
2. Configure the initial LSN (log sequence number) to start processing changed data.
3. Get changed data inside and mark the end of the processing range.

The following steps explain what should be done in SSMS and SSDT to make CDC work:

1. Enable CDC capture functionality through SSMS.
2. Open **SSMS**, select **AdventureWorksLT2012** database and click on **New Query...**.

3. Enable CDC capture on the database `AdventureWorksLT2012` by executing the following SQL statement:

    ```
    EXEC sys.sp_cdc_enable_db
    ```

4. If the previous statement executes successfully, the database name will be shown as activated in the result of the following statement:

    ```
    SELECT name AS Databases, is_cdc_enabled FROM sys.databases
    ```

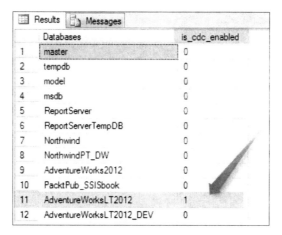

5. Enable CDC capture on the `Customer` table by executing the following SQL statement:

    ```
    EXEC sp_cdc_enable_table 'SalesLT', 'Customer',@role_name = NULL,
    @supports_net_changes =1
    ```

6. Two SQL jobs, shown in the previous screenshot, and several other SQL objects are created to enable CDC on the `Customer` table from the `AdventureWorksLT2012` database.

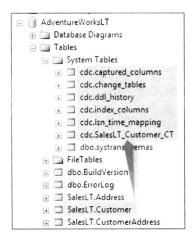

7. If the previous SQL statement executes successfully, the database table `Customer`, will be shown as activated in the result of the following statement:

    ```
    SELECT name, is_tracked_by_cdc FROM sys.tables
    ```

8. In SSDT, create an ADO.Net Connection to the `AdventureWorksLT2012` database sample.

9. In the **Connection Manager** right-click and then click on **New ADO.Net Connection...**.

10. In the **Data Connections** list select the `AdventureWorksLT2012` database. If it is not listed, create a new one by clicking on the **New...** button.

11. Click on the **OK** button and rename the connection to `cmADOAdventureWorksLT`.

12. Add a CDC Control Task to start filling the current log sequence number (LSN) and also configure a SQL table to store the CDC state.

13. Drag-and-drop the **CDC Control** Task from the **SSIS Toolbox | Other Tasks** to the **Control Flow** design area.

14. Open the task for the purpose of editing.

15. Set the **ADO.Net connection** to the connection previously created.

16. Create a new SSIS variable to store the CDC state by clicking on the **New...** button.

17. Select a table to store the CDC state for future extractions. If no table is created to store this information, SSIS will provide a way to create it automatically with the help of the **New...** button.

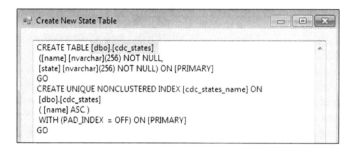

18. Click on **Run** to create the table in the AdventureWorksLT2012 database.

19. Set the **CDC control operation** property to *Mark CDC start*. (This operation will save the CDC state to the SQL table created previously.)

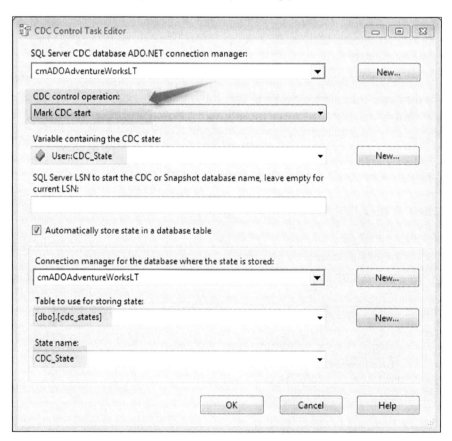

20. Click on **OK** to close the editor.

21. Press *F5* to execute the package and state the current CDC state in the SQL table created previously.

22. In SSMS read the contents of the `[cdc_states]` table with the last access register as the LSN number.

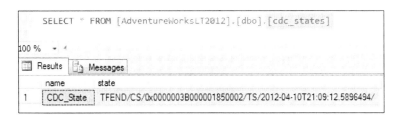

23. Disable this task and proceed with the remaining CDC configuration.

24. Add a CDC Control Task to get the processing range of the data that has changed since the last extraction.

25. Drag-and-drop the **CDC Control Task** from the **SSIS Toolbox | Other Tasks** to the **Control Flow** design area.

26. Open the task for the purpose of editing and use the same configuration of the previous task, changing only the value of the **CDC control operations** property to `Get processing range`. (This operation will allow changes to be made between the LSN stored before and the LSN created by this second CDC Task.)

27. Click on **Ok** to close the editor.

28. Add a **Data Flow** to the **Control Flow** in order to process the changed data since the latest access to the source.

29. Drag-and-drop the **Data Flow Task** from the **SSIS Toolbox | Favorites** to the **Control Flow** design area.

30. Open the **Data Flow** for the purpose of editing.

31. Drag-and-drop the **CDC Source** component from **SSIS Toolbox | Other Sources** to the **Data Flow** design area.

32. Double-click the **CDC Source** component for the purpose of editing.

33. Set the **ADO.Net connection manager** property to *cmADOAdventureWorksLT*.

34. Set the **CDC enabled table** property to the table that was configured to store CDC: `[SalesLT].[Customer]`.

35. Set the **CDC processing mode** property to *Net*. This mode is the most often used mode because it has just the filter records. (For example, the same customer that was inserted and then updated, just generates one row in spite of two rows for each operation.)

36. Set the **Variable containing the CDC state** to the SSIS variable `CDC_State` created and in the CDC Task on the **Control Flow** design area.

37. Drag-and-drop the **CDC Splitter** component from the **SSIS Toolbox | Other Transforms** to the **Data Flow** design area.

38. Link both the components.

39. Drag-and-drop three **Union All** components from the **SSIS Toolbox | Common** to each output provided by **CDC Splitter** component and based on the __$operation:

```
__$operation = 1 Delete
__$operation = 2 Insert
__$operation = 3 Update before change
__$operation = 4 Update after change
```

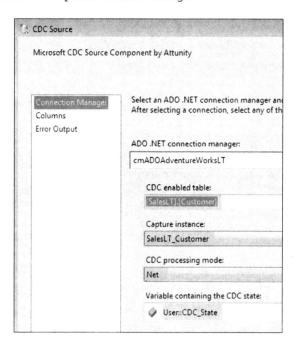

40. In SSMS, simulate some data changes in `Customer` table to see the CDC in action.

41. Insert a new `Customer` in the `Customer` table using the following code:

```
INSERT INTO [SalesLT].[Customer] (NameStyle,FirstName,LastName,Pas
swordHash,PasswordSalt)

VALUES (0,'Peter','Mackensie','','')
```

42. Update an existing customer by using the following code:

```
UPDATE [SalesLT].[Customer] SET LastName='Mourinho'
WHERE CustomerID=3
```

43. Simulate some other changes in this table.

44. Execute the package by pressing *F5* and see the changed data captured components and tasks in action.

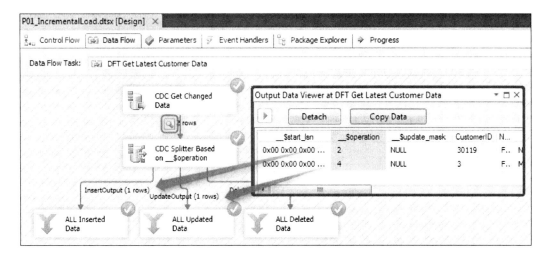

45. The CDC Source component detects the changes applied in the previous SQL statements.

46. If the CDC capture is not updated in the `cdc_states` table, the CDC Source will always read the changes between the last CDC state and the state detected by the CDC Task that get the processing range.

47. Add a CDC Control Task to the **Control Flow** to update the CDC state with the latest LSN access.

48. Drag-and-drop the **CDC Control** Task from the **SSIS Toolbox | Other Tasks** to the **Control Flow** design area

49. Open the task for the purpose of editing and use the same configuration of the previous CDC Task. In the **CDC control operations** property, in spite of **Get processing range**, set the value **Mark processed range** to update the latest CDC state in the `cdc_states` table.

50. After all the changes are replicated in the final destination, execute the package twice by pressing *F5*. You will observe that the second time no changes will be detected by CDC Source inside the **Data Flow**.

How it works...

The previous steps explained in detail how to activate the CDC features under a SSIS package. It was demonstrated how an incremental load can be automated using the new CDC tasks and components.

The first step was to activate the CDC in the SQL database and table. Several objects such as tables, stored procedures, and functions are created under the respective database. The table which CDC was applied to was replicated under the System Tables folder with the suffix :_CT.

For further details about SQL CDC objects created, see the following link:
http://msdn.microsoft.com/en-us/library/bb500353(v=sql.110).aspx.

In SSIS, the CDC capture is prepared for two common scenarios, namely, the initial load and the incremental load. Configure the CDC task under the **Control Flow** appropriately in both the scenarios.

In the initial load CDC Task should be created with the CDC control operation, one with **Mark initial load start** and other with **Mark initial load end** to mark the initial and final access respectively.

In the incremental load (considered in this recipe) CDC Task should be configured to start through **Mark CDC start** and other two tasks to set the range **Get processing range** and to mark the end with *Mark processed range*. Then the CDC Source component under **Data Flow** will work properly and be controlled by the previous created tasks. The final appearance of the **Control Flow** will look similar to the following screenshot:

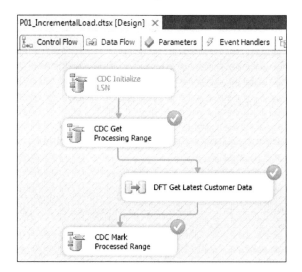

4

Data Flow Task Part 2— Transformations

by Reza Rad and Pedro Perfeito

In this chapter, we will cover the following topics:

- ▶ Derived Column: adding calculated columns
- ▶ Audit Transformation: logging in Data Flow
- ▶ Aggregate Transform: aggregating the data stream
- ▶ Conditional Split: dividing the data stream based on conditions
- ▶ Lookup Transform: performing the Upsert scenario
- ▶ OLE DB Command: executing SQL statements on each row in the data stream
- ▶ Merge and Union All transformations: combining input data rows
- ▶ Merge Join Transform: performing different types of joins in Data Flow
- ▶ Multicast: creating copies of the data stream
- ▶ Working with BLOB fields: Export Column and Import Column transformations
- ▶ Slowly Changing Dimensions (SCDs) in SSIS

Introduction

Transforming data is one of the most important parts of ETL. There are lots of useful transformations that tailor your data just the way you'd like it.

We will take a look at some useful transformations in this chapter and cover some more advanced transformations in the next chapter.

Derived Column: adding calculated columns

Creating customized columns is among the most common requirements in the ETL. The **Derived Column Transform** provides a way to write custom expressions in order to create new columns or replace existing columns. The customization of generated columns is based on expressions.

In this recipe we will get a list of employees from the `EmployeeDepartmentHistory` table. We have two columns that serve as sources: `StartDate` and `EndDate`. We will fetch a value for the `YearsInCompany` field by subtracting the `StartDate` year from the `EndDate` year; and if `EndDate` is Null, then subtracting the `StartDate` from the current date.

Getting ready

Create a new empty file. Name it `R01_Destination.csv` in the `C:\SSIS\Ch03_Data Flow Task-Part 2-Transformations\Files` directory, then save it with `utf-8` encoding. We will use this file as our destination. Select the package created by default and rename it to "P01_DerivedColumn.dtsx"

How to do it...

1. Create a new Integration Services type project and name it `R01_Derived Column`.

2. Drag-and-drop a Data Flow Task into the Control Flow and then go to the **Data Flow** tab.

3. Drag-and-drop an **OLE DB Source** into the **Data Flow** tab, and open the OLE DB Source Editor.

4. Create a new connection to the `AdventureWorks2012` database and set the **Data Access Mode** as *Table or view*, then select *[HumanResources].[vEmployeeDepartmentHistory]* from the list of tables or views.

5. Click on **Preview** and you will see that there is a `StartDate` and an `EndDate` column, but `EndDate` has a Null value in most rows.

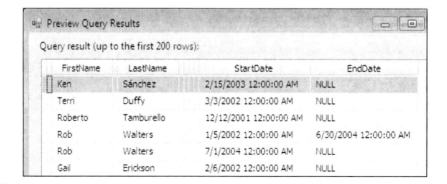

FirstName	LastName	StartDate	EndDate
Ken	Sánchez	2/15/2003 12:00:00 AM	NULL
Terri	Duffy	3/3/2002 12:00:00 AM	NULL
Roberto	Tamburello	12/12/2001 12:00:00 AM	NULL
Rob	Walters	1/5/2002 12:00:00 AM	6/30/2004 12:00:00 AM
Rob	Walters	7/1/2004 12:00:00 AM	NULL
Gail	Erickson	2/6/2002 12:00:00 AM	NULL

6. In the **Columns** tab just select *FirstName*, *LastName*, *StartDate*, and *EndDate*.

7. Go to **SSIS Toolbox**, from the **Common** section, drag-and-drop a **Derived Column** into the Data Flow right after the **OLE DB Source**, and connect the **Data Path** (green arrow) from **OLE DB Source** to **Derived Column**.

8. Double-click on **Derived Column Transform** to open the **Derived Column Transformation Editor**.

9. Write the following expression in the **Expression** field:

```
YEAR(ISNULL(EndDate) ? GETDATE() : EndDate) - YEAR(StartDate)
```

10. In the **Derived Column Name** field enter *YearsInCompany*.

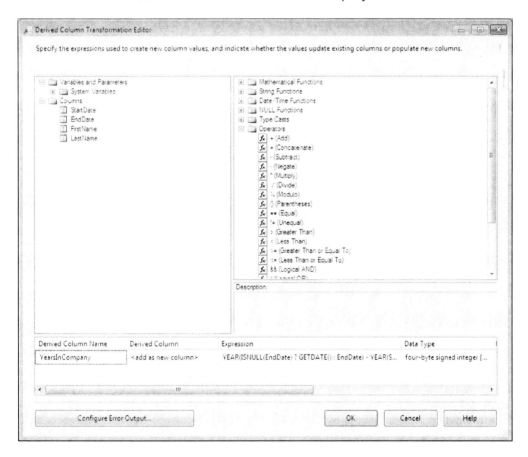

11. Drag-and-drop a **Flat File Destination** right after the **Derived Column** and connect **Data Path** from **Derived Column** to the **Flat File Destination**.

12. In the **Flat File Destination Editor**, click on **New** and set the **Flat File Format** as *Delimited*.

13. Browse the `R01_Destination.csv` file from the following address: `C:\SSIS\Ch03_Data Flow Task-Part 2-Transformations\R01_DerivedColumn\Files`.

14.. Check the column names in the first data row and then go to the **Columns** tab, and confirm whether all required columns are present; you will see the `YearsInCompany` column as well as the other columns there.

15. Close the Flat File connection manager and **Flat File Destination**, and run the package.

16. Go to `C:\SSIS\Ch03_Data Flow Task-Part 2-Transformations\Files` and open `R01_Destination.csv`. You will see the new `YearsInCompany` column with calculated values after all the other columns.

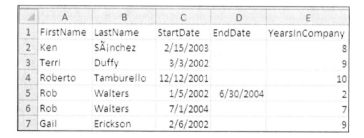

	A	B	C	D	E
1	FirstName	LastName	StartDate	EndDate	YearsInCompany
2	Ken	SÃinchez	2/15/2003		8
3	Terri	Duffy	3/3/2002		9
4	Roberto	Tamburello	12/12/2001		10
5	Rob	Walters	1/5/2002	6/30/2004	2
6	Rob	Walters	7/1/2004		7
7	Gail	Erickson	2/6/2002		9

How it works...

The Derived Column transformation is a basic principle that's very simple to use, and yet, one of the most useful transformations. This transformation provides a way to write a custom snippet of code called an **Expression**.

The Expression is a functional expression similar to C#. The functions that we can use are divided into four categories:

▸ Mathematical functions

▸ String functions

▸ Date/Time functions

▸ NULL functions

There are a variety of functions in each category. In this recipe we used the `ISNULL` function to find out whether the `EndDate` column has a Null value or not. The `YEAR` function will fetch the year part of a date value, and the `GETDATE()` function will return the current date.

There are also many operators that can be used. In this recipe we used a conditional operator, which is similar to what you'd see in C#:

```
«boolean_expression» ? «when_true» : «when_false»
```

There are two other trees in the **Derived Column Transformation Editor**, one for **Variables and Parameters** and another for **Columns**.

In summary, an expression can be a combination of:

▸ Columns, variables, and parameters

▸ Operators

▸ Functions

▸ Type Casts

Not all of these parts need to be together. A list of all expression functions will be discussed in *Chapter 6, Variables, Expressions, and Dynamism in SSIS*.

We can add numerous Derived Columns by adding expressions in the rows of the grid in the **Derived Column Transformation Editor**; the data type of each output column will be set by resolving the data type from the entered expression.

In the Derived Column we can choose between adding a new column or replacing an existing column.

Audit Transformation: logging in Data Flow

When you run SSIS packages through the SSDT environment it's possible to see any unexpected errors, the tasks and components that are currently executing, and the data that is moving within the pipeline, all in real time. All this gives us the impression that everything is under control. In the real world, however, SSIS packages run in batch mode and it's very difficult to know what is happening if the logs are not activated and used.

SSIS provides an automatic logging system that is shown in *Chapter 11, Event Handling and Logging*, and also provides several system variables that could be used to store extra information about the tasks that are running!

Getting ready

To get ready for this recipe, use the following steps:

1. Open **SQL Server Data Tools** (**SSDT**) and create a new SSIS project.
2. Provide a name and a location for the SSIS project and proceed.
3. Select the package created by default and rename it to P01_Audit.dtsx.

How to do it...

Consider a Data Warehousing scenario where system variables need to be added to Staging or even Data Warehouse tables. In this recipe, the Order Details table will be read from the AdventureWorksLT database and transformed with extra columns to be inserted into a destination (in this case the destination is a UNION ALL for demo purposes).

1. Add a **Data Flow** to the **Control Flow** tab and open it.
2. Create an OLEDB connection for the source component to the AdventureWorksLT2012 database sample.
3. In the connection manager right-click to add a **New OLEDB Connection**.
4. In the **Data Connections** list select the AdventureWorksLT2012 database. If it is not listed, create one by pressing the **New** button.
5. Press the **OK** button and rename the connection to cmAdventureWorksLT.
6. Drag-and-drop the **OLE DB Source** component from **SSIS Toolbox | Other Sources** to the **Data Flow** design area.
7. Open the component for editing.
8. The connection created in the previous step will be automatically assigned to the source component. If it is not, select it from the respective drop-down menu.
9. In the **Data access mode** property select **Table or view**. Other options could be applied as explained in the previous chapter.
10. In the **Name of the table or view** property, select *[SalesLT].[SalesOrderDetail]*.

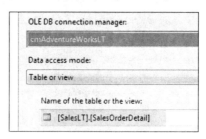

11. Drag-and-drop the **Audit** component from **SSIS Toolbox | Other Transforms** to the **Data Flow** design area.

12. Link this component to the previous one through the red output of the first component.

13. Open the component for editing.

14. Select each system variable available from the drop-down list.

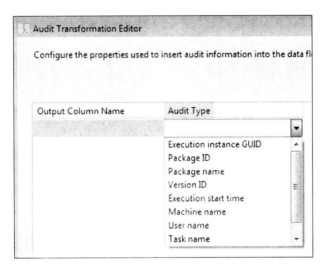

15. After each variable is selected, the final properties should appear as follows:

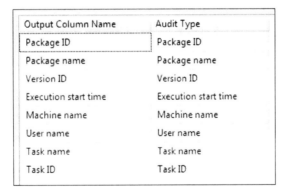

16. Press **OK** to save your changes and close the editor.

17. Drag-and-drop the **Union All** component from **SSIS Toolbox | Common** to the **Data Flow** design area.

18. Link this component to the previous one through the red output of the first component.

19. Under the green row that links **Audit** to **Union All**, right-click and select the **Enable Data Viewer** option to view the data moving through the pipeline.

20. Press *F5* to execute the package and check the extra columns added to the pipeline.

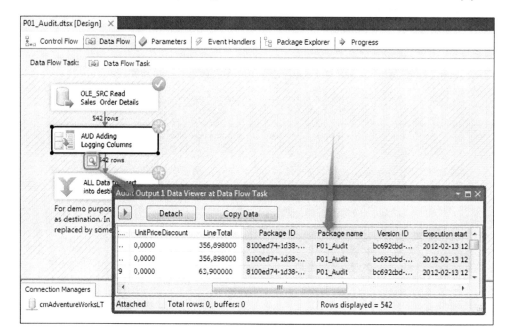

How it works...

The previous steps explain the use of the **Audit** component inside an SSIS package Data Flow. This component adds SSIS System Variables values' into new columns of Data Flow. The available variables are:

- ExecutionInstanceGUID: The GUID that identifies the execution instance of the package
- PackageID: The unique identifier of the package
- PackageName: The package's name
- VersionID: The version of the package
- ExecutionStartTime: The time that the package began running
- MachineName: The computer's name
- UserName: The login name of the person who started the package
- TaskName: The name of the Data Flow Task with which the Audit transformation is associated
- TaskId: The unique identifier of the Data Flow Task

All these system variables can also be included in the SSIS pipeline through the **Derived Column** component.

Aggregate Transform: aggregating the data stream

Aggregate Transform provides a way to group data by column(s) and apply aggregation functions on them.

In this recipe we will fetch each Sales Person according to the start and end date of sales and the sum of their sales quota by resorting to an Aggregate Transform.

How to do it...

1. Create a new Integration Services project and name it `R03_Aggregate`.

2. Add a Data Flow Task and in the **Data Flow** tab add an **OLE DB Source** and then create a connection to the `AdventureWorks2012` sample database. Set the data access mode to *SQL Command* and enter the following T-SQL code in the **SQL Command** field:

```
SELECT SLHST.QuotaDate, SLHST.SalesQuota,
    PER.FirstName, PER.LastName
FROM Sales.SalesPersonQuotaHistory SLHST
  INNER JOIN Person.Person PER
  ON SLHST.BusinessEntityID = PER.BusinessEntityID
```

3. Click on **Preview** and check the structure of your data.

QuotaDate	SalesQuota	FirstName	LastName
7/1/2005 12:00:00 AM	28000	Stephen	Jiang
10/1/2005 12:00:00 AM	7000	Stephen	Jiang
1/1/2006 12:00:00 AM	91000	Stephen	Jiang
4/1/2006 12:00:00 AM	140000	Stephen	Jiang
7/1/2006 12:00:00 AM	70000	Stephen	Jiang
10/1/2006 12:00:00 AM	154000	Stephen	Jiang
1/1/2007 12:00:00 AM	107000	Stephen	Jiang
4/1/2007 12:00:00 AM	58000	Stephen	Jiang
7/1/2007 12:00:00 AM	263000	Stephen	Jiang
10/1/2007 12:00:00 AM	116000	Stephen	Jiang
1/1/2008 12:00:00 AM	84000	Stephen	Jiang
4/1/2008 12:00:00 AM	187000	Stephen	Jiang
7/1/2005 12:00:00 AM	367000	Michael	Blythe
10/1/2005 12:00:00 AM	556000	Michael	Blythe
1/1/2006 12:00:00 AM	502000	Michael	Blythe
4/1/2006 12:00:00 AM	550000	Michael	Blythe
7/1/2006 12:00:00 AM	1429000	Michael	Blythe
10/1/2006 12:00:00 AM	1324000	Michael	Blythe

4. Drag-and-drop an **Aggregate Transform** right after the **OLE DB Source** and connect the Data Path to the aggregate transformation.

5. In the **Aggregate Transformation Editor**, add `FirstName`, `LastName`, and confirm the **Operation** to be *Group by*. Add the `SalesQuota` with **Operation** *Sum* (this will be set by default). Add the `QuotaDate` two times, once with **Output Alias** *StartDate* and **Operation** *Minimum*, another with **Output Alias** *EndDate* and **Operation** *Maximum*.

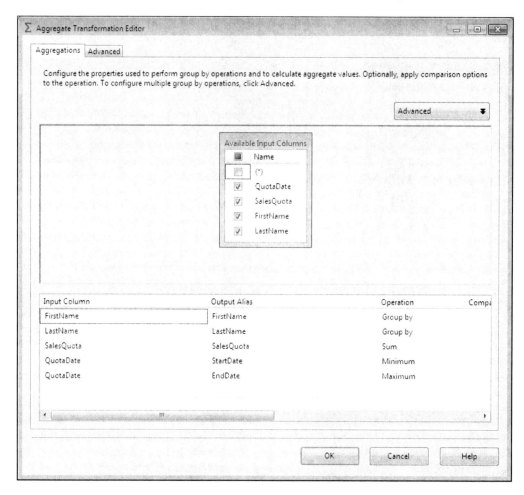

6. Add a **Flat File Destination**; then connect a **Data Path** from **Aggregate Transform** to this destination. Create a new Flat File connection manager with file format as *Delimited*, and add the address to the `Destination.csv` file in `C:\SSIS\Ch03_ Data Flow Task-Part 2-Transformations\Files`. Also verify whether all the necessary columns are present.

7. Close **Flat File Destination** and run the package; there are 163 rows coming out from the **OLE DB Source**, but **Aggregate Transform** will group them in only 17 rows.

8. Open the `R03_Destination.csv` file and check the result; `SalesQuota` shows all sales by specified sales person and start and end date of sales.

FirstName	LastName	SalesQuota	StartDate	EndDate
Michael	Blythe	11162000	7/1/2005 0:00	4/1/2008 0:00
Shu	Ito	7804000	7/1/2005 0:00	4/1/2008 0:00
Ranjit	Varkey Chudukatil	5557000	7/1/2006 0:00	4/1/2008 0:00
Syed	Abbas	205000	7/1/2007 0:00	4/1/2008 0:00
JosÃ©	Saraiva	7098000	7/1/2005 0:00	4/1/2008 0:00
Tsvi	Reiter	8541000	7/1/2005 0:00	4/1/2008 0:00
Jillian	Carson	12198000	7/1/2005 0:00	4/1/2008 0:00
David	Campbell	4025000	7/1/2005 0:00	4/1/2008 0:00
Stephen	Jiang	1305000	7/1/2005 0:00	4/1/2008 0:00
Garrett	Vargas	4365000	7/1/2005 0:00	4/1/2008 0:00
Amy	Alberts	876000	7/1/2006 0:00	4/1/2008 0:00
Lynn	Tsoflias	1687000	7/1/2007 0:00	4/1/2008 0:00
Rachel	Valdez	2287000	7/1/2007 0:00	4/1/2008 0:00
Pamela	Ansman-Wolfe	3551000	7/1/2005 0:00	4/1/2008 0:00
Tete	Mensa-Annan	2753000	10/1/2006 0:00	4/1/2008 0:00
Linda	Mitchell	11786000	7/1/2005 0:00	4/1/2008 0:00
Jae	Pak	10514000	7/1/2006 0:00	4/1/2008 0:00

How it works...

The Aggregate Transform provides a way to use aggregation functions. The **Operation** property defines the aggregation function, which consists of:

- Group by
- Count
- Count distinct
- Sum
- Average
- Minimum
- Maximum

The Aggregate Transform will group input the data stream by those columns that are set up with a *Group by* operation and then generate output columns with aggregate transformation on Sum, Count, Count distinct, Average, Minimum, and Maximum.

In this recipe, an input data stream was grouped by the first name and last name of a sales person, and a sum of the sales quota and the minimum and maximum of the quota date fetched for each group of sales persons.

Comparison Flags is a property that is configurable in the *Group by* fields, and it defines the way string data will be compared. There are four options here:

Comparison Flags	Description
Ignore case	Ignore the case of strings; "ABC" and "abc" will be considered as equal with this option.
Ignore kana type	Ignore the difference between two different Japanese string types; hiragana and katakana.
Ignore non-spacing characters	Treat diacritics; for example, "é" and "e" are equal.
Ignore character width	Ignore the same character in a single byte and double byte presentations as equal.

There is an advanced option in the Aggregate Transformation Editor, which shows the same settings as a default basic view of the Aggregate Transform. There are two extra properties there: **Key** and **Key Scale**.

> Key and Key Scale in the Aggregate Transform are for optimizing the component so that it knows how many rows to expect.

Key Scale can be unspecified, which means that the Key Scale property will not be used. *Low* means that Aggregate can write 500,000 rows. *Medium* means that Aggregate can write 5,000,000 rows, and *High* means that the aggregate can write 25,000,000 rows.

In the Key property we can specify the exact number of output rows. If both Key and Key Scale properties are in use, the Key property will be applied.

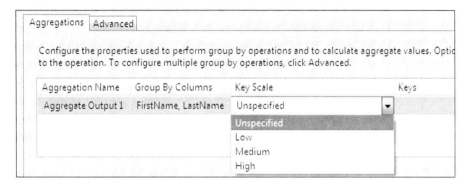

We can use a single Aggregate Transform multiple times on the same data stream and create more than one output for each of them and we can set the Key Scale and Keys.

On the other hand in the **Advanced** tab of **Aggregate Transform Editor**, there are some properties for the **Number of Keys**, **Keys scale**, **Count distinct scale**, and **Count distinct keys**, which will be applied on all outputs.

The **Auto extend factor** defines the percentage of memory that can be extended during this transformation.

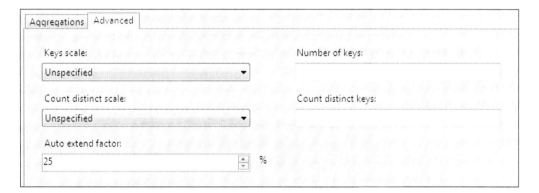

Conditional Split: dividing the data stream based on conditions

This recipe demonstrates the use of the **Condition Split** component, which is one of the most used components and is responsible for splitting data into several destinations. It's applied when data in a specific stage of the pipeline needs to follow a different path based on logical conditions. At a later stage all the data divided could be joined again using the **Union All** or even the **Merge** transformation referred in a later recipe in this chapter.

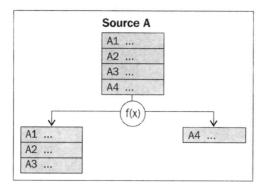

Getting ready

To get ready for this recipe, use the following steps:

1. Open SQL Server **SQL Server Data Tools** (**SSDT**) and create a new SSIS project.
2. Provide a name and location for the SSIS project and then proceed.
3. Select the package created by default and rename it to P01_ConditionalSplit.dtsx.

How to do it...

In a Data Warehousing scenario, this component is not only very useful in order to apply business rules to the data extracted from sources, but also to apply some data quality validations. Consider a scenario where it's necessary to apply business and data quality rules. In the data quality rule, it is required to check if a column is Null whereas for the business rule, is required to check if each row with the column Category has a "VIP" customer. Each of these outputs has a specific procedure to follow during package execution.

	A	B	C	D	E
1	ID	Customer_Name	Customer_Email	Money_Owed	Category
2	10.002	Marc Jacobs	mjacobs@hotmail.com	34,00 €	NULL
3	10.003	Kate Crowford	katec@gmail.com		NULL
4	10.004	John Lewis	jlewis@hotmail.com	NULL	VIP
5	10.005	Stephen Watson	swatson@ebay.com	4.500,00 €	VIP
6	10.006	Richard White	rwhite@hotmail.com	1.040,00 €	VIP

1. Add a **Data Flow** to the **Control Flow** tab and open it.

2. Create an Excel file connection that points to the sample file included in this recipe.

3. In the connection manager, right-click to add a **New Connection**.

4. In the **Connection manager type** list, select the *EXCEL* type and press the **Add** button.

5. Press the **Browse** button and locate the sample Excel file `C:\SSIS\Ch04_Data Flow Task-Part 2-Transformations\FILES\R04_CustomerData.xlsx`.

6. Drag-and-drop an **Excel Source** component from **SSIS Toolbox | Other Sources** to the **Data Flow** design area.

7. Open the component for editing.

8. The connection created in the previous step will be automatically assigned to the source component. If it is not, select it from the respective source drop-down menu.

9. In the **Data access mode** property, select *Table or view* (other options that could be applied are explained in the next section).

10. In the **Name of the Excel sheet** property, select the first worksheet *Sheet1$*.

11. Press the **OK** button to finish editing.

12. Drag-and-drop a **Conditional Split** component from **SSIS Toolbox | Common** to the **Data Flow** design area for the data quality rule.

13. Link this component to the previous one through the green output of the first.

14. Open this component for editing to add the data quality rule.

15. Add the `ISNULL(Money_Owed)` condition to check if the column `Money_Owed` is Null in some of the rows when read through the component. If the condition evaluates to true, then the row is redirected to the output **Case Missing Data** (item **1** in the next screenshot), else the row is redirected to the output **Case Data Ok** (item **2** in the next screenshot):

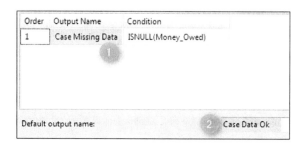

16. Press **OK** to finalize editing.

17. Drag-and-drop a **Union All** component from **SSIS Toolbox | Common** to the **Data Flow** design area for both outputs.

18. Link this component to the previous one through the green output of the first component.

19. Drag-and-drop a **Conditional Split** component from **SSIS Toolbox | Common** to the **Data Flow** design area for the business rule.

20. Link this component to the previous one through the green output of the first.

21. Open the component for editing to add the business rule.

22. Add the rule `Category == "VIP"` to check if the `Category` column has the value *VIP* in the rows read through the component. If the condition evaluates to true, then the row is redirected to the output **Case VIP Customers** (item **1** in the next screenshot), else row is redirected to the output **Case Else** (item **2** in the next screenshot).

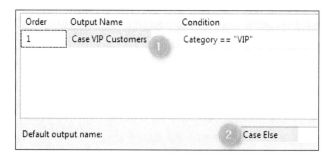

23. Press **OK** to finalize editing.

24. Drag-and-drop a **Union All** component from **SSIS Toolbox | Common** to the **Data Flow** design area of both the outputs.

25. Link this component to the previous one through the green output of the first.

26. Press *F5* to execute the package.

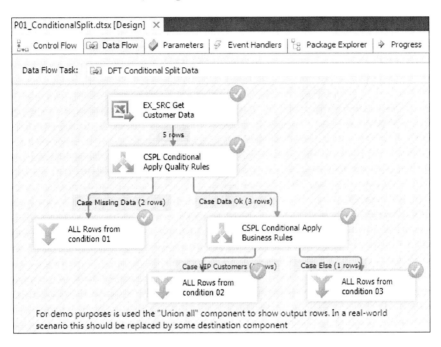

How it works...

The previous steps explain the use of the **Conditional Split** component. It first applied the data quality rule to check whether an amount is filled in and then applied the business rule to split data between the VIP customers and the remaining customers.

Under the Conditional Split, it's possible to add mathematical, string, date/time, and Null functions, operators, and type casts. It is also possible to use SSIS variables and make use of columns previously added to the pipeline.

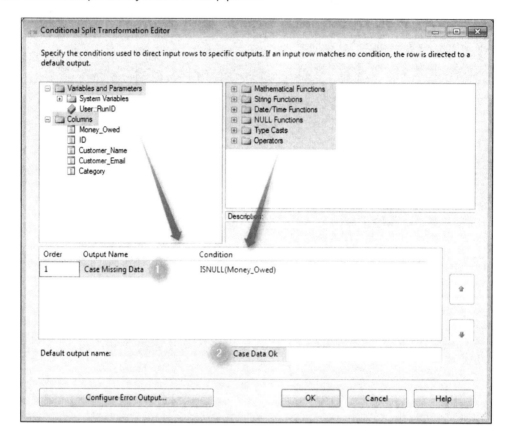

Lookup Transform: performing the Upsert scenario

The Lookup Transform searches for matching records in a reference table. There are lots of uses for this transform; while loading data into a data warehouse, when a fact table gets loaded with data coming from sources with natural key(s) of dimensions, those natural keys should be looked up in the dimension table and their equivalent surrogate key fetched and loaded into the fact table.

There are also many times when an Upsert scenario is needed. **Upsert** means **Up**date existing records and In**sert** new records. We will take a look at an Upsert scenario by resorting to a Lookup Transform and an OLE DB Command Transform. So our example begins in this recipe and will end in the next recipe, and these two recipes together demonstrate an Upsert.

Getting ready

Download `Person.csv` and `Person - second data file.csv` from the source files of this book and create a table in the `PacktPub_SSISbook` database with the following script:

```
CREATE TABLE [dbo].[SalesPerson](
    [ID] [int] IDENTITY(1,1) NOT NULL,
    [NationalID] [nvarchar](10) NULL,
    [FirstName] [nvarchar](50) NULL,
    [LastName] [nvarchar](50) NULL,
    [Email] [nvarchar](50) NULL,
    [Url] [nvarchar](50) NULL,
 CONSTRAINT [PK_SalesPerson] PRIMARY KEY CLUSTERED
(
    [ID] ASC
)WITH (PAD_INDEX = OFF, STATISTICS_NORECOMPUTE = OFF, IGNORE_DUP_KEY =
OFF, ALLOW_ROW_LOCKS = ON, ALLOW_PAGE_LOCKS = ON) ON [PRIMARY]
) ON [PRIMARY]
```

How to do it...

1. Create a new Integration Services project and name it `R05_Lookup`.

2. Add a Data Flow Task in the **Data Flow** tab, then add a Flat File Source and create a new Flat File connection manager to the `Person.csv` file in `C:\SSIS\Ch04_Data Flow Task-Part 2-Transformations\Files`. Check the column names in the first data row.

3. Go to the **Advanced** tab of the Flat File connection manager and change the data type of all columns to *DT_WSTR*; also change `OutputColumnWidth` of the column `NationalID` to 10.

4. Preview the data to get an understanding about the data structure and existing values:

NationalID	FirstName	LastName	Email	Url
1122334455	Reza	Rad		
2233445566	Pedro	Perfeito		

5. Drag-and-drop a Lookup Transform. In the Lookup Transform Editor's **General** tab, set the **Specify how to handle rows with no matching entries** option to *Redirect rows to no match output*.

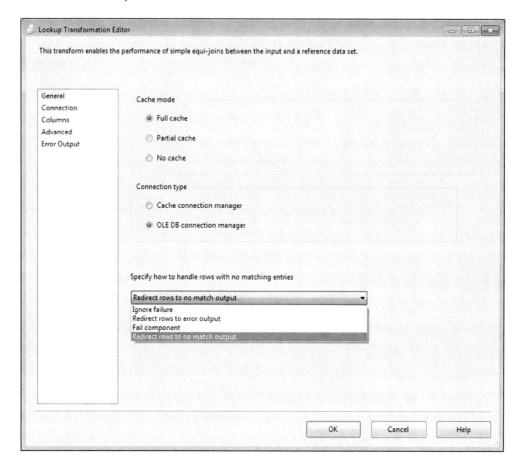

6. In the **Connection** tab, set a new **OLE DB Connection** to the database Ch04_Transformations, and in the **Use table or view** option, choose the SalesPerson table.

7. In the **Columns** tab, drag-and-drop NationalID from **Available Input Columns** to **Available Lookup Columns**. A line between them will appear, which defines the joining key (*NationalID*).

8. Check the ID in **Available Lookup Columns**; this will add the ID from the `Person` table to existing columns in the data stream.

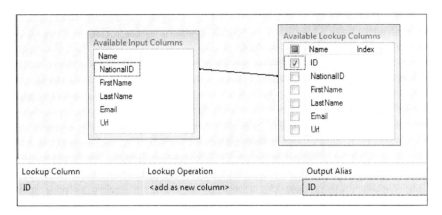

9. Close the Lookup Transform and add an OLE DB Destination. Connect a data path from **Lookup Transform** to the **OLE DB Destination**, and in the **Input Output Selection** dialog box, choose *No Match Output*.

10. Choose an OLE DB Connection to the `PacktPub_SSISbook` database.

11. Choose the `SalesPerson` table in the **Mapping** tab to verify all mappings. The `ID` column in the destination has no equivalent because this is an IDENTITY column and should be ignored during load.

12. Run the package; two rows from the source will load into destination. This is because at first there is no equivalent row in the destination table.

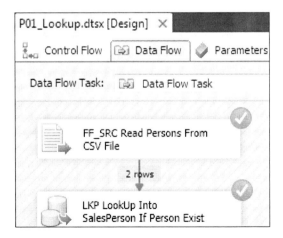

13. We will continue these steps to implement the Update Part of Upsert in the next recipe.

How it works...

In this recipe we implement an Upsert scenario. The source is a Flat File that contains information about sales persons that should be loaded into the destination `SalesPerson` table in our database. Records that do not exist in the destination table should be inserted, and records that exist should be updated in their columns. The field that is our base for detecting existing records is `NationalID`.

Specify how to handle rows with no matching entries

The Lookup Transform will find matching rows by default and return them as matched output. This option specifies how "No match" rows should be handled. The default setting is **Fail Component** and will cause the component to be failed if the lookup doesn't find any matching entries. To use "no match" records and retain them in your output, the *Redirect rows to no match output* option should be selected. There are also other options such as *Ignore* that ignore "No match" records and redirect them as an *Error* output.

Connection tab

Connections to a **lookup table** will be defined in the **Connection** tab. This table has another terminology: **reference table**. We can write our custom T-SQL query as a lookup table too, and one of the most useful scenarios in which to use a T-SQL query as a lookup table is when it will reduce the buffer size if we just select a finite number of columns and rows that we need in the T-SQL query.

Columns tab

In this tab, joining column(s) will be defined by the line between **Available Input Columns** and **Available Lookup Columns**. Checking each column in the **Available Lookup Columns** means that the lookup operation will fetch that record's field from reference table.

Two different outputs

Lookup has two different outputs; one for "Match Output" and another for "No Match Output". We may use one of these outputs, or both, in different scenarios.

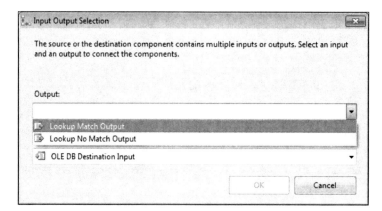

In this recipe we used the **Lookup No Match Output** option to implement the INSERT part of the Upsert scenario.

We will use the **Lookup No Match Output** option in the next recipe in order to implement the UPDATE part.

There's more...

There are some options that are very useful while working with the Lookup Transform; using them will help use the Lookup Transform to its full potential with improved performance in most situations. The next two options reveal these advanced properties.

Cache mode

As Lookup Transform looks for every record from source input inside the reference table, there should be performance tweaks to use during this lookup. SSIS provides a way to use the Cache option and cache the lookup table.

There are three options in the **General** tab of the Lookup Transform Editor's **Cache** mode setting:

- **Full Cache**: The lookup table will be fully loaded in the cache memory.
- This option will be optimal if the lookup table is not very large.
- **Partial Cache**: The lookup table will be loaded in cache memory, but not fully.

  When you select this option, the size of cache can be defined in the **Advanced** tab with the **Cache Size** option.
- **No Cache**: The lookup table doesn't cache in memory.

Connection type

The Lookup Transform only accepts two types of connections: OLE DB connection and Cache connection. An OLE DB connection can be used for OLE DB providers for databases.

For data with no OLE DB providers, such as Flat Files, we can't use the Lookup Transform directly. We can load data from the file into a cache file with Cache Transform in another Data Flow right before this Data Flow, then use the cache connection manager here for lookup.

The Cache Connection type is a handy feature, which has been added to SSIS from 2008 version.

For a quick example of the cache connection manager and Cache Transform, let's perform this recipe's first steps with MySQL database. As you found in the *Working with database connections in Data Flow* recipe in *Chapter 3, Data Flow Task Part 1—Extract and Load*, there isn't any OLE DB Connection type for MySQL databases (at least until the time of writing this book), so we cannot use the OLE DB Connection type in a Lookup Transform, What then is the solution?

The solution is that we should store the data required for a lookup or reference table in a cache file; the Cache Transform will help us do this. Then we can look up through this cache file with the Lookup Transform using the cache connection manager. We obviously need two Data Flow because if we put both parts in one Data Flow there will be no guarantee that the cache file will be written before reading it; maybe the lookup component would read the cache file before the cache transform fills it. For this reason, we need two Data Flow while working with cache connection managers.

Assume that we have the same `Person` table in MySQL. We won't explain how to install MySQL on your machine and create tables and databases because the same operation has already been described in the *Working with database connections in Data Flow* recipe in *Chapter 3, Data Flow Task Part 1—Extract and Load*.

In the first Data Flow we will fetch data from a MySQL table and load it into a cache file with a Cache Transform.

Create a Data Flow Task and name it `DFT_ Load`. We'll use this to load data from a MySQL table into a cache file. Inside the **Data Flow** tab, add an **ADO.NET Source** and connect it to the `PacktPub_SSISbook` database in MySQL (for more information about how to connect from SSIS to MySQL read the Working with database connections in Data Flow recipe in Chapter 3, Data Flow Task Part 1—Extract and Load) after the **ADO.NET Source**, drag-and-drop a **Cache Transform** from **SSIS Toolbox** and connect a data path to it.

In the Cache Transformation Editor, create a new cache connection manager. In the **Cache Connection Manager Editor** window check the **Use file cache** option to fill data into a cache file. Then address the file to the `Files` folder inside the project directory.

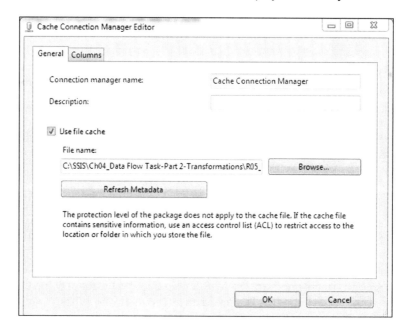

Go to the **Columns** tab. Note that you should always set an index position for columns that you want to use as a lookup key. So in this example, set the *Index* position of the `NationalID` column to *1*. If you have more than one column as index, then you should set the *Index* position starting from 1, for example 1, 2, and so on.

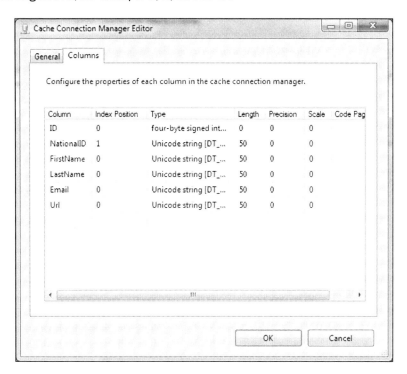

After the first Data Flow add the second Data Flow, name it DFT_ Lookup and hook it into the cache file. Create this Data Flow in the same way as the Data Flow with the SQL Server table that we described in this recipe; just note that in the Lookup Transformation Editor you should set the **Connection type** as *Cache connection manager,* and in the **Connection** tab check the *Cache connection manager* option.

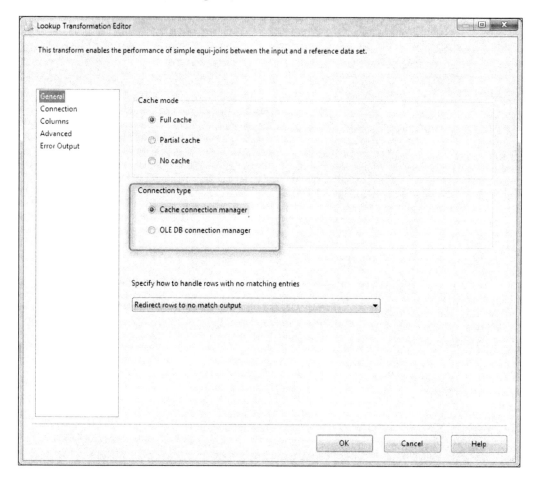

It is obvious that you should use an appropriate destination in the second Data Flow so that you can use an *ODBC* or *ADO.NET* destination.

After running the package, you will see that the cache file is filled up in the first Data Flow with the Cache Transform, and the second Data Flow lookup is filled through this cache file with the Lookup Transform.

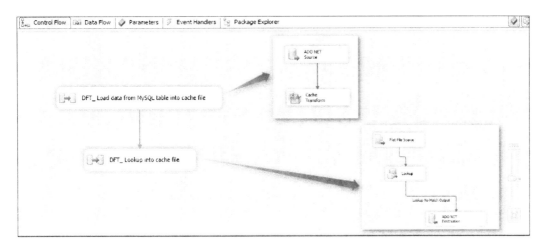

One of the new features of SSIS 2012 is that you can create a shared cache connection manager, and when data loaded into the shared connection manager in the first package, all packages in the project can simply use same data because the data is already exists in system cache memory.

OLE DB Command: executing SQL statements on each row in the data stream

In the Data Flow Task there are times when there is a need to run an SQL statement. This statement may just do something and not return any result, or may get input values and generate output values.

The OLE DB Command provides a way to execute SQL statements on OLE DB connections to databases. We will try to implement the Update part of the previous recipe's Upsert scenario in this recipe.

Getting ready

The previous recipe should be executed before beginning this recipe.

Execute the following command on the `PacktPub_SSISbook` database to create the stored procedure for updates in the `Person` table:

```
Create PROCEDURE dbo.UpdatePerson
    @ID nvarchar(10),
    @FirstName nvarchar(50),
    @LastName nvarchar(50),
    @Email nvarchar(50),
    @Url nvarchar(50)
AS
BEGIN
    UPDATE [dbo].[SalesPerson]
        SET [FirstName] = @FirstName
          ,[LastName] = @LastName
          ,[Email] = @Email
          ,[Url] = @Url
      WHERE [ID]=@ID
END
GO
```

How to do it...

1. Create a new Integration Services project and name it R06_R06_OLE DB Command

2. In the Solution Explorer, add an existent package "P01_LookUp" created in the previous recipe "R05_Lookup"

3. In the connection manager pane, open the Flat File connection manager and browse for `Person`; the second `data file.csv` file this time.

4. Open the Flat File source and preview the data. There are two existing records, which have updated their `Email` and `Url` fields, and there are two new records.

NationalID	FirstName	LastName	Email	Url
1122334455	Reza	Rad	a.raad.g@gmail.com	http://rad.pasfu.com
2233445566	Pedro	Perfeito	pperfeito@hotmail.com	http://pedrocgd.blogspot.com
3344556677	Rafael	Salas		
4455667788	Phil	Brammer		

5. Drag-and-drop an OLE DB Command from the SSIS Toolbox after the Lookup Transform.

6. Connect a Data Path from the Lookup Transform to the OLE DB Command. Because the **Lookup not match output** option is used in OLE DB Destination, **Lookup match output** will be used as input for OLE DB Command.

7. In the OLE DB Command Editor, which is an advanced editor, within the **Connection Manager** pane, select the OLE DB connection manager to the `PacktPub_SSISbook` database there.

8. In the **Component Properties** tab, write the following statement in the **SqlCommand** property:

```
exec dbo.UpdatePerson ?,?,?,?,?
```

9. In the **Columns Mappings** tab, all input columns fetched from Lookup Transform are available on one side, and all parameters of **SqlCommand** on the other side. Map the input columns to appropriate parameters as shown in the following screenshot:

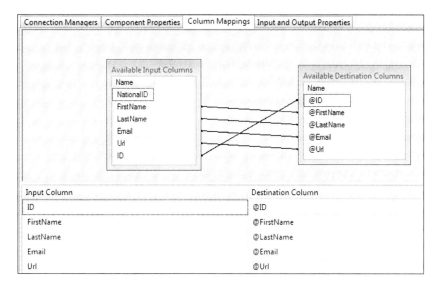

10. Close the OLE DB Command, and run the package. There will be two rows at the **Lookup No Match Output**, which were inserted in the database with **OLE DB Destination**. There will be two rows at the Lookup Match output which were updated in database with OLE DB Command.

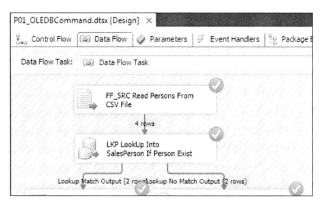

11. Take a look at the `Person` table; you will see all records there: existing, updated, and new inserted rows. If we run the package one more time, we will see no rows in **No Match Output** because all records now exist.

How it works...

The **OLE DB Command** provides a way to run the **Update** parametric command on the `Person` table by resorting to the `UpdatePerson` stored procedure. The **OLE DB Command** will run the SQL statement for each row in the data stream.

OLE DB

The first important thing about the **OLE DB Command** is the **OLE DB** part in its name, stating that this transform only works with **OLE DB** connection managers, so for other connection types you should think about alternative methods such as script components or using a "for each" loop with the Execute SQL Task.

Parameter markers

The **SqlCommand** property contains the statement that should be run; in this recipe we used a parametric statement that executes the `UpdatePerson` statement. Parameter markers in **OLE DB Connection** are question marks, as fully described in the *Executing T-SQL commands: Execute SQL Task* recipe in *Chapter 2, Control Flow Tasks*. So for each parameter marker in the **SqlCommand** there will be a parameter in the columns mappings' **Available Destination Columns** part.

Input Columns should be mapped to their appropriate parameters.

If we don't use stored procedures here and directly specify an update command there will be no problem and everything will work fine. However, the cumbersome part is where parameter names in the column mapping tab will be *Parameter_1, Parameter_2*, and so on, which is really hard to debug for statements with many parameters.

There's more...

Fetching the output parameter into the data stream column

We can use the **OLE DB Command** to run a stored procedure that returns an output parameter, and then use this output parameter's returned value as a column in the data stream. Suppose that we have a scalar function that gets an input parameter from the input data stream and then generates an output value that should appear beside other columns in the data stream.

In such cases we can create a dummy column at first and then map it to the output parameter besides other parameters. A full sample is described in this blog post: `http://www.rad.pasfu.com/index.php?/archives/24-Output-Parameter-of-Stored-Procedure-In-OLE-DB-Command-SSIS.html`.

Merge and Union All transformations: combining input data rows

Merge and **Union All** transformation components are used to join data in the pipeline. This data may come from more than one source, or have been divided previously in the pipeline. The main reason we use these components is to avoid duplicate work in the pipeline because the data at this point forward has the same treatment.

The main differences between the two components are that **Merge** component requires input data sorted and it's not possible to have more than two inputs. There are sufficient reasons from consider this **Merge** component useless.

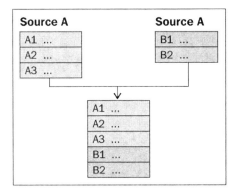

Getting ready

To get ready for this recipe, use the following steps:

1. Open **SQL Server Data Tools** (**SSDT**) and create a new SSIS project.
2. Provide a name and a location for the SSIS project and proceed.
3. Select the package created by default and rename it to `P01_UnionData.dtsx`.

How to do it...

Consider a *Data Warehousing* scenario where data coming from two different sources need to be joined and then transformed and inserted into a Staging Area or Data Warehouse. In this recipe two customer data files are joined using the two approaches through **Union All** and also **Merge**.

1. Add a **Data Flow** to the **Control Flow** tab and open it.
2. Create an Excel File Connection that points to the sample file included in this recipe.

3. In the connection manager right-click to add a **New Connection**.

4. In the **Connection manager type** list, select the *EXCEL* type and press the **Add** button.

5. Press the **Browse** button and locate the sample Excel file `R04_CustomerData.xlsx`.

6. Repeat the previous step to create an Excel file connection that points to the other customer data Excel file.

7. Use the sample Excel file `R07_CustomerData.xlsx` in this connection.

8. Drag-and-drop two **Excel Source** components from **SSIS Toolbox | Other Sources** to the **Data Flow** design area.

9. Open each component for editing and select the *Excel* connection.

10. In the **Data access mode** property, select *Table or view* (other options that could be applied are explained in the next section).

11. In the **Name of the Excel sheet** property, select the first worksheet *Sheet1$*.

12. Press the **OK** button to finish editing.

13. Drag-and-drop the **Union All** component from **SSIS Toolbox | Common** to the **Data Flow** design area for both outputs.

14. Link the two previous connections to this component through the green output of the first component.

15. Drag-and-drop another two **Excel Source** components from **SSIS Toolbox | Other Sources** to the **Data Flow** design area.

16. Open each component for editing and select the *Excel* connection.

17. In the **Data access mode** property, select *Table or view* (other options that could be applied are explained in the next section).

18. In the **Name of the Excel sheet** property, select the first worksheet `Sheet1$`.

19. Press the **OK** button to finish editing.

20. Drag-and-drop two **Sort** components from **SSIS Toolbox | Common** to the **Data Flow** design area.

21. Open each component for editing.

22. Select the column ID as sort order criteria.

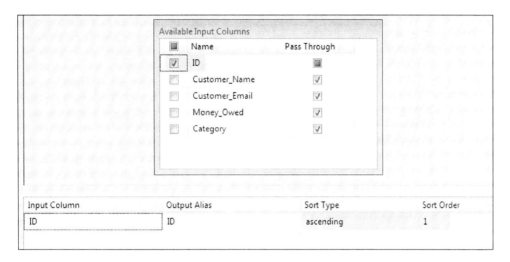

23. Drag-and-drop the **Merge** component from **SSIS Toolbox | Common** to the **Data Flow** design area for both outputs.

24. Link the two previous connections to this component through the green outputs of the first components.

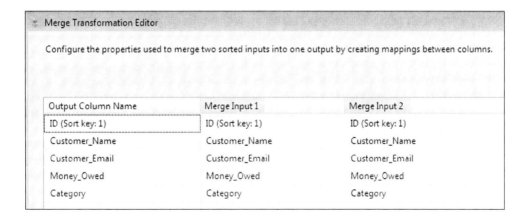

25. Press *F5* to execute the package and check the extra columns added to the pipeline.

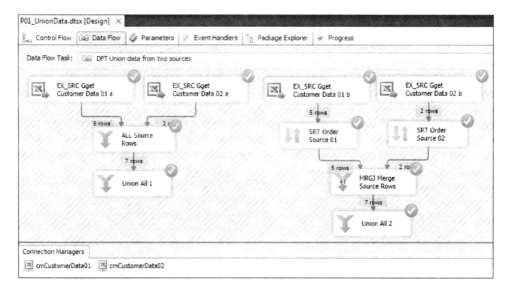

How it works...

The previous steps explain the use of the **Union All** and **Merge** components. Sample data was read from two Excel files and joined using both the approaches. As mentioned before, **Union all** seems to be more useful than the **Merge** component because it does not need to have data sorted and allows more than two inputs to be joined.

Merge Join Transform: performing different types of joins in data flow

If you are familiar with T-SQL you may wonder why this transform exists when we can query source data joined in the T-SQL? Remember that in an ETL we may have source data from different types of sources such as flat files or XML. This transformation provides all types of joins such as Inner, Outer, and Left join.

There are differences between these three types of joins, which are explored in this recipe. In this recipe we have two data sources, from an Excel file and a Flat File, and we want to combine them in rows (join them) with the Merge Join Transform. We need to fetch all records that exist in both files or exist in one of the files but not in the other one.

How to do it...

1. Create a new Integration Services project and name it `R08_Merge Join`.

2. Add a Data Flow Task in the **Control Flow**, then go to the **Data Flow** tab.

3. Add an Excel Source, create a new Excel connection manager, and set the Excel file to `C:\SSIS\Ch04_Data Flow Task-Part 2-Transformations\Files\R08_ExcelSource.xlsx`. Check whether the first row has a column names option.

4. Go to Excel Source Editor and choose `Sheet1$` as the name of your Excel sheet. Preview the data to view the structure of the Excel file's data.

ID	Email	Url
1	a.raad.g@...	http://rad.pasfu.com
2	info@micro...	http://microsoft.com
3	pperfeito@...	http://pedrocgd.blogspot.com
4	info@Packt...	http://packtpub.com

5. Right-click on the Excel source and open the advanced editor. Go to the **Input and Output Properties** tab. Explore the **Excel Source** output. Under **Output Columns** select *ID*, and in the properties pane change the **Data Type** to *DT_I4*.

6. Add a **Flat File Source** in the Data Flow, create a new Flat File connection manager and then browse to `C:\SSIS\Ch04_Data Flow Task-Part 2-Transformations\Files\R08_FlatFileSource.csv` to set the source file. Check the column names in the first data row and go to the **Advanced** tab. Change the data type of the `ID` column to *DT_I4* and change the data type of `Email` and `Url` to *DT_WSTR*.

7. In the Flat File Source, preview the data to find out its structure.

ID	Email	Url
1	a.raad.g@gmail.com	http://rad.pasfu.com
2	info@microsoft.com	http://microsoft.com
3	pperfeito@hotmail.com	http://pedrocgd.blogspot.com
4	info@Packtpub.com	http://packtpub.com

8. Drag-and-drop a Merge Join Transform from the SSIS Toolbox after both sources and connect a data path from **Excel Source** to **Merge Join**. An **Input Output Selection** dialog box will appear, choose *Merge Join Left Input* in the **Input** drop-down.

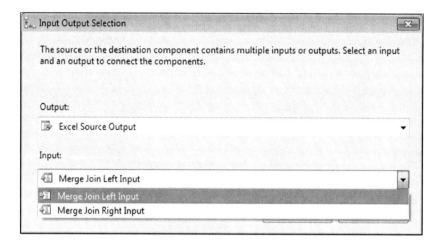

9. Connect a data path from **Flat File Source** to **Merge Join**; this time you don't need to set the **Input** because only **Right Input** is empty and the flat file data is considered as **Right Input**.

10. Double-click on **Merge Join Transform** to open the editor; you will receive an error message that says **Merge Join** inputs should be sorted, and you cannot edit the **Merge Join** before sorting both inputs.

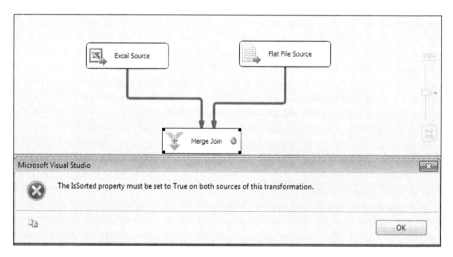

11. Delete both data paths from the sources to **Merge Join**.

12. Add a Sort Transform between **Excel Source** and **Merge Join**, and connect a data path from **Excel Source** to the Sort Transform.

13. In the **Sort Transformation Editor**, check ID as the column to be sorted, and leave FirstName and LastName as *Pass Through*.

14. Connect a data path from the Sort Transform to the Merge Join Transform, and select the input as *Left Input*.

15. Add another Sort Transform between **Flat File Source** and the **Merge Join** transform, go to **Sort Transform Editor**, set ID as a sort column, and leave Email and Url as *Pass Through*.

16. Connect a data path from the second Sort Transform to **Merge Join**; this will be considered as **Right** input.

17. Open the Merge Join Transform, and this time you won't get any error.

18. Set **Join type** as *Full outer join*; verify that the joining key is present as a line between the two inputs, the line connecting ID columns from one source to another.

19. Check all columns from both sources. Just change the **Output Alias** of the IDs to *ID from Excel Source* and *ID from Flat File Source* as shown in the following screenshot:

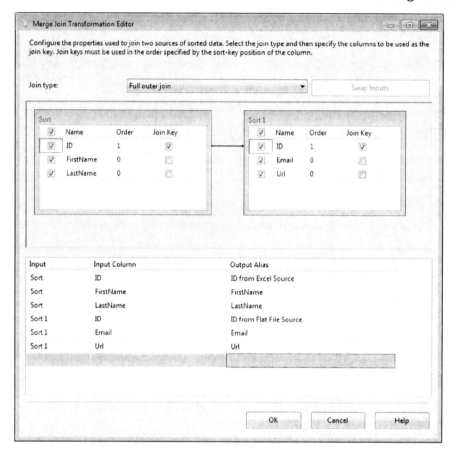

20. Add a **Conditional Split** Transform after the **Merge Join**, and connect a data path from **Merge Join** to **Conditional Split**, right-click on the data path, and *Enable Data Viewer*.

21. Add expressions in the **Condition** parameters as seen in the next screenshot:

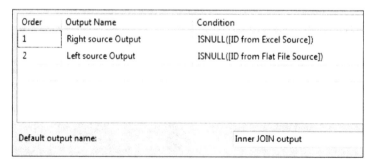

22. Add three **Union All components** after **Conditional Split**. Connect the three outputs from **Conditional Split** to them and check the input columns in each of them. Also enable data viewers in all three data paths from **Conditional Split** to the Union All components.

23. Run the package and check first Data Viewer; you will see the result of the Merge Join Transform there; rows with no matching ID in another source will have NULL in their columns.

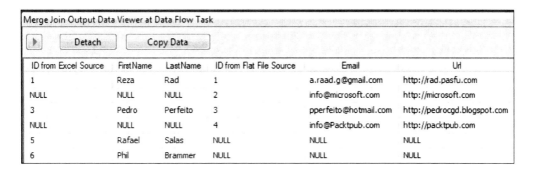

ID from Excel Source	First Name	Last Name	ID from Flat File Source	Email	Url
1	Reza	Rad	1	a.raad.g@gmail.com	http://rad.pasfu.com
NULL	NULL	NULL	2	info@microsoft.com	http://microsoft.com
3	Pedro	Perfeito	3	pperfeito@hotmail.com	http://pedrocgd.blogspot.com
NULL	NULL	NULL	4	info@Packtpub.com	http://packtpub.com
5	Rafael	Salas	NULL	NULL	NULL
6	Phil	Brammer	NULL	NULL	NULL

24. The three outputs from **Conditional Split** show each part of the join, as seen in the next screenshot:

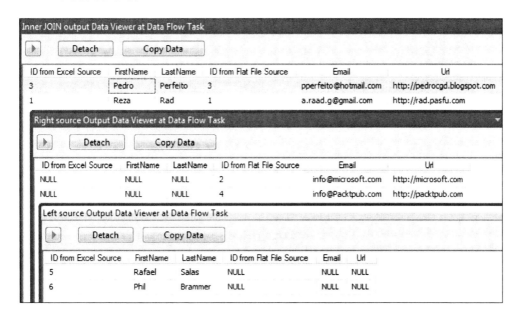

25. Confirm the Data Flow schema with the following screenshot:

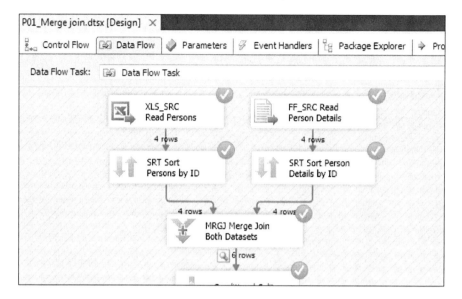

How it works...

This recipe fetched three sets of records: rows whose equivalent ID fields exist in both
R08_ExcelSource.xlsx and R08_FlatFileSource.csv, rows that exist in
R08_ExcelSource.xlsx but not in R08_FlatFileSource.csv, and finally, rows
that exist in R08_FlatFileSource.csv but not in R08_ExcelSource.xlsx.

Joining key(s)

The first important thing about Merge Join is that both inputs should be sorted by their joining
keys. In this recipe we sort both input sources by ID, which is the joining key. The Join Type
will be applied based on the joining key(s).

Join types

We discussed the following types of Joins:

- ▶ Inner Join: records that exist in both sources
- ▶ Left Outer Join: records that exist in Left input, irrespective of whether rows exist in
  the Right input or not
- ▶ Full Outer Join: records from both inputs; contains records that exist in both sources
  (inner join) and records that exist only in the left or right source

In all these Join types, if any row doesn't have a matching row in other inputs, its columns in the output will be filled with NULL.

The role of the **Conditional Split** and **Union All components** in this recipe was just for monitoring records that exist in both sources and in only one of the sources.

There's more...

Performance issue with Sort Transformation

Sort is an asynchronous transformation. **Asynchronous** transforms fetch all of the data from the input, then start processing, and finally generate output; this will use up a considerable amount of memory and slow down the whole operation. On the other hand, Synchronous Transformation will fetch data from input streams record by record, process them, and then generate output record by record.

It would be much better if we could use synchronous transforms in Data Flow and avoid asynchronous transforms, but an asynchronous operation is sometimes unavoidable; pivoting data for example.

Some examples of synchronous transforms are:

- Derived Column
- Copy Column
- Data Conversion

Some examples of asynchronous transforms are:

- Pivot
- Sort

We should avoid Sort Transform as it is an asynchronous transformation. There are cases where we have sorted input, or we can sort data at the source itself. For example, an OLEDB source can use an "Order by" clause in the T-SQL to have sorted input. In these cases we don't need Sort Transform, but we should inform SSIS that the source data is sorted. This is where we use **Sort Properties of Source**.

Order by clause

Assume that we used an Order by clause in our query as follows:

```
Select ID,FirstName,LastName from Person
Order by ID
```

IsSorted

By right-clicking on **OLE DB Source** we can go to the Advanced Editor. In the Advanced Editor go to **Input and Output Properties**, select the output and in the properties pane there will be an **IsSorted** property, which is *False* by default.

Setting the **IsSorted** property to *True* tells SSIS that this output is sorted. However, we need to set how the sorting is organized and by which columns in which order the data is sorted.

SortKeyPosition

SSIS should know in what order sorting is organized: by expanding output columns in the **Input and Output Properties** tab and selecting each column the **SortKeyPosition** property of each column can be set.

SortKeyPosition is set to *0* by default, which means that there is no column that sorting applied on that column. The order of sorting should be set with this property. For the `Order by` clause sample, we should set the **SortKeyPosition** of the `ID` column to *1*.

If we have more than one column on which sorting is applied, we should set a **SortKeyPosition** for those columns with an index numbered from 1, 2, 3, and so on.

Using sort properties at the source has much better performance than an asynchronous Sort Transformation.

Merge Join versus Lookup

Merge Join and Lookup both provide ways to join data and fetch records whether they match or not. So, what are their pros and cons?

As Lookup uses caching for table reference, it can work with better performance, but performance tips should be considered; on the other hand we need a sorting phase before Merge Join, which consumes more memory and time.

As the Lookup Transform works with OLE DB connection managers, working with the Lookup Component and databases using the ODBC connector is impossible. On the other hand, the Merge Join has no limitation in the connection or source type, the only limitation for Merge Join is that inputs should be sorted.

 The Lookup Transform is case sensitive, so "Hello" won't match "hello" in the Lookup Transform.

Sort Transform properties

Listed next are some of the properties that the Sort Transform has:

Remove rows with duplicate sort values

The Sort Transform has a built-in feature to remove records with duplicate sort values. This can be checked in the option with the same name in the Sort Transformation Editor.

Sort Order

Sorting in the Sort Transform can be applied to more than one column; in such a case **Sort Order** defines the order of sorting between columns by index from 1, 2, and so on.

Sort Type

Each column can be sorted in either ascending or descending order; the **Sort Type** option defines the type of sorting to be used.

Comparison Flags

If a column with sort value is a string column, **Comparison Flags** can be used there; for more information about Comparison Flags turn back to the *Aggregate Transform: aggregating the data stream* recipe of this chapter.

Pass Through

Columns that are checked as **Pass Through** will pass through Sort Transform from the input data stream to output. If we uncheck any column there, that column won't appear in sort transformation output columns.

Multicast: creating copies of the data stream

The **Multicast** transformation component is used when the data in the pipeline needs to be transferred to more than one flow. This component receives a single data input and makes multiple copies of that data that are available through as many outputs as needed. Each of the outputs coming out of **Multicast** can be used in different ways. For example one output could make an aggregation on data that joins another output in a later phase, or for example we could create several outputs to insert/load the same data into different destinations.

The difference between the **Multicast** and the **Conditional Split** components (referred in a previous recipe), is that **Multicast** directs each row of the source to every output, whereas **Conditional Split** directs each row to a single output.

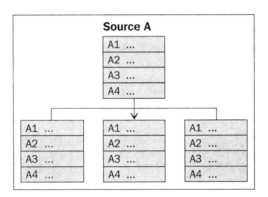

Getting ready

To get ready for this recipe, use the following steps:

1. Open **SQL Server Business Intelligence Development Studio (BIDS)** and create a new SSIS project.

2. Provide a name and a location for the SSIS project and then proceed.

3. Select the package created by default and rename it to `P01_Multicast.dtsx`.

How to do it...

Consider a scenario where data read from a source needs to be loaded into several destinations like, for example, development, testing or production environments.

1. Add a Data Flow to the **Control Flow** tab and open it.

2. Create an Excel file connection that points to the sample file included in this recipe.

3. In the connection manager, right-click to add a **New Connection**.

4. In the **Connection manager type** list, select *EXCEL* and press the **Add** button.

5. Press the **Browse** button and locate the sample Excel file `R09_CustomerData.xlsx`.

6. Drag-and-drop the **Excel Source** component from **SSIS Toolbox | Other Sources** to the **Data Flow** design area.

7. Open the component for editing.

8. The connection created in the previous step will be automatically assigned to the source component. If it is not, select it from the respective drop-down menu.

9. In the **Data access mode** property, select *Table or view* (other options that could be applied are explained in the next section).

10. In the **Name of the Excel sheet** property, select the first worksheet *Sheet1$*.

11. Press the **OK** button to finish editing.

12. Drag-and-drop the **Multicast** component from **SSIS Toolbox | Common** to the **Data Flow** design area.

13. Link this component to the previous one through the green output of the first.

14. Open this component for editing and verify whether it's possible to rename each output.

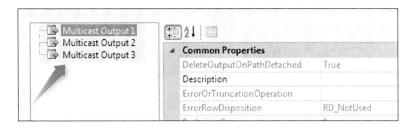

15. Add three **Union All** components, one for each output, and link each with the green output row of the **Multicast** component

16. Press *F5* to execute the package and check whether the Multicast input data is replicated into three output data streams.

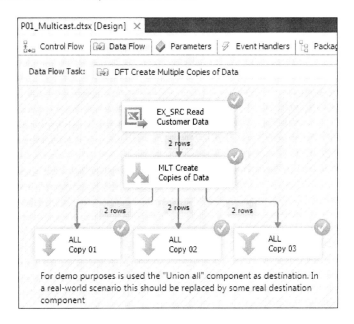

How it works...

The previous steps explain the use of the **Multicast** component that creates several copies (outputs) of the Multicast Transform input. Each output on the transform is broken down into parallel execution paths and this allows those outputs to go out and get their own engine threads.

Working with BLOB fields: Export Column and Import Column transformations

Resorting to BLOB fields as storage medium for physical files is a common need nowadays. SQL Server support BLOB data in two standard types as Image or Varbinary. SSIS also provides two transformations to work with BLOB fields: Export Column and Import Column.

Export Column will fetch physical files from BLOB data, whereas **Import Column** feeds the physical file to an Image or Varbinary field.

In this recipe we use both Export Column and Import Column transformations. With Export Column we fetch actual files from the Document table in the AdventureWorks2012 database. With Import Column, we load physical files into the Image type field of the database table.

Getting ready

Create a new empty file at C:\SSIS\Ch03_Data Flow Task-Part 2-Transformations\ Files and name it R10_files.txt.

How to do it...

1. Create a new Integration Services project in BIDS and name the project R10_Export Column.

2. Create a Data Flow Task; in the **Data Flow** tab, add an OLE DB Source. Create a connection to AdventureWorks2012 and set the data access mode as *SQL Command*. Then write the following statement in the **SQL Statement** textbox:

   ```
   SELECT FileName, FileExtension, Title, Document
   FROM Production.Document
   WHERE (Document IS NOT NULL)
   ```

3. Preview the data and verify whether there is a BLOB field where *System.Byte []*is shown in all rows.

FileName	FileExtension	Title	Document
Introduction 1.doc	.doc	Introduction 1	System.Byte[]
Repair and Service Guidelines.doc	.doc	Repair and Service Guidelines	System.Byte[]
Crank Arm and Tire Maintenance.doc	.doc	Crank Arm and Tire Maintenance	System.Byte[]
Lubrication Maintenance.doc	.doc	Lubrication Maintenance	System.Byte[]
Front Reflector Bracket and Reflector Assembly 3.doc	.doc	Front Reflector Bracket and Reflector Assembly 3	System.Byte[]
Front Reflector Bracket Installation.doc	.doc	Front Reflector Bracket Installation	System.Byte[]
Installing Replacement Pedals.doc	.doc	Installing Replacement Pedals	System.Byte[]
Seat Assembly.doc	.doc	Seat Assembly	System.Byte[]
Training Wheels 2.doc	.doc	Training Wheels 2	System.Byte[]

4. Drag-and-drop a **Derived Column** Transform right after the **OLE DB Source**, and then create a new **Column.** Name it `FullFilePath` and write the following expression there:

    ```
    "C:\\SSIS\\Ch04_Data Flow Task-Part 2-Transformations\\Files\\R10_
    Documents\\" + FileName
    ```

5. Drag-and-drop an **Export Column** in the Data Flow after the **Derived Column**. In the **Export Column** Transform, within the **Extract Column**, select the **Document** field. In the `File Path Column` select *FullFilePath*. Check the **Force Truncate** option and close it.

Extract Column	File Path Column	Allow Append	Force Truncate	Write Byte-Order Mark
Document	FullFilePath	☐	☑	☐

6. Add a **Flat File Destination** after **Export Column**, and create a new flat file connection manager; point it to `R10_Files.txt` at `C:\SSIS\Ch03_Data Flow Task-Part 2-Transformations\Files`. In the **Advanced** tab of the Flat File connection manager delete the `FileName`, `FileExtension`, and `Document` columns; just keep the `Title` and `FullFilePath` columns.

7. Close the Flat File Destination and run the package. The whole package schema is shown in the next screenshot. After running the package, check the following address to find the actual files fetched from the BLOB database field: `C:\SSIS\Ch03_Data Flow Task-Part 2-Transformations\Files`.

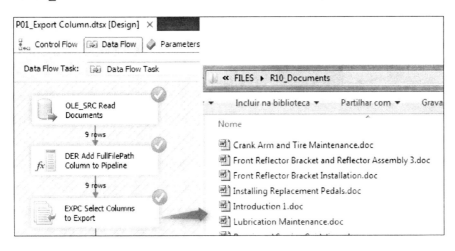

8. Add another SSIS Package to the project and name it `P02_Import Column`.

9. In the **Data Flow** Task, create a new **Flat File Source** and then create a connection to the same R10_Files.txt file that we previously created. Just go to the **Advanced** tab in the Flat File connection manager and change the **OutputColumnWidth** property of the FullFilePath column to *500*.

10. Drag-and-drop an **Import Column** Transform after **Flat File Source**. Then go to the Advanced Editor for Import Column and check the FullFilePath column.

11. Go to the **Input and Output Properties** tab, expand **Import Column Output** and click on **Output Columns**, then click on the **Add Column** button. Name this new column Content. Verify whether the data type of the column is automatically set to *image [DT_IMAGE]*. Keep this window and tab open for the next step.

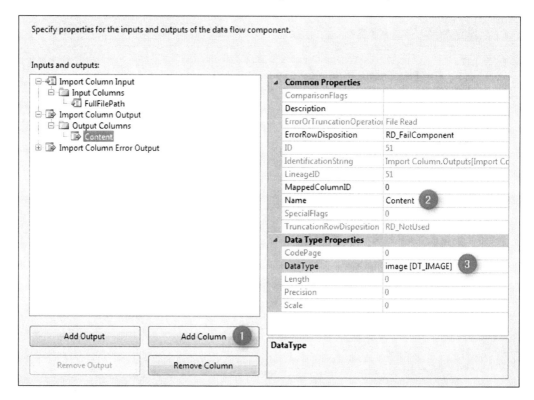

12. Expand **Import Column Input** and under **Input Columns** click on **FullFilePath** then, in the properties pane, set the **FileDataColumnID** with the ID of the Content output column. The **ID** property of the Content column can be found by selecting the Content column and finding the **ID** property. Note that the **ID 51** used here may be different on your environment.

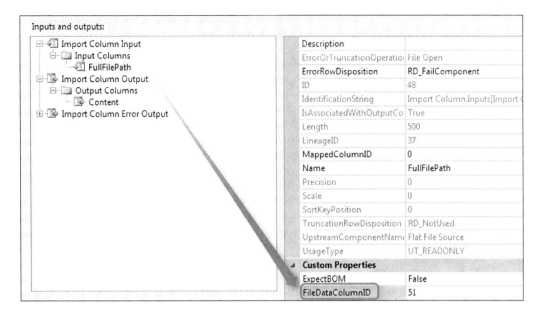

13. Open SSMS. If you didn't create the `PacktPub_SSISbook` database in the previous recipe, create it now. Then run the following statement there to create the `Files` table that will be used to save physical data in BLOG fields with an Image data type:

```
CREATE TABLE [dbo].[Files](
    [ID] [int] IDENTITY(1,1) NOT NULL,
    [Title] [varchar](250) NULL,
    [Content] [varbinary](max) NULL,
 CONSTRAINT [PK_Files] PRIMARY KEY CLUSTERED
(
    [ID] ASC
)WITH (PAD_INDEX = OFF, STATISTICS_NORECOMPUTE = OFF, IGNORE_
DUP_KEY = OFF, ALLOW_ROW_LOCKS = ON, ALLOW_PAGE_LOCKS = ON) ON
[PRIMARY]
) ON [PRIMARY] TEXTIMAGE_ON [PRIMARY]
```

14. In this step we load data from the data stream into this table, so go back to BIDS, drag-and-drop an **OLE DB Destination** into Data Flow after the Import Column, create a connection to the `Ch04_Transformations` database, and then select *Files* in the **Select table** drop-down list. Go to the **Mapping** tab and verify mappings.

15. Run the package. Nine files will be imported in the image field; you can see them in the SSMS query window and verify the whole operation.

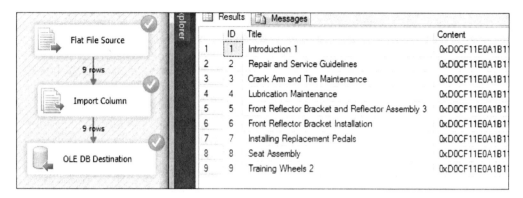

How it works...

Export Column

In this recipe, we first used the `Document` table in the `AdventureWorks2012` database, which contains information about documents, and a **Document** field of type Varbinary(max), which contains the actual document.

Export Column needs an exact and complete file address to fetch out BLOB data as a physical file, so we used a `Derived` column to make a `FullFilePath`. We then fed this `FullFilePath` column and the `Document` column into Export Column. Export Column has some interesting properties, which are described here:

- ▸ Extract Column: The Image field that contains the BLOB data.

- ▸ File Path Column: Full file path with name and extension of the desired output file.

- ▸ Allow Append: Defines whether data should be appended to an existing file or not.

- ▸ Force Truncate: Defines whether the data should be re-written in the destination file.

- ▸ Write Byte-Order Mark: Byte Order Mark is a Unicode character to specify the end of the text file or stream. This option only works with the `DT_NTEXT` and `DT_WSTR` data types.

We have stored **Title** and **FullFilePath** to the `R10_Files.txt` file for the next steps, which are an example of Import Column.

Import Column

From step **8**, we used `R10_Files.txt` which contains the Titles of documents and their
FullFilePath as source and wanted to find the actual files in physical address and load
them into an Image type field in the `Files` database table.

As **Flat File Source** always considers columns as string type with width 50, we changed the
width of the `FullFilePath` column to 500 to cover long data paths.

Then we used an **Import Column** Transform to load physical files into a database BLOB field.
The **Import Column** Transform has no standard editor other than an Advanced Editor.

While working with Import Column, one or more input columns that contain the full file path
should always be selected.

As the Import Column Transform has no built-in Output Column, the Output Column should be
added manually (as described in step **11**). The data type of this column is `DT_Image`
by default.

Each Output Column should be mapped to an input column. In the example we mapped the
`Content` Output Column to the `FullFilePath` Input Column using the **FileDataColumnID**
property of the Input Column, which should be set with the **ID** of the Output Column.

There is also a property called **ExpectBOM** among the Input Column properties, which
indicates whether the transformation should expect a BOM character or not in case
`DT_NTEXT` or `DT_WSTR` data is going to be read from a file.

Slowly Changing Dimensions (SCDs) in SSIS

Slowly Changing Dimensions (**SCDs**) is a term coined by *Ralph Kimball* refer to dimension
tables that have data that slowly changes with time. These changes in data need to be
recorded in order to make dimension table data refreshed and also to enable end user
to analyse historical changes in data. For example, it could be necessary to let the Data
Warehouse "know" when a customer's address changes (to make it possible to analyze sales
by customer locations and have more focused marketing activities), or it could be necessary
to update a product's name.

You could use several techniques to deal with these types of dimensions. One technique is
explained in this recipe through an SSIS component created exclusively for that purpose.

The SCD has four methods to manage changes in a dimension:

- SCD Type 0
- SCD Type 1
- SCD Type 2
- SCD Type 3

SCD Type 0 is a passive approach to managing changes in dimension values; no action is taken because the dimension record remains as it were at the time when the row was added to the table. **SCD Type 1** overwrites old data with new data, and therefore does not track historical data at all. **SCD Type 2** tracks historical data by creating multiple records for a given business key in the dimensional tables with separate surrogate keys. With Type 2, a new record is inserted every time a change is made. **SCD Type 3** tracks history by creating a new column in the dimension table for each change in each column. This type requires changing the physical table structure and is rarely used (the SCD SSIS component will not be prepared for this type of SCD).

After configuring the SCD SSIS component, several components will be automatically generated in the Data Flow. If there are several dimensions then repeating the work dozens of times manually is a waste of time. This component makes life easier, and all the components generated can be reused in custom scenarios.

Getting ready

To get ready for this recipe, use the following steps:

1. Open SQL Server Management Studio (SSMS) and Execute the following SQL Statement:

```
CREATE TABLE [dbo].[DimCustomer](
  [CustomerSK] [int] IDENTITY(1,1) NOT NULL,
  [CustomerID] [int] NULL,
  [FirstName] [nvarchar](50) NULL,
  [LastName] [nvarchar](50) NULL,
  [CompanyName] [nvarchar](128) NULL,
  [City] [nvarchar](30) NULL,
  [CountryRegion] [nvarchar](50) NULL,
  [SCDStartDate] [datetime] NULL,
  [SCDEndDate] [datetime] NULL,
  [SCDStatus] [bit] NULL,
  CONSTRAINT [PK_DimCustomer] PRIMARY KEY CLUSTERED
([CustomerSK] ASC)
) ON [PRIMARY]
```

2. Open SQL Server Business Intelligence Development Studio (BIDS) and create a new SSIS project.

3. Provide a name and a location for the SSIS project and proceed.

4. Select the package created by default and rename it to:
   `P01_SlowlyChangingDimension.dtsx`.

How to do it...

This recipe reads customer data from the `AdventureWorksLT2012` database and updates the `Dimension` customer table created in the PacktPub database with changes that will be fired by an SQL statement.

1. Add a Data Flow to the Control Flow and open it.

2. Create for the source component an OLEDB Connection to the `AdventureWorksLT2012` database sample.

3. In the **Connection Manager** right-click to add a **New OLEDB Connection**.

4. In the **Data Connections** list select the `AdventureWorksLT2012` database. If it is not listed, create a new one by pressing the **New** button.

5. Press the **OK** button and rename the connection to `cmAdventureWorksLT`.

6. Drag-and-drop the **OLE DB Source** component from **SSIS Toolbox | Other Sources** to the **Data Flow** design area.

7. Open the component for editing.

8. The connection created in the previous step will be automatically assigned to the source component. If it is not, select it from its respective drop-down menu.

9. In the **Data access mode** property, select *SQL Command* (other options that could be applied are explained in the previous chapter).

10. In the **SQL Command Text**, add the SQL statement given next:

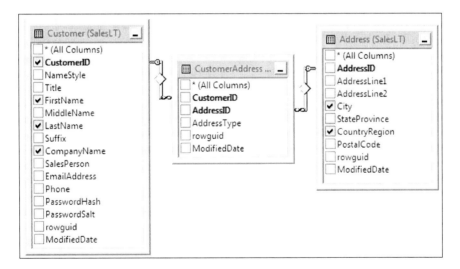

```
SELECT    CUST.CustomerID, CUST.FirstName, CUST.LastName,
          CUST.CompanyName, ADDR.City, ADDR.CountryRegion
FROM      SalesLT.Address ADDR
```

```
INNER JOIN SalesLT.CustomerAddress ADDRC
    ON ADDR.AddressID = ADDRC.AddressID
INNER JOIN SalesLT.Customer CUST
    ON ADDRC.CustomerID = CUST.CustomerID
```

11. Drag-and-drop the **Slowly Changing Dimension** component from **SSIS Toolbox | Other Transforms** to the **Data Flow** design area.

12. Link this component to the previous component through the green output of the first.

13. Open the component for editing.

14. Select the customer dimension business key in the **Key type** column.

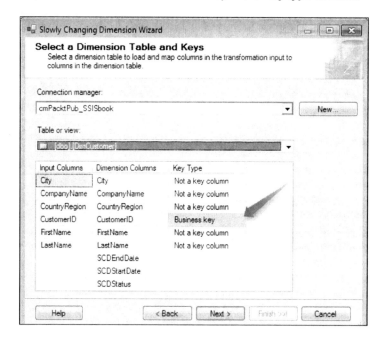

15. Select the SCD type for each column that requires tracking changes (in this example **City** is a SCD Type 2 whereas **CompanyName** and **LastName** are SCD Type 1.

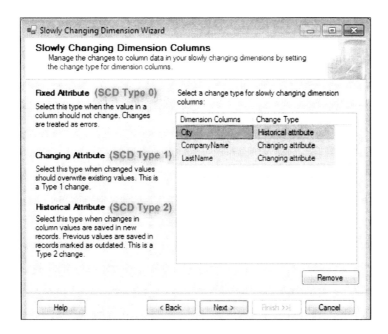

16. Set the start and end date to track historical changes over time. The reference to fill these columns is the **SSIS StartTime** variable.

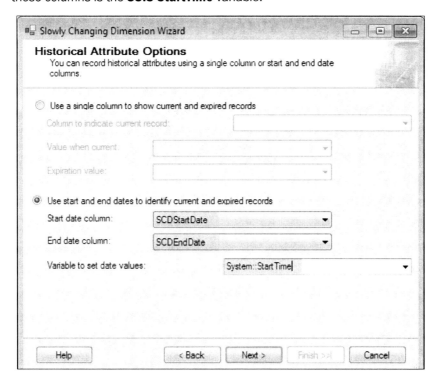

17. Press **OK** to finish configuration and verify all the new components create in the Data Flow.

18. Press *F5* to execute the package and check the new customer data moving in the pipeline.

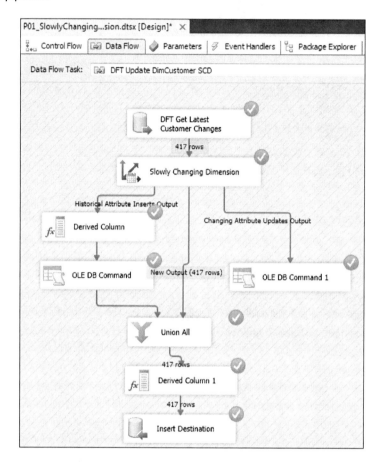

19. Execute the following SQL statement to simulate a change in the source and then execute the package again to verify is the change is updated in the customer dimension.

```
UPDATE DimCustomer SET City='Toronto' WHERE CustomerID=29499
```

How it works...

Using the SSIS SCD component makes everything seem easy, but there is a lot of work to do when dealing with SCD, especially if the dimension has many columns to consider for SCD approach. Some requirements you must fulfill to implement this approach include the creation of a new column ID for the dimension (known as **Surrogate Key**) and three more columns to help control the valid and expired dimension rows. We created the following columns in this example:

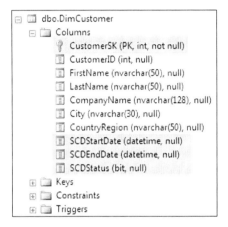

The following figure explains in detail the validations required for the SCD Type 1 approach. Data is read from the respective **Dimension Source**, then **Some Transformations** and business rules can be applied. If the record is **New** (based on the business key(s)) then an **Insert** statement is executed, else it is verified whether the changes were applied to the dimension attributes with SCD Type 1; if false, nothing is done with the record, else an **Update** statement is executed on the dimension table.

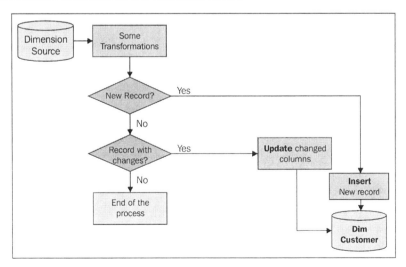

The next figure explains the validation required for the SCD Type 2 approach in detail. This approach is more complex than SCD Type 1 because it's necessary to add an additional row on the dimension wherever a change occurs in some attribute defined as SCD Type 2. After source data has been read and transformations or business rules have been applied, it is necessary to check whether any attributes of SCD Type 1 exist (to ensure that if a new record needs to be added for the SCD Type 2 approach, we will use the latest values from the SCD Type 1 attributes). If so, an update statement is executed for those attributes and we verify if any change for any SCD Type 2 attributes exists. If not, nothing is done with the record; if so, the current record is expired and a new record is added to store the new values of those SCD Type 2 attributes.

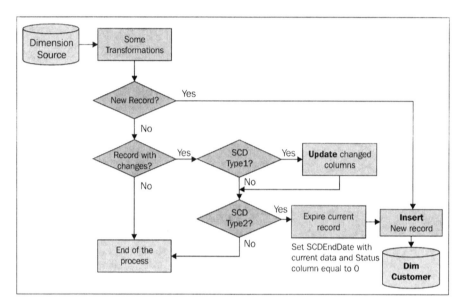

5
Data Flow Task Part 3—Advanced Transformation

by Reza Rad

In this chapter, we will cover:

▶ Pivot and Unpivot Transformations

▶ Text Analysis with Term Lookup and Term Extraction transformations

▶ DQS Cleansing Transformation—Cleansing Data

▶ Fuzzy Transformations—how SSIS understands fuzzy similarities

Introduction

In real-world scenarios different data sources do not provide the same structure, so there is a need to unify them in a unique structure. There are some transformations in the SSIS Data Flow task that use complex ways to apply such changes on the data stream, we call them Advanced Transformations.

There are some times when values in each row in a specified column should be transformed into columns based on a key. The Pivot Transformation comes to our help in this scenario, and in case it is the other way round, the Unpivot Transformation can be applied.

There are many times when data from the source comes in a variety of values in strings, such as "MS SQL Server", "SQLServer", and "MSSQL"—different values but the same meaning. A Fuzzy operation can detect these cases and treat them appropriately. There are two Fuzzy Transformations that will be discussed in this chapter: Fuzzy Grouping and Fuzzy Lookup.

SSIS 2012 provides a new service to cleanse data based on a dictionary. The requirement for cleansing data is always a challenge for loading a data warehouse; the DQS Transformation provides a solution for cleansing data.

Besides nine different data-mining algorithms provided by SQL Server Analysis Services, there is another data mining option for Text, which is referred to as Text Mining. Text Mining is supported by two transformations in SSIS: Term Extraction and Term Lookup. These transformations can find patterns in text and extract terms or apply a look up on them.

All of these transformations come from the previous version of SSIS, which was SSIS 2008, except DQS, which is a new component in SSIS 2012.

Pivot and Unpivot Transformations

Pivoting data means separating different row values from one column into separate columns; if it is the other way round, Unpivot terminology is used. The following screenshot shows a sample of Pivot data:

ProductID	Name	OrderYear	OrderQuantity
879	All-Purpose Bike Stand	2007	119
879	All-Purpose Bike Stand	2008	130
712	AWC Logo Cap	2005	520
712	AWC Logo Cap	2006	1853
712	AWC Logo Cap	2007	3562
712	AWC Logo Cap	2008	2376
877	Bike Wash - Dissolver	2007	1844
877	Bike Wash - Dissolver	2008	1475
843	Cable Lock	2006	676
843	Cable Lock	2007	411
952	Chain	2007	470
952	Chain	2008	304

As the previous data shows, there are multiple rows for each **ProductID**, but different **OrderQuantity** entries for different **OrderYear** entries in each row. A Pivot can be applied on this data and it can fetch out each different **OrderYear** entry as a different column and the value of each equivalent **OrderQuantity** can appear in its appropriate column, and as a result, one row will be needed for each product. The following screenshot shows the pivoting result of such a scenario:

ProductID	Name	2005	2006	2007	2008
879	All-Purpose Bike Stand	NULL	NULL	119	130
712	AWC Logo Cap	520	1853	3562	2376
877	Bike Wash - Dissolver	NULL	NULL	1844	1475
843	Cable Lock	NULL	676	411	NULL
952	Chain	NULL	NULL	470	304

In this recipe, we will use the Pivot Transformation for reading the list of products with their quantity of sales each year from the `AdventureWorks2012` database with **ProductID**, **Name**, **OrderYear**, and **OrderQuantity** columns and then pivot the data into multiple columns for each **OrderYear** entry. The quantity of each product will appear in row values.

Also, we will use Unpivot for reverse operations to combine all columns of order year values into one column.

Getting ready

Create two new tables in the `AdventureWorks2012` database with these scripts; one for the `PivotedData` table:

```
CREATE TABLE [dbo].[PivotedData](
   [ProductID] [int] NULL,
   [Name] [nvarchar](50) NULL,
   [2005] [int] NULL,
   [2006] [int] NULL,
   [2007] [int] NULL,
   [2008] [int] NULL
)
```

And the second one for the `UnPivotedData` table:

```
CREATE TABLE [dbo].[UnPivotedData](
   [OrderYear] [nvarchar](255) NULL,
   [OrderQuantity] [int] NULL,
   [ProductID] [int] NULL,
   [Name] [nvarchar](50) NULL
)
```

How to do it...

1. Create a new project of type **Integration Services** and name it `R01_Pivoting and Unpivoting Data`, rename the package to **P01_Pivot**, drag-and-drop a Data Flow Task into the Control Flow, and then go to the **Data Flow** tab.

2. Drag-and-drop an **OLE DB Source** into the **Data Flow** tab, and open **OLE DB Source Editor**.

3. Create new connection to the `AdventureWorks2012` database, set the **Data Access Mode** to *SQL Command*, and type the following query in SQL Command:

```
SELECT PRD.ProductID, PRD.Name, YEAR(ORD.OrderDate) as OrderYear,
   SUM(ORDDET.OrderQty) as OrderQuantity
FROM Sales.SalesOrderDetail ORDDET
   INNER JOIN Production.Product PRD
    ON ORDDET.ProductID=PRD.ProductID
         INNER JOIN Sales.SalesOrderHeader ORD
    ON ORDDET.SalesOrderID=ORD.SalesOrderID
GROUP BY PRD.ProductID, PRD.Name, year(ORD.OrderDate)
ORDER BY PRD.Name,year(ORD.OrderDate)
```

4. Click on **Preview** and check the data structure. It should be similar to the following screenshot:

ProductID	Name	OrderYear	OrderQuantity
879	All-Purpose Bike Stand	2007	119
879	All-Purpose Bike Stand	2008	130
712	AWC Logo Cap	2005	520
712	AWC Logo Cap	2006	1853
712	AWC Logo Cap	2007	3562
712	AWC Logo Cap	2008	2376
877	Bike Wash - Dissolver	2007	1844
877	Bike Wash - Dissolver	2008	1475
843	Cable Lock	2006	676
843	Cable Lock	2007	411
952	Chain	2007	470
952	Chain	2008	304

5. Drag-and-drop a **Pivot Transformation** after **OLE DB Source** and go to **Pivot Transformation Editor**.

6. In **Pivot Transformation Editor**, set **Pivot Key** to *OrderYear*, set **Set Key** to *Name*, and set **Pivot Value** to *OrderQuantity*. Check the **Ignore un-matched Pivot Key values and report them after DataFlow execution** checkbox as shown in the following screenshot:

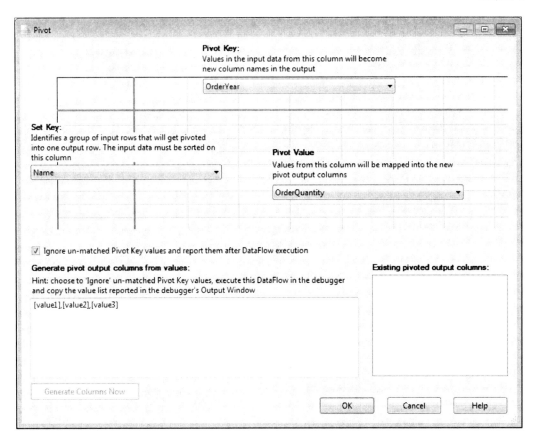

7. Run the package, and then go to the **Progress** or **Execution Results** tab. Find the record that states: **[Pivot [number]] Information** as shown in the following screenshot:

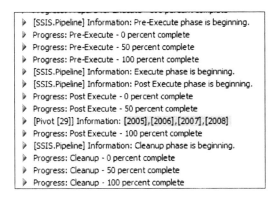

8. Copy the numbers **[2005],[2006],[2007],[2008]** from the **Progress** tab, open the **Pivot Transformation Editor** again and paste the copied text into the **Generate pivot output columns from values** box. Then, click on **Generate Columns Now**, and you will see that output columns will be generated accordingly as shown in the following screenshot:

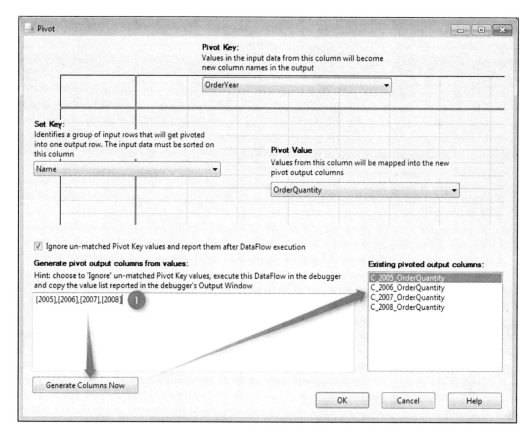

9. Close **Pivot Transformation Editor**, and add an **OLE DB Destination**, set the connection to the AdventureWorks2012 database, and select *PivotedData* as table. Set mappings as shown in the following screenshot, and close **OLE DB Destination Editor**:

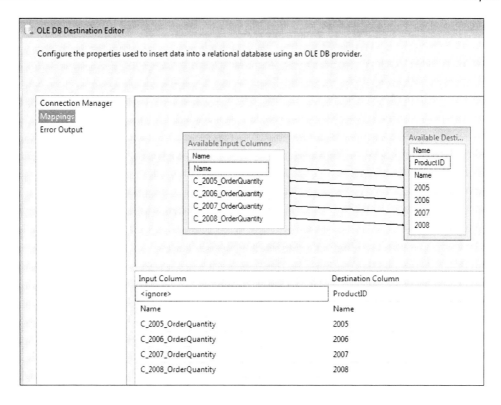

10. Verify the whole schema of the package with the following screenshot:

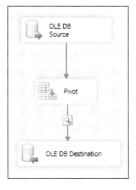

11. Run the package and check the pivoted data in the destination table; an example of the result is showed in the following screenshot:

ProductID	Name	2005	2006	2007	2008
879	All-Purpose Bike Stand	NULL	NULL	119	130
712	AWC Logo Cap	520	1853	3562	2376
877	Bike Wash - Dissolver	NULL	NULL	1844	1475
843	Cable Lock	NULL	676	411	NULL
952	Chain	NULL	NULL	470	304

12. Add another package, name it `P02_Unpivot`, add an OLE DB Source, set the connection to `AdventureWorks2012`, and select the `PivotedData` table as the source table.

13. Add an Unpivot Transformation after the OLE DB Source.

14. In the **Available Input Columns**, just select the 2005 to 2008 columns. Set the **ProductID** and **Name** column as **Pass Through**.

15. Set **Destination Column** for all columns from 2005 to 2008 as **OrderQuantity**.

16. Set **Pivot Key Value** column name as **OrderYear** as shown in the following screenshot:

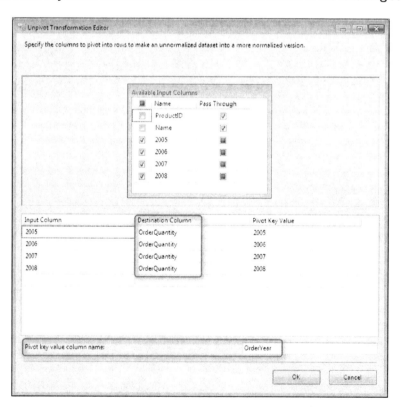

17. Close **Unpivot Transformation Editor**, add an OLE DB Destination, and set the destination table as *UnPivotedData*.

18. Run the package, and check results in the `UnpivotedData` table. The result will be similar to the first screenshot of this recipe.

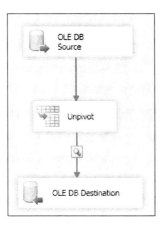

How it works...

Pivot and Unpivot Transformations in SSIS 2012 have a basic editor that helps the developer to create output columns simply. They are explained briefly as follows:

Pivot Transformation

A Pivot Transformation needs four important parts:

▶ **Set Key**: A column with key values, in our example the Set Key column was **Name**.

▶ **Pivot Key**: A column that is the Pivot Column. This column has values that will be the output column names of the pivot transform. In our example the Pivot Key column was **OrderYear**.

▶ **Pivot Value**: Another column that has equivalent values for the Pivot Column. Values from this column will appear under the output columns that are generated by the Pivot Column. In our example the Pivot Value column was **OrderQuantity**.

▶ **Output columns**: Pivot Transform needs to know output columns' names statically, so this is why we set static values [2005],[2006],[2007],[2008] as output columns in steps 8 and 9.

Unpivot Transformation

An Unpivot Transformation has three important parts:

- ▸ **Pass Through**: There are some input columns that should pass through directly as output columns; these columns should be checked as **Pass Through**. In our example **ProductID** and **Name** are set to **Pass Through**.

- ▸ **Destination Column**: All input columns that contain values which should be Unpivoted should be checked as **Input Column**, and their **PivotKeyValue** should be set appropriately. All of the equivalent values that come from these columns' data will be zipped in a new column with the name that is specified in Destination Column.

- ▸ **Pivot key value column name**: All **PivotKeyValue** values will be zipped in a column, which is named in this property. In this example, we set the **Pivot key value column name** to **OrderYear**.

There's more...

The Pivot Transformation has an advanced editor, which is described as follows:

Pivot Transformation; Working with the Advanced Editor

You can configure Pivot Transformation by right-clicking on it and selecting **Show Advanced Editor**. Then, follow the given steps:

1. In the **Input Columns** tab, check all the available input columns.

2. In the **Input and Output Columns** tab, expand **Pivot Default Input**, click on **ProductID** and then in the properties pane, change **PivotUsage** to *0* (*0* is default value; for this case just verify it). Also, set other the **Pivot Usage** property of other input columns as follows:

Input Column	PivotUsage	Equivalent in Basic Editor
ProductID	0	Pass Through
Name	1	Set Key
OrderYear	2	Pivot Key
OrderQuantity	3	Pivot Value

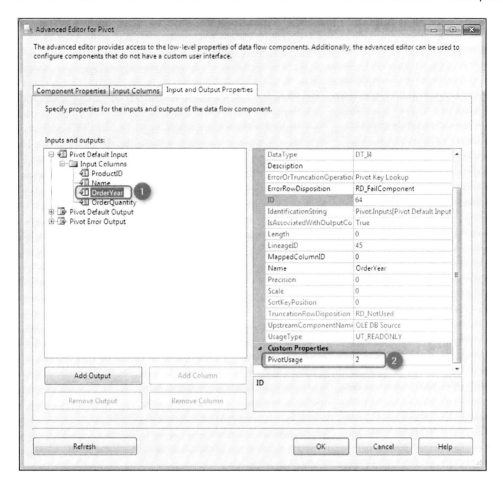

3. Expand **Pivot Default Output**, and under **Output Columns**, add the following columns:

    ❑ **ProductID**
    ❑ **Name**
    ❑ **2005**
    ❑ **2006**
    ❑ **2007**
    ❑ **2008**

4. Under **Pivot Default Input**, under **Input Columns**, select *ProductID*, and in the properties pane, check the **LineageID** value. Remember this value for the next step. Note that the value of **LineageID** may differ from the one shown in the following screenshot:

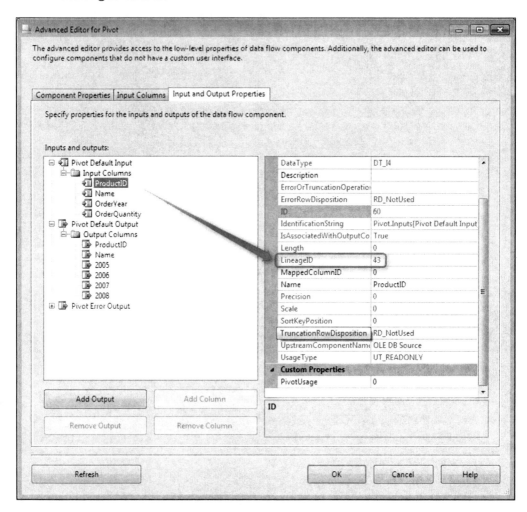

5. Then go back to **Pivot Default Output**, and under **Output Columns**, select **ProductID**, and then enter the **LineageID** property value from previous step in the **SourceColumn** property.

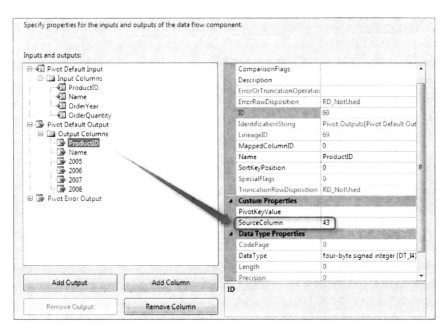

6. Perform the step again for the **Name** column. Note that after setting the **SourceColumn**, the **DataType** property of the **Output Column** will change and will be equivalent to the column to which it refers.

7. Under **Pivot Default Input**, under **Input Columns** select the **OrderQuantity** column (the column with **PivotUsage** value *3*), and copy **LineageID**.

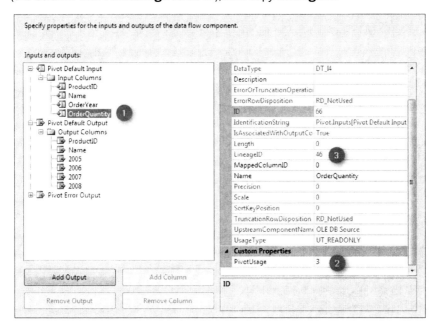

8. Under the **Pivot Default Output**, under **Output Columns**, select the *2005* column, set the source column as **LineageID** from the **OrderQuantity** input column, and also change the **PivotKeyValue** to *2005*.

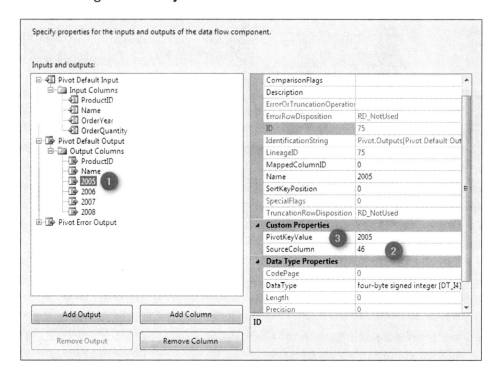

9. Perform the same step for output columns 2006, 2007, and 2008, and set all **SourceColumn** values with the LineageID of the **OrderQuantity** column. Set **PivotKeyValue** for the columns as *2006, 2007,* and *2008* sequentially.

The Advanced Editor settings sound a bit hard to understand but it will be much clearer after reading the following explanation of each configuration:

▶   **PivotUsage**: The Pivot Transform needs three input columns: A column with Key values; in our example the Key column was **Name**; the **PivotUsage** of this column should be set to 1. A column which is the Pivot Column; this column has values that will be output column names of the pivot transform; the **PivotUsage** of this column should be set to 2. Another column that has equivalent values for the Pivot Column; values from this column will appear under the output columns that are generated by the Pivot Column, Transformation, the **PivotUsage** of this column should be 3.

Every other column that appears in the output directly without any changes, and will pass through, should have **PivotUsage** as 0.

For a Pivot Transformation there should be at least one column with **PivotUsage** 2, one column with **PivotUsage** 3, and one column with **PivotUsage** 0 or 1.

- **SourceColumn**: Each output column in the Pivot Transformation should know where the source column data comes from, so the **SourceColumn** property of each output column should be set with the **LineageID** of the appropriate input column. Each column in the Data Flow has a **LineageID** property, which defines this column in the buffer. The **LineageID** may be different than the ID property.

- **PivotKeyValue**: Each value in the Pivot Column will be a column in output, so output columns equivalent for these values should be added manually in the output columns part as we did in step 8. Each output column that has only pass through values or is a pivot key, just needs to have the **SourceColumn** property, but pivoted columns need another property to be set, *PivotKeyValue*. The value of the **PivotKeyValue** property should be equivalent to the Pivot Column for that output column, for example in the output column, which shows the value *2005*, the *PivotKeyValue* should be *2005*.

The **SourceColumn** property for pivoted columns should be set with the LineageID from the input column with the **PivotUsage** *3*, the column that contains values that should appear in output pivoted data rows.

 Note that in the previous versions of SSIS (2005, 2008, and 2008R2) the Pivot Transformation had only the Advanced Editor; this means that if you want to work with earlier versions of SSIS you need to work with the method described here.

Text Analysis with Term Lookup and Term Extraction transformations

There are a lot of transformations that help you to analyze numeric data. You can even use aggregate functions in T-SQL to fetch analytic information from numeric data; but what happens when you want to analyze user comments? Those can be freeform texts without any categorization.

Text Analysis is a complete topic in the data analysis category, which discusses fetching analytical information from text data; the text data can be completely freeform text data. Fortunately SSIS provides two useful and advanced transformations for Text Analysis called Term Extraction and Term Lookup.

In this recipe, we will take a look at how we can analyze and mine free text data. Assume that customers of a company share their experiences with the company products with freefrom text comments on the company's website.

Getting ready

Create a `Product` table in the `PacktPub_SSISbook` database with the following script:

```
CREATE TABLE [dbo].[Product](
  [ID] [int] IDENTITY(1,1) NOT NULL,
  [Name] [nvarchar](128) NULL,
  CONSTRAINT [PK_Product] PRIMARY KEY CLUSTERED
  (
    [ID] ASC
  )) ON [PRIMARY]

GO


USE [PacktPub_SSISbook]
GO

INSERT INTO [dbo].[Product] ([Name]) VALUES ('PX12')
INSERT INTO [dbo].[Product] ([Name]) VALUES ('PX800')
INSERT INTO [dbo].[Product] ([Name]) VALUES ('PX609')
```

Download or copy the `comments.txt` file from the book's online materials and copy it into this address: `C:\SSIS\Ch05_Data Flow Task-Part 3-Advanced Transformations\R02_Text Analysis\Files`.

The content of the `comments.txt` file is as follows:

```
ID,TextData
1,I used PX609 for 5 years that was really good.
2,the PX800 delivered very soon but it was a mistaken delivery so I
asked for a re-send
3,this company has a brilliant support service but everytime I should
spend a lot of time in the long queue, that was my experience with
PX609
4,I recommended PX12 to couple of my friends and they are happy with
its good performance
5,I received my PX12 and PX800 with delayed delivery
6,PX609 was a fair product for me
7,there were no upgrades from PX800 that made me crazy
8,my PX12 had a problem at first turn off but after that I used it for
10 months and it works great
```

How to do it...

1. Create an SSIS Project and name it `R02_Text Analysis`.

2. In the Connection Manager folder in **Solution Explorer**, add an **OLE DB Connection Manager** to **PacktPub_SSISbook**.

3. Add a **Flat File Connection Manager** and connect it to the `comments.txt` file, which is placed at `C:\SSIS\Ch05_Data Flow Task-Part 3-Advanced Transformations\R02_Text Analysis\Files\comments.txt`. Set the format as *Delimited*, check the **Column names in the first data row** checkbox and change the data type of the **TextData** column in **Advanced** tab to **Unicode string [DT_WSTR]**.

 Note that using `DT_WSTR` or `DT_NTEXT` is mandatory if you want to do Term Extraction or Term Lookup because these components only work with these data types.

4. Rename `package.dtsx` to `P1_Term Lookup`, and add a Data Flow Task to the package and go to the **Data Flow** tab.

5. Add a **Flat File Source** and connect it to the **Flat File Connection Manager** that we created in step 3.

6. Drag-and-drop a Term Lookup transformation after the Flat File Source.

7. In the **Term Lookup Transformation Editor**, set **OLE DB connection manager** to the *PacktPub_SSISbook* database, and set **Reference table name** to *[dbo].[Product]* as shown in the following screenshot:

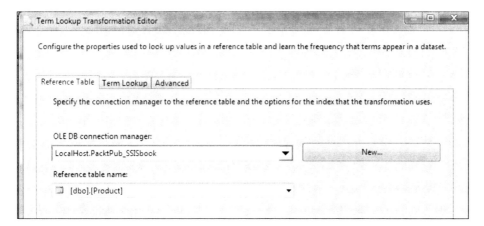

8. Go to the **Term Lookup** tab, and drag-and-drop **TextData** from **Available Input Columns** to **Available Reference Columns**, and check both the **TextData** and **ID** checkboxes from **Available Input Columns** as shown in the following screenshot:

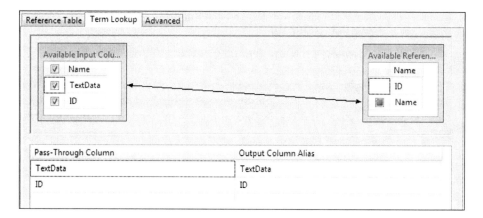

9. Close **Term Lookup Transformation Editor** and drag-and-drop a Union All transformation. Then, right-click on the data path between **Term Lookup and Union All** and click **Enable Data Viewer** (using Union All here is just for viewing data in the data viewer).

10. Run the package, and check the data in Data Viewer. You will see that the result shows each **Term** that is seen in **TextData** and its frequency in each record. For some comments that mention more than one product, there will be two records in the result of Term Lookup.

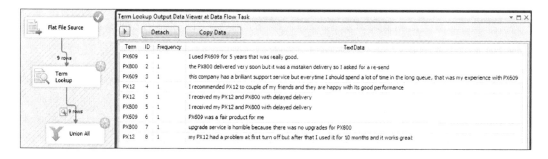

11. Add another package to the project and name it `P2_Term Extraction`, add a **Data Flow Task** there and go to the **Data Flow** tab.

12. Add a **Flat File Source** connecting to the flat file connection manager that was created in step 3.

13. Drag-and-drop a Term Extraction Transformation from the toolbox to the Data Flow after the Flat File Source.

14. In the **Term Extraction Transformation Editor window**, in the **Term Extraction** tab, select *TextData* in the **Available Input Columns**, and leave **Output column name** as is.

15. Go to the **Advanced** tab and in the **Term type** section select *Noun and noun phrase*, set **Score type** to *Frequency*, in the **Parameters** section set **Frequency threshold** to *1* and **Maximum length of term** as 18 as shown in the following screenshot:

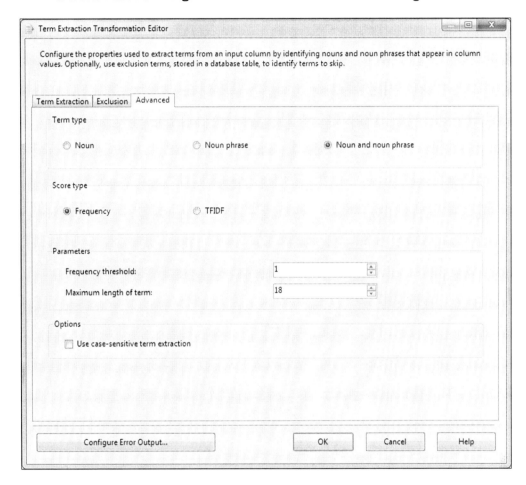

16. Close **Term Extraction Transformation Editor**, and drag-and-drop a **Union All** transformation. Then, right-click on the data path between **Term Extraction** and **Union All** and click on **Enable Data Viewer** (using **Union All** here is just for viewing data in the data viewer).

17. Run the package, and check the data in **Data Viewer**. You will see the terms separated by nouns and noun phrases in different records with their frequency in the whole input **TextData** column.

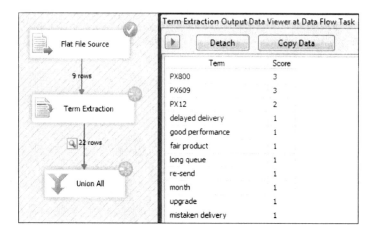

18. Open **Term Extraction Transformation Editor** again and change **Term type** to *Noun phrase* and **Score type** to *TFIDF*. Run the package again; you will see different results. We will discuss it in the *How it works...* section.

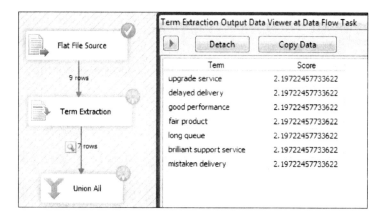

How it works...

We saw how to work with two term transformation components in Data Flow. Term Lookup fetches all terms in the input text record and looks for them in the reference table; if it finds a match then it will return the term and its frequency in the source text column. This transformation can detect case-sensitive data if you check this option in the **Advanced** tab.

Term Extraction will expand each term in a separate row in output and will show its score as well.

Terms can be detected in three ways as follows:

- Noun
- Noun phrase
- Noun and noun phrase

Frequency scores each term based on its frequency in whole data rows, for example take a look at PX800 in the result of step 10; this shows that there are three PX800 nouns in the input file. TFIDF is the abbreviation of **Term Frequency and Inverse Document Frequency**. This algorithm works with the following formula:

```
TFIDF of a Term T = (frequency of T) * log( (#rows in Input) / (#rows
having T) )
```

We can filter the frequency by setting the Frequency threshold parameter; the default value is 2, so every term that has less than 2 occurrences will be omitted in the result by default. We can also set the maximum length of term to prevent having long noun phrases. The Term Extraction component also has the ability to detect words with case.

The **Score** and **Term** provided by the Term Extraction component's result can be used in other tranformations to do more cleansing, for example a conditional split can filter rows with higher TFIDF score results.

There's more...

Term Extraction can use an exclusion list and overlook unwanted terms. We will take a quick look at this option.

Excluding Terms

Term Extraction may fetch many unwanted nouns and noun phrases by default; fortunately we can filter them in the **Exclusion** tab by defining an **OLE DB connection manager** and the exclusion table and column as shown in the following screenshot:

Term Lookup and Term Extraction can be much more powerful if we use them in combination with other transforms such as Fuzzy components and DQS Cleansing.

DQS Cleansing Transformation—Cleansing Data

Data Cleansing is one of the most important parts in every data transfer scenario. There are many scenarios where the source of data is not well structured, and the source is not consistent. For example, Microsoft is not spelled the same in all data sources, in one of them it is "Micsoft", in another case it is "Micro soft" and in some cases "Microsoft". Data Cleansing means maintaining the consistency of data.

SQL Server 2012 comes with a new service, which is named **DQS**. DQS stands for Data Quality Services. DQS is one of the services that can be installed and can listen to requests. You can create knowledge bases in DQS with a tool named DQS Client, and then use SSIS DQS Cleansing Component to check matching data with the knowledge bases and standardize them or report their status.

DQS itself is outside the scope of this book, but we will take a quick look at how to install and use DQS. Lastly, we will run a sample to apply DQS Cleansing on a data source to see how it works.

Getting ready

Prepare the data source; download `source.txt` from the book code bundle, which is available on the book's website. Copy this file to the following address: `C:\SSIS\Ch05_Data Flow Task-Part 3-Advanced Transformations\R03_DQS Cleansing\Files`.

Install DQS in the following way:

1. Go to **Start | All Programs | Microsoft SQL Server | Data Quality Services** and click on **Data Quality Server Installer**.
2. Enter a master key password with conditions provided in the screen.
3. Wait for Data Quality Server to be completely installed.

Create a Knowledge Base using the following steps:

1. Go to **Start | All Programs | Microsoft SQL Server | Data Quality Services** and open **Data Quality Client**.
2. Connect to local (or if you have DQS installed or you are using another machine as the DQS Server use their names).
3. Click on **Open Knowledge Base**.
4. In the right panel, select knowledge base data as **US – State** and click on **Next**.

5. In the **Domain Management** window, go to the **Domain Values** tab and in the **Find** textbox, type in **california**; you will see the list of states includes **California** there as shown in the following screenshot:

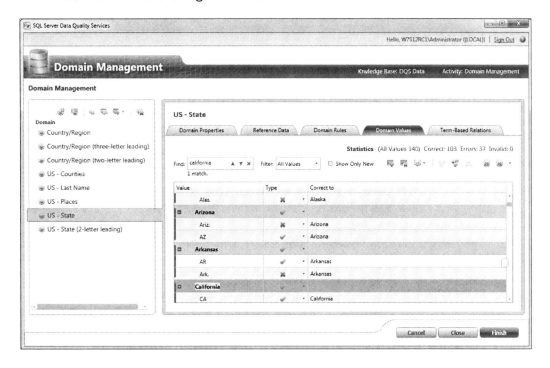

6. Click on **Finish** and publish the knowledge base to the server. Name the knowledge base **DQS Data**.

How to do it...

1. Create an SSIS Project and name it R03_DQS Cleansing. Add a Data Flow Task to the package and go to the **Data Flow** tab.

2. Add a **Flat File Source** and create a connection to the source file, which is available at C:\SSIS\Ch05_Data Flow Task-Part 3-Advanced Transformations\ R03_DQS Cleansing\Files\source.txt.

3. Set the **Text Qualifier** as double quote ("). Check the column names in the first data row.

4. Go to the **Columns** tab and check values in the **StateProvinceName** column:

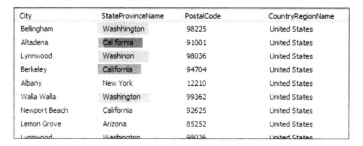

City	StateProvinceName	PostalCode	CountryRegionName
Bellingham	Washhington	98225	United States
Altadena	Cal fornia	91001	United States
Lynnwood	Washinon	98036	United States
Berkeley	California	94704	United States
Albany	New York	12210	United States
Walla Walla	Washington	99362	United States
Newport Beach	California	92625	United States
Lemon Grove	Arizona	85252	United States
Lynnwood	Washington	98036	United States

5. Note that there are some state names that are spelt wrongly, for example we have **Washhington, Washinon,** and **Washington**. (We will apply DQS Cleansing on this data.)

6. Click on **OK**, and close the **Flat File Source**.

7. Drag-and-drop a **DQS Cleansing Transform** from the **SSIS Toolbox** to **Data Flow** after the **Flat File Source**.

8. Open **DQS Cleansing Transformation Editor**, and create a new **Data Quality Connection Manager**. Set the name of DQS Server to the local machine (or the name of any machine that you use as DQS Server). Verify the test connection to be successful.

9. Go back to **DQS Cleansing Transformation Editor** and select *DQS Data* as **Data Quality Knowledge Base** as shown in the following screenshot:

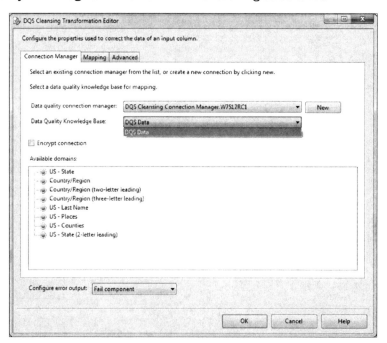

10. Go to the **Mapping** tab, in **Available Input Columns** select **StateProvinceName**, and in the row under it, select **Domain** as *US – State*. Leave the other settings as default as shown in the following screenshot:

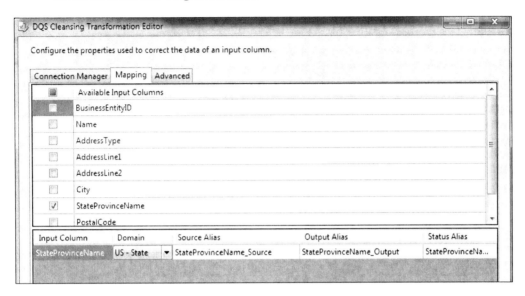

11. Close DQS Cleansing Transformation Editor.

12. Add a Destination (this part is only to show what the result will be; you may need to use different components in your own scenarios). Add an **Object Type** variable, then add a RecordSet Desination after the DQS Cleansing Transform, and select the object variable there. Then enable Data Viewer on the data path between DQS Cleansing and RecordSet Destination (to enable Data Viewer just right-click on the data path and select **Enable Data Viewer**).

13. Run the package and check the results. Note that all the wrong values are corrected already, but with different status; we will discuss these status types in the next section.

StateProvinceName_Source	StateProvinceName_Output	StateProvinceName_Status	PostalCode	CountryRegionName	Record Status
Washhington	Washington	Corrected	98225	United States	Corrected
Cal fornia	California	Auto suggest	91001	United States	Auto suggest
Washinon	Washington	Auto suggest	98036	United States	Auto suggest
California	California	Correct	94704	United States	Correct
New York	New York	Correct	12210	United States	Correct
Washington	Washington	Correct	99362	United States	Correct

How it works...

We saw how DQS Cleansing works in the previous example. To use DQS we need a DQS Server, which can be a local computer or another computer that has DQS Server installed. Note that DQS only exists from SQL Server 2012.

DQS Server has a service which runs and listens to incoming requests to match with knowledge bases. So we need to create or configure knowledge bases when we want to work with DQS. There are some default knowledge bases such as the one with the **US – State** domain that we used. Each knowledge base can consist of Domains. For example, the knowledge base can be Phone numbers, and different domains can be based on different countries.

Creating and managing knowledge bases can be done with DQS Client, which is one of tools that will be installed with SQL Server 2012.

As an SSIS developer, maybe you don't have to work with knowledge bases directly and create or manage them, but obviously you will have to work with DQS Cleansing Transformation in SSIS components. DQS Cleansing Transformation is a component that connects to a knowledge base in a DQS Server and checks similarity of data with the knowledge base, and finally standardizes the data. It also provides useful status information on each value and shows the matching results of comparison and standardization with the knowledge base.

DQS Cleansing Transformation creates an overall column for whole input, which is the **Record Status** column. This column shows the overall status of all columns that participated in DQS Cleansing. Two other columns, which will be shown per each of the input columns that are marked to be cleansed in the **Mapping** tab, are **SourceColumnName_Output** and **SourceColumnName_Status**. (In the screenshot of step 13 you saw **StateProvinceName_Output** and **StateProvinceName_Status**.)

SourceColumnName_Output is a column that has the corrected or matched result after DQS Cleansing, and **SourceColumnName_Status** will show the status of that value (you will read more about it in the *There's more...* section).

There's more...

Using DQS Cleansing Transformation needs a good understanding of its results and feedbacks, and how to configure it to get better results. In this section we will take a look at some advanced topics about DQS Cleansing.

The DQS Cleansing Component acts asynchronously

DQS Cleansing requires heavy processing to be done at the DQS Server, and the processing for a large number of rows will be very time consuming. So be careful when using this transformation and don't feed a large number of data rows into it because it will be time and resource consuming.

Advanced settings

You can customize DQS Cleansing Tranformation with some configuration settings, which are provided in the **Advanced** tab of **DQS Cleansing Transformation Editor**. There are a number of options, which can be seen in the following screenshot:

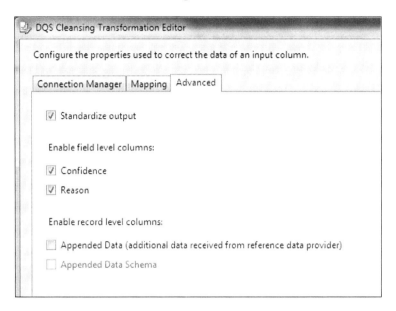

- ▸ **Standardize output**: With this option you can choose if DQS Cleansing should use domain default settings or not. Domain default settings can be set by opening **DQS Client**, clicking on knowledge base settings, and selecting *Domain Management* under the **Domain Properties** tab. Domain default settings can be found there.

- ▸ **Enable field level columns**: There are two columns that can be added to output columns of DQS Cleansing per each field that goes for cleansing. **Confidence** shows the threshold of similarity between incoming value and domain values, and **Reason** shows where the output column's data comes from. The following screenshot shows a sample result of **Confidence** and **Reason** for the **StateProvinceName** column:

StateProvinceName_Source	StateProvinceName_Output	StateProvinceName_Status	PostalCode	CountryRegionName	Record Status	StateProvinceName_Confidence	StateProvinceName_Reason
Washhington	Washington	Corrected	98225	United States	Corrected	0.88	DQS cleansing
Cal fornia	California	Auto suggest	91001	United States	Auto suggest	0.75	DQS cleansing
Washinon	Washington	Auto suggest	98036	United States	Auto suggest	0.7272727	DQS cleansing
California	California	Correct	94704	United States	Correct		Domain value
New York	New York	Correct	12210	United States	Correct		Domain value

- ▸ **Enable record level columns**: In some cases the knowledge base's domain may have additional information about domain values. Enabling record level columns will provide two columns that collect additional information from domain values.

Status Column

The Status Column provides useful information that is a result of DQS matching with the knowledge base.

There are several values that can be seen in this column; these values are described as follows:

- ▸ **Correct**: Data is correctly matched with domain values.
- ▸ **Corrected**: Data didn't match with domain values, but DQS fixed and corrected it.
- ▸ **Auto Suggest**: Data didn't find domain values, and DQS suggested a domain value. This option can be used together with Confidence in the **Advanced** tab of **DQS Cleansing Transformation Editor**.
- ▸ **New**: Data is unknown and new for domain values in the knowledge base.

At some point in the DQS section, running data through the DQS Cleansing component will automatically create a DQS project in the DQS Client. This enables the business to maintain the knowledge base by accepting/rejecting changes. As of RTM, the project created by the SSIS component cannot be opened in the DQS Client. Expect this to be fixed in a patch to SQL Server 2012.

Fuzzy Transformations—how SSIS understands fuzzy similarities

Suppose that input data is a `csv` file with department name information and there is no guarantee that the department names are spelt consistently. So you may have names such as "Management" and "Managmnt" together in the same data file. In such cases an ordinal Lookup Transform cannot detect these similarities, because Lookup checks for terms that are completely identical. This is where we need to apply some Fuzzy operations.

SSIS has two Fuzzy Transformations, which catch fuzzy similarities between terms and help us in master data management, as follows:

- ▸ **Fuzzy Grouping**: This component will create groups of data rows based on their similarity threshold
- ▸ **Fuzzy Lookup**: This component will look at a reference table to find matching keywords based on a predefined similarity threshold

In this recipe, we take a look at two Fuzzy Transformations and how they can help us in real-world scenarios.

Getting ready

Create a `Department` table with the following script in `PacktPub_SSISbook`:

```
CREATE TABLE [dbo].[Department](
  [ID] [int] IDENTITY(1,1) NOT NULL,
  [Name] [varchar](50) NULL,
  CONSTRAINT [PK_Department] PRIMARY KEY CLUSTERED
  (
    [ID] ASC
  ) ON [PRIMARY]
) ON [PRIMARY]

GO

INSERT INTO [dbo].[Department] ([Name]) VALUES ('Information
  Technology')
INSERT INTO [dbo].[Department] ([Name]) VALUES ('Sales')
INSERT INTO [dbo].[Department] ([Name]) VALUES ('Management')
```

Download or copy the `source.txt` file from the code bundle to this folder: `C:\SSIS\Ch05_Data Flow Task-Part 3-Advanced Transformations\R04_Fuzzy\Files`.

How to do it...

1. Create an SSIS Project and name it `R04_Fuzzy`.

2. In the Connection Manager folder in Solution Explorer, add an **OLE DB Connection Manager** to **PacktPub_SSISbook**.

3. Add a **Flat File Connection Manager** and connect it to the `comments.txt` file, which is available at: `C:\SSIS\Ch05_Data Flow Task-Part 3-Advanced Transformations\R04_Fuzzy\Files\source.txt`. Set the format as *Delimited*, and check the **Column names in the first data row** checkbox.

4. Rename `package.dtsx` to `P1_Fuzzy Lookup`, add a **Data Flow Task** to the package, and go to the **Data Flow** tab.

5. Add a **Flat File Source** and connect it to the **Flat File Connection Manager** that we created in step 3.

6. Drag-and-drop a **Fuzzy Lookup Transformation** after the **Flat File Source**.

7. In the **Fuzzy Lookup Transformation Editor**, under the **Reference Table** tab, set the **OLE DB connection manager** to *PacktPub_SSISbook*, and set **Reference table name** to *[dbo].[Department]*. Also, check the **Store new index** checkbox. We will talk about these settings in the *How it works...* section.

8. Go to the **Columns** tab, connect **Department** from **Available Input Columns** to **Name** in the **Available Lookup Columns**, and check both **Name** and **ID** from **Available Lookup Columns** and rename them as **Department Name from DB** and **Department ID from DB** respectively as shown in the following screenshot:

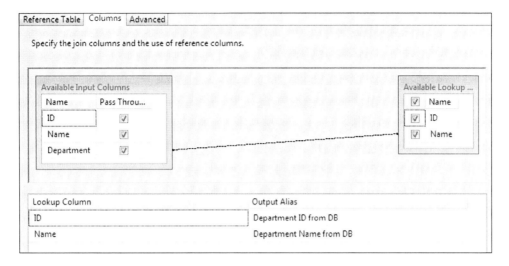

9. Go to the **Advanced** tab and change **Similarity threshold** to **0.70**, leaving the other settings as their default values:

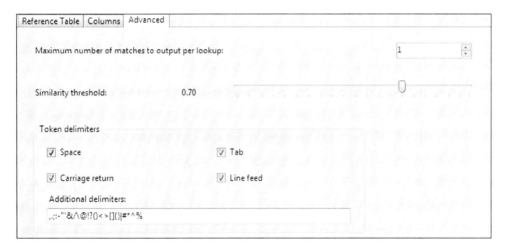

10. Close **Fuzzy Lookup Transformation Editor**, and drag-and-drop a **Union All** transformation. Then, right-click on the data path between **Term Lookup** and **Union All** and click on **Enable Data Viewer** (using **Union All** here is just for viewing data in the Data Viewer).

11. Run the package, and check the data in Data Viewer. You will see that Fuzzy Lookup found similarity of input text with department names in the reference table and cleaned data wherever the similarity was greater than 0.70.

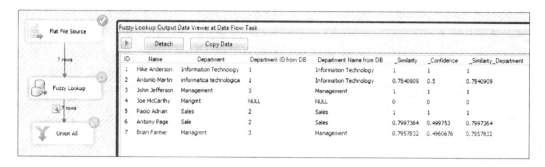

12. Add another package to the project and name it `P2_Fuzzy Grouping`; add a Data Flow Task there and go to the **Data Flow** tab.

13. Add a **Flat File Source** that connects to the **Flat File Connection Manager** that was created in step 3.

14. Drag-and-drop a Fuzzy Grouping transformation from toolbox to the Data Flow after the **Flat File Source**.

15. In **Fuzzy Grouping Transformation Editor,** set the **OLE DB connection manager** to *PacktPub_SSISbook*.

16. Go to the **Columns** tab, and select **Department** from the available columns list; note **Match Type** under the grid should be **Fuzzy** as shown in the following screenshot:

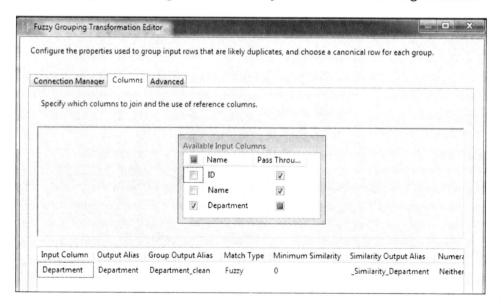

17. Go to the **Advanced** tab and set **Similarity threshold** to **0.70**, leaving the other settings as their default values.

18. Close **Fuzzy Grouping Transformation Editor**, and drag-and-drop a **Union All** transformation. Then, right-click on the data path between **Term Lookup** and **Union All** and **Enable Data Viewer**.

19. Run the package, and check the data in Data Viewer. You will see that there are some new columns in the output: **_key_in**, **_key_out**, **_score**, **Department_clean**, and **_Similarity_Department**.

    ❏ **_key_in** is an auto-generated key that is assigned to each record at execution time

    ❏ **_Similarity_Department** shows similarity of input data with each output group data

    ❏ **_key_out** is the returned and cleaned key after applying fuzzy algorithms

    ❏ **_score** is an average of all similarity columns in the Fuzzy Grouping operation

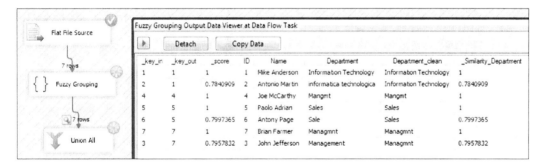

20. Go to **Fuzzy Grouping Transformation Editor**, and in the **Advanced** tab change the threshold to **0.80.** You will see a different result this time.

How it works...

Fuzzy operations are one of the most powerful features in the SSIS, which helps a lot in cleansing data. When we mention the term "Fuzzy" it means that comparison of two terms may results a value between 0 and 1 with decimal points. Ordinal comparisons will result in 0 or 1, where zero means not equivalent and one means equivalent. But there are a lot of times when we need to find all terms that are similar to a specific percentage of our keyword for example with 80 percent similarity.

Fuzzy Transformations in SSIS do fuzzy operations to find similarity between terms. There are two Fuzzy Transformations: Fuzzy Lookup and Fuzzy Grouping.

Fuzzy Lookup processes each row in a way that checks the similarity of a specific column to the predefined column in the reference table and calculates similarity. If the similarity is higher than the threshold then it will return the value from the lookup table as cleaned data. The threshold is what we set in the **Advanced** tab as the similarity threshold property of **Fuzzy Lookup Transformation Editor**.

Fuzzy Grouping creates groups of input keys based on their similarities. It processes each record and creates an output group; if the second input record is similar to the first record in the specific column then it will return the first record's output key otherwise it will create another output group. This is what you saw in step 19 with **_key_in** and **_key_out** columns. Let's simplify with an example; take a look at the first record in the result of step 19, the **_key_in** for the first record is **1**. As there is no output group yet, the input department created an **Department_clean** with the exact input value and the **_key_out** is **1**. But for the second record which has **_key_in** value **2**, the value in **Department** column is similar to the previous output group. So the result of **Department_clean** is **Information Technology** with the **_key_out** value **1**.

Fuzzy operations are very resource-consuming operations. They will take a lot of memory, CPU usage, and time to work with a huge number of records. So be careful when you want to use them and apply the Fuzzy Transformations to only the records that need this operation; for example in our example we could find the "Information Technology" keyword with a Lookup Transformation and the first record doesn't need to be send to Fuzzy Lookup, so with a Lookup Transformation or other transformations we can reduce the load of Fuzzy Transformations.

The Fuzzy Lookup Transformation needs an Index table to perform fuzzy calculations. This is why we chose Generate New Index in step 7 of this recipe. The **Index** table can be stored for future executions of this transformation, so it will be better to store the index as we did in step 7. There is another property **Maintain stored index**; when the reference table's content is changed this property will cause the index to be updated automatically.

As fuzzy operations may create unexpected results in some cases, you may need to play with different settings and similarity thresholds in the **Advanced** tab to find the appropriate configuration. You may need to set the similarity threshold to lower or higher values, if you set it to a higher value, results will be a much more exact match, and if you set it to a lower value, results will be considered as similar with more differences in their values. Note that with 0.70 similarity threshold in the Fuzzy Lookup Transformation "Mangmt" isn't similar to "Management" so you may need to reduce the threshold. Defining the similarity threshold is based on your input data; if it is approximately clean you can raise the similarity threshold, if it is dirty then reduce the threshold.

Fuzzy Grouping has the ability to apply fuzzy operations on different columns of each row; this is what we select in the **Columns** tab of **Fuzzy Grouping Transformation Editor**. Each column that has a **Match type** property of **Fuzzy** will generate two columns in output: **<Input_column_name>_clean** and **_Similarity_<Input_column_name>**. There is also a **_score** column, which shows the average of all **_similarity_*** columns.

There are some **Token delimiters** in the **Advanced** tab of Fuzzy Transformations. You can check or enter any character that you want to be omitted from the terms before applying the fuzzy operations. By default **Space**, **Tab**, and some non-alphanumeric characters will be omitted, but you can change this setting according to your requirements.

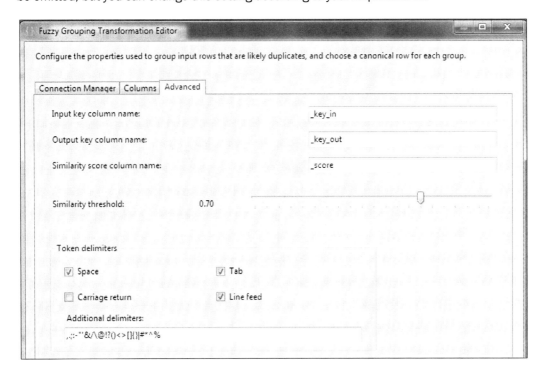

 Fuzzy Transformations are not available in the Standard Edition of SQL Server 2012. You need to buy SQL Server 2012 Business Intelligence or Enterprise Edition to use Fuzzy Transformations in SSIS.

6
Variables, Expressions, and Dynamism in SSIS

by Reza Rad and Pedro Perfeito

In this chapter, we will cover the following topics:

- ► Variables and data types
- ► Using expressions in Control Flow
- ► Using expressions in Data Flow
- ► The Expression Task
- ► Dynamic connection managers
- ► Dynamic data transfer with different data structures

Introduction

A package is executable and acts like an application. One of the basic requirements in every application is to work with variables. SSIS has the following two types of variables:

- ► **System variables**: System variables are used to fetch system information at a specific place in a package
- ► **User variables**: User variables can be used to read and write through their scope in the package

Expressions as we have talked about them till now are a way to provide calculations and write logic in basic semi-functional expressions. The use of expressions is not limited to **Derived Column** or Conditional Split transforms, but they are widely used throughout the package. Expressions provide a method of setting property values dynamically, so using expressions is a way to dynamism in SSIS.

There are different types of dynamism. Control Flow Tasks can work with dynamic properties, for example attachments of a Send Mail Task can be set dynamically based on a variable value or an expression. There is a common scenario in which Connection Manager's Connection String is to be set dynamically. One of the most powerful aspects of a data integration tool is to transfer data dynamically.

The SSIS Data Flow Task provides a way to transfer data but although column mappings should be set statically, there are some ways to create dynamic data transfer with the SSIS package.

In this chapter variables, expressions, and the main aspects of dynamism in the SSIS package will be covered.

Variables and data types

If you've got some experience building Integration Services packages, you probably already know that SSIS has its own representation of different data types. The names of these data types start with **DT_**, followed by the data type such as **I** for Integer, **BOOL** for Boolean, **STR** for String, and so on.

Each time we move data from a source to a destination, conversion between input and output data types is required. The following figure shows a list of the most used data types and their relationship between different environments.

SSIS Data Type	SQL Server Data Type	.NET Type	Range
DT_WSTR	nvarchar, nchar	System.String	
DT_STR	varchar, char		
DT_DBTIMESTAMP	smalldatetime, datetime	System.DateTime	
DT_DBDATE	date	System.DateTime	
DT_NUMERIC	numeric	System.Decimal	
DT_DECIMAL	decimal	System.Decimal	
DT_I1		System.SByte	-127 to 128
DT_I2	smallint	System.Int16	"-2^15 (-32,768) to 2^15-1 (32,767)"
DT_I4	int	System.Int32	"-2^31 (-2,147,483,648) to 2^31-1 (2,147,483,647)"
DT_I8	bigint	System.Int64	"-2^63 (-9,223,372,036,854,775,808) to 2^63-1 (9,223,372,036,854,775,807)"
DT_BOOL	Bit	System.Boolean	0 or 1

To get further details about SSIS data types, refer to the *Working with Data Types in the Data Flow* topic in Microsoft SQL books online at the following URL:

`http://msdn.microsoft.com/en-us/library/ms345165(v=SQL.110).aspx.`

Getting ready

To get started with this recipe, follow these steps:

1. Open SQL Server Business Intelligence Development Studio (BIDS) and create a new SSIS project.

2. Provide a name and a location for the SSIS project and proceed.

3. Select the package created by default and rename it to:
   `P01_VariablesAndDataTypes.dtsx.`

How to do it...

The following steps explain the use of variables and data types under an SSIS package.

To manage variables under a package, SSIS provides a very intuitive interface that displays not only the system variables but also the custom variables created by the user. An important consideration about variables is that each variable has a specific scope, that could be throughout the package under the Control Flow (global) or could be in the scope of a specific Data Flow (private).

1. Open the Variables Editor.

2. Right-click under the **Control Flow** design area and select **Variables** or select the **Variables** menu link.

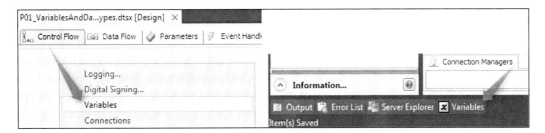

3. Manage SSIS variables. Click on the **Add** button to create a new variable.

4. Enrich the metadata of your variables with two extra columns (**Namespace** and **Description**) that could be added in the variables editor (the **Description** column was included on this SSIS version).

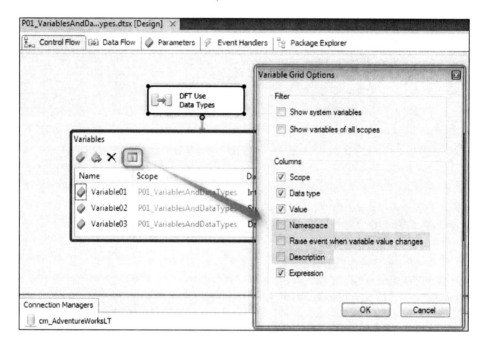

5. The information about the new variables enables a better understanding of all variables during the development and in future enhancements. To raise an event when a value of a specific variable changes enable the **Raise event when variable value changes** checkbox.

6. To avoid creating duplicate variable names and to have an overview of all package variables, just enable the options **Show system variables** and **Show variables of all scopes**.

7. Now it's possible to change the scope of any existent user variable. Select the desired variable to change the scope and click on the button **Move Variable**. The following pop-up will appear. Select the destination scope and click on the Ok button to apply the change to the variable scope.

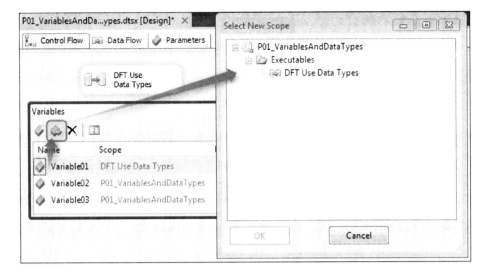

8. To apply an expression for a specific variable, just select the **...** button in the respective row and add the expression on the Expression Editor that will appear on the screen. The property **EvaluateAsExpression** is set automatically to `true` or `false` while an expression is added or removed.

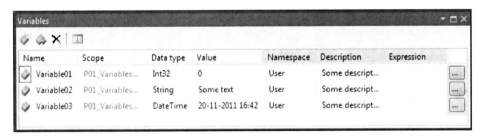

The following steps describe the several options to apply data conversions under a Data Flow Task. In this scenario, the column **ListPrice** from the **Products** table needs to be converted to decimal data type (SSIS suggests a data type applied by default based on source data, but it's not the data type required for some cases). Four data conversion options are highlighted: using source DB engine, using SSIS OLEDB Source component, using Data Conversion component, and using Derived Column component.

1. Add a Data Flow to the Control Flow and open it.

2. Create an OLEDB Connection to query the Adventure Works LT sample database.

3. In **Connection Manager**, right-click to add a **New OLEDB Connection...**.

4. In the **Data Connections** list select the **AdventureWorksLT2012** database. If it is not listed, create a new one pressing the **New...** button.

5. Press the **OK** button and rename the connection to **cmAdventureWorksLT**.

6. Drag-and-drop the **OLE DB Source** component from **SSIS Toolbox | Other Sources** to the Data Flow design area.

7. Open the component for editing.

8. The connection created in the previous step will be automatically assigned to the source component. If it is not, select it from the respective drop-down.

9. In the **Data access mode** property, select *SQL Command*.

10. In the **SQL Command Text**, add a SQL statement to return data from the Products table:

```
SELECT ProductID, ProductNumber, convert(decimal(10,2),ListPrice)
AS ListPrice
FROM SalesLT.Product
```

11. Drag-and-drop from **SSIS Toolbox | Other Sources** another **OLE DB Source** component to the Data Flow design area.

12. Open the component for editing.

13. The connection created in the previous step will be automatically assigned to the source component. If not, select it from the respective drop-down.

14. In the **Data access mode** property, select *SQL Command*.

15. In **SQL Command Text**, add a SQL statement to return data from the Products table:

```
SELECT   ProductID, ProductNumber, ListPrice
FROM     SalesLT.Product
```

16. Close the component and open it again, but this time by selecting and right-clicking the source component through **Show Advanced Editor...**.

17. Select the **Input and Output Properties** tab and drill down the **OLE DB Source Output**.

18. Select the **ListPrice** column under **Output Columns**, and change the **DataType** property in the right panel.

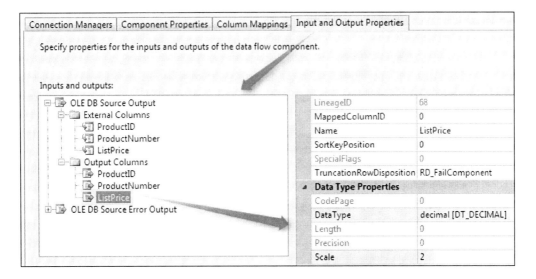

19. Drag-and-drop another **OLE DB Source** component to the Data Flow design area repeating step 3.

20. Drag-and-drop the **Data Conversion** component to the Data Flow design area from **SSIS Toolbox | Common**.

21. Link the previous connection to this component through the green output of the first.

22. Open the component for editing and add an expression into the component to cast the column **ListPrice** into decimal data type.

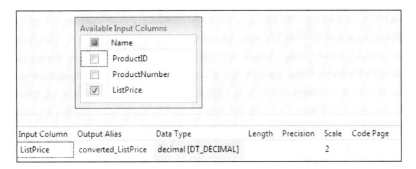

23. Drag-and-drop another **OLE DB Source** component to the Data Flow design area repeating step 3.

24. Drag-and-drop the **Derived Column** component to the Data Flow design area from **SSIS Toolbox | Common**.

25. Link the previous connection to this component through the green output of the first.

26. Open the component for editing and add an expression into the component to cast the column into decimal data type.

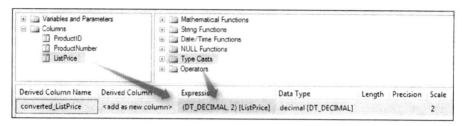

27. Press **F5** to execute the package.

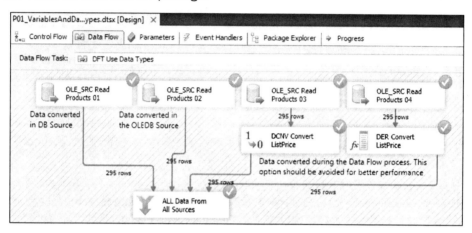

How it works...

Each approach described previously has advantages and disadvantages. Applying conversions during the Data Flow could decrease the performance because an extra column is added to the pipeline (converted column). The first two approaches are the best ones to apply and have the following two specifications to consider:

▸ Using the SQL `convert` function, data is converted using the source server resources and if some row raises any data conversion error, the entire block of data will generate an error

▸ Using the OLE DB Source component, data is converted using SSIS server resources and if some row raises any data conversion error, the specific row could be redirected to an error output

A very common conversion that should be referred to here is the conversion between Unicode and Non-Unicode columns. By default, SSIS uses Unicode data types in the default import behavior and also in all the string functions that expect Unicode strings as input. Unicode is a great protective selection for handling data from import files with special characters but requires more storage space.

Using expressions in Control Flow

Expressions provide a level of dynamism in Control Flow. Working with a Control Flow task can be much more robust when properties of the task can be set dynamically instead of having static values.

Prior to SSIS 2012, you could assign the result of an expression to a variable (writing the expression in the variable's expression property and setting the `EvaluateAsExpression` property of the variable to `true`), but problem with this method is that the value of the variable will be resolved whenever you refer the variable. For example, assume that you have a `User::StartTime` variable which gets the current time with the `GetDate()` expression function, at the end of package you want to use the `User::StartTime` variable to fetch start time of the package and do some calculations, but you will get the current time! This is because the expression will resolve at the time of referring to the variable. So there is a need to specify a step or it makes sense better to say a Control FlowTask to assigns expression result to variable. Expression Task will assign result of the expression to the variable or parameter when this task executed.

In many SSIS Control Flow Tasks, we can use the variables provided in the Task Editor itself, such as reading the SQL statement of an Execute SQL Task from a variable, or working with the File System Task and getting the source and destination from variables.

However, there are many Task properties that cannot be set directly from the Editor Window. Here expressions come into play; we can change majority of each Control Flow Task's properties dynamically using expression property.

In this recipe, we will use the Execute Process Task to compress the content of a directory, but the directory path will be dynamic.

Getting ready

The 7z compressor is needed for this recipe. You can follow the instructions discussed in the recipe *Execute Process Task* in *Chapter 2, Control Flow Tasks*.

How to do it...

1. Create an SSIS project and name it **R02_Using Expressions** in **Control Flow**.

2. Add an Execute Process Task, set the executable as the 7z application in the following path:

   ```
   C:\Program Files\7-Zip\7z.exe
   ```

3. Add the the following to the **Arguments** property:

```
a -t7z files.7z *.txt
```

4. Create a new `String` type variable in the `Package` scope (click on the empty area on Control Flow and then go to the Variables Pane and create a new variable; the variable will be created in package scope in this way), and name it `WorkingDirectory`. Set a default value for the variable as follows:

```
C:\SSIS\Ch06_Variables Expressions and Dynamism\Files
```

5. In the **Execute Process Task Editor**, go to the **Expressions** tab and set the property as *WorkingDirectory* and set the expression as **@[User::WorkingDirectory]**.

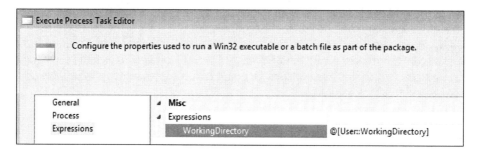

6. Run the package and verify if `files.7z` has been generated in the working directory.

7. Change the `WorkingDirectory` variable's value to another folder and run the package again. The compressed `.7z` file will appear in the new directory.

How it works...

There is an **Expressions** tab in most of the Control Flow Task Editors. The **Expressions** tab provides a method to set each property of the task with an expression made from variables, parameters, operators, and functions.

In this recipe, we set the **WorkingDirectory** property of the Execute Process Task with the *@[User::WorkingDirectory]* variable; this means that every time the Execute Process Task starts it will fetch the working directory from the variable's value. So changing the value of the variable at compile time or runtime will cause the Execute Process Task to work dynamically.

DelayValidation

As SSIS validates metadata at compile time, setting a property with an expression may cause validation errors. This is because the values of the variables will be fetched at runtime, and at compile time they don't have appropriate values. There are two ways of dealing with this:

- ▶ Setting a default valid value for the variable to bypass SSIS Validation
- ▶ Setting the **DelayValidation** property of the task to *True*

The **DelayValidation** property is set to *False* by default, which means that SSIS will validate this task at compile time. If *DelayValidation* is set to **True** then SSIS won't check validation for this task during compile time.

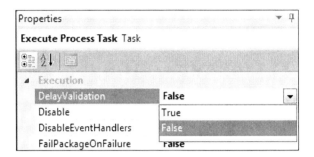

IsVariable

SSIS provides a way to set some of the important properties of each task to work with variables' values. You don't need to work with expressions directly. In these tasks, some properties can be filled by the value of an SSIS variable that can be used at runtime. For example, in the Execute SQL Task, the **SQL Statement** property can be filled at runtime from a variable setting the **SqlSourceType** to the respective variable.

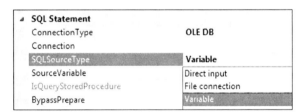

Also, in the File System Task for source and destination there are *IsSourceVariable* and *IsDestinationVariable* properties.

Real-world scenarios

The ability to set properties with expressions provides a way to change properties of the Control Flow Tasks dynamically at runtime. There are lots of real-world scenarios for runtime dynamism. For example, a common scenario with Execute Process Tasks is that a `foreach` loop loops through all CSV files and loads them into database and in the last step we compress each file and rename them with a date part in their name and finally archive them somewhere.

In this recipe, we saw how to change the working directory to compress files with a dynamic runtime working directory. In order to rename a file with a date part, we can use the `GetDate` expression function to fetch the current date and convert it to a string and then finally use the File System Task and set the **IsDestinationVariable** property.

Moving the Files Task has the same operation.

Using expressions in Data Flow

The previous recipe explained in detail the use of expressions under Control Flow. However, expressions can also be used under Data Flow Tasks, mainly for applying data quality and business rules.

Some examples where expressions could be applied are inside variables (that are often used together) and Data Flow components such as **Derived Column, Conditional Split**, and **Script Components**. Since it's possible to have several different components in Data Flow, the properties available under each one can vary and not all of these properties support property expressions. To get further details about which Data Flow component properties support expressions, refer to the section *Data Flow Properties that Can Be Set by Using Expressions* in the Microsoft SQL online book at the following URL:

```
http://msdn.microsoft.com/en-us/library/ms136104(v=SQL.110).aspx.
```

Getting ready

To get started with this recipe, follow these steps:

1. Open SQL Server Data Tools (SSDT) and create a new SSIS project.
2. Provide a name and a location for the SSIS project and proceed.
3. Select the package created by default and rename it to `P01_DataFlow Expressions.dtsx`.

How to do it...

The following steps explain the use of expressions under Data Flow components (**Derived Column** and **Conditional Split**) and the use of property expressions passed dynamically to a component inside Data Flow (**Flat File Destination**).

Here, in a fictitious scenario we are required to transform the customer source data. These data, based on the customer's country, will be divided into two different flat files for marketing purposes.

1. Add a Data Flow to the Control Flow and open it.

2. Create an OLEDB Connection to query the Adventure Works LT sample database.

3. In the **Connection Manager** right-click to add a **New OLEDB Connection...**.

4. In the **Data Connections** list select the **AdventureWorksLT2012** database. If it is not listed, create a new one using the **New...** button.

5. Click on the **OK** button and rename the connection to **cmAdventureWorksLT**.

6. Drag-and-drop the **OLE DB Source** component to the Data Flow design area from the **SSIS Toolbox | Other Sources**.

7. Open the component for editing.

8. The connection created in the previous step will be automatically assigned to the source component. If it is not, select it from the respective drop-down.

9. In the **Data access mode** property, select *SQL Command*.

10. In the **SQL Command Text**, add a SQL statement to return data from the Customer and Address tables or use the **Build Query...** option.

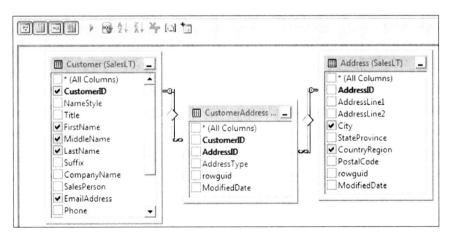

```
SELECT  CUST.CustomerID, CUST.FirstName,
    CUST.MiddleName, CUST.LastName,
    CUST.EmailAddress, ADDR.City, ADDR.CountryRegion
FROM  SalesLT.Customer CUST
    INNER JOIN SalesLT.CustomerAddress ADDRC
      ON CUST.CustomerID=ADDRC.CustomerID
    INNER JOIN SalesLT.Address ADDR
      ON ADDRC.AddressID=ADDR.AddressID
```

11. Drag-and-drop the **Derived Column** component to the Data Flow design area from **SSIS Toolbox | Common**.

12. Link both the components through the green arrow output of the first.

13. Add an expression into the component to concatenate the following customer columns:

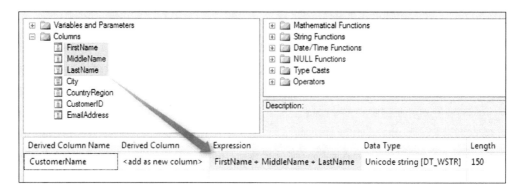

14. Drag-and-drop the **Condition Split** component to the Data Flow design area from **SSIS Toolbox | Common**.

15. Link both the components through the green arrow output of the first.

16. Add an expression into the component to split data based on the country.

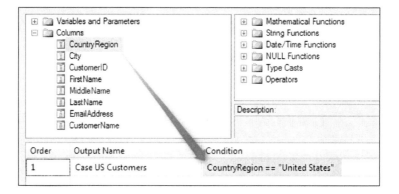

17. The previous expression could be replaced by an SSIS variable to pass the country name dynamically: `CountryRegion==@[User::uvCountry]`.

18. Create two flat file connections one for each customer output dataset.

19. In the **Connection Manager**, right-click to add **New Flat File Connection...**.

20. Browse a location for each of the new flat files and name the connection as **cmDST_USCustomers** for US customers and **cmDST_NonUSCustomers** for non-US customers.

21. Drag-and-drop two **Flat File Destination** components to the Data Flow design area, one for each customer output dataset from **SSIS Toolbox | Other Destination**.

22. Link each component to the previous one through the green output for **USCustomers** and for **NonUSCustomers**.

23. Select each connection created before to the correct customer dataset and ensure that the mappings are correct as shown in the following screenshot:

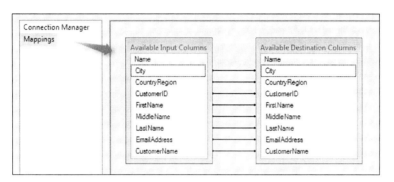

24. Press **F5** to execute the package.

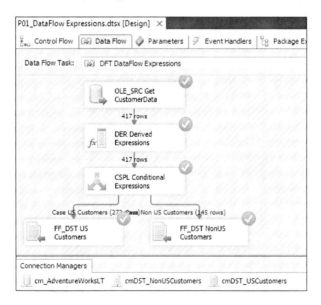

After the explanations of how to use expressions under Data Flow components, it's time to dynamically create an expression to change the property of each flat file component through the Data Flow properties. To configure expressions on a property in a Data Flow component under Control Flow, select Data Flow properties and select the *Expression* property to display the components that could be changed inside Data Flow.

1. In the Control Flow, select the Data Flow created in the previous steps.

2. Select the *Data Flow* and *Expressions* properties to display the component properties that could be changed dynamically.

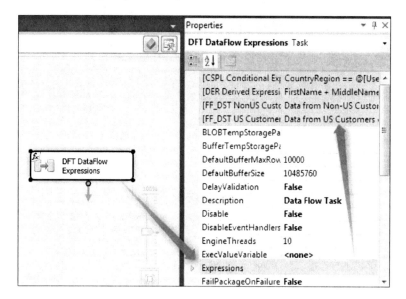

3. Add an expression to the **Header** property of each flat file destination to include some context (mainly a description and the date when the data was collected) as follows:

```
"Data from Non-US Customers collected at" + (DT_WSTR,10) (DT_
DBDATE) GETDATE()
```

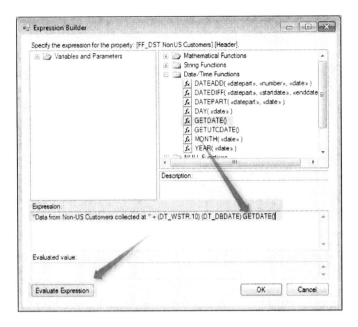

4. Press **F5** to execute the package again and check the result of each flat file.

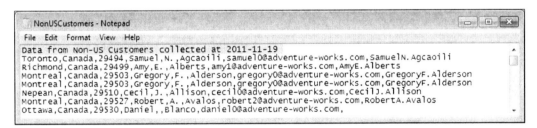

How it works...

The previous steps explained how to create expressions inside the Data Flow Task and also how to create expressions dynamically through the Data Flow Task properties. The expression language is similar to the C# syntax and in some cases it is also similar to the TSQL syntax (for example, the `Getdate()` function). For example, the expression operators are very often used and have the following syntaxes:

```
<A> == <B>  (Equal)
<A> != <B> (Unequal)
<A> && <B>  (Logical AND)
<A> || <B>  (Logical OR)
<boolean condition> ? <true> : <false> (Conditional)
```

Not all components provide the capability of setting their properties using expressions. If they do, then those properties will show up in the Properties pane of the Data Flow Task containing the component.

The Expression Task

The Expression Task is one of the SSIS Control Flow Tasks. The reason why we excluded it from *Chapter 2, Control Flow Tasks,* is that this task works only with expressions and variables and is much more relevant to this chapter.

The Expression Task provides a way of setting a variable's value with an expression. This is a handy task and was added recently in SSIS 2012. Besides the fact that this task didn't exist in the previous versions of SSIS, there was an alternative solution for same cases, which is used frequently.

In this recipe, we will create a filename based on the date of running the package and combine it with a folder path to create a full file path.

How to do it...

1. Create an SSIS project and name it R04_Expression Task.

2. Add two variables to the package scope as shown in the following screenshot:

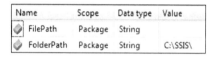

Name	Scope	Data type	Value
FilePath	Package	String	
FolderPath	Package	String	C:\SSIS\

3. Drag-and-drop an Expression Task into Control Flow and double-click on it.

4. Add the following expression in the **Expression Builder** window of the Expression Task Editor, as shown in the following screenshot:

```
@[User::FilePath] = @[User::FolderPath]+
(DT_WSTR,4)YEAR( GETDATE()   )+
RIGHT("0"+ (DT_WSTR,2)MONTH( GETDATE()   ),2)+
RIGHT("0"+ (DT_WSTR,2)DAY( GETDATE()   ),2)
+".txt"
```

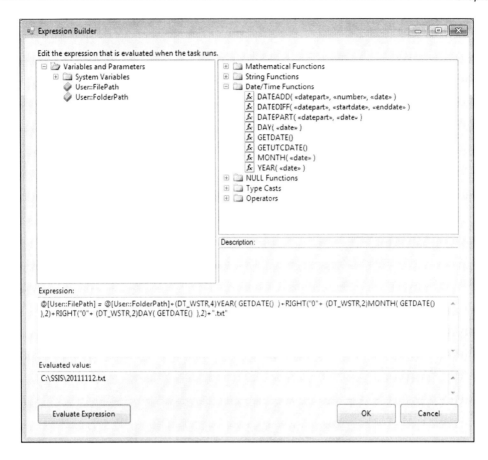

5. Click on the **Evaluate Expression** button to see the expression result.

6. Close the **Expression Builder**; add a **Script Task** right after the **Expression Task**.

7. Set the `FilePath` variable as `ReadOnlyVariables`.

8. In the Script Editor in the first line of the `Main` method, write the following .NET code:

```
MessageBox.Show(string.Format("Generate File Path: {0}",
            Dts.Variables["User::FilePath"].Value));
```

9. Run the package and check the value of **File Path** at runtime.

How it works...

The Expression Task will run the expression at execution time and will store the result of execution into the variable that is set on the left of the expression.

In this recipe, we used the `GetDate()` function to fetch the current date—year, month, and date—and generated the filename in this pattern: `yyyyMMdd.txt`; the result of this expression is to be filled into the `FilePath` variable because the `FilePath` variable is at the left of the expression.

We will use the Expression Task in other samples discussed in this chapter and the next chapter. Also, real-world scenarios for this Task will be explored in the following recipes.

There's more...

Expressions were in use from SSIS 2005 and there was another method to set value of variable with expression. Here you will see the latter method.

Alternative method

As we mentioned earlier, the Expression Task has been added to this SSIS version. There is an alternative way to set the value of a variable based on the result of an expression at runtime which was from SSIS 2005 and is still supported in SSIS 2012.

Each variable has an expression property, which can be set with an expression to be executed at runtime and the result filled into variable's value.

`EvaluateAsExpression` is a Boolean property that declares whether the variable gets its value by executing the expression. The default value is `false`. If we want to fetch the value of variable with an expression, besides writing the expression in the *Expression* property, we should set the **EvaluateAsExpression** property to *true*.

The following steps show how to do it:

1. Create new variable of type string in the package scope and name it `FilePathAlternative`.

2. When the variable is selected in the **Variables** window, go to the **Properties** window and write the following expression in the **Expression** property:

```
@[User::FolderPath] +
(DT_WSTR,4)YEAR( GETDATE()   ) +
RIGHT("0"+ (DT_WSTR,2)MONTH( GETDATE()   ),2) +
RIGHT("0"+ (DT_WSTR,2)DAY( GETDATE()   ),2)
+".txt"
```

3. Set the **EvaluateAsExpression** property to *True*.

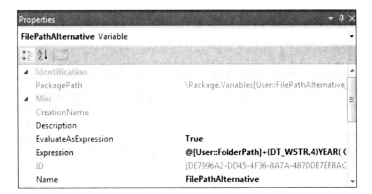

The value of the expression will be fetched at the time of accessing the variable and stored into the variable's value.

Each variable that has the **EvaluateAsExpression** property as *True* will have a small *fx* symbol at the lowest right part of its icon indicating that this variable's value will be fetched from an expression at runtime.

Dynamic connection managers

Connections can be created at package level or project level, and in both cases these connections can be configured to change at runtime. A common scenario where a dynamic connection is required happens when a package should execute against different development or production environments. The option of doing it manually each time a connection change, can be time consuming and even more dangerous.

Getting ready

To get ready for this recipe, follow these steps:

1. Open SQL Server Data Tools (SSDT) and create a new SSIS project.

2. Provide a name and a location for the SSIS project and proceed.

3. Select the package created by default and rename it to: `P01_DynamicConnections.dtsx`.

How to do it...

Imagine the scenario where customer data is read from SQL database and inserted into a flat file. This simple example has two connections that will be configured to be changed at runtime through expressions that use SSIS variables that store the respective connection strings inside.

1. Add a Data Flow to the Control Flow and open it.

2. Create an OLEDB Connection to query the Adventure Works LT sample database.

3. In the **Connection Manager** right-click to add a **New OLEDB Connection...**.

4. In the **Data Connections** list, select the **AdventureWorksLT2012** database. If it is not listed, create a new one by clicking on the **New...** button.

5. Press the **OK** button and rename the connection to **cmAdventureWorksLT**.

6. Drag-and-drop the **OLE DB Source** component to the Data Flow design area from the **SSIS Toolbox | Other Sources**.

7. Open the component for editing.

8. The connection created in the previous step will be automatically assigned to the source component. If it is not, select it from the respective drop-down.

9. In the **Data access mode** property, select *SQL Command*.

10. In **SQL Command Text**, add a SQL statement to return the customer data such as **CustomerName**, **CompanyName**, **SalesPerson**, **Phone**, and **EmailAdress**.

```
SELECT FirstName + ' ' + ISNULL(MiddleName, '') + ' ' + LastName
AS CustomerName, CompanyName,
SalesPerson, Phone, EmailAddress
FROM SalesLT.Customer
```

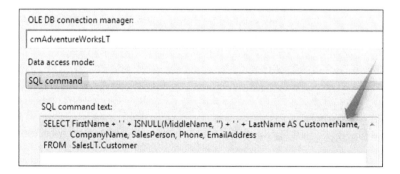

11. Drag-and-drop the **Flat File Destination** component to the Data Flow design area from **SSIS Toolbox | Other Destinations**.

12. Link both components through the green arrow output of the first **OLE DB Source**.

13. Open the **Flat File Destination** component for editing.

14. Create a new connection by clicking on the **New...** button.

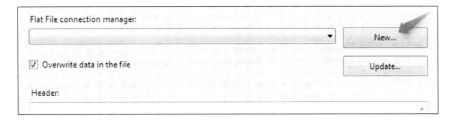

15. Set the destination flat file format as **Delimited**.

16. Set the encoding option to **True** to accept Unicode. (Each Unicode character takes 2 bytes of storage and each non-Unicode character takes 1 byte of storage, but only Unicode can handle special characters such as Japanese or Chinese. If possible, avoid using Unicode.)

17. Set to **True** the option to include column names in the first data row.

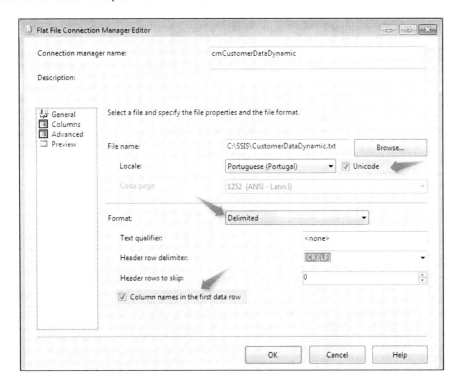

18. Set the file location through the **Browse** button and then click **Open**.

19. Rename the flat file connection at `C:\SSIS\Ch06_Variables Expressions and Dynamism\Files` as `cmCustomerDataDynamic`.

Now that two connections are created, let's change the package to pass connection strings dynamically on each SSIS project execution.

1. The first step is creating SSIS variables that store connection strings that will be called through the expressions of each connection.

2. Create an SSIS variable `uvSRC_SQLConnection` for the source SQL connection and fill it with the following value (replace `BISERVER` with the correct server name):

   ```
   Data Source=.;Initial Catalog=AdventureWorksLT2012;Provider=SQLNCL
   I11.1;Integrated Security=SSPI;Auto Translate=False;
   ```

3. Create an SSIS variable `uvDST_Filename` to store the filename of the destination flat file and fill it with the following value:

   ```
   CustomerDataDynamic.txt
   ```

4. Create an SSIS variable `uvDST_Directory` to store the directory of the destination flat file and fill it with the following value:

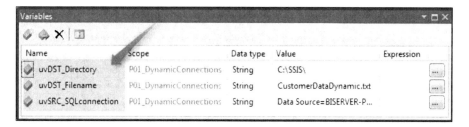

5. Configure the source connection to be passed dynamically.

6. Select the **cmAdventureWorksLT** connection.

7. In the **Properties** panel, change the **DelayValidation** property to *True*.

8. In the **Properties** panel, click on the **...** button inside the **Expressions** property to set the properties of the connection that must be passed dynamically.

9. In the **Property Expressions Editor**, select the **ConnectionString** property and map to it the value of the variable created before **uvSRC_SQLConnection**.

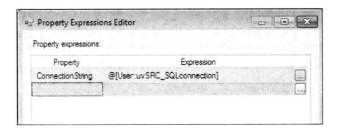

10. Change the destination connection to pass the flat file connection dynamically.

11. Select the **cmCustomerDataDynamic** connection.

12. In the **Properties** panel, change the **DelayValidation** property to *True*.

13. In the **Properties** panel, click on the **...** button inside the **Expressions** property to set the properties of the connection that must be passed dynamically.

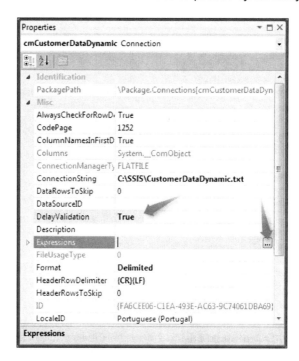

14. In **Property Expressions Editor**, select the **ConnectionString** property and click on the **...** button associated with it.

15. Drag the two variables created before (uvDST_Directory and uvDST_Filename) from the **Variables and Parameters** folder and drop them into the **Expression** area.

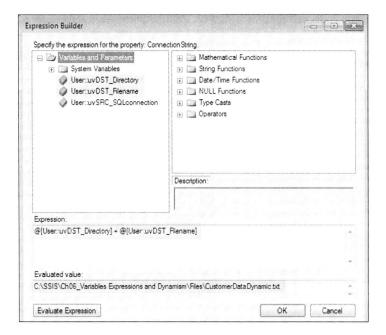

16. Click on the **OK** button.

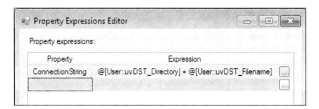

17. Click on **F5** to execute the package.

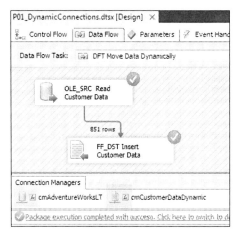

18. Change the SSIS variables to a non-existent connection and execute the package again. If the package is created correctly an error will occur.

How it works...

The previous steps explained how to configure connections to be updated dynamically at runtime each time a package executes. The values of connection properties are stored into SSIS variables that could be updated through a SQL Task, through SSIS package configurations, through a Script Task, through a SSIS parameter, and in other ways.

It's possible to dynamically pass the entire connection string or parts of the connection component, if available, as a property. For example, in the SQL connection, instead of passing the entire connection string, we can pass just the **InitialCatalog** or **Servername**.

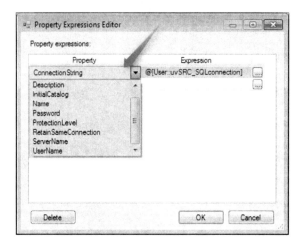

An important step, and common to all connections, is setting the **DelayValidation** property of the connection to **True**. If this property is set to *True*, SSIS will not validate any of the properties set in the task until runtime. The default value for this property is false.

Dynamic data transfer with different data structures

Dynamic data transfer is one of the most challenging tasks in Data Integration tools. This challenge will be much greater when structure of data is different. As you saw in the previous recipe, the SSIS Data Flow Task cannot work with dynamic metadata and this means that if structure of columns (name of columns, data types of columns, and number of columns) changes, the Data Flow Task will fail on validation and stop working.

Good news is that there are alternative ways for data transfer based on source and destination outside the Data Flow Task.

In this recipe, we will see an example of dynamic data transfer from SQL server database to CSV flat files. The source tables may have different data structure. At the end of this recipe, we will talk about other sources and destinations.

Getting ready

Xp_CmdShell should be enabled for this recipe. To enable xp_cmdShell, run the following statements on SSMS on the local default instance of the SQL server:

```
---- To allow advanced options to be changed.
EXEC sp_configure 'show advanced options', 1
GO
-- To update the currently configured value for advanced options.
RECONFIGURE
GO
-- To enable the feature.
EXEC sp_configure 'xp_cmdshell', 1
GO
-- To update the currently configured value for this feature.
RECONFIGURE
GO
```

How to do it...

1. Create an SSIS project and name it R07_Dynamic Data Transfer with different data structures.

2. Create three variables as shown in the following screenshot:

Name	Scope	Data type	Value
BCPCommand	Package	String	
DestinationFolder	Package	String	C:\SSIS\Ch06_Variables Expressions and Dynamism\R06_Dynamic Da...
SourceTable	Package	String	AdventureWorks2008R2.HumanResources.Department

3. Set the default value for SourceTable as AdventureWorks2012. HumanResources.Department and the default value for DestinationFolder as C:\SSIS\Ch06_Variables Expressions, and Dynamism\R06_Dynamic Data Transfer for Different Data Structures\Files\.

4. Add an Expression Task into Control Flow.

5. Write the following expression to create a BCP command there:

```
@[User::BCPCommand] = "bcp "+ @[User::SourceTable] +" out \""+ @
[User::DestinationFolder] +@[User::SourceTable]+".csv\" -c -t, -T
-S."
```

6. Click on **Evaluate Expression** to find out how this expression result will be at runtime.

7. Add an Execute SQL Task right after the Expression Task.

8. Create a connection to the `AdventureWorks2012` database. In the SQL **Statement** property, add the following statements:

```
declare @sql varchar(8000)
select @sql = ?
exec master..xp_cmdshell @sql
```

9. In the **Parameter Mapping** tab, set the variable **BCPCommand** as input variable with parameter name **0** as shown in the following screenshot:

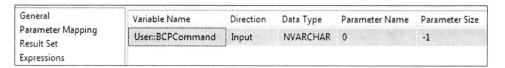

General Parameter Mapping Result Set Expressions	Variable Name	Direction	Data Type	Parameter Name	Parameter Size
	User::BCPCommand	Input	NVARCHAR	0	-1

10. Run the package and check the destination folder for a new CSV file that contains the transferred data.

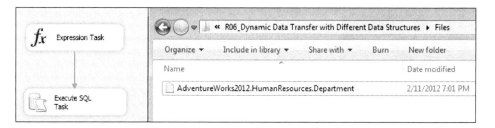

11. Stop execution and change the value of the `SourceTable` variable to `AdventureWorks2012.Sales.SalesTerritory` and run the package again; you will see new `AdventureWorks2012.Sales.SalesTerritory.csv`, which contains different information than the previous CSV file.

How it works...

As we mentioned earlier, SSIS Data Flow Task doesn't support dynamic metadata. So if the structure of the data—name of columns, data type of columns, and the number of columns—may differ in each data transfer we cannot use SSIS Data Flow Task dynamically.

There are alternative methods to implement this dynamism outside the Data Flow Task. In this recipe, we used the SQL Task to run a BCP-generated command.

When working with flat files and SQL server database, BCP is one of the good choices. BCP will copy data from SQL server to flat file or reverse in bulk mode. Full syntax of the BCP command is available at this MSDN link: `http://msdn.microsoft.com/en-us/library/ms162802.aspx`.

As BCP runs under `Xp_CmdShell`, we enabled `xp_cmdshell` in the *Getting ready* section of this recipe.

In this recipe, the Expression Task will generate the BCP command based on the `SourceTable` variable's value, and fill the result of the expression into another variable named `BCPCommand`.

In the Execute SQL Task, the value of the `BCPCommand` variable was passed as input parameter to `xp_cmdshell` to run it.

Other sources and destinations

There are different methods suggested for each source and destination. Some of the most common cases are covered here.

Flat file to SQL server

The BCP command can act in reverse and load data from the CSV file into the SQL server database table. A sample BCP command for this case is as follows:

```
bcp [<database-name.>][<owner.>]<table-name> in <csv-file> [/U<username>]
[/P<password>] [/S<server-name>] /c /t
```

SQL query to flat file

BCP can accept a SQL query and save the output into flat file. The following BCP command line is a sample for this situation:

```
Bcp "Select Name,GroupName FROM AdventureWorks2012.HumanResources.
Department" queryout C:\somefolder\query.csv -c -t, -T -S.
```

SQL server to SQL server on the same server

When both source and destination are the SQL server located on the same server, we can use `Insert Into …. Select From…` to insert data into an existing destination table or the `Select …. Into ….` SQL statement to insert data into a new table.

Excel to SQL server

`OpenRowSet` provides a way to read data from as Excel file with a query. Here is an example:

```
SELECT * INTO XLImport5 FROM OPENROWSET('Microsoft.Jet.OLEDB.4.0',
'Excel 8.0;Database=C:\test\xltest.xls', 'SELECT * FROM [Customers$]')
```

There are many other ways to work with Excel and import into SQL server and they are described completely in the following MSDN article:

`http://support.microsoft.com/kb/321686.`

Other DB engines with SQL server

We can link servers in SSMS and use linked servers. For more information about linked servers refer to `http://msdn.microsoft.com/en-us/library/ms188279.aspx.`

Any other source and destination

There are alternatives for other sources and destinations. Scripting is one of the most powerful ways which provides ability to use full .NET library 4.0 for reading data from any kind of source and load it into any kind of destination.

7
Containers and Precedence Constraints

by Reza Rad and Pedro Perfeito

In this chapter, we will cover:

- ▶ Sequence Container: putting all tasks in an executable object
- ▶ For Loop Container: looping through static enumerator till a condition is met
- ▶ Foreach Loop Container: looping through result set of a database query
- ▶ Foreach Loop Container: looping through files using File Enumerator
- ▶ Foreach Loop Container: looping through data table
- ▶ Precedence Constraints: how to control the flow of task execution

Introduction

Till now we have seen how flow of execution can be defined in the Control Flow. There are trailing arrows after each task which defines the flow of execution. These arrows are called Precedence Constraints.

Precedence Constraint defines the execution flow not only by the state of the first task but also with the help of expressions. Combination of Expressions and Precedence Constraints make a Control Flow a powerful executable.

An important part of each application's Control Flow are the control structures, such as conditions and loop structures. SSIS, as an executable, has the ability to implement conditions with resort of Precedence Constraint. There are three types of containers in the Control Flow as shown in the following screenshot:

With **Sequence Container**, Control Flow Tasks get grouped together and will be considered as an executable object which has some properties. One of the most useful scenarios for sequence container is to use transactions which will be explored in the later chapters of this book.

The **For Loop Container** provides a way to loop through numeric values by using initial value and final condition. The structure of the For Loop is similar to the For Loop structure in programming languages.

Looping through collections is a powerful ability in SSIS which is provided by the **Foreach Loop Container**. This container is a very handy loop structure because it can loop through seven types of enumerators. Enumerators vary from files in a folder, to nodes in an xml document or records in a data source.

We will bring real-world scenarios of each execution flow discussion. In many samples we will use previous chapters' methodologies and will create dynamism.

Sequence Container: putting all tasks in an executable object

Sequence Container is the first container which will be covered in this chapter. SSIS Control Flow Tasks play an executable role and each task is an executable. Every executable can have one or more precedence constraints, and one or more outputs.

The Sequence Container will group one or more executable together and create an executable object. Transactions and some settings can be applied on a Sequence Container. We will discuss this in the later recipes.

In this recipe, we will reveal a sample of the Sequence Container and we will demonstrate when and how a Sequence Container will be helpful.

How to do it...

1. Create a SSIS project and name it as `R01_Sequence Container`.

2. Add a **Sequence Container** from the **Control Flow Toolbox** under the **Containers** section into the **Control Flow**.

3. Add an **Execute SQL Task** inside the Sequence Container and connect it to **AdventureWorks2012**.

4. Type the following statement in the **SqlStatement** property (This statement is for raising an Error):

```
Select 1/0
```

5. Close the **Execute SQL Task** and add a **Data Flow Task** inside the **Sequence Container** right after the **Execute SQL Task**. Connect the precedence constraint from the **Execute SQL Task** to the **Data Flow Task**.

6. Add a **Script Task** inside the **Sequence Container** after the **Execute SQL Task**. Then, connect a green arrow from **Execute SQL Task** to this new **Script Task**, right-click on the green arrow and select **Failure**. The arrow color will change to red.

7. Add another script task after the **Sequence Container**, name it as `script - Final Task`, and connect a green arrow from the **Sequence Container** to the script task.

8. In the last script task, edit the script and type the following script in the main method:

```
MessageBox.Show("Final Task");
```

9. Select the **Sequence Container**, and in the **properties** window set `MaximumErrorCount` to 2.

10. Run the package and check the execution of package; **script – Final Task** will be executed.

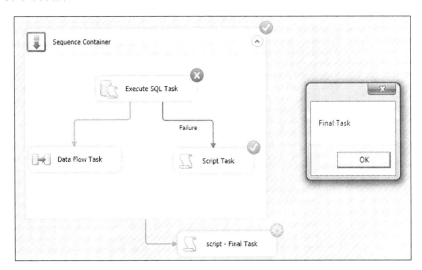

11. Stop the package and open **Execute SQL Task Editor** again. Change the SQL Statement to the following query (We changed the statement so that it runs without an error):

```
Select 1/1
```

12. Run the package again, and you will see that the **Final Task** will be executed again.

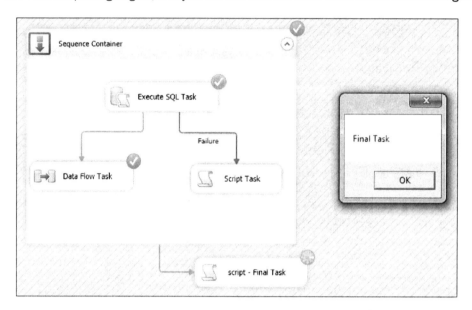

How it works...

In this recipe, one of the usages of a Sequence Container was revealed. A Sequence Container will be considered as an executable. An executable in SSIS means a unit which starts and ends with success or failure. So as this recipe showed we used a Success Precedence Constraint (green arrow) from the Sequence Container, and the Control of execution will be redirected to the Final Task (second script task), if the Execute SQL Task fails and the first **Script Task** runs or if Execute SQL Task succeeds and the Data Flow Task runs.

If you try to connect precedence from a task outside a Sequence Container to another task inside the Sequence Container you will get the following error:

Cannot create a connector.
Cannot connect the executables from different containers.

This is because each container is an executable and you can only work with it as a single component.

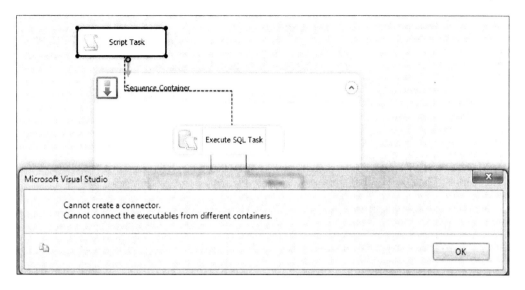

So the only way is to connect precedence constraints to the sequence or from a **Sequence Container** directly. Take a look at the following screenshot to get a better idea:

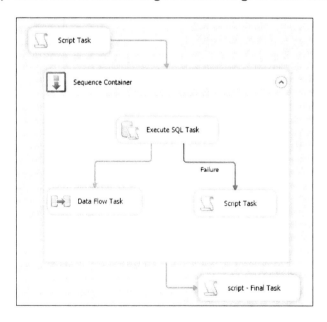

One of the main advantages of the **Sequence Containers** is using transactions and separating Control Flow Tasks in a transaction channel. We will discuss this feature in *Chapter 13, Restartability and Robustness*.

For Loop Container: looping through static enumerator till a condition is met

The **For Loop Container** is a method to create looping in the SSIS package Control Flow and is very similar to the For Loop structure that exists in programming languages. In this looping container, SSIS optionally initializes an expression and repeats its workflow until the expression evaluates to `false`.

As mentioned previously, this container repeats something until a condition in the `EvalExpression` property evaluates to `true`. Some examples could be as follows:

- Doing something *n* times
- Wait for some time (seconds, minutes, hours...) in each interaction until a specific action takes place; for example until a flag stored in a database changes
- Wait until a specific date and time to do something

To configure this container three important properties must be considered:

- `InitExpression`: An optional initialization expression for the loop counter.
- `EvalExpression`: This evaluates an expression and must be `true`, otherwise the container will be completed. It is used to test whether the loop should stop or continue.
- `AssignExpression`: An optional iteration expression that increments or decrements the loop counter.

Getting ready

To get ready for this recipe, use the following steps:

1. Open **SQL Server Data Tools (SSDT)** and create a new **SSIS project**.
2. Provide a name and a location for the SSIS project and proceed.
3. Select the package created by default and rename it: `P01_ForLoopContainer.dtsx`.

How to do it...

The following steps explain how the container should be configured to execute something five times. In this example, three containers are created and are executed five times where one uses the optional and required properties and others use just the required property.

1. Create four SSIS variables for the three containers created as follows:

   ❑ Variable `uvLoopCounter1` to store each iteration of the first container.

   ❑ Variable `uvLoopCounter2` to store each iteration of the second container.

   ❑ Variable `uvLoopCounter3` to store each iteration of the third container.

   ❑ Variable `uvLoopCounter3_End` to store the number of times (n times) the third container should execute (default value is equal to 5).

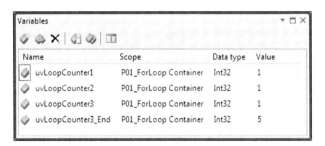

2. Add a **For Loop Container** and configure it to execute five times using the required and optional properties.

3. Drag-and-drop the **For Loop Container** from the **SSIS Toolbox | Containers**, to the **Control Flow** design area.

4. Open the component for the purpose of editing.

5. In the **InitExpression** property, initialize the variable `uvLoopCounter1` to 1.

6. In the **EvalExpression** property, set the evaluation expression *uvLoopCounter1* to less than or equal to 5. (The For Loop will execute until this expression is not true.)

7. In the **AssignExpression** property, increment the variable `uvLoopCounter1` by one unit.

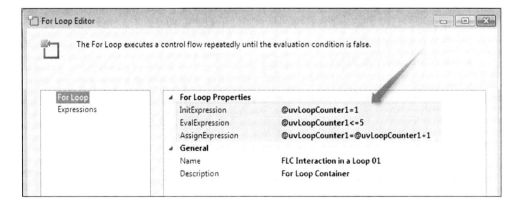

8. Drag-and-drop the **Script Task** inside the **For Loop Container** from the **SSIS Toolbox | Common**, just to display the progress of the **uvLoopCounter1** in each execution.

9. Open the **Script Task** for the purpose of editing, and add the *uvLoopCounter1* to the **ReadOnlyVariables** property.

10. Click on **Edit Script...** and add the following code to the main function

```
MsgBox("LoopCounter = " & CStr(Dts.Variables(" uvLoopCounter1").
Value), MsgBoxStyle.Information, "ForLoop Recipe")
```

11. Add a **For Loop Container** and configure it to execute five times using the required property.

12. Drag-and-drop the **For Loop Container** from the **SSIS Toolbox | Containers**, to the **Control Flow** design area.

13. Open the component for the purpose of editing.

14. In the **EvalExpression** property, set the evaluation expression *uvLoopCounter2* to less or equal to 5. (The For Loop will execute until this expression is not true.)

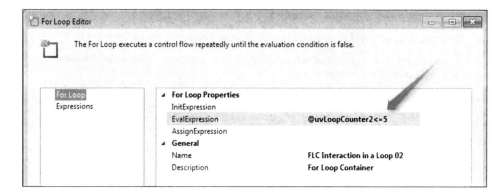

15. Drag-and-drop the **Script Task** from the **SSIS Toolbox | Common**, inside the **For Loop Container** just to display the progress of the **uvLoopCounter2** in each execution.

16. Open the **Script Task** for the purpose of editing, and add the *uvLoopCounter2* to the **ReadOnlyVariables** property.

17. Click on **Edit Script...** and add the following code to the main function:

```
MsgBox("LoopCounter = " & CStr(Dts.Variables("uvLoopCounter2").
Value), MsgBoxStyle.Information, "ForLoop Recipe")
```

18. Drag-and-drop another **Script Task** from the **SSIS Toolbox | Common**, to increment the variable **uvLoopCounter2** in each execution.

19. Open the **Script Task** for the purpose of editing, and add *uvLoopCounter2* to the **ReadWriteVariables** property.

20. Click on **Edit Script...** and add the following code to the main function:

```
Dts.Variables("uvLoopCounter2").Value = CInt(Dts.
Variables("uvLoopCounter2").Value) + 1
```

21. Link both the Script Tasks from the green output row.

22. Add a For Loop Container and configure it to execute five times using the required property dynamically.

23. Drag-and-drop the For Loop Container from the **SSIS Toolbox | Containers** to the **Control Flow** design area.

24. Open the component for the purpose of editing.

25. In the **EvalExpression** property, set the evaluation expression to *uvLoopCounter3* to less or equal to the *uvLoopCounter3_End* variable. (The For Loop will execute until this expression is not true.)

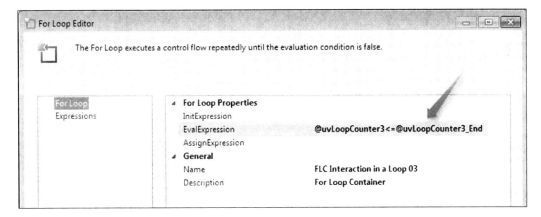

26. Drag-and-drop the **Script Task** from the **SSIS Toolbox | Common**, inside the **For Loop Container** just to display the progress of **uvLoopCounter3** in each execution.

27. Open the Script Task for the purpose of editing, and add *uvLoopCounter3* to the **ReadOnlyVariables** property.

28. Click on **Edit Script...** and add the following code to the main function:

```
MsgBox("LoopCounter = " & CStr(Dts.Variables("uvLoopCounter3").
Value), MsgBoxStyle.Information, "ForLoop Recipe")
```

29. Drag-and-drop another **Script Task** from the **SSIS Toolbox | Common**, to increment the variable **uvLoopCounter3** in each execution.

30. Open the **Script Task** for the purpose of editing, and add *uvLoopCounter3* to the **ReadWriteVariables** property.

31. Click on **Edit Script...** and add the following code to the main function:

```
Dts.Variables("uvLoopCounter3").Value =
    CInt(Dts.Variables("uvLoopCounter3").Value) + 1
If CInt(Dts.Variables("uvLoopCounter3").Value) = 3 Then
    Dts.TaskResult = ScriptResults.Failure
Else
    Dts.TaskResult = ScriptResults.Success
End If
```

32. Link both the **Script Tasks** from the green output row.

33. Select the **For Loop Container** and in the **Properties** panel, change the **MaximumErrorCount** to 5 (or use the **Expressions** property to assign the value of **uvLoopCounter3_End** variable).

34. In the package properties also change the **MaximumErrorCount** to 5. This makes the package succeed in spite of returning a failed result at the end of all iterations through the For Loop Container component.

35. Click on *F5* to execute the package.

36. Verify the value of several messages boxes that will be displayed along the package execution. (Each For Loop Container will be executed five times.)

37. After clicking on **OK** in all the messages boxes, the final result will be similar to the following screenshot:

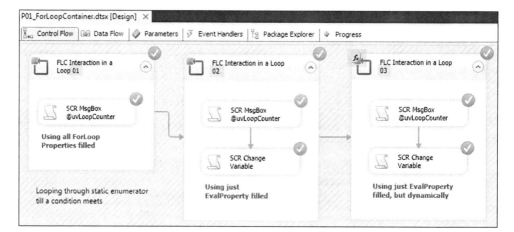

How it works...

The previous steps explained how to configure the For Loop Container that follows the same logic of the For Loop of any programming language. It's required to initialize a variable, increment it on each execution, and also include a condition to check if the execution should be repeated or not. Only the property `EvalExpression` is required to be included in the For Loop Container properties, because the initialization can be done outside the container and the increment/decrement can be done inside the container through a script task or several other tasks or components.

Using the default properties of the For Loop Container, if some execution fails the entire container fails and in consequence the package also fails at the same time. But in real-world scenarios it is often required that some execution failure is tolerated and the container should allow continuing the next step of execution. To make this possible, it is just needed to change the variable `MaximumErrorCount` in the Sequence Container and at the Package level as described in the third **For Loop Container** component created in this recipe.

Foreach Loop Container: looping through result set of a database query

Foreach Loop Container is one of the two loop structures in the SSIS Control Flow, and it can be said strongly that this is the most useful. The Foreach Loop provides a method of looping through seven different types of enumerators and can loop through different types of collections. Collection types vary from files in a folder to nodes in xml data or records in a database table.

In this recipe, we will take a closer look at the ADO enumerator and one of the most useful real world scenarios of using this container.

Suppose that we want to loop through different SQL Server database servers, each server having a different server name and different database name. We read list of all tables with their schema from each database. We want to use a single Data Flow to extract data from an OLE DB Source and load it into an Excel destination, and we need to run this Data Flow for each server and append all the data from all servers into the excel destination.

Getting ready

1. For this recipe we need to have both AdventureWorks2012 and AdventureWorksLT2012 together.

2. Create an Excel file with four column headers: SchemaName, TableName, Server, and DB. Save this file as R03_Destination.xlsx.

How to do it...

1. Create a SSIS project and name it as R03_Foreach Loop Container - ADO Enumerator.

2. Create a R03_DataSources.csv file that contains data similar to the following screenshot:

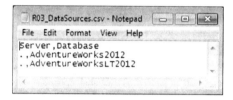

3. Create a package variable of type Object and name it as DataSourcesList.

4. Drag-and-drop a **Data Flow Task** inside the **Control Flow**, this task is supposed to read data from a CSV file and fill it into the Object type variable.

5. Go to the **Data Flow Task**, add a **Flat File Source**, and point it to the R03_DataSources.csv file.

6. Add a **Recordset Destination**, connect data path from **Flat File Source** to the **Recordset Destination**, and go to **Recordset Destination Editor**. Set the DataSourcesList variable in the first tab, and select all the input columns in the second tab.

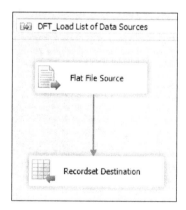

7. Check the schema of the first Data Flow Task; name it as `DFT_Load List of Data Sources`, as shown in the previous screenshot.

8. Return to the **Control Flow**.

9. Create two new variables to store each server name and database name. So create a **Server** and **DatabaseName** variable of type `String` with default valid values.

10. Drag-and-drop a **Foreach Loop Container** right after **DFT_Load List of Data Sources** and connect the precedence constraint (green arrow) from the **Data Flow** to this **Foreach Loop Container**.

11. Open the **Foreach Loop Editor** and go to **Collection** tab.

12. Set **Enumerator** to *Foreach ADO Enumerator*; in the **Enumerator configuration** pane, set the **ADO object source variable** to *User::DataSourcesList*. Leave the **Enumeration mode** as *Rows in the first table*. The configuration should be similar to the following screenshot:

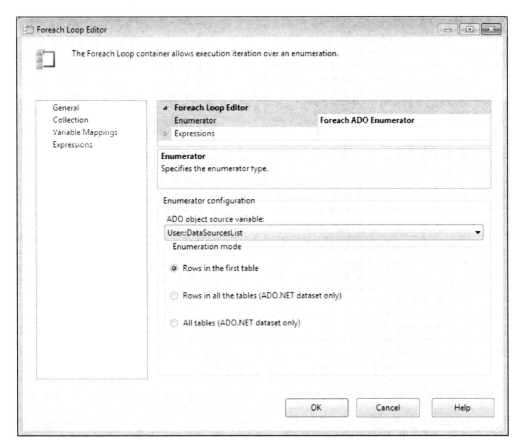

13. Go to the **Variable Mappings** tab and add two records, one for variable **User::Server** and index **0** and another for variable **User::Database** with index **1** as shown in the following screenshot:

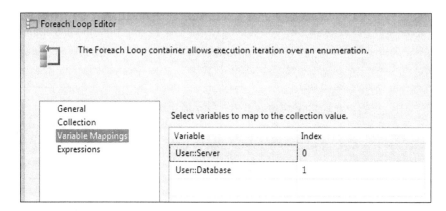

14. Close the **Foreach Loop Editor**.

15. Add another Data Flow Task inside the **Foreach Loop Container**; name it as DFT_Load data into Excel.

16. Go to **Data Flow** tab of the **DFT_Load data into Excel's** task,

17. Add an **OLE DB Source**; create an **OLE DB Connection Manager** to the AdventureWorksLT2012 database on the local system and **Data Access** mode as the **SQL Command**, and type the following command in **SQL Command Text**:

```
select sys.schemas.name as SchemaName,sys.tables.name as TableName
from sys.tables
inner join sys.schemas
on sys.tables.schema_id=sys.schemas.schema_id
```

18. Close the **OLE DB Source**; in the **Connection manager's** pane at bottom of designer window, rename the **OLE DB Connection Manager** to OLEDBConnMgr.

19. Add a **Derived Column** transform after the **OLE DB Source**, and connect a data path between them. In the **Derived Column**, add the following **Expression** columns:

Derived Column Name	Derived Column	Expression	Data Type	Length
Server	<add as new column>	(DT_WSTR,50)@[User::Server]	Unicode string [DT_WSTR]	50
Database	<add as new column>	(DT_WSTR,50)@[User::Database]	Unicode string [DT_WSTR]	50

20. Close the **Derived Column Editor**, and add an **Excel Destination**. Note that you created the R03_Destination.xlsx file in the *Getting ready* section. Point this excel destination to the R03_Destination.xlsx file. Then go to **Mapping** tab and check all mappings between source and destination.

21. The schema of **DFT_Load data into Excel** should be similar to the following screenshot:

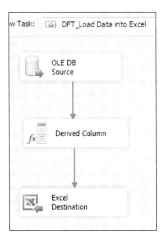

22. Right-click on **OLEDBConnMgr** in the **Connection Manager** pane and select **Properties**. In the properties window, find the **Expression** property, and click on ellipsis(**...**) button besides it. In the **Property Expressions Editor**, set the **ServerName** to @*[User::Server]*, and set **InitialCatalog** to @*[User::Database]* as shown in the following screenshot:

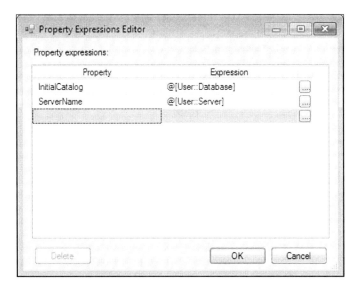

23. Notice the **OLEDBConnMgr** icon after the change. You will see a small **X** there that shows that this connection get its properties from an expression.

24. Go back to **Control Flow**, and run the package.

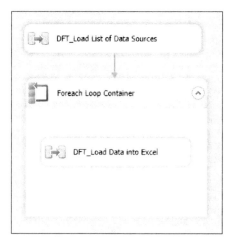

25. Check the Excel destination file and there are two types of records, some of them from one server, and others from another server.

How it works...

In this recipe, we used a stored list of server properties that contains server and database names in a csv file. There is no limit on the storage type, and this list can be stored everywhere from a SQL server database to an xml file. We used the **DFT_Load List of Data Sources** Data Flow Task to fetch data sources information into an Object type variable.

The reason why we used Object type variable is that the **Foreach Loop Container** has the ability to loop through records in an Object type variable with an enumerator called ADO Enumerator.

ADO Enumerator

We set the Enumerator in the Foreach loop as ADO Enumerator. The ADO Enumerator can loop through an Object type variable which is filled with a RecordSet Destination or with an Execute SQL Task with Full Result Set, or from a Script Task that filled data into a Data Table or Data Set and filled the Object type variable with it.

We choose the object variable from the **Collection** tab in the Foreach Loop Container.

When the Object type variable is filled from a RecordSet Destination or from an Execute SQL Task with Full Result Set option, there is only one data stream stored in the variable, so there will be only one table there.

But when a Data Set containing multiple Data Tables is stored into the object variable (from script task and with .NET code), we can choose the Enumeration mode to loop through records of the first table, or records from all tables, or just to loop through table headers.

In situations where the object variable is filled from RecordSet Destination or Execute SQL Task. In this recipe we used the first option **Rows in the first table**. Other options will loop through all rows in all tables, or loop through tables only.

Variable Mappings

Data columns stored in the `Object` type variable have a zero based index, so if we want to fetch them out we need to obey the ordering of columns.

Variable Mappings tab will fetch each column of the data stream stored in the object variable into package variables in the specific enumeration. The only key point is that columns in the data stream should be referred as their index which is zero based.

In this recipe, we load data into the RecordSet Destination in the order Server, Database. So when we want to fetch the Server name we should use index `0` in the variable mapping, and when we want to fetch Database name we should use index `1`.

Type Cast in expressions in the derived column

The reason we used type cast `(DT_WSTR, 50)` before each variable name in the derived column is that, when we work with variables directly in the expressions in the derived column the output column length will be defined by the default value's length. This means that if the default value has four character lengths then the derived column length will be considered as four. The length of the derived column cannot be changed directly, but we can change the predefined length by using `(DT_WSTR, 50)`.

Foreach Loop Container: looping through files using File Enumerator

The most common type of enumerator, the Foreach Loop Container with file enumerator, is used in this recipe. This type of container loops through a list of files in the filesystem and executes some type of action that should be taken inside the respective container.

If a connection exists inside this container, an essential configuration associated with this container type is to pass this connection dynamically creating the connection string based on expressions with the filename provided by the container and read in each execution.

Getting ready

To get ready for this recipe, use the following steps:

1. Open **SQL Server Data Tools (SSDT)** and create a new SSIS project.

2. Provide a name and a location for the SSIS project and proceed.

3. Select the package created by default and rename it to
   `P01_ForEachLoop_Files.dtsx`.

How to do it...

1. Create SSIS variables to pass dynamically the directory and filename of each file that will be processed in each execution of the ForEach Loop Container.

2. Open the **Variables** panel.

3. Create a variable `uvSRC_Directory` to store the files directory.

4. Create a variable `uvSRC_Filename` to store the filename of each file.

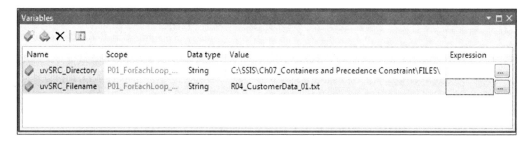

5. Drag-and-drop the **ForEach Loop Container** from the **SSIS Toolbox | Containers**, to the **Control Flow** design area.

6. Open the container for the purpose of editing.

7. Set the value of the **Enumerator** property to *Foreach File Enumerator*.

8. Select the folder where files will be read by the ForEach Container by clicking on the **Browse** button.

9. In the **Files** textbox, enter the extension `*.txt`.

10. Select **Name and extension** for the **Retrieve file name** option.

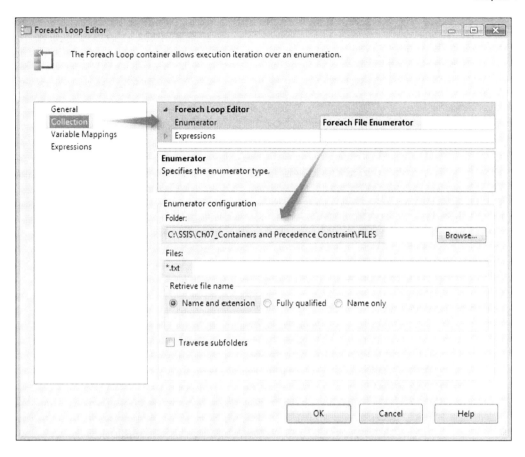

11. In the **Variable Mappings** tab, map the **Name and extension** read in each container iteration with the SSIS variable **User::uvSRC_Filename**.

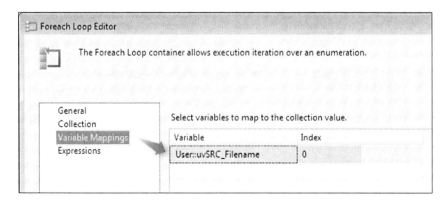

12. Drag-and-drop the **Script Task** from the **SSIS Toolbox | Common**, inside the **For Loop Container** just to display the progress of the **uvLoopCounter3** in each execution.

13. Open the **Script Task** for the purpose of editing and add the SSIS variables uvSRC_Directory and uvSRC_Filename to the **ReadOnlyVariables** property.

14. Click on **Edit Script...** and add the following code to the main function:

```
MsgBox("Directory is " & CStr(Dts.Variables("uvSRC_Directory").
Value) & " and filename is " & CStr(Dts.Variables("uvSRC_
Filename").Value), MsgBoxStyle.Information, "ForLoop Recipe")
```

15. Drag-and-drop the **Data Flow Task** from the **SSIS Toolbox | Favorites**, to the **Control Flow** design area and open it.

16. Create a **Flat File Connection** that points to the sample file included in the recipe.

17. Right-click the **Connection Manager** to select **New Flat File Connection...** to add a new flat file.

18. Add a name to the connection manager property and locate the sample file R04_CustomerData_01.txt by clicking on the **Browse...** button.

19. Accept all the default values and close the editor.

20. In the connection manager, rename the connection to cmCustomerData.

21. In the properties panel, select the **ConnectionString** property and add the following expression to the **Expression** column that concatenates the directory with the filename:

```
@[User::uvSRC_Directory]  +  @[User::uvSRC_Filename]
```

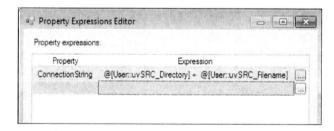

(This expression allows passing the connection dynamically for each container execution.)

22. Drag-and-drop the **Flat File Source** component from the **SSIS Toolbox | Other Sources**, to the **Data Flow** design area.

23. Open the component for the purpose of editing.

24. The connection created in the previous step will be automatically assigned to the source component.

25. Add a **Union All** component to see data moving in the pipeline and link the source to it. Below the row that links the two components, select **Enable Data Viewer**.

26. Press *F5* to execute the package.

27. Several messages will be displayed with the values of the SSIS variables `uvSRC_Directory` and `uvSRC_Filename`. It is then used in conjunction to dynamically read each file located on the filesystem.

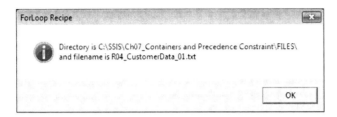

28. After clicking on **OK** in the message box that is similar to the previous screenshot, the data read in each file is displayed in the viewer.

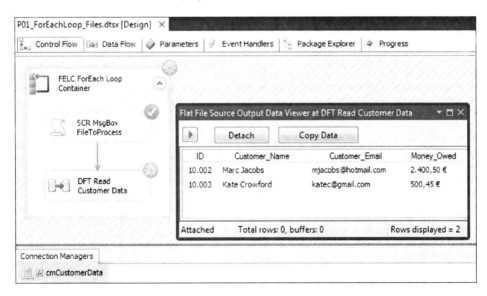

29. Click on play in the data viewer to continue the execution for the next file.

How it works...

The previous steps explained how to configure and use the ForEach Loop Container for file enumerator. This is one of the most common use of this component and it is very useful when a specific task needs to be repeated in several files.

The container configurations should be adjusted to fit the needs of each scenario, such as the extensions of the files to be considered and mainly the **Retrieve file name** option that needs to be retrieved. If the option selected is **Name and extension**, the filename and extension is retrieved; if the option selected is **Fully qualified**, the absolute path and filename is retrieved; and if the selected option is **Name only**, the filename (without extension) is retrieved.

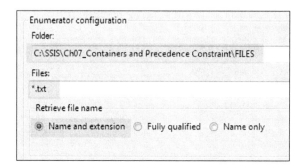

Foreach Loop Container: looping through data table

One of the enumerators in Foreach Loop is the Item Enumerator. This enumerator has the ability to create a temporary table in the SSIS Foreach Loop Container itself to use as the iteration list. This option will remove the need for an external temporary storage as we saw in the *Foreach Loop Container: looping through result set of a database query* recipe of this chapter.

In this recipe, we will reveal another real world sample with Item Enumerator. We will loop through the list of servers with different database names, and load the same data structure from the same table but onto different servers into different excel files which will be named based on the data sources.

Getting ready

1. For this recipe we need to have both `AdventureWorks2012` and `AdventureWorksLT2012` together.

2. Create a `R05_Template.xlsx` file that only contains two column headers namely, `SchemaName` and `TableName`.

How to do it...

1. Create a SSIS project and name it `R05_Foreach Loop Container-Item Enumerator`.

2. Create a `TemplateFilePath` variable of type `String` in the package scope, and set a default value for it as: `C:\SSIS\Ch07_Containers and Precedence Constraint\Files\R05_Template.xlsx`.

3. Create a `DestinationFolderPath` variable of type `String` in the package scope, with a default valid value.

4. Add an **Expression Task** into the **Control Flow** and name it `ET_Generate Destination Folder Name`. Write this expression in the expression editor:

   ```
   @[User::DestinationFolderPath]=
           SUBSTRING( @[User::TemplateFilePath] , 1,
           FINDSTRING(@[User::TemplateFilePath], "\\",
           TOKENCOUNT(@[User::TemplateFilePath],"\\")-2)
           )+"FILES\\GeneratedFiles\\"
   ```

5. Evaluate the **Expression**; you should be able to verify the folder address here.

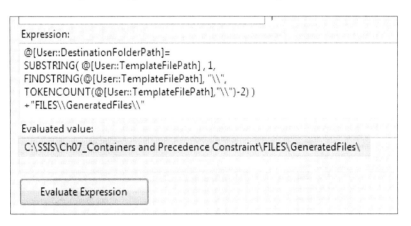

6. Add a **File System Task** after the **Expression Task** and name it `FST_Create Destination Folder If Not Exists`.

7. In the **File System Task Editor**, set **Operation** to *Create directory*; set **IsSourcePathVariable** to *True*; and set **SourceVariable** to *User::DestinationFolderPath*. Also, set the **UseDirectoryIfExists** to *True*. The configurations should be similar to the following screenshot:

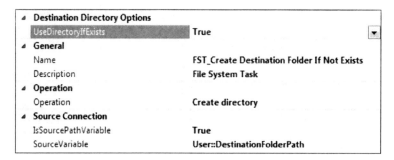

8. Add two package variables in the package scope of type `String`, and with valid default values, name them as `Server` and `Database`.

9. Add a **Foreach Loop Container** after the **File System Task**.

10. In the **Foreach Loop Editor**, in the **Collection** tab set the **Enumerator** as *Item Enumerator*.

11. In the **Enumerator Configuration** pane, click on the **Add** button, and add two columns, leave both the data types as **String**, and note that you cannot set the column names.

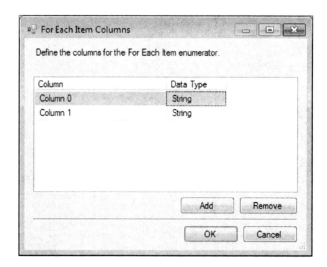

12. Close the **For Each Item Columns** window, and you will see two column names as the columns header In the **Enumerator configuration** generated table, type in two records for two different data sources and different databases. For this recipe we used the same server and database names as the *Foreach Loop Container: looping through result set of a database query* recipe of this chapter.

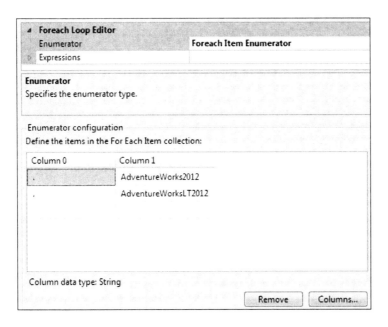

13. Go to the **Variable Mappings** tab of the **Foreach Loop Editor**, and set the index of **User::Server** to *0*, and the index of **User::Database** to *1*.

14. Go back to **Control Flow**, create another package variable of type `String` and name it as `DestinationFilePath`, remember to set a default value for this variable.

15. Add another **Expression Task** inside the **Foreach Loop Container**; name this task as `ET_Generate Destination File Path` and type the following expression there:

    ```
    @[User::DestinationFilePath] = @[User::DestinationFolderPath]
    +
    REPLACE( @[User::Server] ,"\\", "-" )+"_"+ REPLACE( @
    [User::Database]   ,"\\", "-" )+".xlsx"
    ```

16. Evaluate the expression and close the expression editor.

17. Add a **File System Task** inside the **Foreach Loop Container** after the expression task, and name it as `FST_Copy Destination Files from Template File`.

18. In the **File System Task Editor**, set the **Operation** to *Copy file*. Set **IsSourceVariable** to *True*, and set *User::TemplateFilePath* as the **SourceVariable**. Also set the **IsDestinationVariable** to *True*, and set the **User::DestinationFilePath** as *DestinationVariable*. Set the **OverwriteDestination** to *True*.

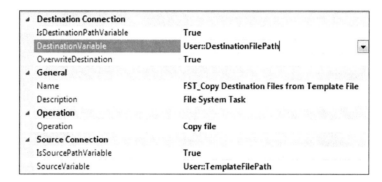

19. Add a **Data Flow Task** inside the **Foreach Loop Container** after the filesystem task, and go to **Data Flow** tab.

20. Add an **OLE DB Source** and create a connection to the local instance of SQL Server, and the `AdventureWorksLT2012` database. Set the data access mode as **SQL Command**, and type the following command in SQL command text:

```
select sys.schemas.name as SchemaName,sys.tables.name as TableName
from sys.tables
inner join sys.schemas
on sys.tables.schema_id=sys.schemas.schema_id
```

21. Rename the connection manager as **OLEDBConnMgr**.

22. In the properties of **OLEDBConnMgr**, set the **ServerName** to *@[User::Server]*, and **InitialCatalog** to *@[User::Database]*. Use the expressions in the same way as described in the *Foreach Loop Container: looping through result set of a database query* recipe of this chapter.

23. Add an Excel Destination, and point it to a copy of the `R05_Template.xlsx` file. (you can create a copy of `R05_Template.xlsx` file for generating the data flow task's structure and delete the file after this step.)

24. Rename the **Excel Connection Manager** to `ExcelConnMgr`.

25. Right-click on **ExcelConnMgr**, and in the **Properties** window, set the **ExcelFilePath** expression property to *@[User::DestinationFilePath]*.

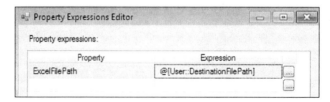

26. Go back to **Control Flow** and run the package.

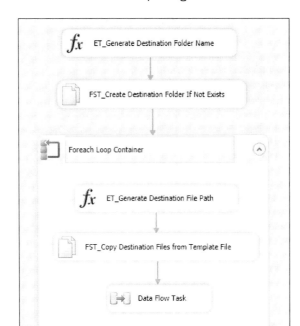

27. Check the `GeneratedFiles` folder that will be available at `C:\SSIS\Ch07_ Containers and Precedence Constraint\Files\GeneratedFiles`. There will be two generated Excel files with the data from each server as shown in the following screenshot:

How it works...

Item Enumerator is one of the seven useful enumerators in the Foreach Loop Container which provides the ability to loop through a static defined data table. The structure of a data table should be defined in the **Collection** tab of the Foreach Loop Editor.

In step 11 of this recipe, we created a table with two columns of type `String` and used this table as a temporary storage of data sources information. The data types of columns can be defined from the list of data types but column names are not changeable.

After defining the structure, data rows can be added in the Enumerator Configuration pane as we did in step 13.

The advantage of this method is that, Item Enumerator doesn't need an external storage for temp data such as server and database names, because it uses its own data table. But this option also has a disadvantage. When working with package in a dynamic mode, the list of data sources should be changeable from outside the package, and this can be done only if storage of data is outside of package as an external storage.

In this recipe, first of all we fetched out the folder path from the `TemplateFilePath` variable. To fetch out the folder path we used `TokenCount`, `FindString`, and `SubString` methods:

- ▶ `TokenCount`: Finds a specific string (called token) number of occurrences in the primary string
- ▶ `FindString`: Finds a position of specific string in the primary string and returns an integer defining the position
- ▶ `SubString`: Fetches part of the primary string with first index of separator and length

We used File System Task to create the folder that does not exist with the **UseDirectoryIfExists** option.

Inside the Foreach Loop Container, there is another Expression Task which generates the specific file name based on server and database name.

Another File System Task is responsible to create copies of `R05_Template.xlsx` with new generated names.

And finally, the Data Flow Task will load data from sources into Excel Destination File, the connection of the Excel file will be changed based on the generated Destination file name.

DelayValidation

There are times when setting an expression can cause a validation error in the SSIS Compile time, the reason is that one or more variables which participate in the expression has no default valid values, and the SSIS will check the expression at compile time for compile time validation.

We can suppress this compile time validation and postpone the validation to runtime by setting `DelayValidation` to `true` for that task or Connection Manager.

On setting the `DelayValidation` to `true`, SSIS will postpone the validation phase for this task or connection manager to runtime. So be careful to set the `DelayValidation` to `true` only when you are sure that there is no logical validation error in the designed task or connection manager.

Precedence Constraints: how to control the flow of task execution

Precedence Constraints are arrows in the Control Flow which define execution priority of tasks and other executables in the Control Flow. In the samples of this book till now we used simple Precedence Constraints a lot.

In this recipe, we will explore a new way of using Precedence Constraints and we will implement an `if` condition in the Control Flow with Precedence Constraints.

Also, we will reveal options to work when there are multiple Precedence Constraints for each executable.

How to do it...

1. Create a SSIS project and name it as `R06_Precedence Constraints`.

2. Create a `RecordCount` package variable of type `int32`. Set the default value to `0`.

3. Add an **Execute SQL Task** into the **Control Flow**, create an OLE DB Connection to the `AdventureWorks2008R2` database.

4. Type the following query in the SQL Statement property:

```
SELECT COUNT(*) AS Cnt
FROM Sales.Customer
WHERE DATEDIFF(Day, ModifiedDate, GETDATE()) < 0
```

5. As the previous statement will return the number of records that have a modified date later than the current date, set the **ResultSet** property in the **General** tab to *Single Row*.

6. In the **Result Set** tab, set the **ResultName** to *Cnt* and the **Variable Name** to *User::RecordCount*.

7. Add a **Data Flow Task** after the **Execute SQL Task**, connect Precedence Constraint from the Execute SQL Task to the Data Flow Task.

8. Right-click on Precedence Constraint and select **Edit**. A **Precedence Constraint Editor** will open.

9. In the **Constraint options** set **Evaluation operation** to *Expression and Constraint* and **Value** to *Success*. Type the following code in the **Expression** textbox:

```
@[User::RecordCount] >0
```

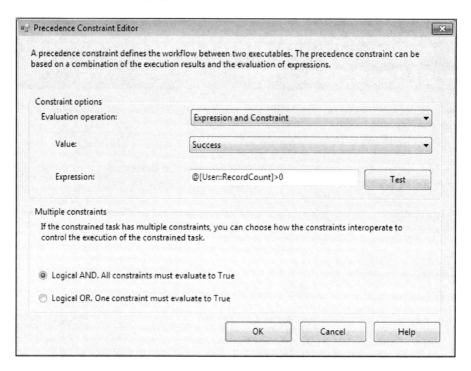

10. Close the **Precedence Constraint Editor**.

11. Drag-and-drop a **Script Task** after the **Execute SQL** Task and connect Precedence Constraint from the **Execute SQL Task** to this **Script Task**. Right-click on **Precedence Constraint** and select **Edit**.

12. In the **Constraint options**, set **Evaluation operation** to *Expression and Constraint* and **Value** to *Success*. Type the following code in the **Expression** textbox:

```
@[User::RecordCount] <=0
```

13. Note that when we write an expression in the Precedence Constraint a *fx* icon will appear on the Precedence Constraint.

14. In this Script Task's main method insert the following code:

```
MessageBox.Show("There is no New or Updated Records");");
```

15. Add another **Script Task** at the bottom of all other tasks, connect the **Precedence Constraint** from both the **Data Flow Task** and the first **Script Task** to the second **Script Task**, and name this task as `Log`.

16. Right-click on one of the Precedence Constraints and choose **Edit**. In the **Precedence Constraint Editor**, in the **Multiple constraints** pane select the **Logical OR. One constraint must evaluate to True** option.

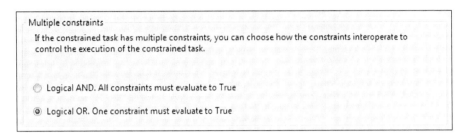

17. Run the package, and you will see a message box that pops up (this means that **Script Task** ran successfully), and after clicking on **OK**, control flow goes to **Log** task.

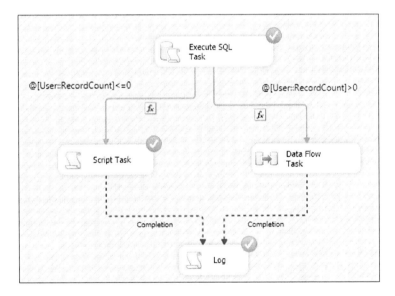

18. Stop the package, and go to **SSMS**, open the `AdventureWorks2012` database and open the `Sales.Customer` table.

19. Change **ModifiedDate** of the first row to a date greater than the current date of system, and run the package again.

20. The Control Flow will go to **Data Flow Task** and **Log** task this time.

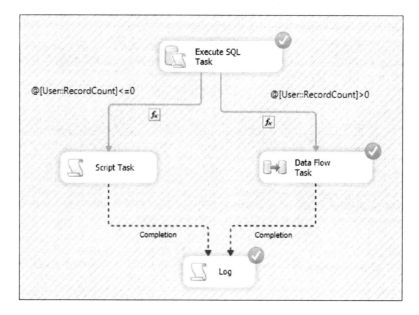

How it works...

In the first 15 steps of this recipe, we implemented an `if` condition with Precedence Constraints. The scenario is that the Execute SQL Task will query `sales.customer` table to find a customer with `modifiedDate` greater than the current date of system. If there were no new or updated customers, a Script Task with a `messageBox` will appear, but if there were some records, a Data Flow Task will start.

The `if` condition is implemented with the help of Expression in Precedence Constraints. We used a variable to fetch the record count from a SQL statement and wrote an expression based on the value of this variable.

Types of Constraints

There are three types of Constraints:

 ▸ **Success**: This means the next task will run only if the first task succeeds

 ▸ **Failure**: This means the next task will run only if the first task fails

 ▸ **Completion**: This means the next task will run if the first task succeeds or fails

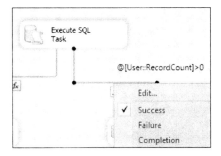

We can choose the Precedence Constraint type by right-clicking on the **Precedence Constraint** and selecting **Type**.

Evaluation operation

This option defines how the constraint will be evaluated. There are four types for this option as follows:

► **Constraint**: This is a default option. It means that the Precedence Constraint will only use success, failure, or completion for evaluation.

► **Expression**: This means that the Precedence Constraint will redirect to the next task only if an expression is met; the expression here should be resolved to `true`.

► **Expression and constraint**: This is a combination of expression and constraint and both should be met. For this recipe the Execute SQL Task should succeed and the expression should resolve to `true`.

► **Expression or constraint**: Each of expression or constraint is enough for redirecting to the next task.

Multiple constraints

Does more than one constraint redirect the same final task when execution of the final task occurs? This is the question which will be answered here.

There are two options here:

► **Logical AND. All constraints must evaluate to True**: All the incoming Precedence Constraints should meet together and then the final task will be executed. This is the default option.

► **Logical OR. One constraint must evaluate to True**: Each incoming Precedence Constraint meets and then the final task will be executed.

8

Scripting

by Reza Rad

In this chapter, we will cover the following topics:

- ▶ The Script Task: Scripting through Control Flow
- ▶ The Script Component as a Transformation
- ▶ The Script Component as a Source
- ▶ The Script Component as a Destination
- ▶ The Asynchronous Script Component

Introduction

In previous chapters, many aspects of SSIS Development Components were revealed. SSIS has a bunch of Tasks and Transformations that help ETL or Data Integration developers to create their package faster, more easily, and with greater reliability. However, there are times when a requirement cannot be met with built-in tasks and transformations. Every ETL Tool should have a way to overcome this common problem.

SSIS provides a way to write your own custom code in a .NET language and execute it during Control Flow or Data Flow. A combination of SSIS and the Microsoft .NET Framework makes scripting in SSIS a great way to handle anything in custom code.

Our scripting language could be C# or VB.NET, and the .NET 4.0 Framework is fully supported in this version of SSIS. This is one of the main advantages of SSIS 2012 over the 2008 version, because in SSIS 2008 only VSTA 2.0 was supported. In SSIS 2005, a developer had no choice but to write code in VB.NET.

There are two locations for writing custom code in SSIS, and these locations provide scripting in two major parts in SSIS—Control Flow and Data Flow. Scripting in Control Flow can be done with the Script Task, and scripting in Data Flow can be done using the Script Component.

Access to variables, connection managers, and other package information are available during scripting, and some of them will be explored during upcoming recipes in this chapter.

Scripting in Data Flow is completely different from scripting in Control Flow because SSIS Data Flow consists of **Sources**, **Transformations**, and **Destinations**. Fortunately, the SSIS Script Component can be used for each of those types of components. There are also times when a transformation should work asynchronously; all of these actions can be done with the Script Component, and we have a complete series of Script Component examples in this chapter.

The Script Task: Scripting through Control Flow

The first, and most easy-to-use scripting component in SSIS is a Script Task during Control Flow, which works with .NET scripts in both C# and VB.NET, which can be written inside the Script Task with its own scripting editor.

Besides the fact that SSIS has a complete and fully functional series of Control Flow Tasks, there are times when some requirements cannot be fulfilled with built-in Control Flow Tasks; this is when the Script Task comes into play.

In this recipe, we will use a simple example to demonstrate how the Script Task works. The **Send Mail** Control Flow Task has a few limitations; for example, if you want to send an e-mail in HTML with special formatting, you cannot use the Send Mail Task. In this recipe, we will implement such functionality with a Script Task and C# code.

How to do it...

1. Create a new SSIS project and name it `R01_ScriptTask`.

2. Create a package variable of type `String` and name it `Receiver`; in the default value field write a valid e-mail address. This is the receiver's e-mail address.

3. Add a Script Task from the SSIS Toolbox into the **Control Flow**.

4. Open Script Task Editor and confirm that the **ScriptLanguage** is set as *Microsoft Visual C# 2010*.

5. Leave the **EntryPoint** as **Main**.

6. In the **ReadOnlyVariables** click on the ellipsis button and select *User::Receiver* from the list of variables.

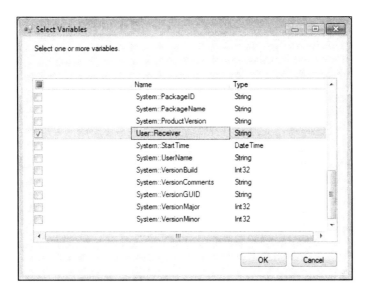

7. Add an Execute SQL Task inside the sequence container, then connect it to the `AdventureWorks2012` database.

8. Click on **Edit Script** and wait for new **Script Editor** to open.

9. Add the following `using` statements at the beginning of the new script:

```
using System.Net.Mail;
using System.Net;
```

10. Write the following code in the `Main()` method:

```
public void Main()
{
    try
    {
        MailMessage message = new MailMessage(
            "sender@somedomain.com",
            Dts.Variables["User::Receiver"].Value.ToString()
            );
        message.IsBodyHtml = true;
        message.Subject = "From SSIS Script Task";
        message.Body = "<html>"
            + "<h1> Automatic mail from SSIS Script Task</h1>"
            + "<BR> This message generated "
            + "<span style='font-size:110%;color:#115588;'>
                  Automatically</span>"
```

```
        + " by SSIS Script Task"
        + "<BR>"
        + "</Html>";

    SmtpClient mailClient =
        new SmtpClient("mail.somedomain.com");
    mailClient.Credentials = new NetworkCredential(
        " sender@somedomain.com ", "password");
    mailClient.Send(message);

    Dts.TaskResult = (int)ScriptResults.Success;
}
catch (Exception ex)
{
    Dts.TaskResult = (int)ScriptResults.Failure;
    Dts.Events.FireError
        (-1, "Script Task Send Mail",
            ex.Message,string.Empty,0);
}
}
```

11. Save your script and close the Script Task Editor.

12. Run the package and check whether the e-mail was received.

Automatic mail from SSIS Script Task

This message generated Automatically by SSIS Script Task

How it works...

The Script Language can be either C# or VB.NET, and the supporting framework in SSIS 2012 is the Microsoft .NET 4.0 Framework. Each Script Task in a package can have a different script language, but whenever we choose a script language and click on **OK** there is no way to turn back and change the language for that Script Task.

ReadOnlyVariables

There is no access to package variables in a Script Task by default. To read variables in a Script Task they should first be selected in ReadOnlyVariables. The syntax for working with variables in C# is:

```
Dts.Variables["User::VariableName"].Value
```

And in VB.NET is:

```
Dts.Variables("User::VariableName").Value
```

Note that variable name should include the namespace part (`User`), and that the variable name is case sensitive.

ReadWriteVariables

To write into variables, you need to select them as `ReadWriteVariables`.

Script

Your `Main()` method is the Entry Point, and this means that the method will be executed.

Code description

In this recipe, we used the `MailMessage` class in `System.Net.Mail` to create an e-mail message with a sender and a receiver address. The next three lines of script generate the message subject and HTML body with special formatting. For more information about the HTML tags used in this recipe, you should read about HTML tags; a basic description of these parts is beyond the scope of this book.

For sending SMTP e-mails, we used `SmtpClient` in the same namespace; the host address and credentials to log in to the `smtp` host were configured in two lines of code, and we finally called the `Send` method in the `SmtpClient` object to send the message.

Script results

The results of a Script Task are important for precedence constraints; there should be a `ScriptResult` at least. If you want to return failure as the result of Script Task, you can use `ScriptResults.Failure`

```
Dts.TaskResult = (int)ScriptResults.Failure;
```

Fire Events

The last line of the previous script snippet shows us how to fire special events from a Script Task with `Dts.Events.FireError`. You can read more about raising events in a Script Task here: `http://msdn.microsoft.com/en-us/library/ms136054.aspx`.

The Script Component as a Transformation

Writing scripts in Data Flow is another major aspect of scripting in SSIS. The Script Component is one of the most powerful components in SSIS Data Flow and is usable as *Source*, *Transformation*, and *Destination*.

In this recipe, we will use a *Transformation* Script Component to create a row number, besides other columns in the data stream, because there is no Row Number *Transformation* in SSIS Toolbox.

How to do it...

1. Create an SSIS project and name it `R02_ScriptComponent` as `Transformation`.

2. Add a Data Flow Task from the SSIS Toolbox and go to the **Data Flow** tab.

3. Add an **OLE DB Source**, create a **Connection** to the `AdventureWorks2012` database, and set the **Data Access Mode** as *Table or View*, and choose `HumanResources.Department` as your source table.

4. Connect a Data Path from **OLE DB Source** to **Script Component** and go to the Script Transformation Editor.

5. Set the **Script Language** as *Visual C# 2010*.

6. Go to the **Inputs and Outputs** tab and expand **Output 0**, then under **Output Columns** add a column with data type `DT_I4` and name it `RowNumber`.

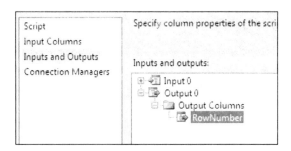

7. Go back to the **Script** tab, and click on **Edit Script**.

8. In the `ScriptMain`'s class body, write the following code:

```
public class ScriptMain : UserComponent
{
    int RowNumber = 0;
```

9. In the `Input0_ProcessInputRow` method, write the following code:

```
public override void Input0_ProcessInputRow(Input0Buffer Row)
    {
        RowNumber++;
        Row.RowNumber = RowNumber;
    }
```

10. Save and close the editor.

11. Add a **Recordset Destination** to the Data Flow and write the results to an object variable. Also enable data viewers on the Data Path between **Script Component** and **Recordset Destination**.

12. Run the package and verify the new `RowNumber` column in the output data stream.

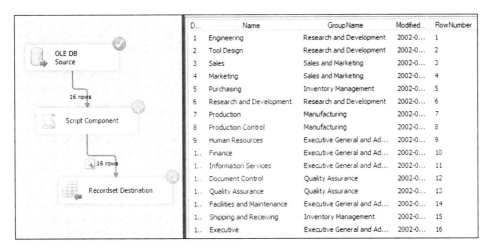

How it works...

First and foremost, the Script Component is the only component in the Data Flow that can play three roles—*Source*, *Transformation*, and *Destination*. In this example, we used the *Transformation* Script Component simply as a synchronous transformation. You will learn more about synchronous and asynchronous transform in this chapter's last recipe The *Asynchronous Script Component*. Decisions about the Script Component's role should be made during the first drag-and-drop dialog of this component's **Select Script Component Type** dialog box in the Data Flow tab.

When a Script Component is set as *Transformation*, it has no default output column and input column. For choosing input columns, we can go to the **Input Columns** tab in **Script Component Editor** and select every column that we need to access inside the script.

Advanced settings for inputs and outputs in the Script Component can be done in the **Inputs and Outputs** tab. As the first default schema shows, there is only one input named **Input 0** and one output named **Output 0**. When we choose input columns in the **Input Columns** tab, there is no need to do anything in the **Inputs and Outputs** tab. For output columns, however, we need to add them here in this tab directly.

There is an **Add Output** button in this tab where you can add as many outputs as you want to this transform. One of the many powerful features of the Script Component is its ability to work with multiple inputs and/or multiple outputs.

Under each output, we can define output columns with names, data types, and other properties. In this recipe, we just need an extra column after the Script Component that holds the row numbers, so we just added a single column of the `Integer` data type named `DT_I4`.

The **Connection Manager** tab is where we can add every connection manager that we need to access in the script; the Script Component has no access to package connection managers by default, so we need to add them if we need to use them in the Script Component.

`ReadOnlyVariables` and `ReadWriteVariables` are like their counterparts in a Script Task within the Control Flow, and provide the ability to access package variables in the script.

Script

The `script` class of the Script Component is completely different from the Script Task. In the Script Task, there is only one `Main` method that has the execution code, but in the Script Component there are a number of methods with each of them playing a role in Script Component behavior.

In this recipe, we used a simple **Transformation** Script Component, so we have only three events and two properties as described next:

- ▶ **PreExecute**: The `PreExecute` method, as its name indicates, will execute before the execution of the Script Component. Connections to resources can be made and streams can be opened in this method. This method will execute once for each Script Component.

- ▶ **PostExecute**: This method will run after execution of the Script Component. We will mostly use this method to release resources that we acquired in the `PreExecute` method and then close connections and streams. This method will execute once for each Script Component.

- ▶ **InputName_ProcessInputRow**: This method will be executed based on the number of rows in the incoming data stream to the Script Component. In other words, this method will execute for each row in the data stream. The `Row` parameter has the type `InputNameBuffer` and holds all data form the current row.

This method is one of the most useful methods in the Script Component because of its special behavior. In this recipe, we declared an `Integer` variable in the Script Component's `class` body and then incremented its value inside the `ProcessInputRow` method. So, in each iteration, the value will increase. And in the second line, we assign the value of this variable to `Row.RowNumber`.

▸ **InputNameBuffer**: The `Row` parameter in `ProcessInputRow` has data from the corresponding record in the data stream. We can change the value of each row or simply read them by using the `Row.ColumnName` method. There is no difference between input and output column names, and you should mention the naming rules that distinguish them in your script as well.

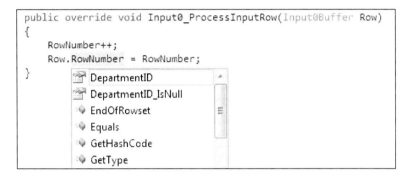

▸ **ColumnName, ColumnName_IsNulll**: For each Input or Output Column in the Script Component, there will be two properties in the `Row` object—`ColumnName` and `ColumnName_IsNull`. The `ColumnName` property contains the actual value of that column in your current row, and the `ColumnName_IsNull` property will identify whether the column has a Null value or not.

See also

▸ The _Script Component as a Destination_
▸ The _Script Component as a Source_

The Script Component as a Source

In the previous recipe we had a real-world example of using a Transformation Script Component. Using a Script Component can be more effective when it plays the role of a Source in Data Flow.

There are times when default built-in sources within Data Flow cannot open a special source—some sources may be very old or very rarely used, and there are no appropriate connection providers or sources for them. In some cases, they could be source structures in special formats that the built-in sources couldn't open correctly. In such scenarios, later in this chapter *Script Component as a Source* will help us to write custom code and fetch data from every source in the way we need.

In this recipe, we have a Flat File with special formatting (this file is generated in the output of the next recipe), so the built-in Flat File source couldn't open it as we require. We will use a Script Component as *Source* and create outputs as well.

The following screenshot is a sample of our Source File content:

```
data.txt - Notepad
File  Edit  Format  View  Help
Employees Information
Start Time: 2011-11-21 01:46:40

NationalIDNumber
FirstName|LastName|Gender|MaritalStatus
JobTitle;HireDate;DepartmentName;DepartmentGroupName;StartDate;EndDate
---------------------------------
295847284
Ken|Sánchez|M|S
Chief Executive Officer;2003-02-15 00:00:00;Executive;Executive General and Administration;2003-02-15 00:00:00;
---------------------------------

.
.

---------------------------------
134219713
Ranjit|Varkey Chudukatil|M|S
Sales Representative;2006-07-01 00:00:00;Sales;Sales and Marketing;2006-07-01 00:00:00;
End Of Data
Finish Time: 2011-11-21 01:46:40
Number of records : 296
```

The file has a few header and footer lines, which should be ignored, and some data rows, which are separated into three rows. In the first row, there is only a single employee **NationalIDNumber**, while in the second and third rows, personal information and professional information of that employee is listed respectively. We need to read this special file content and create two outputs; one for the employee's personal information and another for the employee's professional information.

Getting ready

A sample `data.txt` file for this recipe will be created as the result of the next recipe (The *Script Component as a Destination*), but if you want to follow the book's sequence of recipes you can find the file in this title's downloadable content under `Ch08_Scripting\ R03_ScriptComponent As Source\Files`.

How to do it...

1. Create a new SSIS project and name it `R03_ScriptComponent as Source`.
2. Add a new Data Flow Task, and in the **Data Flow** tab, add two object type package variables and name them `PersonalInf` and `ProfessionalInf`.

3. Add a `String` type variable and name it `SourceFilePath`. Set the value of this variable as `C:\SSIS\Ch08_Scripting\R03_ScriptComponent As Source\Files\data.txt`.

4. Drag-and-drop a Script Component into the Data Flow and in **Select Script Component Type,** select *Source*.

5. In the Script Component Editor, select the `SourceFilePath` variable under the **ReadOnlyVariables** section in the **Script** tab.

6. Go to the **Input and output** tab. Note that there is no **Input** when you work with a Script Component as *Source*.

7. Change the default **output 0** name to **PersonalInformationOutput**.

8. Add these output columns under this output; **NationalIDNumber**, **FirstName**, **LastName**, **Gender**, and **MaritalStatus**. Set the data type of all columns to `DT_WSTR` and leave the default length as 50.

9. Add another output and name it `ProfessionalInformationOutput`.

10. Add these columns under the output as `DT_WSTR` data type; `NationalIDNumber`, `JobTitle`, `DepartmentName` and `DepartmentGroupName`. And add these columns as `DT_DBDate` data type; `HireDate`, `StartDate`, and `EndDate`.

11. Check whether your **Inputs and outputs** configuration concurs with the following screenshot:

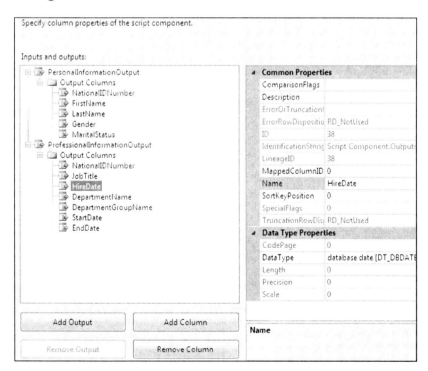

12. Go back to the **Script** tab and click on **Edit Script**.

13. In the `ScriptMain` class body add these variable declaration lines:

```
StreamReader reader = null;
    int RowIndex = 0;
```

14. In the `PreExecute` method, open the `StreamReader` class and instantiate the `reader` variable as follows:

```
public override void PreExecute()
{
    base.PreExecute();
    reader = new StreamReader(this.Variables.SourceFilePath);
}
```

15. In the `CreateNewOutputRows` method, write the following code (for a complete description of the code, refer to the *How it works...* section of this recipe):

```
public override void CreateNewOutputRows()
{
  while (!reader.EndOfStream)
  {
  RowIndex++;
  if (RowIndex > 6)
  {
    string data = reader.ReadLine();
    if (data == "End Of Data")
      {
        reader.ReadToEnd();
        break;
      }

      string NationalIDNumber = reader.ReadLine();
      //Generate Personal Information Output Row
      string PersonalInformation = reader.ReadLine();
      string[] personalInfArray =
        PersonalInformation.Split('|');
      PersonalInformationOutputBuffer.AddRow();
      PersonalInformationOutputBuffer.NationalIDNumber =
        NationalIDNumber;
      PersonalInformationOutputBuffer.FirstName =
        personalInfArray[0];
      PersonalInformationOutputBuffer.LastName =
        personalInfArray[1];
      PersonalInformationOutputBuffer.Gender =
        personalInfArray[2];
```

```
    PersonalInformationOutputBuffer.MaritalStatus =
      personalInfArray[3];

    //Generate Professional Information Output Row
    string ProfessionalInformation = reader.ReadLine();
    string[] professionalInfArray =
      ProfessionalInformation.Split(';');
    ProfessionalInformationOutputBuffer.AddRow();
    ProfessionalInformationOutputBuffer.NationalIDNumber =
      NationalIDNumber;
    ProfessionalInformationOutputBuffer.JobTitle =
      professionalInfArray[0];
    ProfessionalInformationOutputBuffer.HireDate =
      DateTime.ParseExact(professionalInfArray[1],
      "yyyy-MM-dd HH:mm:ss", new CultureInfo("en-US"));
    ProfessionalInformationOutputBuffer.DepartmentName =
      professionalInfArray[2];
  ProfessionalInformationOutputBuffer.DepartmentGroupName =
      professionalInfArray[3];
    ProfessionalInformationOutputBuffer.StartDate =
      DateTime.ParseExact(professionalInfArray[4],
      "yyyy-MM-dd HH:mm:ss", new CultureInfo("en-US"));
    if (professionalInfArray[5] == string.Empty)
  ProfessionalInformationOutputBuffer.EndDate_IsNull =
      true;
    else
        ProfessionalInformationOutputBuffer.EndDate =
          DateTime.ParseExact(professionalInfArray[5],
            "yyyy-MM-dd HH:mm:ss",
            new CultureInfo("en-US"));
  }
  else
  {
      reader.ReadLine();
  }
}
}
```

16. In the `PostExecute` method, close the reader object as follows:

```
public override void PostExecute()
  {
      base.PostExecute();
      reader.Close();
  }
```

17. Add two **Recordset Destination**s after the Script Component; name them **Personal Information** and **Professional Information**. Connect outputs from the Script Component to their corresponding Destinations. In the `variableName` of each **Recordset Destination**, select appropriate variables (`PersonalInf` and `ProfessionalInf` sequentially) and select all input columns in the **Input columns** tab. Also enable **Data Viewer** on each data path to **RecordSet** Destinations.

18. Run the package and check both outputs; you will see two different outputs. First of all, there is a `NationalIDNumber` column in each output, and in **PersonalInformationOutput** only personal columns showed up.

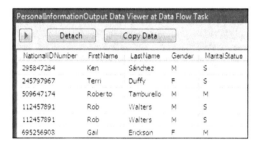

19. And there is another output for **ProfessionalInformationOutput** as the following screenshot shows:

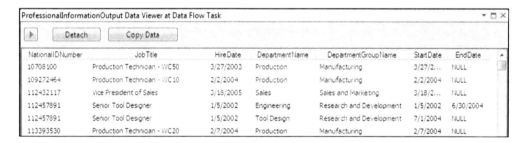

20. The following screenshot shows the complete schema:

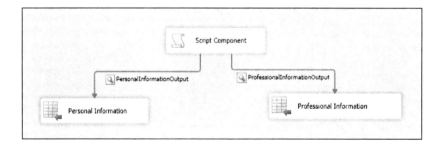

How it works...

Using the Script Component as a *Source* is a bit different from using it as a *Transformation*. Primarily, there is no **Input Columns** tab in the Script Component as *Source*.

The **Inputs and Outputs** column is only for configuring outputs and their columns.

In this recipe, we used the `PreExecute` method to open the `StreamReader` method in order to connect the text file and open it as a reader. The following code will open the text file:

```
reader = new StreamReader(this.Variables.SourceFilePath);
```

Note the special signature of working with variables in the Script Component in the preceding code. This signature is different from the way we worked with variables in the Script Task. The difference is that in the Script Component, variables that are checked as `ReadOnlyVariables` or `ReadWriteVariables` appear as properties under `this.Variables`, and their data type is fetched correctly from package variables.

As the `PreExecute` method runs just one time at the first execution of Script Component, so the best place to open `StreamReader` is in this method.

CreateNewOutputRows

This method is responsible for creating output records. This method will run just once, so if we want to create a bunch of output rows, we should implement our own looping structure inside the method.

In this recipe, we use a `while` loop till `StreamReader` hits the "end of stream" with the following line of code:

```
while (!reader.EndOfStream)
```

As the Script Component, it should read the data; so we should separate useful data and not-so-useful data. This is why we reject the first six rows, because there is no useful information in our scenario's file headers.

```
if (RowIndex > 6)
```

The end of useful information is labeled with `"End Of Data"` so checking this label will end our loop structure.

```
if (data == "End Of Data")
    {
        reader.ReadToEnd();
        break;
    }
```

The first line of each triple data row in the text file is `NationalIDNumber`, and the second line represents `PersonalInformation` that is delimited with a vertical line (|); we fetch this information in the following lines of code:

```
string NationalIDNumber = reader.ReadLine();
    //Generate Personal Information Output Row
    string PersonalInformation = reader.ReadLine();
    string[] personalInfArray = PersonalInformation.Split('|');
```

AddRow

The `AddRow` method will create a new output row. After adding the output row, we can set the column data.

```
PersonalInformationOutputBuffer.AddRow();
        PersonalInformationOutputBuffer.NationalIDNumber =
          NationalIDNumber;
        PersonalInformationOutputBuffer.FirstName =
          personalInfArray[0];
        PersonalInformationOutputBuffer.LastName =
          personalInfArray[1];
        PersonalInformationOutputBuffer.Gender =
          personalInfArray[2];
        PersonalInformationOutputBuffer.MaritalStatus =
          personalInfArray[3];
```

The same process needs to be followed for **ProfessionalInformationOutput**.

Finally, `StreamReader` is closed in the `PostExecute` method.

See also

> ▸ The *Script Component as a Destination*

The Script Component as a Destination

Writing data at non-ordinal destinations and in special formats creates a need for some custom destinations in the Data Flow. The Script Component as *Destination* will help SSIS Developers get rid of such problems.

In this recipe, we read some data rows from a database query and load them into a text file destination in a specific format as shown here:

```
NationalIDNumber
FirstName|LastName|Gender|MaritalStatus
JobTitle;HireDate;DepartmentName;DepartmentGroupName;StartDate;EndDate
```

The first data row should have `NationalIDNumber`, the second data row should have personal information that's delimited by a vertical line (|), and finally the third row has professional information delimited by a semi colon (;). Each data stream row will be separated into three output rows with different formatting. The regular Flat File Destination cannot handle this format of output, so we handle this problem using a Script Component as *Destination*.

How to do it...

1. Create a new SSIS project and name it `R04_ScriptComponent As Destination`.

2. Create a package variable of the `String` data type, name it `DestinationFilePath` and set its default value to `C:\SSIS\Ch08_Scripting\R04_ScriptComponent As Destination\data.txt`.

3. Add a Data Flow Task and go to the **Data Flow** tab.

4. Add an **OLE DB Source** and link it to the `AdventureWorks2012` database. Set data access mode to *SQL Command* and write the following query in the **SQL Command** textbox:

```
SELECT EMP.NationalIDNumber, EMP.JobTitle, EMP.MaritalStatus,
   EMP.Gender, EMP.HireDate, DEP.Name, DEP.GroupName, DEPHST.
StartDate,
       DEPHST.EndDate, PER.FirstName, PER.LastName
FROM HumanResources.Department AS DEP
INNER JOIN HumanResources.EmployeeDepartmentHistory AS DEPHST
 ON DEP.DepartmentID = DEPHST.DepartmentID
INNER JOIN HumanResources.Employee AS EMP
 ON DEPHST.BusinessEntityID = EMP.BusinessEntityID
INNER JOIN Person.Person AS PER
 ON EMP.BusinessEntityID = PER.BusinessEntityID
```

5. Preview your columns and review the data structure.

NationalIDNumber	JobTitle	MaritalStatus	Gender	HireDate	Name	GroupName	StartDate	EndDate	FirstName	LastName
480168528	Tool Designer	M	M	1/11/2002 12:00:00 AM	Tool Design	Research and Development	1/11/2002 12:00:00 AM	NULL	Thierry	D'Hers
486228782	Tool Designer	M	F	1/23/2005 12:00:00 AM	Tool Design	Research and Development	1/23/2005 12:00:00 AM	NULL	Janice	Galvin
42487730	Senior Design Engineer	S	M	1/30/2005 12:00:00 AM	Engineering	Research and Development	1/30/2005 12:00:00 AM	NULL	Michael	Sullivan
24756624	Marketing Manager	M	M	1/26/2002 12:00:00 AM	Marketing	Sales and Marketing	5/16/2003 12:00:00 AM	NULL	David	Bradley
253022876	Marketing Assistant	S	M	2/28/2001 12:00:00 AM	Marketing	Sales and Marketing	2/26/2001 12:00:00 AM	NULL	Kevin	Brown
222969461	Marketing Specialist	S	M	3/10/2005 12:00:00 AM	Marketing	Sales and Marketing	3/10/2005 12:00:00 AM	NULL	John	Wood
52541518	Marketing Assistant	S	F	3/17/2005 12:00:00 AM	Marketing	Sales and Marketing	3/17/2005 12:00:00 AM	NULL	Mary	Dempsey
323403273	Marketing Assistant	M	F	2/7/2005 12:00:00 AM	Marketing	Sales and Marketing	2/7/2005 12:00:00 AM	NULL	Wanida	Benshoof
243222160	Marketing Specialist	M	M	4/3/2003 12:00:00 AM	Marketing	Sales and Marketing	4/2/2002 12:00:00 AM	NULL	Terry	Eminhizer
95958230	Marketing Specialist	S	M	1/13/2003 12:00:00 AM	Marketing	Sales and Marketing	1/13/2003 12:00:00 AM	NULL	Sariya	Harnpadoungsataya
767955365	Marketing Specialist	M	F	2/13/2003 12:00:00 AM	Marketing	Sales and Marketing	2/13/2003 12:00:00 AM	NULL	Mary	Gibson
72636981	Marketing Specialist	M	M	2/19/2005 12:00:00 AM	Marketing	Sales and Marketing	2/19/2005 12:00:00 AM	NULL	Jill	Williams
519999904	Vice President of Production	S	M	3/7/2002 12:00:00 AM	Production	Manufacturing	3/7/2003 12:00:00 AM	NULL	James	Hamilton
277173473	Production Control Manager	M	M	1/2/2002 12:00:00 AM	Production Control	Manufacturing	1/2/2003 12:00:00 AM	NULL	Peter	Krebs
446466105	Production Supervisor - WC60	S	F	3/30/2002 12:00:00 AM	Production	Manufacturing	3/30/2002 12:00:00 AM	NULL	Jo	Brown
14417807	Production Technician - WC60	M	M	7/31/2000 12:00:00 AM	Production	Manufacturing	7/31/2000 12:00:00 AM	NULL	Guy	Gilbert

6. Drag-and-drop a Script Component and set the **Select Script Component Type** as *Destination*.

7. In `ReadOnlyVariables`, check the `User::DestinationFilePath` variable.

8. Check all columns in the **Input Columns** tab.

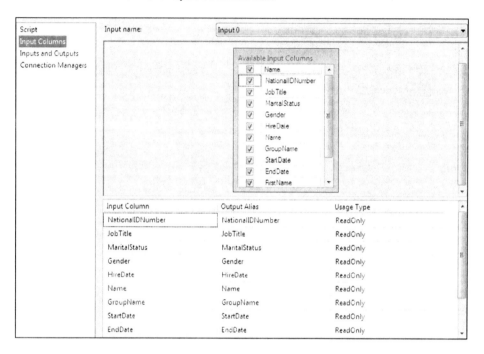

9. Go back to the **Script** tab and click on **Edit Script**.

10. In the `ScriptMain`'s class body, add a declaration of variables with the following lines:

```
StreamWriter writer = null;
    int RecordCount = 0;
```

11. In the `PreExecute` method, add header lines for the destination text file as follows:

```
public override void PreExecute()
{
  base.PreExecute();
  writer = new StreamWriter(
      this.Variables.DestinationFilePath,
      true);
  //write header rows
  writer.WriteLine("Employees Information");
  writer.WriteLine("Start Time: "
```

```
        + DateTime.Now.ToString("yyyy-MM-dd HH:mm:ss"));
    writer.WriteLine();
    writer.WriteLine("NationalIDNumber");
    writer.WriteLine("FirstName|LastName|Gender|MaritalStatus");
    writer.WriteLine("JobTitle;HireDate;DepartmentName;
      DepartmentGroupName;StartDate;EndDate");


}
```

12. In the `Input0_ProcessInputRow` method, add the following lines of code to write data into the text file as follows:

```
public override void Input0_ProcessInputRow(Input0Buffer Row)
{
    RecordCount++;

    writer.WriteLine("----------------------------");
    string firstdataRow =
        string.Format(
        "{0}",Row.NationalIDNumber);
    string seconddataRow =
        string.Format(
        "{0}|{1}|{2}|{3}"
        , Row.FirstName
        , Row.LastName
        , Row.Gender
        , Row.MaritalStatus);
    string thirddataRow =
        string.Format(
        "{0};{1};{2};{3};{4};{5}"
        , Row.JobTitle
        , Row.HireDate.ToString("yyyy-MM-dd HH:mm:ss")
        , Row.Name
        , Row.GroupName
        , Row.StartDate.ToString("yyyy-MM-dd HH:mm:ss")
        , Row.EndDate_IsNull ? string.Empty :
            Row.EndDate.ToString("yyyy-MM-dd HH:mm:ss"));
    writer.WriteLine(firstdataRow);
    writer.WriteLine(seconddataRow);
    writer.WriteLine(thirddataRow);
}
```

Scripting

13. In the `PostExecute` method, add footer lines to the end of the file and close the stream writer as follows:

```
public override void PostExecute()
{
    base.PostExecute();
    writer.WriteLine("End Of Data");
    writer.WriteLine("Finish Time: "
        + DateTime.Now.ToString("yyyy-MM-dd HH:mm:ss"));
    writer.WriteLine("Number of records : "
        + RecordCount.ToString());
    writer.Flush();
    writer.Close();
}
```

14. Close the Script Editor and run the package. After running the package check `data.txt` at the address which is set in the `DestinationFilePath` variable.

15. The complete package schema is shown here:

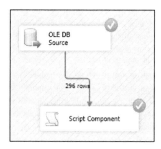

How it works...

Special destination formats such as what was required in this recipe are one of the most common scenarios of using the Script Component as a *Destination*. As expected, there is no need to have an output for the Script Component when its used as *Destination*, but there is no limitation here and we can add outputs to this kind of *Destination*.

The Script Component, when used as *Destination*, is similar to when using it as a *Transformation*, and there is an `InputName_ProcessInputRow` method there, which will be run for each row in the input data stream.

A destination is responsible for writing data out as expected, so we used the `ScriptWriter` class in `System.IO` to write data lines out to a text file. First of all, we instantiate the `ScriptWriter` class in the `PreExecute` method.

In the `PreExecute` method, some header lines for the text file will also be written with the `WriteLine` method from `StreamWriter`.

In the `Input0_ProcessInputRow` method, three data lines for output were generated using the `string.Format` method along with `Row.ColumnNames` and special delimiters, and we then wrote out to a text file with the `WriteLine` method.

Finally in the `PostExecute` method, some footer lines such as the "End Of Data" label and the number of records that were fetched from `ProcessInputRow` were added and the `StreamWriter` method closed.

The Asynchronous Script Component

As we discussed in previous chapters, Data Flow transformations are categorized into two categories based on their synchronization behavior: Synchronous and Asynchronous.

Synchronous Transformations process each input row, generate an output row at the same time, and then go to the next row. Asynchronous transformations stack incoming data and generate output based on some input records. An example of synchronous transformation is a Derived column, and an example of asynchronous transformation is Sort, because all rows have to be accumulated in order to sort them.

It's obvious that synchronous transformations are much better in terms of performance as compared to asynchronous transformations, but there are some cases where the only solution is an asynchronous transform.

The SSIS Script Component, when used in transformations, can act in both a synchronous and an asynchronous manner. In this recipe, we have a special type of input, which has its data in four rows, and we need to create a single output row with all of the combined data that's gathered from the four rows; so an asynchronous transformation should generate output records after reading every four rows.

Getting ready

Create a text file with the following data lines and name it `source.txt`; we will "Flat" this file data based on each person's information.

```
FirstName: Reza
LastName: Rad
Age: 31
Email: a.raad.g@gmail.com
FirstName: Pedro
LastName: Perfeito
Age: 31
```

```
Email: pperfeito@hotmail.com
FirstName: Phil
LastName: Brammer
Age: 34
Email: phil.brammer@gmail.com
```

How to do it...

1. Create a new SSIS project and name it R05_ScriptComponent Asynchronous.

2. Add a Data Flow Task from the SSIS Toolbox and go to the **Data Flow** tab.

3. Add a **Flat File Source** and create a connection to source.txt; don't check the column names in the first data row. In the **Columns** tab, set **Column delimiter** as *Colon {:}* and reset columns. In the **Advanced** tab, name the first column NameColumn and second column ValueColumn.

4. Close the Flat File Connection Manager and Flat File Source.

5. Drag-and-drop a Script Component as *Transformation* after the Flat File Source.

6. In the Script Component Editor, select all input columns in the **Input Columns** tab.

7. In the **Inputs and outputs** tab select *Output 0* and in the **Properties** pane set the **SynchronousInputID** property to *None*. We will discuss more about this setting in the *How it works...* section later.

8. Add these columns under **Output 0** with the `DT_STR` data type for **FirstName**, **LastName**, and **Email**. Add two other columns with the `DT_I4` data type and name them `Age` and `BirthYear`.

9. Confirm whether all your configurations conform to the following screenshot:

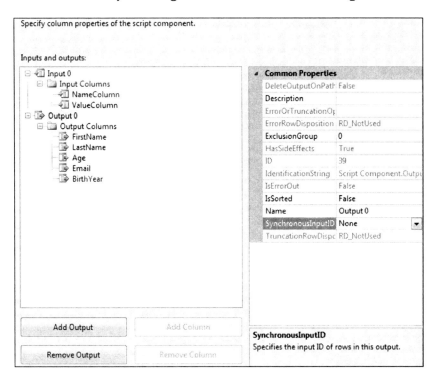

10. Go back to the **Script** tab and click on **Edit Script**.

11. In the script, override the `Input0_ProcessInput` method with the following code:

```
public override void Input0_ProcessInput(Input0Buffer Buffer)
    {
        while (Buffer.NextRow())
        {
            Input0_ProcessInputRow(Buffer);
        }

        if (Buffer.EndOfRowset())
        {
            Output0Buffer.SetEndOfRowset();
        }

    }
```

12. Add some lines of code to fetch appropriate `ValueColumn` values into the `Output0Buffer` columns in the `Input0_ProcessInputRow` method as follows:

```
public override void Input0_ProcessInputRow(Input0Buffer Row)
    {
        if (Row.NameColumn.Trim() == "FirstName")
            Output0Buffer.AddRow();

        switch (Row.NameColumn.Trim())
        {
            case "FirstName":
                Output0Buffer.FirstName = Row.ValueColumn;
                break;
            case "LastName":
                Output0Buffer.LastName = Row.ValueColumn;
                break;
            case "Age":
                int age = int.Parse(Row.ValueColumn);
                Output0Buffer.Age = age;
                Output0Buffer.BirthYear =
                    DateTime.Now.AddYears(0-age).Year;
                break;
            case "Email":
                Output0Buffer.Email = Row.ValueColumn;
                break;
        }
    }
```

13. Close the Script Component Editor, add an object type variable to the package, and then drag-and-drop a **Recordset Destination** after **Script Component**. Set the variable name there, select all input columns, and enable data viewers.

14. Run the package, and you will see output generated rows as shown in the next screenshot:

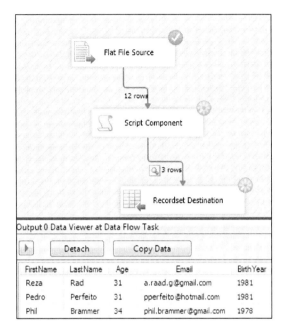

How it works...

The input text file in this recipe has a special format and four values sequentially stored in four different rows; the expected result is to combine all these rows into a single row within seperate columns. As the input text content's name and values are delimited by a colon, we used a Flat File Source with a colon delimiter to fetch **NameColumn** and **ValueColumn**.

SynchronousInputID

A Script Component as *Transformation* will act asynchronously if the **SynchronousInputID** property of the output is set to *None*. This property is set to input data stream ID by default, so this means that a Script Component as *Transformation* will work synchronously by default.

InputName_ProcessInput

This method will define how to process the input data stream. The method will execute once for `InputBuffer`.

In this recipe, we used a `while` structure to navigate between rows with the `Buffer.NextRow` method and called `Input0_ProcessInputRow` for each incoming data stream.

```
while (Buffer.NextRow())
    {
       Input0_ProcessInputRow(Buffer);
    }
```

When inputting records is completed, the rows generated as output should also be marked as finished, something that the `SetEndOfRowset` method used in this recipe took care of.

```
if (Buffer.EndOfRowset())
    {
       Output0Buffer.SetEndOfRowset();
    }
```

In the `Input0_ProcessInputRow` method, we defined the **FirstName** label as a starting row for each person's data, so when a row is found by **NameColumn** as **FirstName**, a new output row with `Output0Buffer.AddRow()` will be generated.

Other lines of code in `Input0_ProcessInputRow` find the appropriate row based on **NameColumn**'s data and feed the corresponding **ValueColumn**'s data into the output columns as defined earlier.

There's more...

Up to now, we have discussed some Script Component methods such as `PreExecute`, `PostExecute`, `ProcessInputRow`, and so on. The complete collection of methods in the Script Component provides more flexibility for programming; using each of these methods, however, is beyond the scope of this book. We will just take a quick look at each method and what it provides in the next part of this recipe.

Script component methods

We will now look at some Script Component methods:

AcquireConnection

Creating a script-side connection based on the package's connection managers can be done in this method.

Log

Log entries can be written to log providers with this method. `MessageCode`, `dataCode`, and `dataBytes` are the main parts of log entries.

PostExecute

The code for this method will run after processing inputs and outputs.

PreExecute

The code of this method will run before processing inputs and outputs.

ProcessInput

Process input data stream from inputs.

ReleaseConnection

Release the connection to the connection manager.

9
Deployment

by Reza Rad

In this chapter, we will cover the following topics:

- Project Deployment Model: Project Deployment from SSDT
- Using Integration Services Deployment Wizard and command-line utility for deployment
- Package Deployment Model: Using SSDT to deploy packages
- Creating and running Deployment Utility
- DTUTIL—the command-line utility for deployment
- Protection level: Securing sensitive data

Introduction

Till now you have read many chapters on the development of packages; this chapter focuses on another phase of ETL or data transfer implementation, which is **deployment**. Every package and project that we created in the previous chapters works correctly on SSDT. However, note that a production environment probably doesn't have SSDT installed, so we should deploy our packages to production on the SSIS server.

The SSIS packages and projects are saved on the local machine at the time of development. If we want to use them in the production environment, we need to save them in other locations considering the parameters. This process called deployment. There are two deployment models for SSIS packages. Project Deployment Model, which is a new model of deployment presented by SSIS 2012. Project Deployment works with SSIS Catalog. In this chapter, we will see how to deploy projects in this model using the SSIS Catalog.

The other deployment model, which is Package Deployment Model, has been available from SSIS 2005 and 2008. In this mode, packages work separately, so deployment can be done package by package, or by creating a deployment utility for all the packages in the project. There are three locations for storing packages in this mode: the file system, SQL Server, and the SSIS package store. We will explore this deployment model and will discuss SSIS locations and their pros and cons.

As SSIS packages contain sensitive data like connection passwords besides structural data like ETL approach and implementation details, accessing these types of data should be controlled. Protection Level is a method to protect access to a package's information. There are six types of Protection Level, each of which can be used in particular situations, and we will take a look at some of the most important types of Protection Level in this chapter.

Project Deployment Model: Project Deployment from SSDT

SSDT is not a tool only for SSIS Package Development, but also for deployment of packages. There are two types of deployment models in SSIS 2012. In this recipe, we will take a look at Project Deployment Model with SSDT and in the fourth recipe of this chapter we will take a look at Package Deployment Model.

To use Project Deployment Model, we need an SSIS Catalog. SSIS Catalog is a repository for SSIS projects, which also manages their versioning and parameters. We will take a look at how to execute packages and get reports from SSIS Catalog in the next chapters.

Getting ready

Create an SSIS Catalog as follows:

1. Open SSMS from **Start | Microsoft SQL Server | SQL Server Management Studio**.

2. Connect to **Database Engine** (default instance like machine name or instance name such as machine_name\instance_name).

3. In the **Object Explorer**, expand the **Integration Services Catalogs** under the database server node. If there is no SSIS Catalog there, right-click on it and click on **Create Catalog** as shown in the following screenshot:

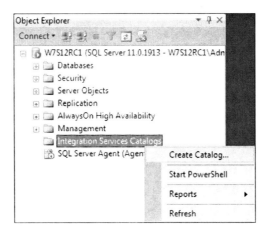

4. The **Create Catalog** window will open. Note that CLR integration should be enabled to use catalogs, so check the **Enable CLR Integration** option. Catalogs use encryption to protect their data, so you need to set a password for encryption.

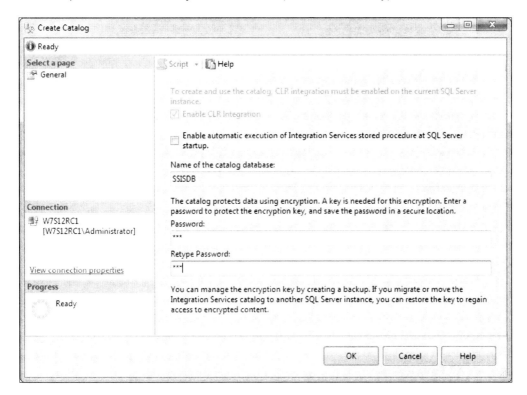

5. SSISDB Catalog will appear under the **Integration Services Catalogs** folder after successful operation.

How to do it...

1. Create an SSIS project and name it `R01_Deployment from SSDT`.

2. Rename `Package.dtsx` to `P01_Master.dtsx`.

3. Add a new package (right-click on the SSIS `Packages` folder in the Solution Explorer and add a new package) and name it `P02_Child.dtsx`.

4. In the `P02_Child.dtsx` package, add the following variable:

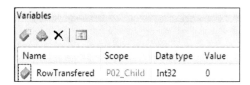

5. Add a **Data Flow** task from the toolbox and name it `DFT - Export Sales Order Headers to CSV`.

6. Inside the **Data Flow** tab, add an **OLE DB Source** and create a connection to the `AdventureWorks2012` database, and select `[Sales].[SalesOrderHeader]` as source table.

7. Add a **Row Count Transformation** after the OLE DB Source and select the **User::RowTransfered** variable there.

8. Add a **Flat File Destination** after the **Row Count Transform**, set **File type** as **Delimited**, and create a new flat file connection to `Destination.csv` file in this folder: `C:\SSIS\Ch09_Deployment\Files`. Note that this file shouldn't exist; just the path and filename should be set.

9. The whole schema of Data Flow should look similar to the following screenshot:

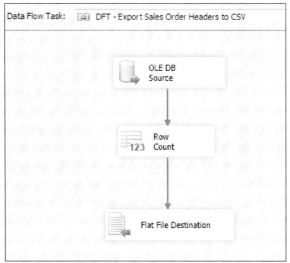

10. Run this script to create a table in the PacktPub_SSISbook database:

```
CREATE TABLE [dbo].[TransferLog](
   [ID] [int] IDENTITY(1,1) NOT NULL,
   [ExportDateTime] [datetime] NULL,
   [RowTransfered] [int] NULL,
 CONSTRAINT [PK_TransferLog] PRIMARY KEY CLUSTERED
(
   [ID] ASC
)WITH (PAD_INDEX = OFF, STATISTICS_NORECOMPUTE = OFF, IGNORE_
DUP_KEY = OFF, ALLOW_ROW_LOCKS = ON, ALLOW_PAGE_LOCKS = ON) ON
[PRIMARY]
) ON [PRIMARY]
```

11. Add an **Execute SQL Task** after the Data Flow Task and rename it to `SQL - Log into TransferLog Table`.

12. In the **Execute SQL Task Editor**, create a new OLE DB connection to `PacktPub_SSISbook`, and in the SQL statement write the following SQL statements:

```
INSERT INTO [dbo].[TransferLog]
            ([ExportDateTime]
            ,[RowTransfered])
      VALUES
            (getdate()
            ,?>)
```

13. Add a Script Task and connect Failure Precedence Constraint from Data Flow Task to Script Task; rename this task to `SCR - Send Mail`. We don't explain the details of the Script Task, but you can refer to the recipe *Script Task; Scripting through Control Flow* discussed in *Chapter 8, Scripting*, to implement it.

14. The whole schema of the child package's Control Flow should look similar to the following screenshot:

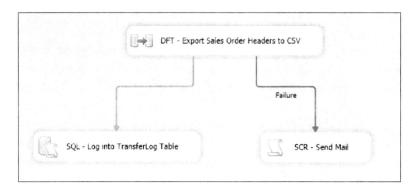

15. Open the master package and add an Execute Package Task in Control Flow and rename it to `EPT - Transfer Sales Order Header`.

16. In the **Execute Package Task Editor's Package** tab, set **ReferenceType** as **Project Reference**, and select **P02_Child.dtsx** as shown in the following screenshot:

17. In the previous step, we created the SSIS project as a working sample and now we will deploy this project into SSIS Catalog.

18. In the Solution Explorer, right-click on **Project name** and select **Deploy**.

19. **Integration Services Deployment Wizard** will be opened; skip the first step, which is the introduction step.

20. In the **Server name**, select the computer to which you want to deploy the package; we used local machine for this sample.

21. In the **Path**, click on **Browse**, and select the folder you want to deploy to. Create a new folder under **SSIDB** and name it DeployedFromSSDT. Select this folder and go to the next step.

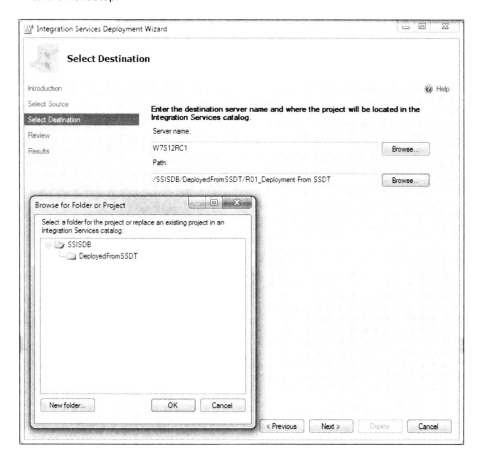

22. The next step will review all settings; you can check everything you've done and return back and change them if you want. Go to the next step.

23. The final step is the **Results** step; deployment results like success or error message will show up here.

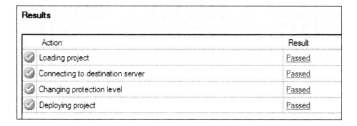

24. To verify deployment, open SSMS. Expand **Integration Service Catalogs**, under **SSISDB** and under the `DeployedFromSSDT` folder the **R01_Deployment From SSDT** project exists and under it you will find all packages (`P01_Master` and `P02_Child`).

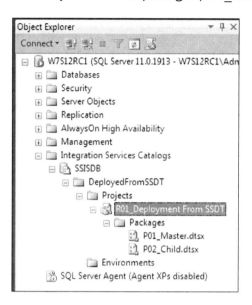

How it works...

Deployment is the next phase after development and test of SSIS packages. There are two different models for deployment in SSIS 2012. The model that was used in this recipe was the Project Deployment Model, which is the latest model provided by SSIS 2012.

In Project Deployment Model, the whole SSIS project will be deployed as a project and the dependent items such as packages, connection managers, and parameters will be deployed under the project. In this deployment model, SSIS packages can relate together simply with their names. Note that we used Execute Package Task with **Reference Type** as **Project Reference** (step 16); with this configuration we just need to select the name of the package that we want to execute, not the whole physical address for the package file.

The Project Deployment Model will deploy the whole SSIS project into SSIS Catalog. Note that we cannot deploy the project to any other place than SSIS Catalog because this is the only location available when we want to use Project Deployment Model. Package Deployment Model, which will be discussed in the next recipes, has more options for choosing location. However, SSIS Catalog provides a way to control the whole SSIS project as a single object, working with parameters, and configuring the whole package and the project is much simpler here. We will take a look at the advantages of SSIS Catalog in *Chapter 12, Execution*.

SSIS Catalog also provides a lot of reports, which help maintain, support, and check the execution process of SSIS packages; we will take a brief look at different reports provided by SSIS 2012 and their usages.

Using Integration Services Deployment Wizard and command-line utility for deployment

The deployment of a project from SSDT is very easy but not very common, because it needs SSDT to be installed somewhere. It is very common that SSIS projects are developed under a development machine in the company but the production environment is in another workplace or network, so SSDT can't be used in these situations. We need to deploy the project without having SSDT.

There are two ways to deploy a project in Project Deployment Model: one of them is through SSDT, which was described in the previous recipe. Another way is to use the Integration Services Deployment Wizard to deploy the project from ISPAC files; we will deploy the same project from the previous recipe in this way without SSDT.

Getting ready

This recipe needs the project from the previous recipe.

How to do it...

1. Open the `R01_Deployment From SSDT` project in **SSDT**.
2. Right-click on **Project** and select **Build**.
3. Go to the project folder at `C:\SSIS\Ch09_Deployment\R01_Deployment From SSDT\bin\Development`.
4. You will see a file with the `.ispac` extension. The name of the file by default is the same as the project name. Double-click on it to run the wizard.

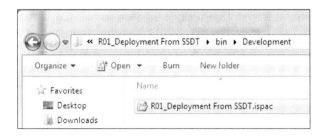

5. The **Integration Services Deployment Wizard** will open. In the **Select Source** step, the default option is the **project deployment file**. You don't need to change this setting; this will point to the ISPAC file.

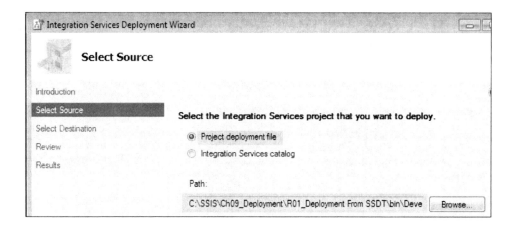

6. In the **Select Destination** step, select the deployment server and then create a new folder in the path under SSISDB and name it DeploymentFromWizard. Follow the remaining steps to complete the wizard.

7. Check the deployed project in SSMS under **Integration Services Catalog**.

8. Till now we deployed the project by running the ISPAC file directly; running the ISPAC file will open the **Integration Services Deployment Wizard**, now we will see how to open this wizard without the need of an ISPAC file.

9. Go to C:\Program Files\Microsoft SQL Server\110\DTS\Binn and open the ISDeploymentWizard.exe file.

10. The same Integration Services Deployment Wizard will open. We don't want to run the steps again. Just note that we can use ISDeployomentWizard to deploy a source project to SSIS Catalog. The source also can be another project under the SSIS Catalog.

11. Another way to deploy the project is using the ISDeploymentWizard command-line utility; this will help to deploy the project in silent mode.

12. Open a command prompt (Type cmd in the **Run** window), go to this path: C:\Program Files\Microsoft SQL Server\110\DTS\Binn, and then type the following statement:

    ISDeploymentWizard /?

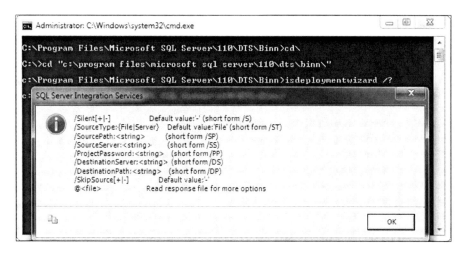

13. You will see a window showing all available switches for running the wizard in the command-line mode.

14. Leave the command prompt window open and open SSMS and under **Integration Services Catalogs** under **SSISDB** add a folder and name it `DeployedInSilentMode`.

15. Go back to the command prompt window, close the **Help** window, and then type the following statement to deploy the project to a folder named `DeployedInSilentMode`:

```
ISDeploymentWizard /S:+ /SP:"C:\SSIS\Ch09_Deployment\R01_
Deployment From SSDT\bin\Development\R01_Deployment From SSDT.
ispac" /DS:. /DP:"/SSISDB/DeployedInSilentMode/R01_Deployment From
SSDT"
```

16. Go to SSMS and check the created folder and deployed project there.

How it works...

This is a very common case that the production machine has no SSDT installed; the production machine is intended to run packages and projects and not for development or debugging. So it is an essential requirement that we can deploy our projects without SSDT.

In this recipe, we walked through two different ways of deploying an SSIS project in Project Deployment Model:

▶ Deployment using Integration Services Deployment Wizard graphical user interface

▶ Deployment using Integration Services Deployment Wizard command-line utility

ISPAC file

After building an SSIS project, it will be compiled and stored in an ISPAC file. Typically this file has the same name as the project and its extension is `.ispac`. We can use this file for deploying the project without the need for SSDT. With this file in hand, the source SSIS packages and other project files are not needed anymore.

You can change the ISPAC filename by right-clicking on the project name in **Solution Explorer** and selecting **Properties**. In the left panel, select **Project** under the **Common Properties**, and in the right pane, change the **Name** property.

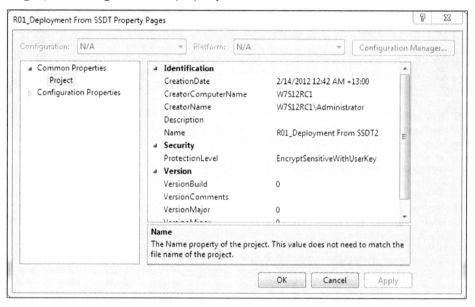

Integration Services Deployment Wizard graphical user interface

The Integration Services Deployment Wizard provides a graphical user interface with very easy steps to follow and deploy an SSIS project. This tool will be installed with SSIS installation on a machine. The steps are very easy: the first step is to select the source. In the Select source step, we can choose the source from a project file, which is a `*.ispac` file, or from a server, which can be another project under the SSIS Catalog on an integration services server. The destination can be a location under the SSIS Catalog.

Integration Services Deployment Wizard command-line utility

The graphical user interface is easy to use, but it needs to be run by a user who knows the SSIS Catalog and ISPAC files, and note that in many cases the production machine user doesn't know anything about SSIS. So the Integration Services Deployment Wizard has a command-line utility part, which can be run under silent mode without interaction with the user. You can just create a `.bat` file and give it to user and say *Run it!* There are some switches for the Integration Services Deployment Wizard command-line utility.

For using Silent mode (Silent mode means running the wizard without any user interaction and dialog boxes), you should use `/S:+`. for setting the source you can use `/ST` for source type which can be File (which means an ISPAC file), or Server (which means a project under the SSIS Catalog). All other switches are very simple and easy understand. You can to get help by running `ISDeploymentWizard.exe /?`.

Another example of using the command-line utility is :

```
ISDeploymentWizard /S:+ /ST:Server /SS:Server1 /SS:"/SSISDB/FolderX/
ProjectY" /DS:Server2 /DP:"/SSISDB/ProjectZ"
```

This command will create another copy of `ProjectY` from the source address Server1 to Server2 with the new name `ProjectZ` and all operation will be in silent mode.

The Package Deployment Model, Using SSDT to deploy package

There is a legacy Deployment Model, which is the Package Deployment Model. The Package Deployment Model is completely based on packages instead of projects. So each package deploys independently and there is no advantage to having all packages in one project for deployment purposes.

Package Deployment Model was the only deployment model for SSIS 2005 and 2008. As we discussed earlier, the Project Deployment Model is much better for a project environment, but as we are working legacy models with SSDT, we should know how to deploy in legacy model.

In this recipe, first we convert a project to Package Deployment Model, and then we deploy the child package with SSDT.

Getting ready

Convert the project to the Package Deployment Model:

1. Create a project and name it `R03_Package Deployment Model`.
2. Remove the `package.dtsx` file and copy `P02_Child.dtsx` from the `R01_Deployment from SSDT` project to this one.

3. Right-click on the project name in Solution Explorer and select **Convert to Package Deployment Model**.

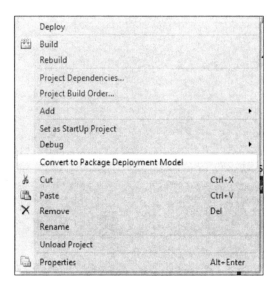

4. Follow a few steps to complete the wizard. The steps are very easy because we don't have any special Project Deployment Model usage in the P02_Child.dtsx package so conversion should be very simple to do.

5. After conversion, check the changes in Solution Explorer; the Project icon will have been changed already and in parenthesis you will see **(package deployment model)**.

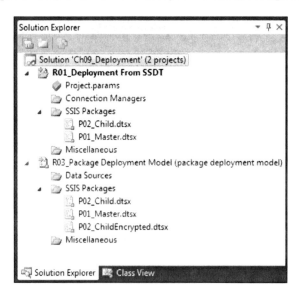

How to do it...

1. After changing to Package Deployment Model, Open the `P02_Child.dtsx` package.

2. Click on an empty area in **Control Flow** and then go to the **File** menu and select **Save Copy of P02_Child.dtsx As ...**.

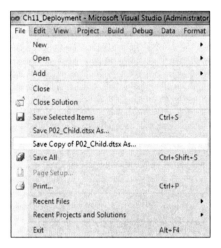

3. Next the **Save Copy of Package** window will open. Leave **Package Location** as **File System**, and set the package path as `C:\SSIS\Ch09_Deployment\Files\ PackageFromSSDT.dtsx`. Click on the **OK** button.

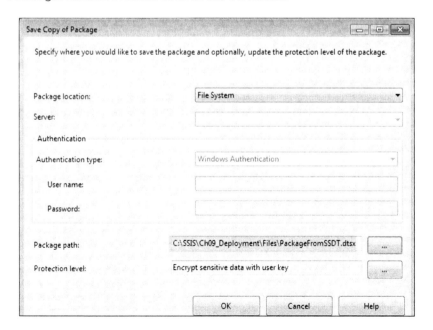

4. The package will be copied to the `C:\SSIS\Ch09_Deployment\Files\PackageFromSSDT.dtsx` path; you can check it with Windows Explorer. Choosing the **File System** as location will copy the package to another location.

5. We want to deploy the package to another location this time. Open the **Save Copy Of Package** window as we described in step 2. Set **Package Location** as **SQL Server**. Choose the **Server** name, which is the SQL Database Engine Server name. Set the authentication mode appropriately. (Authentication mode is the way you connect to SQL Server. In all the samples in this book we used Windows authentication, which needs the current user to have appropriate privilege on SQL Server.)

6. Finally, set the package path. Note that when you click on **Browse**, you will see a tree of folders; set the destination folder and **Package path** as:

   `/PackageFromSSDTToSQLServer.`

7. Open SSMS, and connect to Integration Services. Set **Server name** as the name of the computer that is the SSIS Server. (We used computer name in many of our samples in this book as server name.)

8. In the Object Explorer, under **Stored Packages** and under **MSDB** you will find the deployed package. In this mode, the package will be deployed to a table in the MSDB database in SQL Server.

How it works...

Package Deployment Model is the legacy deployment model, which was in use in SSIS 2005 and 2008. This deployment model has some problems: Packages are not related together in one project and they should be deployed separately, deployed packages have no versioning and other historical records in the server, and some other problems.

Project Deployment Model is intended to solve these problems and it actually does its duty very well, but SSIS needs to be backward compatible, which is the reason why we need to use Package Deployment Model. So if you develop an SSIS project that doesn't need to be backward compatible, use the Project Deployment Model.

Package Deployment Model, as we explained till now, is based on single packages. Each single package is a core item in deployment. There are other ways to deploy multiple packages together in this model, and we will discuss them in the next recipes.

There are three ways to deploy packages in Package Deployment Model. The easiest way is to use SSDT and use the **Save a Copy of Package.dtsx as** window, which we described in this recipe. The other two are described in the next recipes of this chapter: Deployment Utility and DTUTIL.

In this model, we need to select **Package Location**. **Package Location** can be three different spaces:

File system

Packages are XML coded files with the .dtsx extension. These files can be simply located in a physical folder in network storage or the local computer. Using a file system location is exactly copying the .dtsx file into a physical location. The location can be anywhere; the only restriction is that write permission to the folder should exist.

SQL Server

SQL Server provides a way to store SSIS packages in the database. In this mode, the SSIS package will be stored in the MSDB database, which is one of the SQL Server system databases. The table name is sysssispackages. There are also some virtual folders under MSDB for storing packages; these folders are stored in the sysssispackagefolders table.

In this mode if you want to get a backup of SSIS packages to move them to another server you just need to back up the MSDB database, and restore it on destination.

SSIS package store

This mode is the combination of file system and SQL Server. In the following screenshot, there are two folders under the SSIS package store: one of them is **MSDB**, which is the same as SQL Server storage, which we described earlier. The other one is **File System**. The only difference with the ordinary file system storage is that in this mode deployment will be done to the default physical folder that is addressed in `MsDtsSrvr.ini.xml`. The XML file can be found here: `C:\Program Files\Microsoft SQL Server\110\DTS\Binn`.

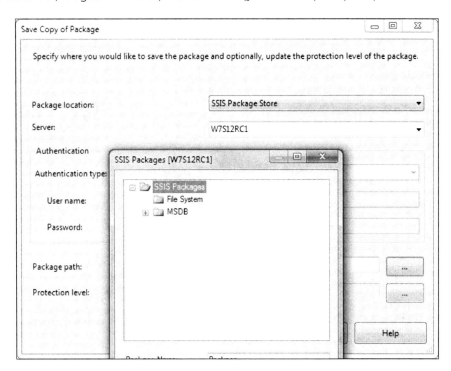

Creating and running Deployment Utility

SSDT provides a very easy way to deploy packages, but one of the big cons of this method of deployment is that if we have 100 SSIS packages then we should do 100 times *Save Copy of package as*!

We need to create a setup for all packages in the project. Fortunately, SSDT provides a way to create a setup kit named Deployment Utility. Deployment Utility contains all packages and their relevant files in the project with an `SSISDeploymentManifest` file, which is something like an installation file.

In this recipe, we will create a Deployment Utility and run it to deploy packages.

How to do it...

1. Open the `R03_Package` Deployment Model project in SSDT.

2. In Solution Explorer, right-click on the project's name and select **Properties**.

3. On the **Project Property** page, under **Configuration Properties** click on **Deployment**.

4. Set **CreateDeploymentUtitlity** to *True*.

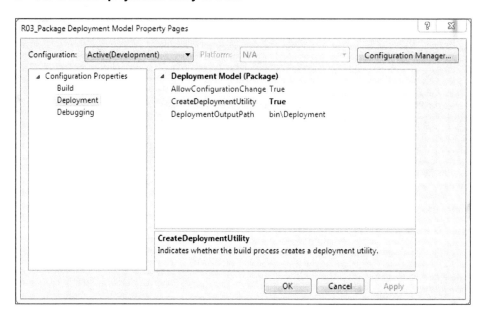

5. You can also change deployment folder in the `DeploymentOutputPath` property. However, for the sake of simplicity we leave this property as default.

6. Close the **Property** page, right-click on the project in Solution Explorer again and select **Build**. This will create Deployment Utility.

7. Go to the project folder and you will see two files there; one of them is the package file with the `.dtsx` extension and the other one is named with the SSIS project's name with the `.SSISDeploymentManifest` extension.

8. Double-click on the **R03_Package Deployment Model.SSISDeploymentManifest** file and the **Package Installation Wizard** will open. Skip the first step, which is an introduction. In the **Deploy SSIS Packages** step, choose **SQL Server deployment**.

9. In the **Specify Target SQL Server** step, enter the details of the SQL Server to which we want to deploy as destination, set SQL Server instance, and set Package Path as single slash: / . This will deploy to root.

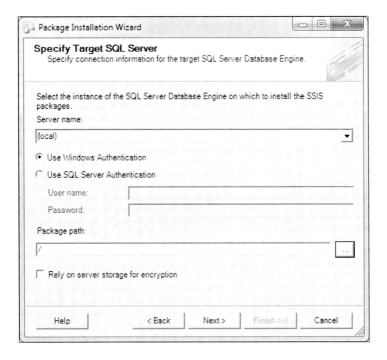

10. The **Select Installation Folder** step is the step to store other files that are relevant to SSIS packages, like configuration files. Leave the default settings; in this sample we don't have any other file than the package itself.

11. Confirm Installation and Finish deployment. Now you can check the Integration Service in SSMS to see the deployed package.

How it works...

Deployment Utility works like a setup kit for SSIS packages in a project. We can create the Deployment Utility simply by setting the `CreateDeploymentUtility` property of the project to *true*, as we did in step 4 of this recipe, and then building the project.

Be careful about this property (`CreateDeploymentUtility`), as long as this property set to *true*, with every compile, build, or run in SSDT, the Deployment Utility will build again. So remember to always turn this property to *false* after creating Deployment Utility.

Deployment Utility Ingredients

1. The SSIS deployment manifest file is a setup file, which can be run with every machine that has the appropriate version of SSIS installed.

2. SSIS Packages—all SSIS packages in the project will be present besides the deployment manifest.

   ❏ Configuration Files—in SSIS 2005 and 2008 there were some configuration files, which helped packages to read the values of variable, task, and component properties and configuration manager properties from outside of the package. One of these configuration types is XML configuration, which stores values in an XML config file. If the package uses this type of configuration, then all XML configuration files will be in the deployment kit.

3. Any file which is in the `Miscellaneous` folder of the SSIS project.

This method of deployment is much more in use than the previous method with SSDT, because SSDT isn't available in many production environments.

DTUTIL—the command-line utility for deployment

Package Deployment Model is based on packages and this means that every package should be deployed independently, but Deployment Utility can help to create one setup kit for all packages. Deployment Utility is helpful but it needs a user who is familiar with SSIS to choose destination type, set server properties, and other things which were in Package Installation Wizard. There should be a method to deploy everything without interaction with the user in silent mode.

Fortunately, SSIS provides a command-line utility—DTUTIL.exe—for Package Deployment Model. We can write statements on DTUTIL to deploy packages in silent mode.

In this recipe, we take a look at how to deploy packages with DTUTIL.

How to do it...

1. Open the command-prompt window and go to the following path in the command prompt:

    `C:\Program Files\Microsoft SQL Server\110\DTS\Binn`

2. Type the following command:

    `DTUTIL /?`

3. A list of switches for DTUTIL will appear.

4. Now enter the following command:

    `DTUTIL /SQL \P02_Child /COPY SQL;\PackageDeployedFromDTUtil`

5. Open SSMS and connect to Integration Services; under MSDB and under **Stored Packages** you will see PackageDeployedFromDTUtil created already.

6. This command deploys a package from SQL Server to another location in SQL Server.

7. Run the following statement in the command prompt:

   ```
   DTUTIL /SQL \PackageDeployedFromDTUtil /Exists
   ```

8. You will see that the result says that *The specified package exists*.

9. This command checks the existence of a package in SQL Server with a specific path.

10. Run the following command:

    ```
    DTUTIL /SQL \P02_child /COPY File;C:\SSIS\NewPackage.dtsx
    ```

11. Then check the `C:\SSIS` folder; you will see `newpackage.dtsx` there.

12. This command deploys a package from SQL Server to file system.

13. Run the following command:

    ```
    DTUTIL /FC SQL;\;myDepFolder
    ```

14. Check SSMS and you will see `myDepFolder` created under **MSDB | Stored Packages**.

15. This command creates a folder in SQL Server under the root with the name `myDepFolder`.

16. Run the following command:

    ```
    DTUTIL /File C:\SSIS\NewPackage.dtsx /DestServer . /Copy SQL;\
    myDepFolder\AnotherPackage
    ```

17. Check SSMS again and you will see `AnotherPackage` deployed under `myDepFolder`.

18. This command deploys a package from the file system to SQL Server specifying the destination server.

19. Run the following command:

    ```
    DTUTIL /help Copy
    ```

20. You will see a quick help message for the Copy switch.

```
Administrator: C:\Windows\system32\cmd.exe

C:\Program Files\Microsoft SQL Server\110\DTS\Binn>dtutil /help copy
Microsoft (R) SQL Server SSIS Package Utilities
Version 11.0.1913.37 for 32-bit
Copyright (C) Microsoft Corporation 2012. All rights reserved.

C[opy] {SQL | FILE | DTS};Path

Operation. Copy the package to the specified location and path.

Examples:
o Copy from a SQL server to a SSIS store's MSDB folder on the local machine.
        dtutil /SQL srcPackage /Copy DTS;MSDB\destPackage

o Copy from a file system to a file system.
        dtutil /File c:\developmentpackages\package.dtsx
                /Copy file;c:\testpackages\newpackage.dtsx

o Copy from a file system to a SQL server on another machine.
        dtutil /File c:\developmentpackages\package.dtsx /DestServer myotherserver
                /copy SQL;newpackage

Note: Windows Authentication is used since /DestU[ser] and /DestP[assword]
        were not used.

C:\Program Files\Microsoft SQL Server\110\DTS\Binn>_
```

How it works...

DTUTIL is a simple command-line utility that provides all the deployment options in Package Deployment Model. We can use this command line for deploying packages, creating and removing folders, checking existence, and every other operation related to deployment.

The syntax of DTUTIL is very simple. There are some switches, the description of which you can find with a simple `DTUTIL /Help <Switch Name>`. The list of all switches and their usages and examples can be found in BOL at the following address:

`http://msdn.microsoft.com/en-us/library/ms162820.aspx`

We tried to use examples of the most common usages of DTUTIL in this recipe. You can play with their options and switches to become more familiar with this command-line utility.

There's more...

Using DTUTIL commands requires understanding more aspects in production environments. We will take a look at these aspects.

DTUTIL exit codes

Running DTUTIL from other applications will return some codes to show what happened after running the command; these are **DTUTIL exit codes**. A list of all codes with their descriptions is in the following table:

Value	Description
0	The utility executed successfully.
1	The utility failed.
4	The utility cannot locate the requested package.
5	The utility cannot load the requested package.
6	The utility cannot resolve the command line because it contains either syntactic or semantic errors.

The preceding table directly comes from the following URL: `http://msdn.microsoft.com/en-us/library/ms162820.aspx`.

Multiple packages deployment

DTUTIL can only deploy one package at a time, so if you want to use it like a setup kit, you can create a BAT file (a file with the `.bat` extension), and write DTUTIL commands one after another. Or you can write a .NET application (or use any other language and framework) to loop through SSIS packages and deploy them all.

Protection level: Securing sensitive data

Packages are XML files; all Control Flow and Data Flow settings, every task and component are listed in the XML file. So accessing this file needs to be considered before deployment.

SSIS provides a way to protect information stored in packages with encryption. There are a number of options for how that encryption can be opened. Packages contain two types of data: data related to structure of data transfer, like Data Flow components or Control Flow tasks, and connection string passwords or any other information that is very important and shouldn't be easy to access; this information is called **sensitive data**.

There are a number of protection levels to protect a package's information. In this recipe, we will talk about protection levels and how to use them and their differences.

How to do it...

1. Open **R03_Package Deployment Model project in SSDT**.

2. Open `P02_Child.dtsx`, click on an empty area in Control Flow, then go to the **File** menu and then **Save Copy of Package**.

3. Set **Package location** as *SQL Server*, set server name (in this sample we used the current machine default instance so it is only single dot: .), set **Authentication**, and set **Package path** as */P02_ChildEncrypted*.

4. The default **Package protection level** is *Encrypt sensitive data with user key*; click on the ellipsis button beside it and set the protection level as *Encrypt Sensitive data with Password*. Enter the password as *123* and its confirmation in the relevant boxes.

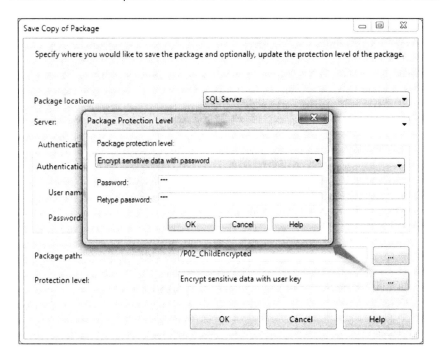

5. After deployment, you can go to SSMS and see the `P02_ChildEncrypted` package there.

6. Go back to SSDT, add another package to the project and name it `P01_Master.dtsx`.

7. Add an Execute Package Task to Control Flow and in the Execute Package Task Editor, set **Location** as **SQL Server**, and create a connection to the server on which **P02_ChildEncrypted** is deployed. Set the package name as *\P02_ChildEncrypted*.

8. Leave the other boxes as their default values, and run the package.

9. You will get an error message after running the `P01_Master` package, which is:

```
Error 0xC0012050 while preparing to load the package. Package
failed validation from the ExecutePackage task. The package cannot
run
```

10. The error is because we need to set the password to run the package, so open the Execute Package Task Editor and set the password as *123*.

11. Run the package again and verify that everything is now successful.

12. Till now we have tried to run an encrypted package. Now we try to open an encrypted package to see what happens if someone who doesn't know the password tries to open the package.

13. In SSDT, right-click on SSIS `Packages` folder and click on **Add Existing Package**.

14. The **Add Copy of Existing Package** window will open; set the package location as SQL Server, set server name as the machine on which `P02_ChildEncrypted` is deployed, and set the package name as */P02_ChildEncrypted*.

15. Next click on the **OK** button. You will see a dialog box with the header **Package Password**. As the package is encrypted you need to enter the password to open it.

16. Type a wrong password there, like `321`, the package won't open, but if you click on the **Cancel** button in this dialog box then the package will be added to the project.

17. Open the `P02_ChildEncrypted` package, and open OLE DB Connection Manager. Note that every connection that used SQL Server authentication has no saved password now, and if you don't enter the password you cannot run the package.

How it works...

Protection level is a way of protecting a package's information. To use protection levels properly it is better to first describe what the sensitive data is.

Sensitive data

Sensitive data is any of the following information:

- ▶ Password parts of connection strings
- ▶ Parameters that are set as sensitive

Protection level types

There are six protection level types which are described as follows:

Do Not Save Sensitive

In this mode, all sensitive information will be removed before deploying the package; this mode can be useful when you want to use Windows Authentication in connection managers.

Encrypt Sensitive with User Key

This mode will encrypt sensitive data and it can only be decrypted if the same user with the same user profile opens the package. If another user with another profile tries to open this package, all sensitive information won't be shown to him/her and the user should enter the sensitive information again. This is the default type so every package that has no protection level will use this protection level by default and no one except the original user can see the sensitive data.

Encrypt Sensitive with Password

Sensitive data will be encrypted. Everyone who wants to use the package needs the password with which the package was deployed. If someone does not have the password then the package will be open but the sensitive data won't show up. This is one of the most useful protection levels. Note that we used this type in our recipe.

Encrypt All with User Key

All information will be encrypted and only the same user with same profile which developed and published the package can open it. Other users cannot open this package.

Encrypt All with Password

All information will be encrypted and only users who have the password can open the package. Without the correct password no one can open the package.

Rely on Server Storage

In this mode, all package information will be stored without any encryption. The benefit of this mode is that this mode relies on SQL Server security. Note that you can only use this mode if you deploy the package on SQL Server.

There's more...

Protection level can be set from other locations other than at the time of deployment. Described next you will find two other places to set the protection level.

The ProtectionLevel property of a package

Click on an empty area in the package's Control Flow and then go to the **Properties** window. You will see the **ProtectionLevel** property there.

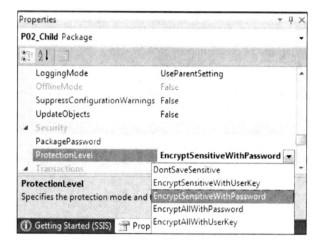

Protection level in project properties

With Project Deployment Model, you can set the protection level at project's properties. In Solution Explorer, right-click on the project (**R01_Deployment** from **SSDT**), and select **Properties**.

In the **Property Page** window, click on **Common Properties** in the left pane, and in the right pane you will see the **ProtectionLevel** property and you can set it as needed.

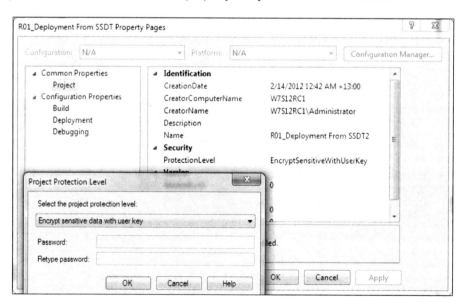

Protection level in DTUTIL

You can set the protection level of the package at the time of deployment with the DTUTIL command-line utility. The switch for encryption is **Encrypt**, which can be used with the following options:

Option code	Protection level
0	Do Not Save Sensitive
1	Save Sensitive with User Key
2	Save Sensitive with Password
3	Save All with Password
4	Save All with User Key
5	Rely on Server Storage

10

Debugging, Troubleshooting, and Migrating Packages to 2012

by Reza Rad and Pedro Perfeito

In this chapter, we will cover:

▸ Troubleshooting with Progress and Execution Results Tab

▸ Breakpoints, Debugging the Control Flow

▸ Handling errors in Data Flow

▸ Migrating packages to 2012

▸ Data Tap

Introduction

SSIS is a Rapid Application Development tool that helps developers to create data transfer packages with designers and needs less coding, so that the development speed will be much faster. On the other hand, a development tool needs debugging and error-handling features. Fortunately SSIS has a debugging feature in Control Flow scope, also error handling fortified SSIS packages.

In this chapter, we will take a deep look at debugging in Control Flow and error handling in Data Flow. More event handler options will be discussed in a separate chapter later in this book.

SSIS 2012 provides some Views and Stored Procedures that monitor SSIS packages and helps SSIS administrator in some administrative tasks. This feature is one of the advantages of SSIS 2012 over its prior versions. In this chapter, we will discuss these management views.

Migrating from the earlier versions of SSIS such as 2005, 2008, and 2008R2 to 2012 is fully supported in SSIS 2012. There is a migration wizard which helps the migration process to be much faster and more reliable. Also, we should note that a few tasks in 2012 are no longer supported such as, ActiveX Task and Execute DTS 2000 Package Task. We will take a look at the migration wizard and how to troubleshoot migration issues in this chapter.

Troubleshooting with Progress and Execution Results tab

Progress and **Execution Results** tab shows some useful information about the package running, validation phases, warnings and errors, and their description. For a SSIS developer who wants to troubleshoot his package these tabs have a lot of useful information.

In this recipe, we will take a look at how this information can be useful and how we can use it in debugging and troubleshooting of packages.

Getting ready

Create a text file named `R01_source.txt`. Enter the following data lines in the file and then place it in the **Files** folder in the **SSIS Project** folder, `C:\SSIS\Ch09_Debugging Troubleshooting and Migrating Packages to 2012`:

```
ID,Firstname,LastName
1,Reza,Rad
2,Pedro,Perfeito
three,Mark,Dastin
```

How to do it...

1. Create a SSIS project and name it `R01_Progress and Execution Results Tab`.

2. Rename the existent `package.dtsx` to `P01_Error` in Control Flow.

3. Add an **Execute SQL Task** in **Control Flow**; create a new OLE DB Connection to `AdventureWorks2012` in the **SQL Statement** property and enter the following script:

   ```
   Select 1/0
   ```

   This script will cause error in control flow.

4. Run the package. A red cross will appear on right top of **Execute SQL Task** at runtime.

5. You will see a new tab named **Progress**; click on it. The details of execution consisting of information about each step of package and warning and error messages will be displayed.

6. In some cases when the error message is long we cannot see the entire message, but by right-clicking on every message, selecting **Copy Message Text**, and then pasting it in a text editor, such as notepad or Word, we can see the whole message. The following is the entire message for this sample:

```
[Execute SQL Task] Error: Executing the query "select 1/0" failed
with the following error: "Divide by zero error encountered.".
Possible failure reasons: Problems with the query, "ResultSet"
property not set correctly, parameters not set correctly, or
connection not established correctly.
```

7. Stop the package. Note that the **Progress** tab will be renamed to **Execution Results**, but all messages for the last run are present—same as it was in **Progress** tab.

8. Create another package and rename it to P02_Error In Data Flow.dtsx.

9. Add a **Data Flow Task**, in the **Data Flow** tab; add a **Flat File Source** and point it to the source.txt file in this address which was created in the *Getting ready* section: C:\SSIS\Ch10_Debugging Troubleshooting and Migrating Packages to 2012\Files\R01_source.txt.

10. Just check the **column names in the first data row** checkbox, and accept all other default values in the **Flat file Connection Manager**.

11. Add a **Data Conversion Task** and convert the **ID** column from **DT_STR** to **DT_I4**. Note that the third data row from the source file cannot convert the String ID to int so we will get an error in this row.

12. Run the Package. An error transformation will be highlighted through the red X icon on the right-top corner of the Derived Column component as shown in the following screenshot:

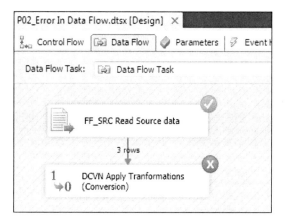

13. The **Progress** tab shows error messages similar to the following screenshot:

14. The following is the error message:

[Data Conversion [2]] Error: Data conversion failed while converting column "ID" (17) to column "Copy of ID" (6). The conversion returned status value 2 and status text "The value could not be converted because of a potential loss of data.".

How it works...

One of the essentials of every development environment is a log viewer of execution messages, information, warnings, and errors. SSDT also has the **Progress** tab which shows all messages such as validation messages, warning message, and error messages that took place during execution of the package.

The **Progress** tab shows messages coming from both Control Flow and Data Flow. At the start there are some log validation messages. Note that there may be some warning messages in different steps. Resolving warning messages isn't mandatory but they will always suggest best practices which help in performance tuning.

For example, in the second package there are some warning messages about columns which aren't in use and should be removed from the data flow such as the following message:

```
[SSIS.Pipeline] Warning: The output column "Copy of ID" (6) on output
"Data Conversion Output" (5) and component "Data Conversion" (2) is
not subsequently used in the Data Flow task. Removing this unused
output column can increase Data Flow task performance.
```

The reason for this message is that we created Data Flow without a destination. When there are some columns in the Data Flow which are not in use, it will be much better to remove them in order to suppress the extra memory usage.

In both examples there are error messages which show the cause of error. But error messages do not always provide enough details, for example, the number of the data row which caused the error isn't clear in the **Progress** tab. For finding out such information, we need other methods to handle data rows in Data Flow; there is an example of such error handling later in this chapter.

Another point to note is that the **Progress** tab will be shown by the first run of the package in SSDT. By stopping the package, this tab will be renamed to **Execution Results** but the details of data will be the same as the latest run of the package.

When an error occurs, you may find some error messages in the **Progress** or **Execution Results** tab, but all of them don't have useful information. In many cases, the first error message shows the main reason, but the other messages might be helpful in some cases.

Breakpoints, Debugging the Control Flow

The debugging environment needs more powerful features than a simple logging such as the **Progress** or **Execution Results** tab. Breakpoints is one of the popular debugging methods which is very well known by software developers. Fortunately the SSIS has the ability to use breakpoints in Control Flow and in Script Task.

In this recipe, we will show how to use breakpoints in Control Flow. The scenario is that in an Excel file, connection properties of some SQL Servers exists. In a Foreach Loop, we will find out the server which has the most up-to-date version of SQL Server.

Getting ready

Create an Excel file which has connection information (**Servername**, **Username**, **Password**) of more than one existing SQL Servers. Name it `serverConnections.xlsx`, and place it in the **Files** folder in the **SSIS Project** folder.

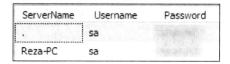

How to do it...

1. Create a SSIS project and name it `R02_Breakpoints Debugging the Control Flow`.

2. Add the following variables with data types and valid default values:

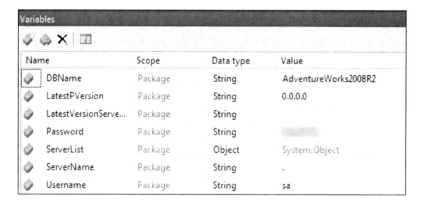

3. Add a **Data Flow Task**. In the **Data Flow** tab, add an **Excel Source** and connect it to the `serverConnections.xlsx` file. Add a **Recordset Destination** and fill the incoming data stream from excel source into the Object variable. In the **Recordset Destination** editor, set the variable to **User::ServerList** and check all the input columns:

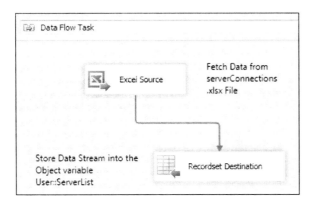

4. Go back to **Control Flow** and add a **Foreach Loop Container**. Set the enumerator to *ADO enumerator* and set **User::ServerList** to *Source Variable*.

5. In the **Variable Mappings** tab, map package variables to the enumerator column indexes as shown in the following screenshot:

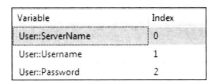

6. Add an **Execute SQL Task** inside the **Foreach Loop Container**; create an OLE DB Connection to the master database in the local SQL Server with username and password for SQL authentication.

7. Type the following script in the **SQL Statement** property:

```
select SERVERPROPERTY('productversion') as pversion
```

8. The previous code will fetch the version of SQL Server installed and then set the **Result Set** property to *Single Row*. In the **Result Set** tab, set **Result Name** to *pversion* and **Variable Name** to *User::PVersion*.

9. Add a script task inside the **Foreach Loop Container** right after the **Execute SQL Task**.

10. Set these variables as *ReadOnlyVariables*: User::PVersion,User::ServerName.

11. And these variables as *ReadWriteVariables* (Note that variable names are case sensitive, both here and inside the script task): `User::LatestPVersion,User::LatestVersionServerName`

12. Type the following script in script editor:

```
public void Main()
{
  Regex reg =
    new Regex
(@"(?<Class1>\d*).(?<Class2>\d*).(?<Class3>\d*).(?<Class4>\d*)");
            int Class1, Class2, Class3, Class4,
                LatestClass1,LatestClass2,LatestClass3,LatestCla
ss4;
            Match result=reg.Match(Dts.
Variables["User::PVersion"].Value.ToString());
                Class1 = int.Parse(result.Groups["Class1"].Value);
                Class2 = int.Parse(result.Groups["Class2"].Value);
                Class3 = int.Parse(result.Groups["Class3"].Value);
                Class4 = int.Parse(result.Groups["Class4"].Value);

                result=reg.Match(Dts.Variables["User::LatestPVersi
on"].Value.ToString());
                LatestClass1 = int.Parse(result.Groups["Class1"].
Value);
                LatestClass2 = int.Parse(result.Groups["Class2"].
Value);
                LatestClass3 = int.Parse(result.Groups["Class3"].
Value);
                LatestClass4 = int.Parse(result.Groups["Class4"].
Value);

                if (Class1 > LatestClass1)
                    UpdateLatestInfo();
                else if (Class1 == LatestClass1 &&
                    Class2 > LatestClass2)
                    UpdateLatestInfo();
                else if (Class1 == LatestClass1 &&
                    Class2 == LatestClass2 &&
                    Class3 >LatestClass3)
                    UpdateLatestInfo();
                else if (Class1 == LatestClass1 &&
                    Class2 == LatestClass2 &&
                    Class3 == LatestClass3 &&
                    Class4 >LatestClass4)
                    UpdateLatestInfo();

    Dts.TaskResult = (int)ScriptResults.Success;
}
```

```
private void UpdateLatestInfo()
{
    Dts.Variables["User::LatestVersionServerName"].Value =
        Dts.Variables["User::ServerName"].Value;
    Dts.Variables["User::LatestPVersion"].Value =
        Dts.Variables["User::PVersion"].Value;
}
```

13. Add a break point on the first `if` statement line. To add a break point, click on the gray bar at the leftmost of script editor window of the specified line.

14. Save the script and close the editor. Click on **OK** in the script task editor.

15. In the **Connection Manager** pane, right-click on **OLE DB Connection** and select **Properties**. In the **Properties** window, set the **Expression** values for the following properties with package variables (Note that you should set default valid values for package variables):

Property	Expression
Password	@[User::Password]
ServerName	@[User::ServerName]
UserName	@[User::Username]

16. Right-click on **Foreach Loop Container** and click on **Edit Breakpoints**.

17. In the **Set Breakpoints** window, set the breakpoint to *Break when the container receives the OnPostExecute event* condition and *Break at the beginning of every iteration of the loop* condition.

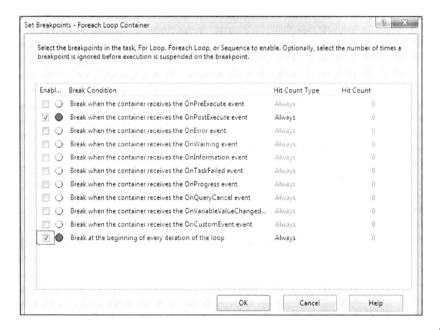

18. Run the package. When the script task hits breakpoint, the script editor window will open and the flow of execution will pause at the line of breakpoint. There are a windows such as watch window which can be used to trace variable values.

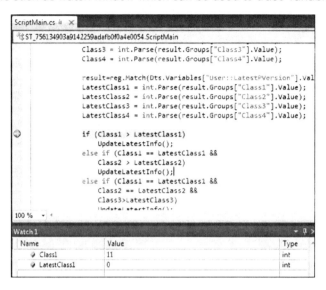

19. Click on **Continue**(*F5*). At final breakpoint, when **Foreach Loop** has finished executing, you can see the value of variables in the locals or watch window. The following screenshot is a sample of the watch window:

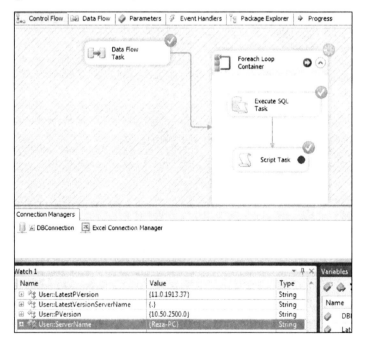

How it works...

Breakpoints are pause points in execution and at those points the developer can watch user and system variable values at runtime, also line by line trace in script task and Task by Task trace on Control Flow is available.

How to enable breakpoints

To use breakpoints, just right-click on the task and click on **Edit Breakpoints**, and in the **Set Breakpoints** window, select the event or events on which you want to set breakpoint. More information about events and their usages will be revealed in a separate chapter later in this book.

Breakpoints window

At runtime, the list of breakpoints and their information can be found in a window in SSDT named **Breakpoints** window. In this window, you can set or remove breakpoints at runtime, set a condition, or hit count on them by right-clicking on each breakpoint.

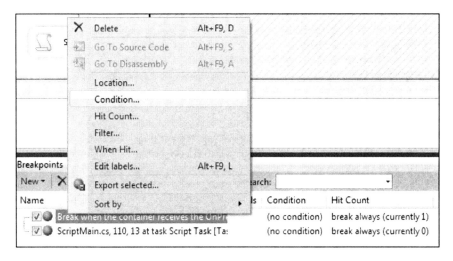

Breakpoint menu options

In SSDT, there are a few menu options for breakpoints which help developers. The menu options can be found under the **Debug** menu at design time or runtime. There are options to control execution. Hitting *F5* will continue execution till the next break point and hitting *F10* will go to the next task; also there are some options in the **Script Task**.

The following screenshot shows a sample of the **Debug** menu in Control Flow.

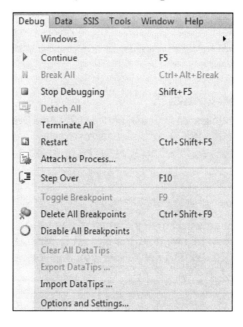

Monitoring windows

There are three windows which help the developer to find out values of system or user variables and other built-in objects at runtime.

- ▶ **Watch Window**: In this window the developer can add any variable by dragging-and-dropping or the writing full name of variable.

- ▶ **Locals Window**: List of all variables will be shown here and by expanding it developer can see every variable's value.

- ▶ **Autos Window**: This window will always show a scope of variables in the current execution step. For example, when you debug a script in a function, variables in that function will be at Autos window.

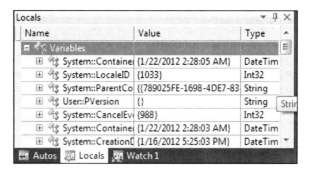

Breakpoints limitation in SSIS

Breakpoints are very useful for debugging but they have a big limitation in SSIS. We cannot use breakpoints inside the Data Flow. None of the sources, transformations, and destinations participate in breakpoints. But don't worry about it. There are other ways to debug the Data Flow; one of them is Data Viewer which is discussed earlier in many recipes and another method is error output configuration which will be discussed in the next recipe. Note that the only place in Data Flow that accepts breakpoints is Script Component.

Script breakpoint support

One of the most powerful aspects of breakpoints in SSIS is that they can be used at script level. As the recipe showed we can put the breakpoint on each line of script in Script Task or Script Component, and at runtime the script editor will be open and line by line tracing and debugging will be available.

Handling errors in Data Flow

Data Flow is the most important and useful part of SSIS packages. Data will transfer there, and if errors occur, there should be an error catching method. The importance of such error catching feature is mostly due to the fact that data flows will transfer millions of data rows in nightly schedule, and maybe re-producing an error which occurred at night can't be possible for a second time.

Fortunately SSIS Data Flow uses a powerful error catching mechanism which will act on every data row on most of the transformations, sources, and destinations. When a transformation hits an error on one or more specific data rows, those rows will be caught and we can develop scenarios on how to deal with those rows.

Most of the sources, transformations, and destinations in Data Flow have an Error Output. Data rows which cause error can be redirected in the error output.

In this recipe, we will use a simple ETL scenario. A flat file data row is inserted into a database table, the data of which has an age field which should be converted to integer before feeding into the database table, and also the database table has an ID field which has a unique constraint as it is a Primary Key. There are some points of error in this scenario namely, when a value wants to convert from string to integer, and when duplicate ID is detected.

Getting ready

Create a `R03_source.txt` file which has delimited information about people, such as `ID`, `FirstName`, `LastName`, and `Age`. Place `R03_source.txt` in the **Files** folder in SSIS project's folder, `C:\SSIS\Ch09_Debugging Troubleshooting and Migrating Packages to 2012\FILES`.

```
ID,FirstName,LastName,Age
```

```
1,Reza,Rad,31
2,Pedro,Perfeito,33
3,Mark,Jones,fifty
2,Richard,Koper,12
4,Rafael,Salas,34
```

Create a `Visitor` table in `PacktPub_SSISbook` in SQL Server database with the following script:

```
CREATE TABLE [dbo].[Visitor](
[ID] [int] NOT NULL,
[FirstName] [varchar](50) NULL,
[LastName] [varchar](50) NULL,
[Age] [int] NULL,
 CONSTRAINT [PK_Visitor] PRIMARY KEY CLUSTERED
(
[ID] ASC
)WITH (PAD_INDEX = OFF, STATISTICS_NORECOMPUTE = OFF, IGNORE_DUP_KEY =
OFF, ALLOW_ROW_LOCKS = ON, ALLOW_PAGE_LOCKS = ON) ON [PRIMARY]
) ON [PRIMARY]
```

How to do it...

1. Create a SSIS project and name it as `R03_Handling Errors in Data Flow`.

2. Add a **Data Flow Task** inside the package.

3. In the **Data Flow** tab, add a **Flat File Source** and create a **Flat File Connection Manager** to the `R01_source.txt` file, just check the column names in the first data row, and accept all other defaults.

4. Add a **Data Conversion Transformation** after **Flat File Source** and change the data type of **ID** and **Age** column from `DT_STR` to `DT_I4`.

5. Add an **OLE DB Destination** after the **Data Conversion Transform**, set **Data Access Mode** as **Table or View** (Don't use **Table or View Fast Load** in this recipe), and set table name as **Visitor**.

6. Run the package, you will get an error and execution of the package will stop. The error in the **progress** tab is because of a value which can't be converted to integer in the **Age** column, but the exact row of error and exact value which caused error isn't specified.

7. Stop the execution, go back to **Data Flow** and double-click on **Data Conversion Transform**, click on **Configure Error Output**.

8. In the **Configure Error Output** window you will see a row per each column in data stream, so there will be two rows; **Copy of ID** and **Copy of Age**. Set the **Error** column for both of them as **Redirect row**.

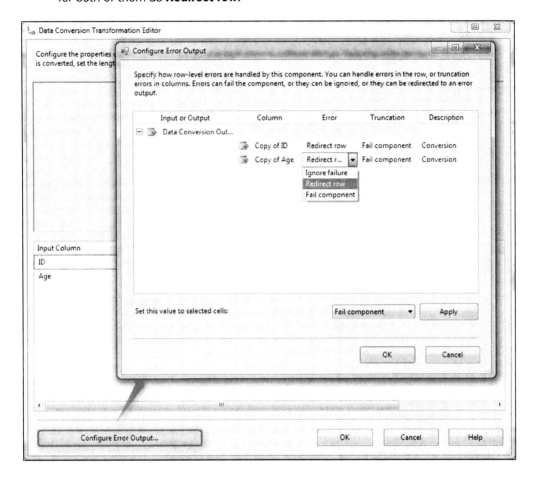

9. Click on **OK** and close the **Configure Error Output** and **Data Conversion Transformation Editor**.

10. In the Data Flow add a Flat File Destination, after Data Conversion Transform and connect red arrow (Error Output) from Data Conversion Transform to the Flat File Destination.

11. Edit the Flat File destination, connect it to a new delimited flat file, name it `dataConversionErrorLog.txt`, and in the flat file destination check the mappings of columns.

12. As there may be some duplicate IDs in data stream, add another flat file destination for error output of duplicate IDs, and place it after **OLE DB Destination**.

13. Connect Error Output from OLE DB Destination to the Flat File Destination (Note that OLE DB Destination only has red arrow output, this means that a destination has no output except the error output).

14. Edit the flat file destination, connect it to a new delimited flat file and name it as `DestinationErrorLog.txt`.

15. Run the package, you will see five data rows fetched out from `R01_source.txt`, but four of them will appear as valid output of data conversion transform and one row will redirect to error output.

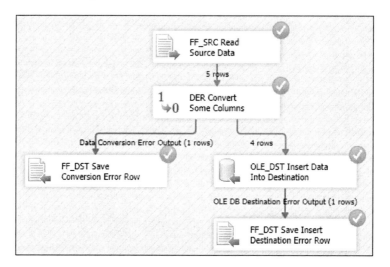

16. In the **Error output** of **OLE DB Destination**, also there is also one row which shows the row which has a problem at the time of inserting to the database table.

17. To find out more about bad data rows (data rows which caused error), open the `dataConversionErrorLog.txt` file. You will see the exact row which caused an error in the data conversion transform. The problem was in "fifty" which cannot be converted to integer.

   ```
   ID,FirstName,LastName,Age,ErrorCode,ErrorColumn
   3,Mark,Jones,fifty,-1071607681,10
   ```

18. Open the `DestinationErrorLog.txt` file, the row here is because of Primary Key Violence because ID "2" is duplicate.

   ```
   ID,FirstName,LastName,Age,Copy of ID,Copy of
   Age,ErrorCode,ErrorColumn
   2,Richard,Koper,12,2,12,-1071607683,0
   ```

How it works...

In this recipe, we explored a sample usage of Error Output. Error output is a very useful way to face bad data rows. In real world SSIS packages there maybe one error output per each source, transformation, or destination, because real-world scenarios may have bad data rows in every operation from Extract and Transformation to Load.

Error Output is available in most of the sources, transformations, and destination as a red arrow. The default Error Output Configuration is Fail Component. This is why when an error occurs the Data Flow component will fail.

In the example of this recipe before step 7, when there is no error output used, occurrence of an error in data conversion will cause failure in data conversion and other data rows won't parse. In the real-world scenarios, a robust system should be developed which will be fault-tolerant and which not only doesn't fail by bad data rows, but also catches them and stores them somewhere for future troubleshooting.

There are three options for error output in the **Configure Error output** window which appears when we want to use error output. They are as follows:

▶ **Ignore Failure**: As its name describes, the bad data row will be ignored and the next row will be processed. When it ignores a value, it replaces it with a NULL.

▶ **Redirect Row**: Bad data rows will be redirected to the error output so a new data stream in error output will be created and bad data rows will transfer during it.

▶ **Fail Component**: This is the default option and will cause the component to fail when a bad data row is found.

Note that Error Output Configuration should be made for each column in the data stream separately, for example if you are sure that the ID column from flat file always has an integer value there is no need to configure error output for the **Copy of ID** column, but there should be a configuration for error output on **Copy of Age** of course.

In the **Configure Error Output** window, there is also a **Truncate** column. The **Truncate** error happens when the input columns of data stream do not fit long enough in the output column. This option is mostly in use with string columns.

If you want to apply an error output configuration on some columns you can select as many rows as you want and then use the combo box under the window to apply the same configuration on multiple cells.

The behavior of execution when error output is configured is that; when a bad data row is found the component won't fail but the bad data row will be redirected or ignored based on configuration made at implementation, and then other rows will be processed.

So using the **Error** output provides a way to catch bad data rows and store them somewhere for future troubleshooting. Also, a detailed logging will be created on Data Flow, for example all bad data rows that stored in a flat file can be attached to an e-mail and sent to an appropriate supervisor.

There are a few transformations that don't have the error output such as **Multicast** and **Copy Column**. The reason is obvious. It is because there wouldn't be any error at the time when copy data is set in the memory.

In this recipe, we didn't configure error output on flat file. Note that in a real-world scenario this may be needed, for example Flat File file columns are of type DT_STR with length 50, so if a column's data exceeds this length it will cause truncation error.

You can combine error outputs with the same structure with Union All to a single destination if you want to reduce the number of error output log files.

Error columns and understanding them

There are two default error columns in error output; **ErrorCode** and **ErrorColumn**. These columns provide useful information about which error occurred in each data row.

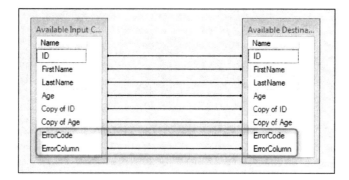

ErrorCode shows number of SSIS errors which is based on a reference table available at `http://msdn.microsoft.com/en-us/library/ms345164.aspx`. And **ErrorColumn** will show the index of column in data stream, the index is zero based.

For example, in the `DestinationErrorLog.txt`, the ErrorCode was -1071607683 (step 17 in the *How to do it* section) and ErrorColumn was 0. This information means that an Integrity Violation happened at Column ID.

Migrating packages to 2012

SSIS 2012 is the latest version of SSIS and packages which were developed and created by SSIS 2005 and 2008 can be converted to the 2012 version simply with help of the Project Conversion Wizard. But there are a few exceptions.

As we mentioned earlier, the ActiveX Script Task and Execute DTS 2000 Package Task are no longer supported in SSIS 2012, so packages with these tasks should use alternative options. For ActiveX Script Task a much better alternative is Script Task with support of .NET 4.0 Framework. And the alternative for Execute DTS 2000 Package Task is Execute Package Task which works with SSIS packages.

Another thing to note in SSIS 2012 package is that configurations no longer exist in Project Deployment Model, but are replaced by parameters. If you want to use package configuration you can still be on legacy Package Deployment Model. But don't worry, because parameters in Project Deployment Model do everything package configuration did earlier and also much more. Also Execute package task has a new option for project reference. These options can be detected by Project Conversion Wizard and replaced.

In this recipe, we will convert two SSIS packages from SSIS 2008 to 2012. Packages have parent child relation with the execute package task and use package configurations.

How to do it...

1. Copy the **Files** folder from the companion media to the local computer in this address: C:\SSIS\Ch10_Debugging Troubleshooting and Migrating Packages to 2012\R04_Migrating Packages to 2012\Files.

2. Go to **Start | All Programs | Microsoft SQL Server 2012 | Integration Services**, and select **Project Conversion Wizard**.

3. When the **Integration Services Project Conversion Wizard** window appears click on **Next** to pass the introduction step.

4. In the **Locate Packages** step, we should provide the source of packages. In this recipe we use file system as source, and the folder should be C:\SSIS\Ch10_Debugging Troubleshooting and Migrating Packages to 2012\R04_Migrating Packages to 2012\Files\Integration Services Project2.

5. **Select Packages** step shows a list of SSIS packages found under the path specified in the previous step.

6. There will be two packages; **Package.dtsx** and **P_msg.dtsx**. The **Package.dtsx** package has the password `123`, so enter it in **Password** column. Check both packages. Then go to the next step.

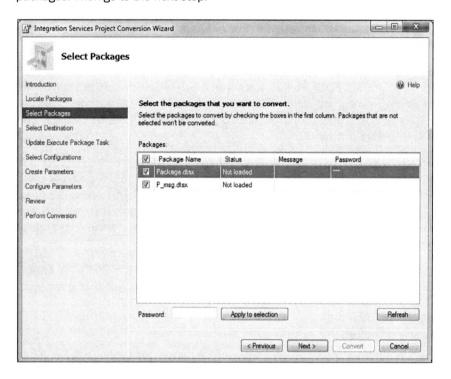

7. When you click on **Next** all packages which were checked in the previous step will be loaded.

8. The **Output of Project Conversion Wizard** is a `*.ispac` file, `.ispac` files will be discussed more in the later chapters. In the **Select Destination** step we should set an address for the new `.ispac` file, name the project as `converted`, and accept other defaults.

9. In the **Update Execute Package Task** tab, a list of execute package tasks in all packages will be shown and their reference type trying to change to project reference. Select **P_msg.dtsx** in the assign reference combo box and go to next step.

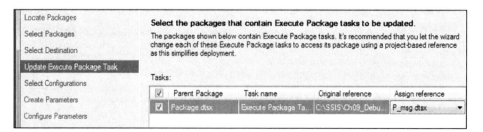

10. The **Select Configuration** tab will show a list of all configuration used in packages and their types. If the configuration can be found then an **OK** message will appear in the **Status** column, otherwise the message will show the reason why configuration is not accessible.

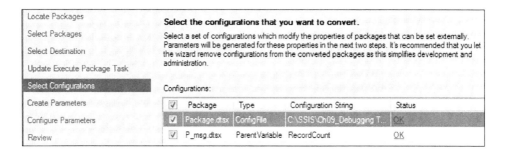

11. The **Create Parameters** tab will create a parameter for each configuration value from the selected configurations in the previous step. The name and scope of parameters can be changed.

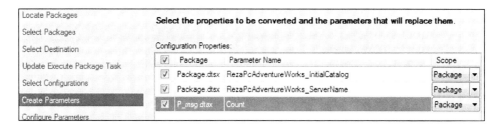

12. The **Configure Parameters** tab will set the default value for parameters.

13. The **Review** tab will show a summary of all settings.

14. Click on **Convert** to perform the conversion. If there was any error in this step an error message will help us find the problem.

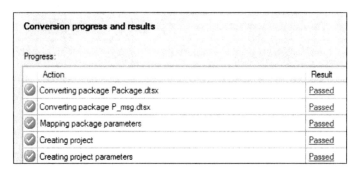

15. After the successful completion of **Project Conversion Wizard**, the converted. ispac file will appear at the destination path. Now, it's time to open the SSIS project from that file.

16. Create a new **Project** of type **Integration Service Import Project Wizard**. This type will open a * . ispac file and create a SSIS project based on it.

17. The **Integration service Import Project Wizard** will appear, pass the first introduction step.

18. In the **Select source**, use the **Project Deployment File** option and set address of converted.ispac there as: C:\SSIS\Ch10_Debugging Troubleshooting and Migrating Packages to 2012\R04_Migrating Packages to 2012\ Files\Integration Services Project2\converted.ispac:

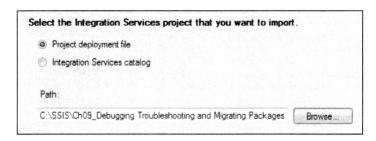

19. The next step has a summary review of project in the `.ispac` file and finally the **Import** button will import all packages in a new project.

20. Now in the new project open `Package.dtsx`, and go to the **Parameters** tab. Two parameters will appear in substitution of configuration values in the legacy SSIS project.

21. In **Control Flow**, open **Execute Package Task Editor**, verify that the reference type is **Project reference**, and in **Parameter Binding** the **RecordCount** and **Count** are bound together.

22. In the **P_msg.dtsx** task also there is a count parameter.

How it works...

Migration from the previous versions of SSIS to 2012 is simple and as we see in this recipe, the Project Conversion Wizard will detect legacy reference types in the execute package tasks and try to convert them to project reference type. It will also fetch out configuration values and convert them to package parameters.

Project Conversion Wizard will create a `*.ispac` file which is a project deployment file, we will discuss this file more in *Chapter 11, Deployment*. This file can be used as a source for **Import Project Wizard** project type in SSDT.

The **Integration Services Import Project Wizard** type will fetch packages metadata from `.ispac` file and import them as a SSIS project.

There will be messages during migration which helps you to troubleshoot migration problems.

Data Tap

Those who normally use the data viewer (to identify the records that go along the pipeline) will be now surprised. In this new version, it's possible to have data viewers dynamically created without having to open and edit a particular package. This type of data viewer is named **Data Tap** and is one of the best features included in this release. During a batch package execution, it is possible to identify the records that are flowing between any components under any Data Flow Task.

This new feature is just available in the Project Deployment Model approach, because the data stored from the **Data Tap** is stored in **SSISDB Catalog**.

Getting ready

To get started with this recipe, follow these steps:

1. Open **SQL Server Data Tools (SSDT)**.

2. Add a new SSIS project to open the SSIS solution and name the project **R05_Data tap**.

How to do it...

The next steps will explain how to create a simple **Data Viewer** under a data flow and then a **Data Tap** in the exact same location.

1. In **Solution Explorer**, locate the project **R05_Data Tap**.

2. Remove the package created by default **Package.dtsx**.

3. Add an existing package **P01_HandlingErrors.dtsx** (created in an earlier recipe) to the package through **Solution Explorer**.

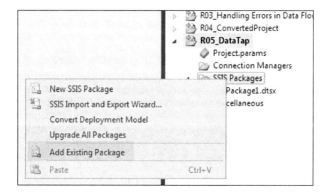

4. Open the Data Flow Task **DFT Handling Errors** for editing.

5. Add a data viewer between **Flat File Source** and the **Derived Column** component.

6. Execute the package pressing *F5* and see the rows flowing in the pipeline:

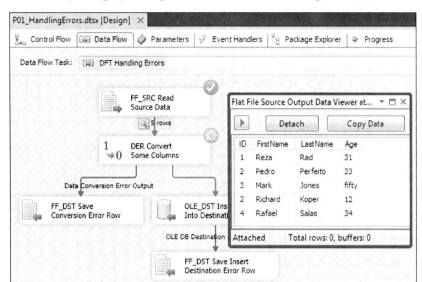

Since in the production environment almost all SSIS packages are executed in the batch mode, you cannot see this data viewer if troubleshooting is required. Fortunately, this new version includes a **Data Tap** to view the rows that pass between any components under a Data Flow. The next steps explain how to add a **Data Tap** in the same place the Data Viewer was added.

7. Since this feature only works in the Project Deployment Model, the first step should be project deployment.

8. Deploy the **R05_DataTap** project to **SSISDB Catalog** under the folder `PacktPub_Chapter09`:

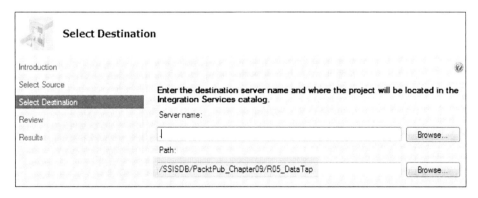

9. Open SQL Server Management Studio (SSMS) and verify if the project was deployed to **Integration Services Catalogs (SSISDB Catalog)**:

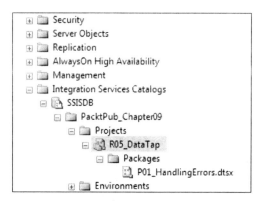

Now that the project is successfully deployed to SSISDB Catalog, let's create the **Data Tap** through the SQL statements.

10. Open the SQL script file **R05_DataTap_Scripts.sql** with all the SQL statements required. The file is located at C:\SSIS\Ch09_Debugging Troubleshooting and Migrating Packages to 2012\FILES\.

11. Execute the entire SQL statements and verify the return result of each step (zero means succeed). Also, take note of the **@execution_id** and **@data_tap_id** to query this execution on the SSISDB database, if needed:

12. Go to the file system location C:\Program Files\Microsoft SQL Server\110\DTS\DataDumps and open the new file created with the data passed in the Data Flow Task.

13. As can be seen, the data in the Flat File (CSV) is exactly the same as the data presented in the data viewer in the SSDT:

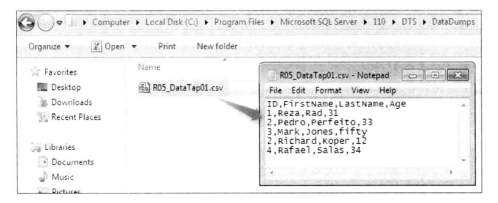

How it works...

The previous steps explained how to configure the **Data Tap** through SQL Server Management Studio (SSMS). This feature has similar functionality as the Data Viewer when used in design mode in the SQL Server Data Tools (SSDT) designer. It's a big improvement for troubleshooting a package that is under a production environment, because without the need to change the package it is possible to dynamically add Data Taps to see which data is passed between each component.

Basically it's necessary to create a project execution, create the **Data Tap** in the desired location, and complete it running the package.

Create the execution

To create the execution, the stored procedure `[catalog].[create_execution]` of the `SSISDB` database should be called with the following most important input parameters: `@folder_name`, `@project_name`, and the `@package_name`:

```
EXEC    @return_value = [catalog].[create_execution]
        --Folder in SSIS server where package is deployed
        @folder_name = N'PacktPub_Chapter09',
        --Project in SSIS server where package is deployed
        @project_name = N'R05_DataTap',
        --Package being executed
        @package_name = N'P01_HandlingErrors.dtsx',
        @execution_id = @execution_id OUTPUT
```

Create the Data Tap

To create the **Data Tap**, the stored procedure [catalog].[add_data_tap] of the SSISDB database must be called with the following most important input parameters: @task_package_path, @dataflow_path_id_string, and @data_filename:

```
EXEC    @return_value = [catalog].[add_data_tap]
        @execution_id = @execution_id,
        -- task path
        @task_package_path = N'\Package\DFT Handling Errors',
        -- Arrow ID
        @dataflow_path_id_string = N'Paths[FF_SRC Read Source Data.Flat File Source Output]',
        -- Filename that will store data
        @data_filename = N'R05_DataTap01.csv',
        @data_tap_id = @data_tap_id OUTPUT
```

@task_package_path is the Data Flow Task where the **Data Tap** will be created while @data_filename is the name of the file that will store the data from the **Data Tap**. @dataflow_path_id_string is the arrow location and you need to know the identification string of the arrow where the **Data Tap** will be placed:

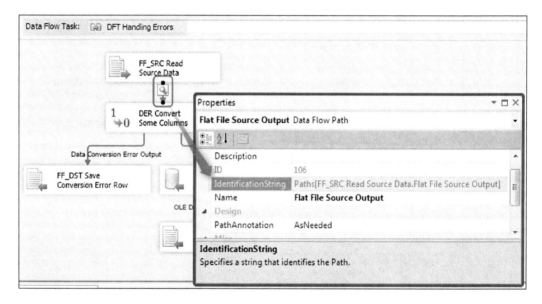

Running the package

To run the package, the stored procedure [catalog].[start_execution] of the **SSISDB** database must be called. If everything succeeds, the **Data Tap** is available on the file system and the troubleshooting will be, without any doubt, easier.

11

Event Handling and Logging

by Pedro Perfeito

In this chapter, we will cover the following topics:

- ▸ Logging over Legacy Deployment Model
- ▸ Logging over Project Deployment Model
- ▸ Using event handlers and system variables for custom logging

Introduction

The logging information is very important and often underestimated. When everything works perfectly, nobody remembers that logging exists, but if it does not reverse, all eyes will be focused on logging to know what went wrong. In the production environment, the **SQL Server Data Tools** (**SSDT**) user interface, which provides useful information in real time about the rows passing through the Data Flow pipeline, will not be available. Packages are normally executed in batch mode at late night hours and if the logging saves just basic information, there will be less logging data to identify the cause of an unexpected error. In the previous versions, logging in SSIS was very basic and more detailed information required extra and duplicated work for developers, who spent too much time creating their own frameworks for SSIS logging. (Rest assured all those developers as your frameworks will still work on this version.) In SSIS 2012, two approaches for dealing with logging are possible: the approach used in the previous versions of SSIS (Legacy Deployment Model) and the new approach known as **Project Deployment Model**. It's possible to use both the approaches and the conversion between them could be done at any stage of development.

The recipes in this chapter will focus on both the approaches (Legacy and Project Deployment Models) and different ways to apply custom logging using event handlers and system variables to each one.

A common example involving three packages will be used in the recipes to update the Product and Customer dimensions created on the `PacktPub_SSISbook` database over previous chapters based on the Adventure Works case study. The example has a package (known as master) that calls two other packages (known as children) that are responsible for updating the `Product` and `Customer` dimensions respectively.

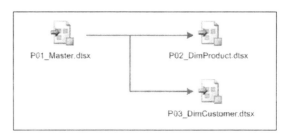

The details about what each package does to update the dimension is not the focus of this chapter, but it is the understanding of how to apply logging functionalities over SSIS projects.

Logging over Legacy Deployment Model

The approach used in the previous version of SSIS is called Legacy Deployment Model or Package Deployment Model. By default, in an empty solution, SSIS sets the SSIS solution using the **Project Deployment Mode**, but converting can easily be done as the following screenshot demonstrates:

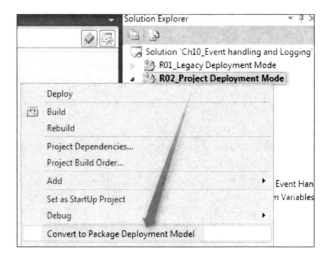

All the SSIS logging created through the SSIS Log Provider or even through custom logging is still very useful if the deployment approach is Legacy. However, the new deployment approach has a new SSIS Catalog that automatically logs all package execution activity along with some built-in reports that provide a more intuitive perspective over log activity and also provide information about all deployments and configurations done to the SSIS Catalog.

Getting ready

To get ready for this recipe, follow these steps:

1. Open SQL Server Management Studio (SSMS) and execute the SQL Statement included in the file `C:\SSIS\Ch02_Control Flow Tasks\Files\R09_CreateDimProduct.sql`

2. Open SQL Server Data Tools (SSDT) and create a new SSIS project.

3. Provide a name and a location for the SSIS project and proceed.

4. Select the package created by default and rename it to **P01_Master.dtsx**.

5. Add an existing package to the solution that will update the Product dimension from the Adventure Works case study used in the book. Under SSIS Solution add the existing package located at `C:\SSIS\Ch11_Event handling and Logging\FILES\P02_DimProduct.dtsx`.

6. Add an existing package to the solution that will update the Customer dimension. Under SSIS Solution add the existing package located at `C:\SSIS\Ch11_Event handling and Logging\FILES\P03_DimCustomer.dtsx`.

How to do it...

The next steps will explain how to create a simple master and child package structure and the respective logging using the Legacy Deployment Model approach.

We will open the Master package and create two Execute packages for calling the packages that will update the Product and Customer dimensions of the *Adventure Works* case study:

1. Open the package **P01_Master.dtsx**.

2. Drag-and-drop two **Execute Package** tasks from the **SSIS Toolbox | Common** to the **Control Flow** design area.

3. Link both the components through the green output of the first one.

4. Rename the first task to **Call DimProduct** and the second to **Call DimCustomer**.

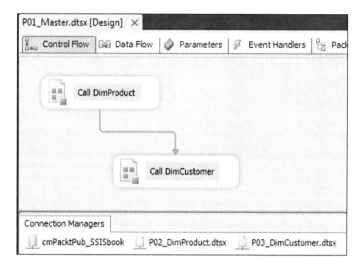

5. Open the first task for editing and set it to the package previously added **P02_DimProduct.dtsx**.

6. Open the second task for edition and set it to the package previously added **P03_DimCustomer.dtsx**.

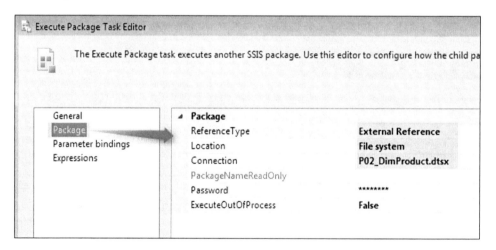

7. Configure SSIS for logging (using Legacy Deployment Model).

8. In the main menu, select the **SSIS | Logging...** option to configure SSIS Packages.

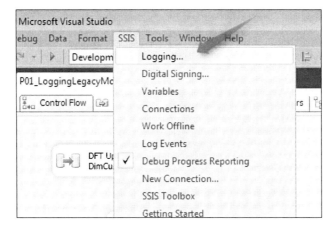

9. In the containers area, select both Data Flows (containers) that should be included in this SSIS logging.

10. In the **Providers and Logs** tab, select the **Provider Type** as **SSIS log provider for SQL Server** that will record all the SSIS events chosen in the next step and click on the **Add...** button.

11. Confirm the provider type in the grid that is available below, and set the connection associated, and already used in the Product and Customer dimension update packages, to **cmPacktPub_SSISbook**.

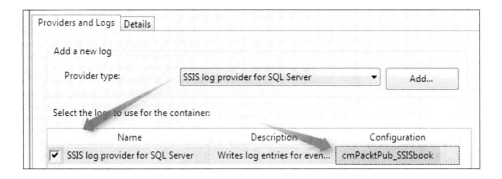

12. In the **Details** tab, select the events required to be recorded during the SSIS package execution. In this case, in the **Events** list, set the most critical and often used events on the event details provider list: **OnError** and **OnWarning**.

13. Execute the SSIS package by pressing *F5*.

14. The logging objects, **sysssislog** and **sp_ssis_addlogentry**, will be created during the package execution.

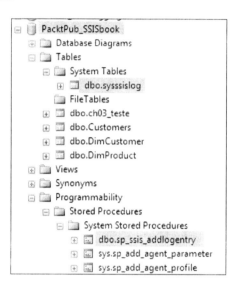

15. Read the contents of **sysssislog** and see the logging information stored:

```
SELECT * FROM sysssislog
```

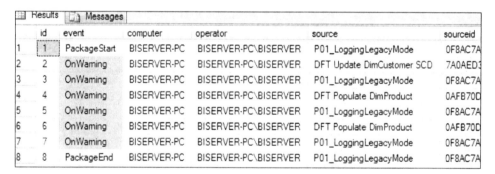

How it works...

The general explanation that can be provided for this approach is that there exist two fundamental SQL objects that follow the configuration settled on each SSIS package through the SSIS Logging wizard. When a package starts the stored procedure, **sp_ssis_addlogentry** is called and the logging data is inserted into sysssislog. (The logging data will record just those events configured in the previous steps).

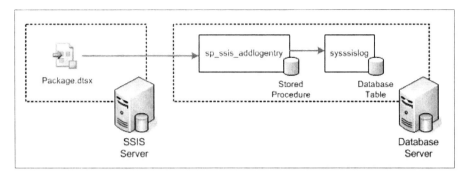

It's possible to enrich the logging information through the use of the exclusive events associated with some tasks. These tasks are the Data Flow Task, SQL Task, and several others listed and explained in the following Microsoft link:

`http://msdn.microsoft.com/en-us/library/ms345174(v=SQL.110).aspx.`

If an SSIS project has a master and child architecture, it's only required to configure SSIS logging (described in the preceding steps) at the master package level. However, if some custom messages task needs to be recorded in a specific child package, the logging should also be activated in this child package.

If there is a need to add or remove some events from the SSIS Log Provider details list, it'll be required to open and edit each package to apply this change. If the project is in production, editing an existing package can increase the risk for unexpected errors and also it can take some time until the change is replicated to production and maybe you will want to edit the package again to go back. A possible solution to figure out this issue is to manually change the stored procedure `sp_ssis_addlogentry` responsible for inserting logging data into the `sysssislog` table, but the performance could decrease.

Logging over Project Deployment Model

While in the Legacy Deployment Model approach the logging data was recorded in the Sysssislog table, in this new model approach all logging data is stored in tables under a new database created exclusively for this approach and named `SSISDB`. This database supports the SSIS catalog, which is the central storage and administration point for Integration Services projects, packages, parameters, and environments.

This means that data is centralized, more complete, and anyone (with the respective permissions to the SISDB database) has the ability to build their own custom reports based on the log data. The SSIS catalog provides four different log levels—**Basic** (default log level), **None**, **Performance**, and **Verbose**.

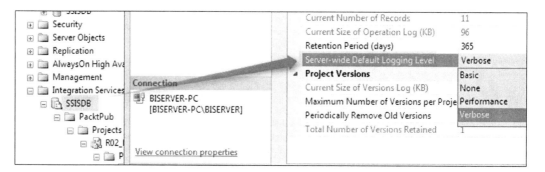

▸ **None level**—Captures enough generic information to inform whether the package succeeded or failed and other generic information.

▸ **Basic level**—Captures the same generic information as **None** level and all SSIS event types except the **OnProgress** and **OnCustomEvent** events.

▸ **Performance**—Captures information to track performance from tasks and components in each execution. The logging information is limited to **OnError** and **OnWarning** event types and captures less logging information than the **Basic** level.

▸ **Verbose**—Captures all log events (including the **Basic** and **Performance** levels). This logging level can introduce some overhead on performance because some of the SSISDB tables will increase significantly on each execution (mainly the `operation_messages` and `event_messages` tables).

The logging level must be set at the SSIS Catalog level and it's not possible to have different levels under the same SSISDB Catalog. However, each project execution can be configured to run any of the four logging levels independently of the default settled at the catalog level.

Getting ready

To get ready for this recipe, follow these steps:

1. Open SQL Server Management Studio (SSMS) and create the SSIS Catalog on the server.

2. Connect to the SQL Server Database Engine.

3. In Object Explorer, expand the server node, right-click on the **Integration Services Catalogs** node, and then click **Create Catalog**.

4. Enable **CLR integration** and enter a password to be used as master key to encrypt sensitive data in the SSISDB database.

5. Open SQL Server Data Tools (SSDT) and create a new SSIS project.

6. Provide a name and a location for the SSIS project and proceed.

7. Select the package created by default and rename it to `P01_Master.dtsx`.

8. Add an existing package to the solution that will update the Product Dimension from the Adventure Works case study used throughout the book. Under **SSIS Solution**, add the existing package located at `C:\SSIS\Ch11_Event handling and Logging\FILES\P02_DimProduct.dtsx`.

9. Add an existing package to the solution that will update the Customer Dimension. Under **SSIS Solution**, add the existing package located at `C:\SSIS\Ch11_Event handling and Logging\FILES\P03_DimCustomer.dtsx`.

How to do it...

The following steps will explain the logging approach using the Project Deployment Model. This recipe uses the same example as the previous recipe where a master package calls two child packages to update the Customer and Product dimensions.

1. Open the package `P01_Master.dtsx`.

2. Drag-and-drop two **Execute Package** tasks from the **SSIS Toolbox | Common** to the **Control Flow** design area.

3. Follow the same steps as in the previous recipe to configure both **Execute Package** tasks.

4. Press *F5* to execute the package and ensure that everything is alright.

   Before you can deploy the projects to the Integration Services server, the server must contain the SSISDB catalog explained in the previous section. As the installation program for Microsoft SQL Server 2012 does not automatically create the catalog, the next section explains how to create it manually.

5. Deploy the project to the server to make use of all new SSIS Catalog features.

6. In the Solution Explorer, select the project **R02_Project Deployment Mode** and click **Deploy**.

7. Enter the destination server and the respective path on the SSIS Catalog.

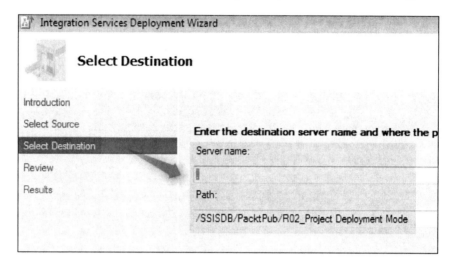

8. Click **Deploy** to start deployment. The progress result will be displayed next as shown in the following screnshot:

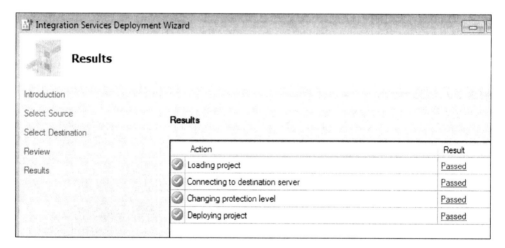

If the deployment is executed successfully, the SSIS project is now displayed under SSIS Catalog, which is created during the recipe.

9. Execute the master package.

10. Locate the P01_Master.dtsx package under the PacktPub folder on the **Integration Services Catalogs** and under the R02_Project Deployment Model folder project.

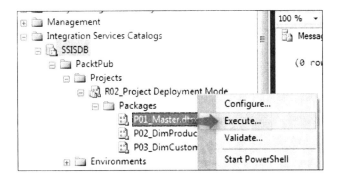

11. After execution, a message box will appear with a message asking if you wish to open the new SSIS Dashboard that displays all information about the SSIS project execution (including all the packages under the project).

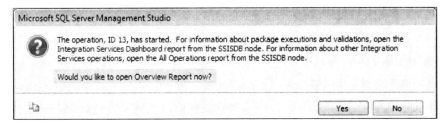

12. The final dashboard has the following appearance:

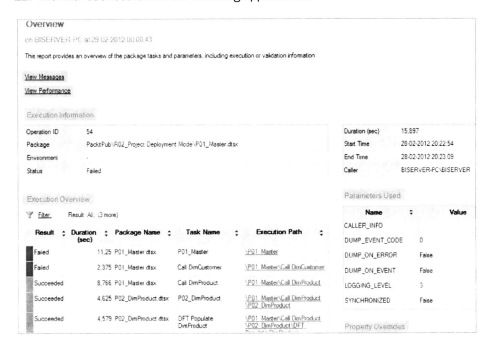

How it works...

It's not possible to ensure that this entire SSIS Catalog will replace all the custom hard work created in SSIS frameworks from previous versions. However, this is an initial and very important step to make use of more centralized logging information and provide better control of all SSIS executions. Naturally, the information available will depend on the logging level selected from the SSIS Catalog. The **None** level is the level that captures least information, while **Verbose** is the level that captures the most information. In the middle are the **Basic** and **Performance** levels that could be applied in scenarios that do not require too little or too much information but just enough logging information.

With this new approach and after the SSIS project is deployed to the SSIS Catalog, it is possible to know the following (depending on the logging level defined) through standard reports and views (without any extra work):

- Generic information execution
- Overview of execution and executables
- Performance execution
- Data flow component details and several other interesting information

However, one feature that should be very important for SSIS developers is the possibility of getting the rows sent between each component under a **Data Flow** component. This information is captured by the **rows_sent** column placed in the [internal].[execution_data_statistics] table and is only possible using the **Verbose** logging level. (Also, refer to the next recipes for further information.)

There's more...

We will now look at few other things.

The SSISDB database

The SSISDB database supports the SSIS Catalog created in SQL Management Studio. This database has several objects that will have importance depending on the logging level defined in the SSIS Catalog. There are several tables, views, stored procedures, and functions that provide a better control over every SSIS project executed under the SSIS Catalog. Some tables are updated when a deployment or a configuration change is made to the SSIS Catalog and others are updated during a project execution. Views are created to better organize logging information and some of the most important views are described as follows:

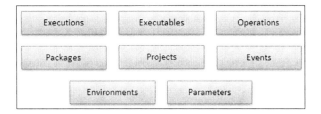

- The [catalog].[projects] view captures generic information (folder, description, creation date, last deployment date, version, and so on) about each project stored in the SSIS catalog. (The result of this view will not change during the execution.)

- The [catalog].[packages] view captures the major and minor versions of a package. (The result of this view will not change during the execution.)

- The [catalog].[executions] view captures the package start time and end time, and the respective status. The [catalog].[execution_data_satistics] view captures the number of rows sent between a source and destination component.

- The [catalog].[executables] view captures information about each executable (task, container, or package) that gets executed in an execution. [catalog].[executable_statistics] captures more detailed information about each executable like start time and end time, duration and status.

- The [catalog].[event_messages] view captures information from executing packages and is the most similar to the [sysssislog] table provided in the earlier versions of SSIS and in the Legacy Deployment Model.

- The [catalog].[operations] view captures information about all operations in the Integration Services Catalog. These operations could be of 10 different types like for example: deploy project, restore project, stop operation, configure catalog, and others.

- For further details about Integration Services Catalog views, follow the link: http://msdn.microsoft.com/en-us/library/ff878135(v=sql.110).aspx.

The SSIS dashboards

There are several standard reports (dashboards) available in the SSIS Catalog that could provide important information about the SSIS projects under the SSIS Catalog in a very intuitive interface. The most aggregated information is displayed in **Integration Services Dashboard** and can be broken down to reports with more detailed information such as **Executions**, **Validations**, **Operations**, or **Connections**.

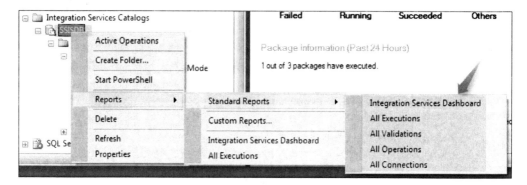

Some useful SSIS Catalog features

On right-clicking the subfolders of SSIS Catalog, the direct links to the important features will be visible that is described and highlighted as follows:

1 SSISDB

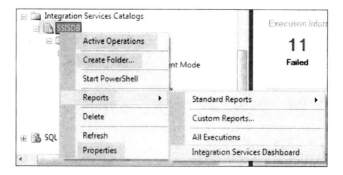

▶ **Active Operations**—Captures the information about the active operations being executed

▶ **Create Folder**—Creates folder to organize one or more projects

▶ **Reports**—Generates reports at the SSIS Catalog level (applied in the report filters)

▶ **Properties**—Changes SSIS Catalog properties, for example logging level

2 PacktPub

▶ **Reports**—Generates reports at the PacktPub folder level (applied in the report filters)

3 Projects

▶ **Deploy Project**—Deploys project to the SSIS Catalog

▶ **Import Packages**—Imports a specific package to an existing project

▶ **Reports**—Generates reports at the Projects folder level (applied in the report filters)

4 R02_Project Deployment Mode

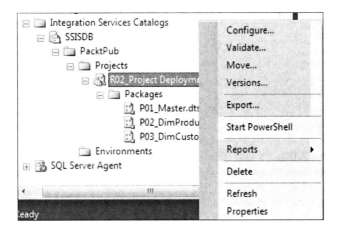

▶ **Configure**—Configures parameters, connection managers, and environments

▶ **Validate**—Validates the entire package

▶ **Move**—Moves the package to another location

▶ **Versions**—Manages project versions and very importantly provides the possibility to restore a previous version

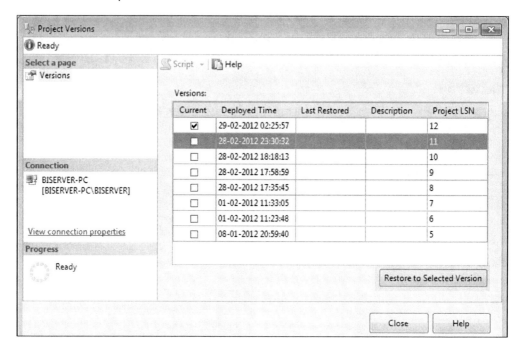

▶ **Export**—Exports the current package

▶ **Reports**—Generates reports at the R02_Project Deployment Mode level (applied in the report filters)

Using event handlers and system variables for custom logging

The previous recipes described two different approaches to manage and control SSIS packages, projects, and executions. If everything works successfully, nothing more needs to be done, but if something goes wrong with data or more information is required, maybe another step should be taken, which could be from simple to very complicated. Imagine the case if some record fails a lookup or even an unexpected error arises. The previous logging information is enough to detect the data quality problem, but may not be enough to troubleshoot and identify the origin of the problem. There are several reasons that custom logging can be applied:

▶ Accessing error records could be needed

▶ Default logging information is too much or too little (independently of the deployment approach followed)

▶ SSIS administrators may be interested to take control of SSIS packages through SSIS frameworks they manually created before

▶ There may be a need to create custom logging information to fit a specific scenario

▶ There may be a desire to control everything that happens in batch mode under an SSIS project or package

Custom logging will be easier since this new SQL version, and will maintain an important position in logging SSIS projects and packages. For that reason, this recipe will explain how to integrate custom logging with the logging mechanism provided by SSIS in both approaches.

The big improvement, and maybe the one that required least effort to include in this version, is the `ExecutionID` (also known by other names such as `RunID`, `ETL_ID`, and so on.) used before that we can now get through the SSIS system variable `[System::ServerExecutionID]` in spite of generating a new one on each package execution. This ID can then be linked to logging tables created by SSIS on SQL databases and even can be included in destination tables to know the source of each row, for example in dimension tables under Data Warehousing scenarios.

Getting ready

To get ready for this recipe, follow these steps:

1. Open SQL Server Management Studio (SSMS) and create the SSIS Catalog on the server.

2. Connect to the SQL Server Database Engine.

3. In Object Explorer, expand the server node, right-click on the **Integration Services Catalogs** node, and then click **Create Catalog**.

4. Enable CLR integration and enter a password to be used as master key to encrypt sensitive data in the SSISDB database.

5. Open SQL Server Data Tools (SSDT) and create a new SSIS project.

6. Provide a name and a location for the SSIS project and proceed.

7. Select the package created by default and rename it to `P01_Master.dtsx`.

8. Add an existing package to the solution that will update the Product Dimension from the Adventure Works case study used throughout the book. Under SSIS Solution, add the existing package located at `C:\SSIS\Ch11_Event handling and Logging\FILES\P02_DimProduct.dtsx`.

9. Add an existing package to the solution that will update the Customer Dimension. Under SSIS Solution, add the existing package located at `C:\SSIS\Ch11_Event handling and Logging\FILES\P03_DimCustomer.dtsx`.

How to do it...

The following steps will explain an example of a custom logging approach using the Legacy and Project Deployment Modes. This recipe uses the same example as the previous recipes where a master package calls two child packages to update the Customer and Product dimensions.

1. Open the package `P01_Master.dtsx`.

2. Drag-and-drop two **Execute Package** tasks from the **SSIS Toolbox | Common** to the **Control Flow** design area.

3. Follow the same steps as in the previous recipe to configure both **Execute Package** tasks.

4. Press *F5* to execute the package and ensure that everything is alright.

Traditional approach

1. Create SQL objects to store custom logging for the traditional approach.

2. Open SQL Server Management Studio (SSMS) and execute the SQL Script `SQLObjects_TraditionalLogging.sql` located at `C:\SSIS\Ch11_Event handling and Logging\FILES` to generate one SQL table and three stored procedures.

3. Go back to the SQL Server Data Tools (SSDT) and open the package `P02_DimProduct.dtsx` of the existing project.

4. Drag-and-drop one **Execute SQL task** from the **SSIS Toolbox | Favorites** to the **Control Flow** design area.

5. Rename the Execute SQL task to `SQL START SSISCustomLog`.

6. Open the **Execute SQL** task for editing.

7. Fill the **Connection** property to with `cmPacktPub_SSISbook` connection.

8. Add the following SQL statement to the `SQLStatment` property:

```
EXEC uspStart_SSISLegacyCustomLog @myPackage=?, @myMachineName=?,
@myVersionBuild=?, @myStartTime=?, @myExecutionId=?, @myRunID=?
OUTPUT
```

9. Map SSIS variables to the input and output stored procedure parameters as described:

General	Variable Name	Direction	Data Type	Paramet...	Parameter ...
Parameter Mapping	System::PackageName	Input	VARCHAR	0	100
Result Set	System::MachineName	Input	VARCHAR	1	15
Expressions	System::VersionBuild	Input	LARGE_INTEGER	2	4
	System::StartTime	Input	DATE	3	12
	System::ExecutionInstanceGUID	Input	VARCHAR	4	50
	User::RunPackageID	Output	LONG	5	8

10. Close the editor and link this task to the **Data Flow** task.

11. Drag-and-drop one **Execute SQL task** from the **SSIS Toolbox | Favorites** to the **Control Flow** design area.

12. Rename the Execute SQL task to `SQL FINISH SSISCustomLog`.

13. Open the **Execute SQL** task for editing.

14. Fill the `Connection` property with the `cmPacktPub_SSISbook` connection.

15. Add the following SQL statement to the `SQLStatment` property:

    `EXEC uspFinish_SSISLegacyCustomLog ?`

16. Map the SSIS variables to the input stored procedure parameter as described in the following screenshot:

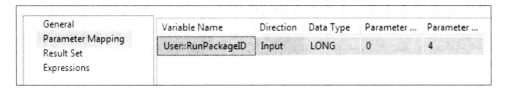

17. Close the editor and link the **Data Flow** task to this **Execute SQL** task.

18. Configure event handlers to be executed each time an error occurs in the package.

19. Select the **Event Handlers** tab.

20. In the **Executable** drop-down property, select **P02_DimProduct**.

21. In the **Event hander** drop-down property, select **OnError** event.

22. Click on the existing link as shown in the following screenshot:

> Click here to create an 'OnError' event handler for executable 'P02_DimProduct'

23. The event handler now created is just required to add the procedure to update the custom log table in SQL database.

24. Drag-and-drop one **Execute SQL task** from the **SSIS Toolbox | Favorites** to the **Control Flow** design area.

25. Rename the **Execute SQL** task to `SQL FAIL SSISCustomLog`.

26. Open the **Execute SQL** task for editing.

27. Fill the `Connection` property with the `cmPacktPub_SSISbook` connection.

28. Add the following SQL statement to the **SQLStatement** property:

```
EXEC uspFail_SSISLegacyCustomLog ?
```

29. Map the SSIS variables to the input stored procedure parameter `RunID` as done before.

30. Close the editor.

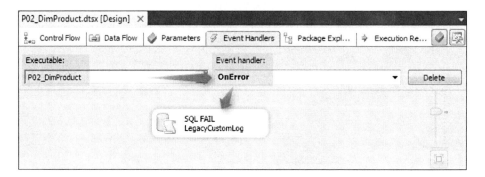

31. Execute the package selecting it on the Solution Explorer.

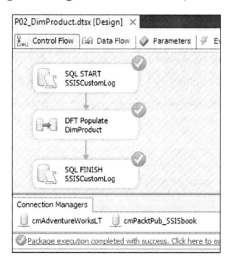

32. Read the contents of **SSISLegacyCustomLog** through SQL Server Management Studio (SSMS).

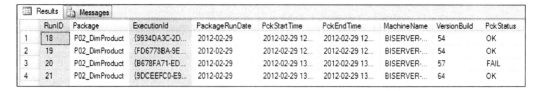

	RunID	Package	ExecutionId	PackageRunDate	PckStartTime	PckEndTime	MachineName	VersionBuild	PckStatus
1	18	P02_DimProduct	{9934DA3C-2D...	2012-02-29	2012-02-29 12...	2012-02-29 12...	BISERVER-...	54	OK
2	19	P02_DimProduct	{FD6778BA-9E...	2012-02-29	2012-02-29 12...	2012-02-29 12...	BISERVER-...	54	OK
3	20	P02_DimProduct	{B678FA71-ED...	2012-02-29	2012-02-29 13...	2012-02-29 13...	BISERVER-...	57	FAIL
4	21	P02_DimProduct	{9DCEEFC0-E9...	2012-02-29	2012-02-29 13...	2012-02-29 13...	BISERVER-...	64	OK

Project Deployment Mode

The previous custom log steps could be applied also to the Project Deployment Model. However, if the new approach is used, the link to the `sysssislog` table log is not useful; it's better to connect directly to the operation table with `[System::ServerExecutionID]`, which is a unique sequential identifier that makes the *bridge* between custom logging and all the tables inside the SSISDB database.

The `[System::ServerExecutionID]` variable gets populated when running the package on the server. For that reason, it is not possible to run the package in the debug mode.

How it works...

SSIS system variables assume an important role in custom logging. These variables are listed in the following screenshot and the ones highlighted enable the link between custom logging and SSIS logging in the two approaches:

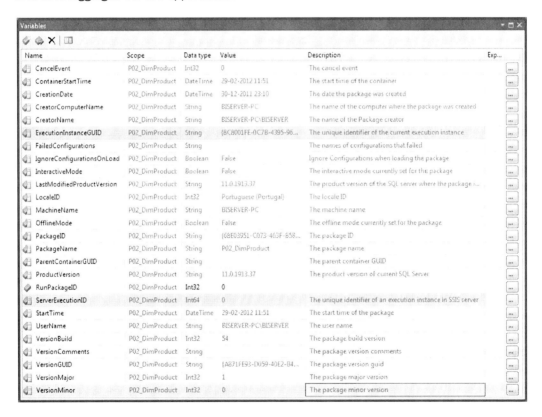

From the previous list, two new system SSIS variables are highlighted. One is very important and already referred to before, the [System::ServerExecutionID] (which provides the execution ID that the SSIS Catalog assigned to the current execution) and the other is the [System::IgnoreConfigurationsOnLoad] (a Boolean value that indicates if the package should ignore configurations or not).

There's more...

We will now look at a few other things.

The traditional approach—Legacy Deloyment Model

This traditional approach for custom logging uses the old sysdtslog90 logging table and could still be used in both deployment model approaches. However, while in the Legacy Deployment Model the SSIS variable that should be used to link custom logging with SSIS logging is [System::ExecutionInstanceGUID], in the Project Deployment Model the suggested SSIS variable is [System::ServerExecutionID] (although it would be possible to still link to the old sysssislog table.) Another difference is that while in the Legacy Deployment Model [System::ExecutionInstanceGUID] represents a unique identifier for each package execution, in the Project Deployment Model [System::ServerExecutionID] represents the unique identifier for the project execution.

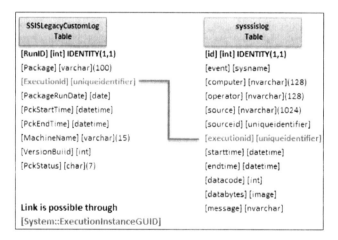

The new approach—Project Deployment Model

As already mentioned, the new approach has an SSIS Catalog that is responsible for automatically storing almost all of the logging information. If more logging data is required, custom tables and views could be added to SSISDB, which supports the catalog.

Enriching default views

One important consideration to enrich the default SSISDB database is to include some views with contextual descriptions that are currently missing on the SSISDB. The views described below have several columns with just ID values that are not yet intuitive information, because the respective meaning is not present there. For example, the status of a specific execution is displayed in the table executions with an ID. It would be better if the description **Succeed** were displayed.

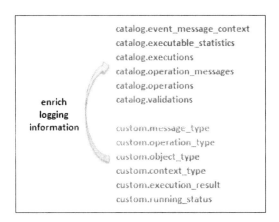

The suggested custom tables to enrich the logging information could be the following ones:

custom.message_type catalog.operation_messages		custom.operation_type catalog.operations		custom.object_type catalog.operations	
message type value	**message type description**	**operation type value**	**operation type description**	**object type**	**object type description**
-1	Unknown	1	Integration Services initialization	10	folder
10	Error	2	Retention window (SQL Agent job)	20	project
11	Warning	3	MaxProjectVersion (SQL Agent job)	30	package
12	Information	101	deploy_project (Stored procedure)	40	environment
20	Pre-validate	106	restore_project (Stored procedure)	50	Instance of execution
21	Post-validate	200	create_execution and start_execution (SPs)		
22	Pre-execute	202	stop_operation (Stored procedure)		
23	Post-execute	300	validate_project (Stored procedure)		
24	Progress	301	validate_package (Stored procedure)		
50	Status change	1000	configure_catalog (Stored procedure)		
51	Query canceled				
52	Task failed				
100	Custom				

custom.execution_result
catalog.executable_statistics

execution result	execution result description
0	Success
1	Failure
2	Completion
3	Cancelled

custom.running_status
catalog.operations
catalog.validations
catalog.executions

status	status description
1	created
2	running
3	canceled
4	failed
5	pending
6	ended unexpectedly
7	succeeded
8	stopping
9	completed

Get row counts

It's possible to get rows that move from one source to a destination component under a Data Flow component through the **rows_sent** column located in the [internal].[execution_ data_statistics] table and explicit in the following SQL statement:

```
SELECT  execution_id, data_stats_id, package_name,
        task_name, source_component_name,
        destination_component_name,
rows_sent
FROM    catalog.execution_data_statistics
ORDER BY  data_stats_id,execution_id,
        source_component_name, destination_component_name
```

	execution ..	package_name	packa...	task_name	d	source..	destination_component_name	rows_sent	created_time
1	56	P02_DimProduct.dtsx	project	DFT Populate DimProduct	O	OLE_...	LKP LookUp for Product Category	295	2012-02-29 01:4
2	56	P02_DimProduct.dtsx	project	DFT Populate DimProduct	L	LKP L...	LKP Check If Product exists in DimProduct	295	2012-02-29 01:4
3	56	P02_DimProduct.dtsx	project	DFT Populate DimProduct	O	OLE_...	LKP LookUp for Product Category	0	2012-02-29 01:4
4	56	P02_DimProduct.dtsx	project	DFT Populate DimProduct	L	LKP L...	LKP Check If Product exists in DimProduct	0	2012-02-29 01:4
5	56	P02_DimProduct.dtsx	project	DFT Populate DimProduct	L	LKP C...	OLE_DST Insert DimProduct data	0	2012-02-29 01:4
6	56	P03_DimCustomer.dtsx	project	DFT Update DimCustomer SCD	O	DFT G...	Slowly Changing Dimension	417	2012-02-29 01:4
7	56	P03_DimCustomer.dtsx	project	DFT Update DimCustomer SCD	N	Slowly...	Union All	0	2012-02-29 01:4
8	56	P03_DimCustomer.dtsx	project	DFT Update DimCustomer SCD	O	DFT G...	Slowly Changing Dimension	0	2012-02-29 01:4
9	56	P03_DimCustomer.dtsx	project	DFT Update DimCustomer SCD	C	Slowly...	OLE DB Command 1	0	2012-02-29 01:4

The most often required information under this context is usually the rows read from source and the rows inserted into destination and not all the rows passing between several components (although this is also important). However, the type of component (**Source**, **Destination**, or **Transform**) is not identified; for that reason, a good and consistent naming convention is recommended. This could be done by filtering the **destination_component_name** column, for example OLE_SRC to get rows from the Source or OLE_DST to get rows inserted into destination.

Custom reporting services reports

To get more from the SSIDB Catalog, it is possible to call custom reports created through the reporting services project. The data source for these custom reports could be some of the views created by default by the SSISBD database or even by the custom tables mentioned before to better contextualize logging information.

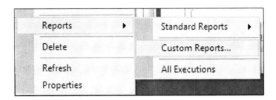

Each approach has advantages and disadvantages, and the decision to choose one will depend on each scenario. The new approach avoids redundant work and has more control over what is happening under the project, while the traditional approach has years of proved work.

12

Execution

by Reza Rad

In this chapter, we will cover the following topics:

- ▶ Execution from SSMS
- ▶ Execution from a command-line utility
- ▶ Execution from a scheduled SQL Server Agent job

Introduction

SSIS packages and projects should be run on a machine that is usually called an SSIS server. In some scenarios companies decide to use the same database server as an SSIS server, and in some cases, companies decide to use a dedicated server as an SSIS server. Choosing between a dedicated SSIS server or using an existing database server as an SSIS server is a decision that requires the consideration of resource consumption for running SSIS packages, expected load, and availability of servers.

Running, or in the other words, the *execution* of SSIS packages and projects should be different in a production environment because production environments do not have SSDT installed in most cases. In this chapter, we will discuss and illustrate the different methods of executing a package and project.

In most cases, SSIS packages are executed on a scheduled basis, but there are some cases where an administrator or authorized user needs to run the package "on demand". SSIS packages can be executed from an external application, which can be in any programming language. For .NET programming languages, we can use a specific library for the execution of a package, a process that will be described in *Chapter 14*, *Programming SSIS*. For other programming languages, command-line utilities can be used to execute the package.

Execution of a package creates some logs and entries, which help troubleshooting. We will take a look at how to troubleshoot package execution in this chapter.

One of the execution methods is executing a package or project from SSDT. We will not discuss this method any more, as we had many examples in this book in which execution was performed directly from SSDT, but we will discuss other methods briefly.

Execution from SSMS

In a production environment, there will be some cases where an administrator or an authorized user wants to execute a package; and note that the production environment will not have SSDT installed in many cases. Hence, execution from SSMS is one of the easy options that is handy for users.

In this recipe we run an SSIS project from SSMS. We deployed the project on SQL Server in *Chapter 9, Deployment*.

Getting ready

We need to have the SSIS project deployed on SSMS from the previous chapter.

How to do it...

1. Open SSMS from **Start | All Programs | Microsoft SQL Server | SQL Server Management Studio**.

2. Connect to the database engine and set the server name as `local` (or if you used another instance or server name provide that as server).

3. In **Object Explorer**, under your server name, expand **Integration Services Catalogs** and then under **SSISDB**, from **R01_Deployment From SSDT** right-click on **P02_Child.dtsx** and click on **Execute**.

4. In the **Execute Package** window, just click on **OK** to execute the package (we will work with some settings of this window in the next steps).

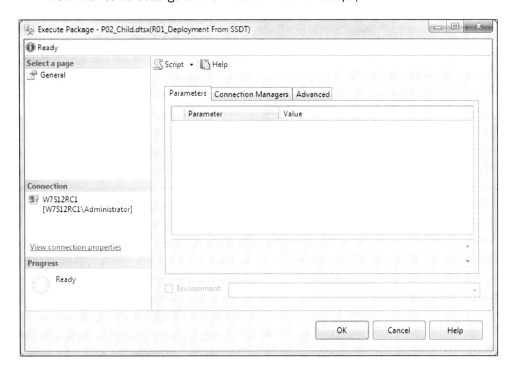

5. You will see a message that says the package started processing and if you want to see the detailed activities list click on **Yes**.

6. In the **Overview** report, you will see list of execution overviews, which shows the order of execution of tasks, and in the **Execution Information** table you will see the ID of each package and the status of execution, duration, start, and end time of the package and the user that runs the package. There is a list for parameters, which we will discuss briefly in *Chapter 13, Restartability and Robustness.*

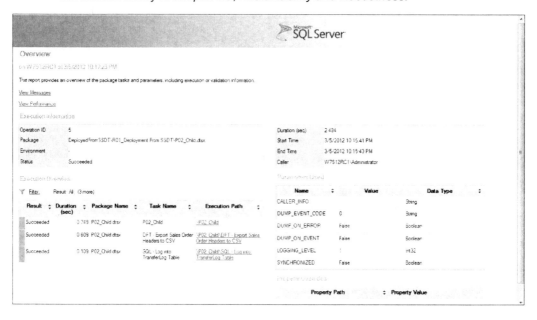

7. In the top left-part of the overview window click on the **View Messages** link; you will see details of activities that are performed at execution time and their properties.

8. In **Object Explorer**, go under **Databases** and expand **PacktPub_SSISbook**, and under **Tables**, right-click on **TransferLog** and click on **Select Top 1000 Rows**; you will see a value in **RowTransfered** and the time of execution of the package (note that this is not related to every package execution, this is what is implemented in P02_Child to track the execution of packages and the number of rows transferred).

9. Open a query window in SSMS and run the following query:

```
USE [PacktPub_SSISbook]
GO
CREATE SCHEMA [Sales] AUTHORIZATION [dbo]
GO
```

And then run the following query:

```
select top 120 *
into [PacktPub_SSISbook].[Sales].[SalesOrderHeader]
from [AdventureWorks2012].[Sales].[SalesOrderHeader]
```

This statement will create a snapshot of SalesOrderHeader in PacktPub_SSISbook with only 120 rows. We will use this as the source data for the next run of P02_Child.dtsx in the next step.

10. In **Object Explorer** right-click on the P02_Child.dtsx package and select **Execute** (in the same way we described in step 3).

11. In the **Execute Package** window, go to the **Connection Managers** tab, and select LocalHost.AdventureWorks2012.sa from the left-hand side panel, and in the right-hand side panel click on the ellipsis button next to the **ConnectionString** property, and change the **Initial Catalog** from *AdventureWorks2012* to *PacktPub_SSISbook*.

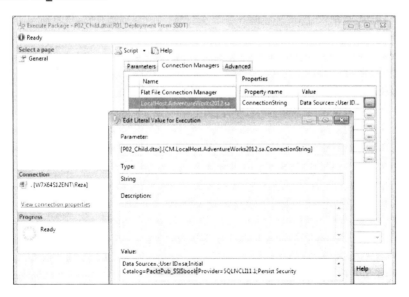

12. Click on **OK** and run the package. Before clicking on **OK** note that if you used SQL Authentication in the connection string then you might also have to set a password.

13. After running the package successfully, browse on rows in the `TransferLog` table in the `PacktPub_SSISbook` database and you will see that the number for `RowTransfered` changed this time to 120. This means that the package connected to another connection string during the second execution.

How it works...

Executing packages from SSMS is one of the most common methods of SSIS package execution. We can run a package from SSMS, change the Connection Manager's connection string properties before execution, and view results and logs of execution.

There's more...

Execution from SSMS has some specific features such as viewing execution reports, changing logging options, running in legacy mode, and validation, which will be discussed in this section.

Logging level

We can change the logging level at the time of execution in this way: In the **Execute Package** window, under the **Advanced** tab, change the logging level.

There are four options for logging level:

1. None
2. Basic
3. Performance
4. Verbose

Logging level goes into deeper detail as you change from *None* to *Verbose*. Logging levels are discussed in *Chapter 11, Event Handling and Logging*.

Package validation

We can validate packages with SSMS. Validating a package helps an authorized user to be assured about the correctness of configurations made on a package. To validate a package just right-click on the package and select **Validate**. You can change the connection string and advanced settings as well in the **Execute Package** window.

Execution and validation reports

You can open summary of execution or validation reports by right-clicking on the package under **Reports,** and then under **Standard Reports** selecting **All Executions** or **All Validations**.

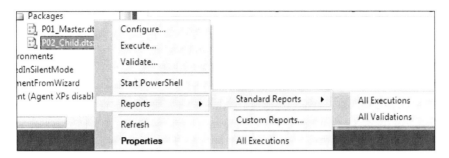

A sample of an Execution Summary Report showed is shown next:

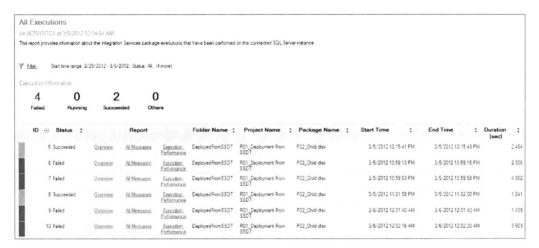

Legacy package execution from SSMS

There is another way of executing a package through SSMS, which is a legacy method. In this method we connect to Integration Services through SSMS and then use DTEXECUI to run the package. DTEXECUI will be discussed more in the next recipe.

Execution from a command-line utility

Execution of a package from SSMS is very easy and handy, but there are many cases where you might want to execute a package from the command line in silent mode, or you may want to run it from an external application or you may want to run some SSIS packages within a batch file. SSIS provides a Command Line Utility to support such cases and execute a package without need of any specific GUI.

In this recipe we will execute a package from the Command Line Utility and will discuss different options for execution.

Getting ready

We need to have an SSIS project deployed on SSMS from *Chapter 9, Deployment*.

How to do it...

1. Open the Command Prompt and go to this path:

   `C:\Program Files\Microsoft SQL Server\110\DTS\Binn`

   And run this command:

   DTExec /?

2. Then run this command:

   DTExec /SQL P02_Child

   P02_Child package will be run and its execution log will appear in the command prompt window. This command runs a package from SQL Server storage.

3. Then run the following command:

   DTExec /SQL P02_Child /Conn LocalHost.AdventureWorks2012.sa;"
   Data Source=.;User ID=sa;Password=*;Initial Catalog=PacktPub_**
   SSISbook;Provider=SQLNCLI11.1;Persist Security Info=True;Auto
   Translate=False;"

   This command runs the P02_Child package from SQL Server with a specific connection string for the connection manager LocalHost. AdventureWorks2012.sa.

4. Run this command:

   DTExec /ISServer "\SSISDB\DeployedFromSSDT\R01_Deployment From
   SSDT\P02_Child.dtsx"

   This command runs the P02_Child.dtsx package from the specified path from SSIS Catalog.

5. Run the following command next:

   DTExec /SQL P02_ChildEncrypted

   You will see that the package causes a failure; this is because the package needs a password to run successfully (recall the *protection level* recipe from *Chapter 9, Deployment*).

6. Then, run this command:

   DTExec /SQL P02_ChildEncrypted /De 123

   The package runs successfully; this command runs the package, decrypting with the provided password.

How it works...

Using a command-line utility for running packages is very common. A wide variety of DTEXEC switches will help to run packages from different sources with flexible configurations, logging, and other settings. DTEXEC will be available with installation of SSIS on the machine.

DTEXEC

The Command Line Utility is a binary file with the name DTEXEC.exe in C:\Program Files\Microsoft SQL Server\110\DTS\Binn.

There's more...

There is another way of executing a package that uses DTEXEC on the backend, but with a GUI on the frontend; we will take a look at this method next.

Execution with DTExecUI

DTExecUI is a GUI tool that runs DTEXEC on the backend. To run a package in this manner, use the following steps:

1. Open **Run** and type DTExecUI.

2. In the **Execute Package Utility** window, set **Package source** as *SQL Server*, set **Server** name as local or your machine's name (or *SQL Server*, you have your SSIS packages there), and select the **Package** under it.

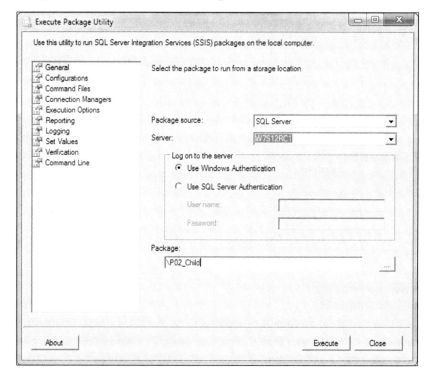

3. Go to the **Connection Managers** tab and select the LocalHost. AdventureWorks2012 database from the left-hand side panel, and change the connection string in the right-hand side panel with **Initial Catalog=PacktPub_ SSISbook**.

4. Go to the command-line window; you will see the DTEXEC command-line switches and their options, which are automatically set based on configurations that you made in DTExecUI.

5. Click on **Execute** and run the package; the results of package execution will be shown in the **Package Execution Progress** window.

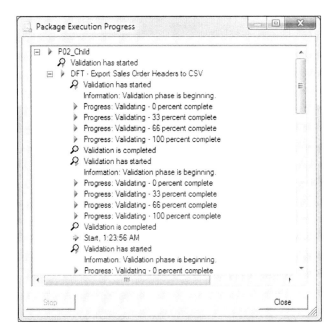

Note that this method only can be applied on a Legacy Deployment Model and doesn't extend to the new Project Deployment Model.

Execution with SSIS catalog procedures

SSIS 2012 provided some stored procedures besides the SSIS Catalog to execute packages; you can use them as follows:

1. Right-click on a package under SSIS Catalog and click on **Execute** (recall the previous recipe about *Execution from SSMS*).

2. In the **Execute Package** window, click on **Script** at the top of the window and then click on **New Query Editor Window**.

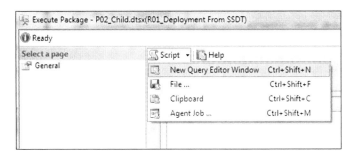

3. SQL statements to run the package appear in a query window as follows:

```
Declare @execution_id bigint
EXEC [SSISDB].[catalog].[create_execution] @package_name=N'P02_
Child.dtsx', @execution_id=@execution_id OUTPUT, @folder_
name=N'DeployedFromSSDT', @project_name=N'R01_Deployment From
SSDT', @use32bitruntime=False, @reference_id=Null
Select @execution_id
DECLARE @var0 smallint = 1
EXEC [SSISDB].[catalog].[set_execution_parameter_value] @
execution_id, @object_type=50, @parameter_name=N'LOGGING_LEVEL',
@parameter_value=@var0
EXEC [SSISDB].[catalog].[start_execution] @execution_id
GO
```

4. Run the statements; the Package ID will be returned, and then you can check the **Execution Report** to see the results of the execution of this package.

Note that this method is only for executing packages that are deployed in the new Project Deployment Model and won't work with the Legacy Package Deployment Model. SSIS Catalog has many stored procedures, which will be completely described in *Chapter 13, Restartability and Robustness*.

32-bit / 64-bit issue

Jet engine has some problems in 64-bit so we need to work with Excel and Access files under 32-bit in most cases. When we run SSIS from SSDT there is an option in the project's **Properties** window which, is **Run64BitRuntime**; we can set this property to *False* in order to run packages in 32-bit mode.

When we want to run packages with DTEXEC and we need to run them under 32-bit modes, we can use DTEXEC 32-bit from this address:

```
C:\Program Files (x86)\Microsoft SQL Server\110\DTS\Binn\DTEXEC.exe
```

Note that the 32-bit providers should be installed at the time of SQL Server installation.

Execution from a scheduled SQL Server Agent job

ETL processes can be executed on a schedule, and this schedule can be daily, weekly, or at larger intervals of time. ETL or any Data Transfer process is better done during off-peak times in order to reduce resource and memory consumption; for example a database engine may have a lot of requests during daytime hours. So if the ETL process runs at daytime, this will cause long responses to requests, which will affect the performance of your server, so this process probably should be run late at night when the number of requests to the server is much lower.

SQL Server has a service that provides scheduling tasks; this service is named SQL Server Agent. The SQL Server Agent service can be installed with SQL Server setup media. This service should be running if we want to use scheduled jobs. SQL Server Agent Service isn't just for SSIS scheduling but is for scheduling T-SQL commands as well, for backing up, restoring, and many other things that are beyond the scope of this book.

In this recipe we will take a look at how to schedule a package with an SQL Server Agent job. There are some common problems when SSIS packages run under an SQL Server Agent job; we will consider them and discuss how to solve them.

Getting ready

To get ready for this recipe, use the following steps:

1. The SSIS Project from the previous chapter needs to be deployed.

2. The SQL Server Agent Service should be started; you can start it as follows:

   ❑ Go to **Start | All Programs | Microsoft SQL Server | Configuration Tools** and open **SQL Server Configuration Manager**.

   ❑ In the left-hand side pane, click on **SQL Server Services** and in the right-hand side pane right-click on **SQL Server Agent** and click on **Start** (if it is not started already).

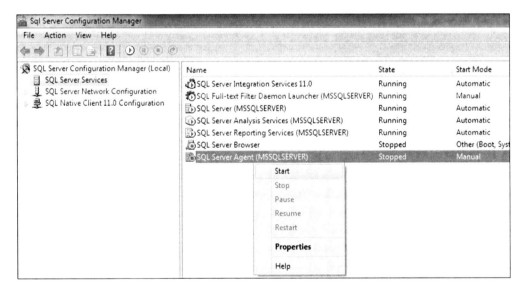

How to do it...

1. Open SSMS and **Connect** to **Database Engine**.

2. In **Object Explorer**, expand the server's name and then expand the **SQL Server Agent** node, and under it right-click on **Jobs** and then click on **New Job**.

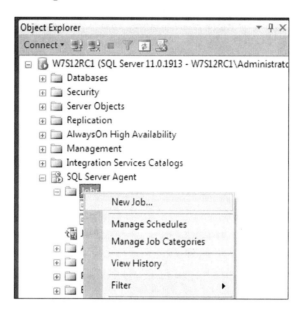

3. In the **New Job** window, set the name of the job as `Ch12_R03`.

4. Go to the **Steps** tab and click on **New**; in the **New Job Step,** name the step `RunSSISPackage`.

5. In the **Type** drop-down list, select **SQL Server Integration Services Package**. Leave the **Run as** drop-down as it is (we will discuss it later in this recipe).

6. Set **Package source** as *SSIS Catalog* (this is the default option), set **Server name** as local or your computer's name (or any other server that you used as an SSIS server), and set **Package** as follows:

   ```
   \SSISDB\DeployedFromSSDT\R01_Deployment From SSDT\P02_Child.
   dtsx
   ```

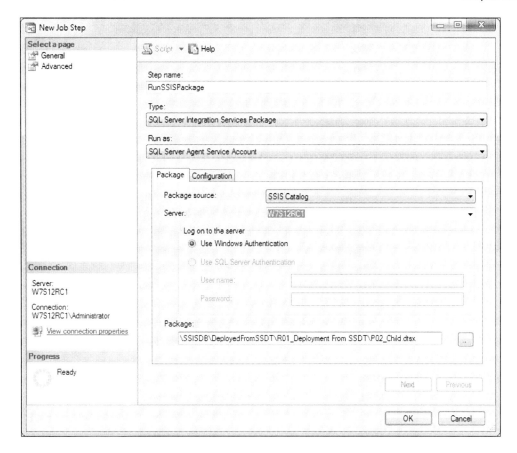

7. Click on **OK** and close the **Job Step** window. Go to the **Schedule** tab and click on **Create New Schedule**, name it OneTimeTestSchedule, and then change the schedule type to *One Time*. Set the time to two minutes after your system's current time.

8. After two minutes, right-click on the **Ch12_R03** job under **Jobs** in SSMS, and select **View History**. In the **Log File Viewer** window you can see the execution log of the SQL Server Job that shows the SQL Server job running successfully.

How it works...

The previous steps showed how to create a job in SQL Server Agent to run a package. SQL Server has an Agent service, which is responsible for running scheduled tasks.

Running a package under SQL Server Agent can be configured within a **Job Step** window. If you choose *SSIS Catalog* as **Package Source** then the configuration tab will show as an **Execute Package** window in the Project Deployment model type and if you choose another **Package Source** then the configuration tab will show as an **Execute Package Utility** window in the Package Deployment model; the next screenshot depicts the **Configuration** tab of the P02_Child package.

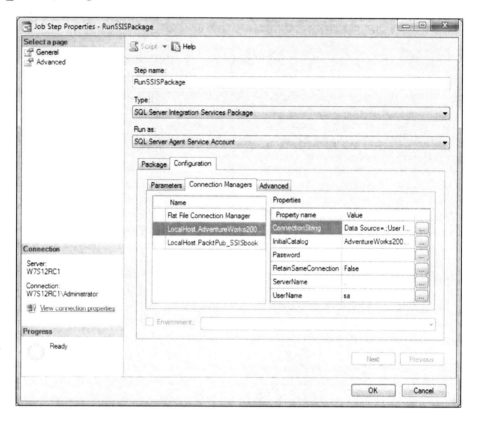

We can set the schedule as *Recurring Daily, Weekly*, or *Monthly*. Also, we can set the schedule type to be run whenever the SQL Server Agent starts or whenever the CPU becomes idle.

Each Job in SQL Server Agent has a history log that can be seen simply by right-clicking on **Job** in SSMS and opening **View History**; details of the job log can be seen there.

There's more...

Running SSIS packages under an SQL Server Agent job is very handy and useful; you will see many SSIS packages that are scheduled and run under an SQL Server Agent job. However, there may be some problems when you run packages under SQL Server Agent; we will take a look at those issues and how to solve them.

Running SQL Server Agent job under a proxy account

One of the most common problems when you run SSIS packages under an SQL Server Agent job is the authentication and permissions related to account problems. Every job will be run under an SQL Server Agent Service account by default. So, if you run an SSIS Package under an SQL Server Agent Service account, it will cause two kinds of problems:

- If you use Windows Authentication in connections in the SSIS package then the SSIS package will connect to an underlying database with the account that runs the package, so in the job's default configuration it will be run under an SQL Server Agent Service. And, if the SQL Server Agent Service Account doesn't have access to the underlying database (which is usually the case), then you will get connection errors after running the job in **Job History**.

- If you used a deployed SSIS package under user-dependent Protection Levels **Encrypt All With User Key** or **Encrypt Sensitive With User Key** (default option), then only the user who developed and deployed the package can run it successfully, so you will need to run SQL Server Job under another account than SQL Server Agent's default Service Account.

In both the above cases, we need to run SQL Server jobs under a specific Windows account. To run a job step under a specific Windows account we need to create a Proxy Account. The steps given next illustrate how to create a proxy account and run an SQL Server job step under this proxy account:

1. Open SSMS, expand the server name in **Object Explorer**, and then under **Security** right-click on the **Credentials** node and click on **New Credential**.

2. In the **New Credential** window, set **Credential name** as `myTestUserCred` and set **Identity** as your current user (the user who has access to run the package and also has access to underlying databases); you can set a password for this credential as well.

3. In **Object Explorer**, under **SQL Server Agent**, right-click on **Proxies**, and click on **New Proxy**.

4. In the **New Proxy Account** window, set the **Proxy name** as *myTestSSISProxy*, and select **myTestUserCred** in the **Credential name** field; in the **Active to the following subsystems** section, just select *SQL Server Integration Services Package*.

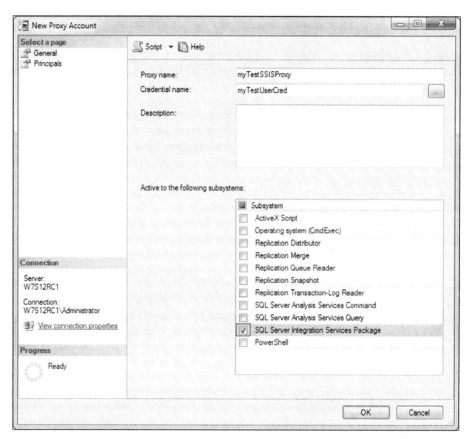

5. Open the `Ch12R03` job under **Jobs** in SSMS, and double-click on **Job Step** to open the **Job Step Properties** window, and then in the **Run as** drop-down list you will see the proxy account, which you created in the previous step; just select **myTestSSISProxy** there. This will guarantee that this job step will be run under the account that is connected to the credential that is connected to this proxy account.

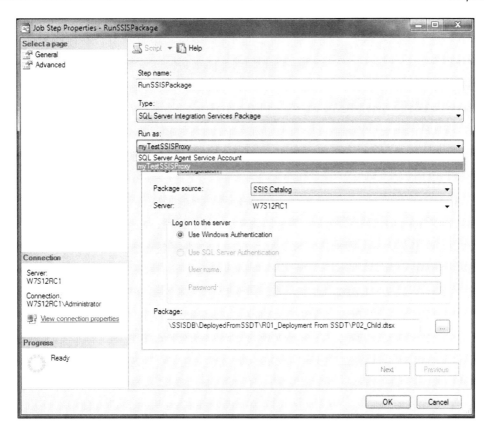

Note that this is highly recommended to run an SSIS package that is running jobs under a proxy account because it will reduce the risk of the problems that we discussed earlier.

Creating an SQL Server job more easily

You can create an SQL Server job from the **Execute Package** window in a simple and easy way, with just a single click on the **Script** button in the top left-hand side corner of the **Execute Package** window and selecting **Agent Job**, as shown in the following screenshot:

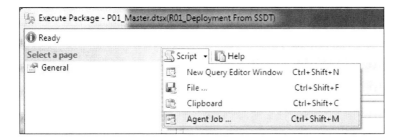

You can set a schedule after that and the job will be created. An example of a created job can be seen here:

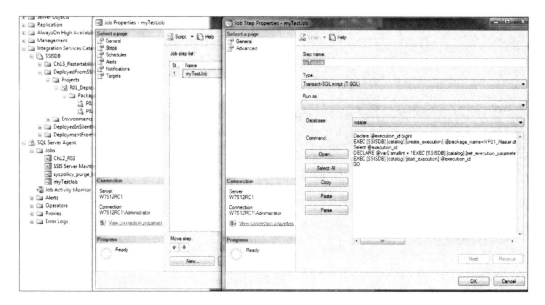

Note that this is only for creating the job, not the proxy. You will need to create a proxy account once each for all jobs.

13

Restartability and Robustness

by Reza Rad

In this chapter, we will cover the following topics:

- ▶ Parameters: Passing values to package from outside
- ▶ Package configuration: Legacy method to inter-relation
- ▶ Transactions: Doing multiple operations atomic
- ▶ Checkpoints: The power of restartability
- ▶ SSIS reports and catalog views

Introduction

Data transfer packages should be robust in design. There are times that a package can get values from outside and set some ETL parts based on input variable. You learned how to create dynamic SSIS packages in the previous chapters, but to run a package dynamically, you may need to pass some values from outside of the package. Package parameters provide a way to get values from outside of the package. With changing parameter values, the package doesn't need to recompile.

Parameters differ from variables. Variables are designed to work inside the package but parameters are designed to get values from outside. Parameters are only available in new Project Deployment Model.

Legacy Package Deployment Model used package configuration for inter-relation between SSIS packages. As the legacy deployment model is in use in many environments, we will discuss related topics of this method and take a look at the package configurations and their differences in this chapter.

An SSIS package needs to save the state of Control Flow, and if one of the tasks fails, the whole package fails. Then in some cases, we just need to continue with remaining tasks instead of all tasks. Checkpoints can be applied on SSIS packages for this purpose.

One of the essential parts of each data-related system is to work with transactions. Transaction means that some of the tasks are atomic. **Atomic** means that tasks should be all successful, and if one of them fails then other operations should be rolled back. We will take a look at how to use transactions in SSIS.

As you saw in *Chapter 9, Deployment,* SSIS Catalog provides a lot of useful features to work with packages in production environments. In this chapter, we will see SSIS Catalog Views which provide all information about packages under SSIS Catalog and can be used in wide range of areas, in custom applications and custom reports.

SSIS Catalog also provides a wide range of reports from package information which is very helpful for an administrator or power user in production environment. Reports can show which reports run successfully or not, and which tasks take longer time than other tasks and other useful information. In this chapter, we will see an overview of SSIS reports.

Parameters: Passing values to packages from outside

Packages need to be configurable from outside. Different environments may need different configuration for executing SSIS packages. Parameters are designed to get values and configuration from outside of package, and their main benefit is that they can be configured after deployment, so there will be no need to compile the package after changing the parameter's values.

Parameters can be used within SSIS packages in expressions or as variables, but don't use them counterproductively. Variables are designed to pass values inside package, and parameters are designed to pass values from outside of package.

SSIS Catalog has the ability to pass parameter values with predefined configuration which is called environment. Environments are designed to add multiple configurations and use them as needed.

In this recipe, we will create a data transfer scenario to log all tables' name and number of rows into a database table. We will create two packages and transfer values from master package to child. Finally, we will deploy the project and execute from SSMS with different source database.

Getting ready

Create a table for log entries in `PacktPub_SSISbook` with the following script:

```
CREATE TABLE [dbo].[DbTablesInfo](
  [ID] [int] IDENTITY(1,1) NOT NULL,
  [Connection] [varchar](500) NULL,
  [TableName] [varchar](500) NULL,
  [RowNumber] [int] NULL,
  [DateTime] [datetime] NULL,
 CONSTRAINT [PK_DbTablesInfo] PRIMARY KEY CLUSTERED
(
  [ID] ASC
)WITH (PAD_INDEX = OFF, STATISTICS_NORECOMPUTE = OFF, IGNORE_DUP_KEY =
OFF, ALLOW_ROW_LOCKS = ON, ALLOW_PAGE_LOCKS = ON) ON [PRIMARY]
) ON [PRIMARY]
```

How to do it...

1. Create an SSIS project and name it as `R01_Parameters`.

2. In **Solution Explorer**, right-click on **Connection Managers**, and add new connection manager of type **OLE DB**. Set the connection to the `PacktPub_SSISbook` database.

3. Create another **Connection Manager** in **Solution Explorer** of type **OLE DB**, set the connection to master database. After the creation rename the **Connection Manager** to `custom.conmgr`.

4. Rename `Package.dtsx` to `P2_Child.dtsx`. Double-click on it.

5. In **Connection Managers** pane of **P2_Child.dtsx**, right-click on **(project) custom** connection manager and select **Parameterize...**.

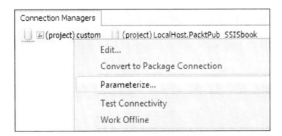

6. In the **Parameterize** window, set the **Property** as *ConnectionString*, and select the **Create new parameter** radio button. Name it as **ConnectionStr**, leave the default value as is. Set **Scope** as **Project**, and check the **Required** check box. We will talk about these settings later in the *How it works* section.

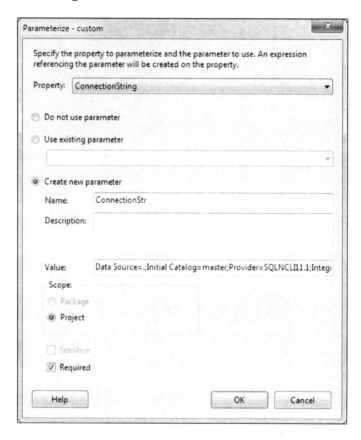

7. Click on the **OK** button and close the window. You can double-click on **Project. params** in **Solution Explorer** and check if the parameter is created there correctly. Note that we can create or delete parameters in this window directly and then use them in the **Parameterize** window in **Use existing parameter** radio button.

8. Go back to the P2_Child package and go to the **Parameters** tab, create a new parameter and name it as **TableName** with String data type. We will use this parameter to get table name from outside of package.

9. Go back to Control Flow and create two variables as follows:

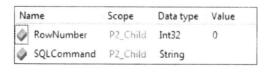

Name	Scope	Data type	Value
RowNumber	P2_Child	Int32	0
SQLCommand	P2_Child	String	

10. Add an Expression Task to Control Flow, rename it to `EXT - Create SQL Command`, and write the following expression:

    ```
    @[User::SQLCommand]= "select count(*) as cnt from "+ @
    [$Package::TableName]
    ```

11. Note the specific signature of parameters, they can be used in this format:

    ```
    @[$<scope of parameter>::<name of parameter>]
    ```

12. Add an Execute SQL Task after the **EXT – Create SQL Command**, and name it as **SQL - Fetch Row Number**.

13. In Execute SQL Task Editor, set connection to *Custom* Connection Manager, set **SQLSourceType** as *Variable*, and set **SourceVariable** as *User::SQLCommand*. Also set **ResultSet** property to *Single Row*. In the **Result Set** tab, add a **Result Name** `cnt` and map it to the variable name `User::RowNumber`.

14. Add another Execute SQL Task after it, and name it as **SQL - Log Info in DB**.

15. In Execute SQL Task Editor, set connection to the `PacktPub_SSISbook` database, and write this statement in the `SQLStatement` property:

    ```
    INSERT INTO [dbo].[DbTablesInfo]
                ([Connection]
                ,[TableName]
                ,[RowNumber]
                ,[DateTime])
          VALUES
                (?
                ,?
                ,?
                ,getdate())
    ```

16. Go to the **Parameter Mappings** tab and add the following mappings:

Variable Name	Direction	Data Type	Parameter Name	Parameter Size
$Project::ConnectionStr	Input	VARCHAR	0	-1
$Package::TableName	Input	VARCHAR	1	-1
User::RowNumber	Input	LONG	2	-1

17. Now the P2_Child package is completed. This package gets connection string and table name from parameters and fetches number of table's records and logs it into DbTablesInfo table in PacktPub_SSISbook. The following is the whole schema of P2_Child.dtsx.

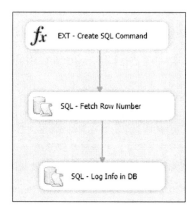

18. Add another package and name it as P1_Master.dtsx.

19. Open the P1_Master package, drag-and-drop an Execute SQL Task and rename it to SQL - Empty Log Table.

20. In Execute SQL Task Editor, set connection to PacktPub_SSISbook and write this statement in the SQLStatement property:

    delete from DbTablesInfo

21. After closing the Execute SQL Task Editor, right-click on **SQL – Empty Log Table** and select **Parameterize**.

22. In the **Parameterize** window, set the **Property** as *Disable*, and select **Create new parameter**, name the parameter as **AppendToLogTable**. Set the **Scope** as *Package* and leave other settings as they are. This setting will create a parameter to control the **Disable** property of Execute SQL Task.

23. Add two variables in P1_Master package as follows:

Name	Scope	Data type	Value
TableName	P1_Master	String	
TablesList	P1_Master	Object	System.Object

24. Add a Data Flow Task after the Execute SQL Task and name it as DFT - Fetch Tables List.

25. In the Data Flow Task, add an **OLE DB Source**, set the connection to *Custom Connection Manager*, set **Data Access Mode** as *SQL Command*, and write the following statement in the `SQL Command Text` property:

```
select sys.schemas.name+'.'+sys.tables.name as TableName
from sys.tables
inner join sys.schemas
on sys.tables.schema_id=sys.schemas.schema_id
```

26. Add a **Recordset Destination** after **OLE DB Source**, and in Recordset Destination Editor, set **Variable Name** as *User::TablesList* and in the **Input Columns** tab select **TableName**.

27. This is the whole schema of Data Flow (This data flow loads list of tables from data source and loads them into an object type variable):

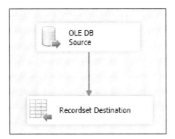

28. Go back to Control Flow, add a Foreach Loop Container after the Data Flow Task.

29. In Foreach Loop Editor, set enumerator as *Foreach ADO Enumerator*, and set **ADO object source** variable as *User::TablesList*. In the **Variable Mappings** tab, set the variable **User::TableName** with index *0*.

30. Drag-and-drop an Execute Package Task into the Foreach Loop Container, and name it as `EPT - Execute Child`.

31. In Execute Package Task Editor, go to the **Package** tab, set **ReferenceType** as *Project Reference*, and **PackageNameFromProjectReference** as *P2_Child.dtsx*.

32. Go to the **Parameter Bindings** tab and add new binding as follows:

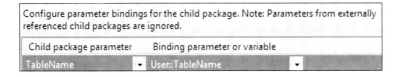

33. Now the `P1_Master` package is complete. This package gets a connection string, loops through list of its tables and executes the `P2_Child` package for each table to log in to the `DbTablesInfo` table. Note that we create an option to append log entries, so we can choose to append them or re-write them. The following is the whole schema of `P1_Master.dtsx`:

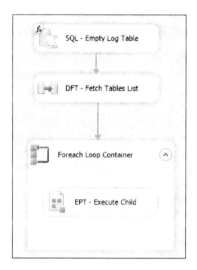

34. Run `P1_Master.dtsx` to check everything is correct. After execution of the package go to SSMS, open `DbTablesInfo` in the `PacktPub_SSISbook` database and see that there are rows which contain information about master database tables.

35. We are going to deploy the project and run it from SSMS but with different configuration at runtime.

36. Right-click on project in **Solution Explorer** and select **Deploy**. In **Select Destination** just set the **Server name** as *Local* (you can use any other server name which has SSIS Catalog, we just used local for many samples in this book), and set the path as `/SSISDB/Ch13_Restartability and Robustnetss/R01_Parameters`. (Create the folders if they don't exist before setting the path).

37. Complete the wizard to finish the deployment successfully.

38. Open SSMS and connect to Database Engine. In Object Explorer, expand the server and under `Integration Services Catalogs` under **Ch13_Restartability and Robustness**, expand **Projects** and right-click on **R01_Parameters** and select **Configure**.

39. In the **Configure** window, you will see a list of all parameters in project and package scope which are used in the project. Change the **ConnectionStr** parameter's value and just change the **Initial Catalog** name to **AdventureWorks2012**. Also, change the value of **AppendToLogTable** parameter to **True**.

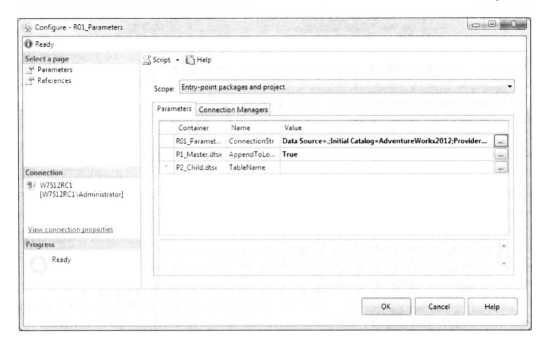

40. Close the **Configure** window, and right-click on the `P1_Master` package under the `Packages` folder in **SSMS** and execute it with default settings. Before execution just check that you can change parameter values in the **Execute Package** window also, and if you can't it will use the values which are set in the **Configure** window in earlier step.

41. After running the package, check the `PacktPub_SSISbook` table entries and you will see log entries from `AdventureWorks2012` tables which are appended to other logs.

	ID	Connection	TableName	RowNumber	DateTime
1	258	Data Source= .;Initial Catalog=master;Provider=SQLNCLI11.1;Integrated Security=SSPI..	dbo.spt_fallback_db	0	2012-03-15 16:46:09.263
2	259	Data Source= .;Initial Catalog=master;Provider=SQLNCLI11.1;Integrated Security=SSPI..	dbo.spt_fallback_dev	0	2012-03-15 16:46:09.500
3	260	Data Source= .;Initial Catalog=master;Provider=SQLNCLI11.1;Integrated Security=SSPI..	dbo.spt_fallback_usg	0	2012-03-15 16:46:09.700
4	261	Data Source= .;Initial Catalog=master;Provider=SQLNCLI11.1;Integrated Security=SSPI..	dbo.spt_monitor	1	2012-03-15 16:46:09.920
5	262	Data Source= .;Initial Catalog=master;Provider=SQLNCLI11.1;Integrated Security=SSPI..	dbo.MSreplication_options	3	2012-03-15 16:46:10.127
6	263	Data Source= .;Initial Catalog=AdventureWorks2012;Provider=SQLNCLI11.1;Integrate...	Production.ScrapReason	16	2012-03-15 16:46:50.890
7	264	Data Source= .;Initial Catalog=AdventureWorks2012;Provider=SQLNCLI11.1;Integrate...	HumanResources.Shift	3	2012-03-15 16:46:51.130
8	265	Data Source= .;Initial Catalog=AdventureWorks2012;Provider=SQLNCLI11.1;Integrate...	Production.ProductCategory	4	2012-03-15 16:46:51.307
9	266	Data Source= .;Initial Catalog=AdventureWorks2012;Provider=SQLNCLI11.1;Integrate...	Purchasing.ShipMethod	5	2012-03-15 16:46:51.527
10	267	Data Source= .;Initial Catalog=AdventureWorks2012;Provider=SQLNCLI11.1;Integrate...	Production.ProductCostHistory	395	2012-03-15 16:46:51.783
11	268	Data Source= .;Initial Catalog=AdventureWorks2012;Provider=SQLNCLI11.1;Integrate...	Production.ProductDescription	762	2012-03-15 16:46:51.967
12	269	Data Source= .;Initial Catalog=AdventureWorks2012;Provider=SQLNCLI11.1;Integrate...	Sales.ShoppingCartItem	3	2012-03-15 16:46:52.120
13	270	Data Source= .;Initial Catalog=AdventureWorks2012;Provider=SQLNCLI11.1;Integrate...	Production.ProductDocument	32	2012-03-15 16:46:52.303

How it works...

In this recipe, we created a scenario which gets an OLE DB database connection string from parameters and logs all tables from that database with their number of records into a log table.

Parameters are a new feature in SSIS 2012 and provide a way to get values from outside of package or project. There are two different scopes for parameters; project and Package scope. Package parameters can be used only inside the package, but project parameters can be used everywhere in the project.

Parameters can be marked as **Required**, which means that value for the parameter is mandatory. So if a parameter is marked as Required, the package won't run before setting a value for that parameter.

Parameters can be marked as **Sensitive**, and this property will apply encryption on the value of the parameter. Note that parameters aren't sensitive by default, so their values will be stored directly in project or package files and if you want to secure them you may need to mark them as sensitive.

Parameters can be used inside package to parameterize properties of package, connection managers, and tasks. To parameterize these properties, you can simply right-click on the object (package, task, and so on) and select **Parameterize**.

Parameters can be used in expressions with the following signature:

```
@[$<scope of parameter>::<parameter name>]
```

You can use parameters as variables in many locations in package, but don't do that! Parameters are designed to get values from outside of package. Variables are designed as a structure for passing values inside the package between tasks and components. So use package variables for inbound relations in the package and use parameters for outbound relations from outside of the package.

Parameter's value can be set at execution time of package, or as you saw within the **Configure** window which keeps parameter's values information for every execution.

There's more...

Setting parameter values from the **Configure** window is very handy but in many environments you may need to store multiple configurations and run the package with each of them as needed.

Environment

SSIS 2012 comes with a new feature called **environment**. An environment is a configuration which is predefined for parameter or connection manager's values and can be used in execution. We can create multiple environments for example for development, test, and production configurations and this is very useful in real-world scenarios.

The following steps show how to create an environment and use it:

1. In SSMS, select **Integration Services Catalogs | SSISDB** and under specific folder right-click on **Environment** and select **Create Environment**.

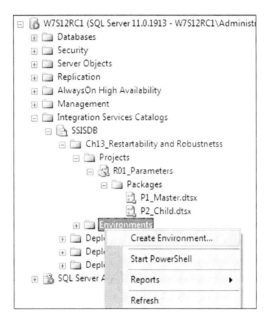

2. Name the environment as `Test`.

3. Double-click on **Test**, and in **Environment Properties** in the **Variables** tab, create two variables as shown in the following screenshot (Note that variable names here shouldn't be similar to package's variables or parameters. These variables are completely different, but we can map them to parameters and connection managers).

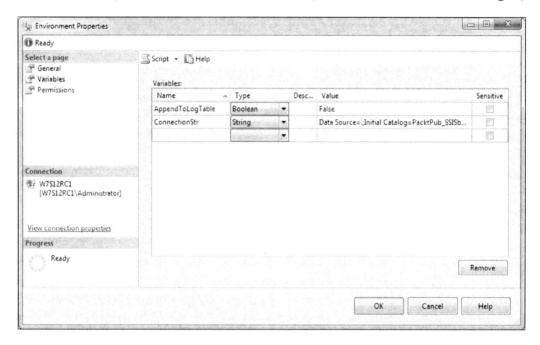

4. Right-click on the project name (R01_Parameters) in SSMS, and select **Configure**. In the **Configure** window, go to the **References** tab and add a reference to the **Test** environment.

5. Then go back to the **Parameters** tab and change parameter value. In the **Set Parameter Value** window select **Use environment variable**, and select **ConnectionStr** variable there. You can do the same for the AppendToLogTable parameter.

Note that you can use environment variables to set connection manager's properties in the **Configure** window.

6. At the time of execution of the package in the **Execute Package** window, you can choose between environments which were added as reference in the **Configure** window earlier.

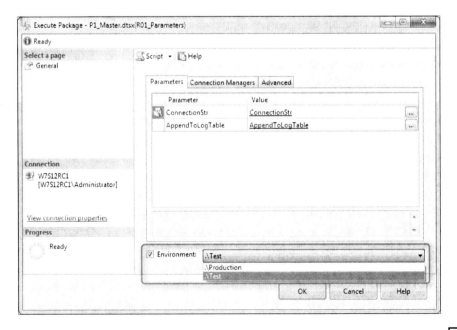

Package configuration: Legacy method to inter-relation

Legacy Package Deployment Model has the ability to configure packages also. Package configuration is the way we handle configuration in Legacy Deployment Model. Packages are different objects in legacy model which has no relation to the project, so we cannot apply project scope parameters or such things for them. However, package configuration solved this problem in another way.

Package configuration consists of properties and values which will be set outside of the package and can be used inside the package simply. There are five types of package configurations, four of them are based on the location of configuration values, and one of them is for passing values between packages.

We will take a look at some of the most common package configurations in this recipe with a sample like what we generated in the very previous recipe (*Parameters*), but this time we work with package configuration instead of parameters.

Getting ready

In this recipe, we need the same `DbTablesInfo` table from the previous recipe, so if you already created it, just run the `truncate table DbTablesInfo` statement, otherwise create a table for log entries in `PacktPub_SSISbook` with the following script:

```
CREATE TABLE [dbo].[DbTablesInfo](
  [ID] [int] IDENTITY(1,1) NOT NULL,
  [Connection] [varchar](500) NULL,
  [TableName] [varchar](500) NULL,
  [RowNumber] [int] NULL,
  [DateTime] [datetime] NULL,
 CONSTRAINT [PK_DbTablesInfo] PRIMARY KEY CLUSTERED
(
  [ID] ASC
)WITH (PAD_INDEX = OFF, STATISTICS_NORECOMPUTE = OFF, IGNORE_DUP_KEY =
OFF, ALLOW_ROW_LOCKS = ON, ALLOW_PAGE_LOCKS = ON) ON [PRIMARY]
) ON [PRIMARY]
```

How to do it...

1. Create an SSIS project and name it as `R02_Package Configuration`.

2. As we want to deal with configurations we need to use Legacy Deployment Model, so right-click on the project in **Solution Explorer** and select **Convert to Package Deployment Model**. Follow the conversion steps and complete the wizard.

3. Rename the `package.dtsx` to `P2_Child.dtsx`.

4. Create variables as shown in the following screenshot:

Name	Scope	Data type	Value	Expression
ConnectionStr	P2_Child	String	Data Source=.;Initial Catalog=master;Pr...	
RowNumber	P2_Child	Int32	0	
SQLCommand	P2_Child	String	select count(*) as cnt from	"select count(*) as cnt from "+ @[User::TableName]
TableName	P2_Child	String		

5. Set the default values for `ConnectionStr` as follows (note that you can set any other server name or database name as you want):

   ```
   Data Source=.;Initial Catalog=master;Provider=SQLNCLI11.1;Integrat
   ed Security=SSPI;Auto Translate=False;
   ```

6. Don't set the default value for the `SQLCommand` variable, just in the **Properties** window set the **Expression** property of **SQLCommand** variable to:

   ```
   "select count(*) as cnt from "+ @[User::TableName]
   ```

   Also, set the **EvaluateAsExpression** property of this variable to *true*. This is another type of setting variable value with expression, which doesn't need Expression Task.

7. Create an OLE DB connection manager, connect it to `PacktPub_SSISbook`.

8. Create another OLE DB connection manager, name it as `Custom` (you can change name of connection manager in the **Properties** window). Also, in the **Expression** property of this connection manager, set the **ConnectionString** property with the *User::ConnectionStr* variable.

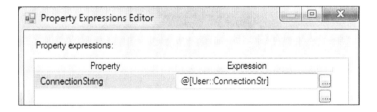

9. Add an Execute SQL Task to the `P2_Child` package's Control Flow, and name it as **SQL - Fetch Row Number**.

10. In Execute SQL Task Editor, set connection to *Custom* connection manager, set **SQLSourceType** as *Variable*, and set **SourceVariable** as *User::SQLCommand*. Also, set the **ResultSet** property to *Single Row*. And in the **Result Set** tab, add a **Result Name** cnt and map it to **Variable Name User::RowNumber**.

11. Add another Execute SQL Task after it, and name it as **SQL - Log Info in DB**.

12. In Execute SQL Task Editor, set the connection to `PacktPub_SSISbook` database, and write the following statement in the `SQLStatement` property:

```
INSERT INTO [dbo].[DbTablesInfo]
           ([Connection]
           ,[TableName]
           ,[RowNumber]
           ,[DateTime])
    VALUES
           (?
           ,?
           ,?
           ,getdate())
```

13. Go to the **Parameter Mappings** tab and add the following mappings:

Variable Name	Direction	Data Type	Parameter Name	Parameter Size
User::ConnectionStr	Input	VARCHAR	0	-1
User::TableName	Input	VARCHAR	1	-1
User::RowNumber	Input	LONG	2	-1

14. Now the `P2_Child` package is complete. This package gets connection string, table name, and fetch number of the table's records and logs them into the `DbTablesInfo` table in `PacktPub_SSISbook`. The following is the whole schema of `P2_Child.dtsx`:

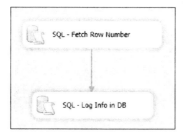

15. Add another package and name it as `P1_Master.dtsx`.

16. Add two variables in `P1_Master` package as shown in the following screenshot: (set the default value for the `ConnectionStr` variable the same as step 5).

Name	Scope	Data type	Value	Expression
ConnectionStr	P1_Master	String	Data Source=.;Initial Catalog=AdventureWorks2012;Pro...	
TableName	P1_Master	String		
TablesList	P1_Master	Object	System.Object	

17. Add two OLE DB connection managers; the same as we did in steps 7 and 8 to `P1_Master`.

18. Drag-and-drop an Execute SQL Task into the `P1_Master` Control Flow and rename it to `SQL - Empty Log Table`.

19. In Execute SQL Task Editor, set the connection to *PacktPub_SSISbook* and write the following statement in the `SQLStatement` property:

    ```
    delete from DbTablesInfo
    ```

20. Add a Data Flow Task after the Execute SQL Task and name it as `DFT - Fetch Tables List`.

21. In the Data Flow Task, add an OLE DB Source, set connection to *Custom* connection manager, set **Data Access Mode** as *SQL Command*, and write the following statement in the **SQL Command Text** property:

    ```
    select sys.schemas.name+'.'+sys.tables.name as TableName
    from sys.tables
    inner join sys.schemas
    on sys.tables.schema_id=sys.schemas.schema_id
    ```

22. Add a Recordset Destination after OLE DB Source, and in Recordset Destination Editor, set **Variable Name** as *User::TablesList* and in the **Input Columns** tab select **TableName**.

23. Go back to Control Flow, add a Foreach Loop Container after the Data Flow Task.

24. In Foreach Loop Editor, set **Enumerator** as *Foreach ADO Enumerator*, and set **ADO object source variable** as *User::TablesList*. In the **Variable Mappings** tab, set the variable **User::TableName** with index *0*.

25. Drag-and-drop an Execute Package Task into the Foreach Loop Container, and name it as **EPT - Execute Child**.

26. In Execute Package Task Editor, go to the **Package** tab, set the **ReferenceType** as *External Reference*, and set **Location** as *File System*, and create a connection to **P2_Child.dtsx** there.

27. Till now the `P1_Master` package is complete. This package gets a connection string, loops through list of its tables and executes the `P2_Child` package for each table to log in to the `DbTablesInfo` table. Note that we create an option to append log entries, so we can choose to append them or rewrite them. The following is the whole schema of `P1_Master.dtsx`:

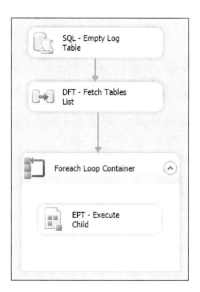

28. Now it's the time for setting **Configuration**. In `P1_Master`, click on an empty area in Control Flow and then go to SSIS menu and then Package Configurations. In the **Package Configuration Organizer** check the **Enable Package Configuration** check box. Then click on the **Add** button.

29. The **Package Configuration Wizard** will appear, skip the introduction step. In the next step, set **Configuration type** as *XML configuration file*. And set the configuration filename as `C:\SSIS\Ch13_Restartability and Robustness\R02_Package Configuration\R02.dtsConfig.`

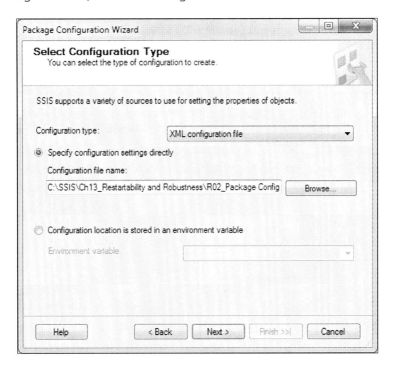

30. In the next step, in the **Objects** tree, select the following two items:

  ❑ **P1_Master | Executables | SQL – Empty Log Table | Properties | Disable**.

  ❑ **P1_Master | Variables | ConnectionStr | Properties | Value**.

[The second is not shown in the following screenshot because of the image size.]

31. In the next step, name the configuration as XML Configuration and finish the wizard. We will talk about these configuration settings and types in the *How it works* section later.

32. Open the P2_Child package and go to the SSIS menu, and then **Package Configurations**, and **Enable Package Configurations**, and click on the **Add** button.

33. In the next step, set **Configuration type** as *Parent package variable*, and in the **Parent variable** box write *User::ConnectionStr*.

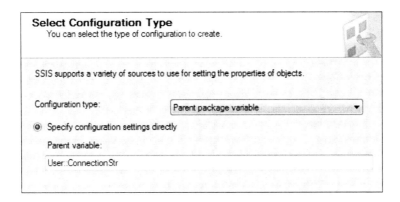

34. In the next step, select **P2_Child | Variables | ConnectionStr | Properties | Value**.

35. Name the configuration as `ConnectionStrFromMaster`.

36. Add another configuration to this page, with configuration type **Parent package variable**, set **Parent variable** as *User::TableName*, and set **Target** property as *P2_Child | Variables | TableName | Properties | Value*, name the configuration as **TableNameFromMaster**.

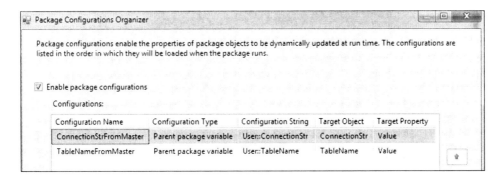

37. Run `P1_Master.dtsx` to check everything is correct. After the execution of the package go to SSMS. Open `DbTablesInfo` in the `PacktPub_SSISbook` database and see that there are rows which contain information about master database tables.

38. Open the Windows Explorer and go to the folder `C:\SSIS\Ch13_Restartability and Robustness\R02_Package Configuration`.

39. You will see a file `R02.dtsconfig` there. Open it with notepad, you will see that the file contains XML contents. Change `Initial Catalog` from `master` to `AdventureWorks2012`, and change `Disable` value property from `0` to `1` as highlighted in the following script:

```
</Configuration><Configuration ConfiguredType="Property" Path="\
Package.Variables[User::ConnectionStr].Properties[Value]" Valu
eType="String"><ConfiguredValue>Data Source=.;Initial Catalog=Advent
ureWorks2012;Provider=SQLNCLI11.1;Integrated Security=SSPI;Auto
Translate=False;</ConfiguredValue></Configuration><Configuration
ConfiguredType="Property" Path="\Package\SQL - Empty Log Table.
Properties[Disable]" ValueType="Boolean"><ConfiguredValue>0</
ConfiguredValue></Configuration>
```

40. Save the file and run the `P1_Master` package again.

41. After running the package, check the `PacktPub_SSISbook` table entries and you will see log entries from `AdventureWorks2012` tables which are appended to other logs.

How it works...

Package configurations are a way of sending values from outside of package without the need to recompile the package in SSDT. In this recipe, you will see how to use package configuration to set connection string from outside of package and also how to send values between two different packages.

One of the main benefits of package configuration is that you just set it once at the development time and then you can change every value in the configuration and the package will use these values at the start time and load them all and then execute. As you don't need to rebuild the package, this will help you to create a dynamic package.

Package configuration is only available in Legacy Package Deployment Model, so you probably don't need to use it in your new SSIS projects which are in Project Deployment Model. So If you want to use package configuration, you need to convert package to Package Deployment Model.

We can pass properties of variables, executable, and the package with package configurations. Some of the configurations can store multiple values and some of them only accept single values.

Each configuration can be used in multiple packages. You just need to be sure that all of those packages should have same properties that are listed in the configuration.

In this recipe, we used two types of package configuration. There are five types of package configuration and each of them has its own usage. In the following section, you will read a brief description about each of them.

XML configuration file

Properties and their values will be stored in XML-based file with `.dtsConfig` extension. These files are the only files which needed to be deployed besides the SSIS packages in Package Deployment Model. Each XML configuration file can store multiple properties and their values. You saw an example of XML configuration in this recipe to set value of the `ConnectionStr` variable and also the `Disable` property of SQL—Empty Log Table's task (steps 28 to 31).

SQL server

Configuration properties and their values will be stored in a SQL server database table. Here you will find how to configure SQL server configuration for the package:

1. In the Package Configuration Wizard, set **Configuration Type** as *SQL Server*, and then set a connection to SQL server database.

2. In front of the configuration table's box when you click on the **New** button, create table script of configuration table will appear; you can change table's name or leave it as is.

   ```
   CREATE TABLE [dbo].[SSIS Configurations]
   (
     ConfigurationFilter NVARCHAR(255) NOT NULL,
     ConfiguredValue NVARCHAR(255) NULL,
     PackagePath NVARCHAR(255) NOT NULL,
     ConfiguredValueType NVARCHAR(20) NOT NULL
   )
   ```

3. You can set the **Configuration filter**—this is for categorizing different configurations which works with same configuration table.

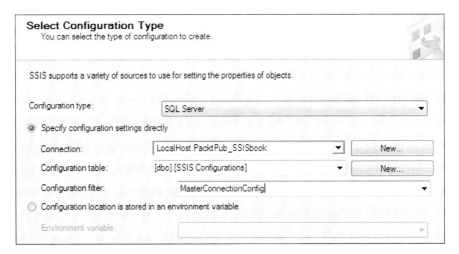

SQL server configuration can store multiple values and properties like XML configuration file. This configuration can be a better option if you need to deploy SSIS packages on different servers and all of them have access to a database engine in a network.

Environment variable

Windows provides a space to define variables called environment variable. You can define these variables in this address:

1. Click on **Start**.
2. Right-click on **Computer** and select **Properties**.
3. Go to **Advance System Settings** in left pane, in **System Properties** window.
4. Then go to the **Advanced** tab. And then click on **Environment Variables**.

An environment variable can store only one property with its value.

Registry entry

You can store property and its value as a registry entry also, and this configuration will store single value only.

Parent package variable

This configuration is a bit different from others, and will be used only in passing values from one package to another package with Execute Package Task. Each parent package variable can read value from one parent package and map it to a single target property in child package. We used this configuration to send values of two variables; `ConnectionStr` and `TableName` from `P1_Master` to `P2_Child` in this recipe (steps 32 to 36).

There's more...

There are some special combinations of options which are very commonly in use in real-world scenarios about package configuration. We will discuss them in the following section.

Indirect configuration

XML configuration file is very handy and a useful type of configuration, but it needs to be dynamic. If you take a deeper look into our example in this recipe then you will find that the address of the XML configuration file is static. This is not a good way of building a dynamic package with XML configuration file that has a static address!

However, you don't need to worry about it, because SSIS provides a way to use Indirect XML Configuration which is easy to create but very handy and useful. We can set the address of XML configuration file with an environment variable, and this is called **Indirect XML Configuration**. So whenever you change XML file's address you just need to change value of Environment variable only.

To create an Indirect XML Configuration you can choose configuration location stored in an environment variable option in the Package Configuration Wizard, and bind it to an environment variable.

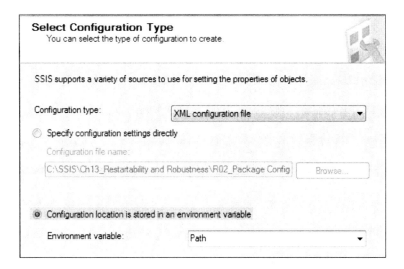

Note that you should be careful to create same environment variable at the production environment if you used indirect configuration.

Configuration priority

We can apply more than one configuration to a package and those configurations have priority of load. Priority of configurations is from top to bottom. So the first configuration on the list will be loaded first and then the second configuration and so on.

Transactions: Doing multiple operations atomic

Doing multiple operations atomic is one of the fundamentals of each application which works with data. Many applications have transaction support; transactions are operations that will be run as one unique atomic operation. An **atomic operation** means that all operations will be run successfully or if an error happens and one of them caused the error all of them will rollback.

SSIS supports transactions also, but SSIS transaction differs from database transaction. SSIS can do most of the tasks atomically, you can copy files from source place to destination, extract them, transfer them to database, and if any error occurs you can rollback all operations.

SSIS uses the Microsoft Distributed Transaction Coordinator service (MS DTC) for transactions. Microsoft applications use this service for handling their transactions, for example you will see that WCF uses this service for managing transactions also. So for using transactions in SSIS this service should be running.

In this recipe, we will start some operations which contain running logging SQL statement, transfer data from flat file to database, and run a SQL statement. You will see that if SQL statement fails then the whole operation will roll back at the time of using operations. We will show difference of transaction options and their usages in this sample.

Getting ready

Copy the `source.txt` file from book materials from this recipe's folder into this address: `C:\SSIS\Ch13_Restartability and Robustness\R03_Transaction\Files`. Content of `source.txt` is as follows:

```
ID,FirstName,LastName
1,Reza,Rad
2,Pedro,Perfeito
3,Phil,Brammer
```

We use the same `Person` table which we used in our earlier recipes in `PacktPub_SSISbook`, if you have this table already. So just run a simple `truncate table person` statement, and if you didn't create it, run the following statements to create the `Person` table:

```
CREATE TABLE [dbo].[Person] (
  [BusinessEntityID] [int] NULL,
  [FirstName] [nvarchar](50) NULL,
  [LastName] [nvarchar](50) NULL
) ON [PRIMARY]
```

Create a table for log operations in `PacktPub_SSISbook` with the following script:

```
CREATE TABLE [dbo].[OperationLog] (
  [ID] [int] IDENTITY(1,1) NOT NULL,
  [logText] [varchar](500) NULL,
  [CreatedTime] [datetime] NULL,
 CONSTRAINT [PK_OperationLog] PRIMARY KEY CLUSTERED
(
  [ID] ASC
)WITH (PAD_INDEX = OFF, STATISTICS_NORECOMPUTE = OFF, IGNORE_DUP_KEY =
OFF, ALLOW_ROW_LOCKS = ON, ALLOW_PAGE_LOCKS = ON) ON [PRIMARY]
) ON [PRIMARY]
```

How to do it...

1. In the first step, we should run MS DTC Service—Open **Control Panel | Administrative Tools | Services** and start the **Distributed Transaction Coordinator**, if it is not running.

2. Create an SSIS project and name it as `R03_Transaction`.

3. Add an Execute SQL Task, name it as `SQL - Start Log`, connect it to `PacktPub_SSISbook`, and write the following statement in the `SQLStatement` property:

    ```
    insert into OperationLog (logtext,createdtime) values ('package
    started',getdate())
    ```

4. Add a Data Flow Task after the first task and name it as `DFT - Transfer Data`.

5. In the Data Flow Task, create a Flat File Source and Flat File Connection Manager, connect it to `source.txt` in OLE DB Source and connect it to this file: `C:\SSIS\Ch13_Restartability and Robustness\R03_Transaction\Files \source.txt`. Check the **Column names in the first data row** check box. In the **Advanced** tab of Flat File Connection Manager, change data type of `FirstName` and `LastName` columns to `Unicode string [DT_WSTR]`.

6. After the Flat File Source, add an OLE DB Destination, connect it to the `PacktPub_SSISbook` database, and choose the `Person` table as destination table and accept mappings as default.

7. Go back to Control Flow. Add another Execute SQL Task after the File System Task, and name it as `SQL - Error Task`. Create a connection to the `PacktPub_SSISbook` database and write the following statement in the `SQLStatement` property:

    ```
    Select 1/0
    ```

    Note that this statement will raise an error at runtime.

8. Add another Execute SQL Task after the `SQL - Error Task` and name it as `SQL - End Log`. Connect it to `PacktPub_SSISbook` and write the following statement in the `SQLStatement` property:

    ```
    insert into OperationLog (logtext,createdtime) values ('package
    completed',getdate())
    ```

9. Right-click on precedence constraint between `SQL - Error Task` and `SQL - End Log` and choose **Completion**. (this is because control flow goes to `SQL - End Log` either SQL – Error Task failed or succeed)

10. Till now we created a regular package without any transaction, we want to run this package first without supporting transaction to see what happens and then apply transaction on it.

11. Run the package.You will see that all tasks except the `SQL - Error Task` will run successfully.

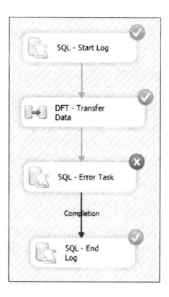

12. Check the `OperationLog` table records in SSMS, you will see two records created there, and also check the `Person` table and you will find the flat file content transferred correctly to this table.

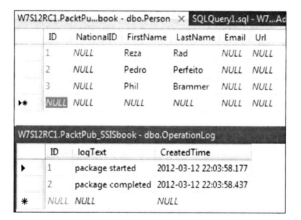

13. Now we want to do all the preceding operations in a Transaction. First of all, delete data from both tables with the following SQL statements in SSMS:

```
Truncate table Person
Truncate table OperationLog
```

14. Add a **Sequence Container** into the package and move all tasks into the **Sequence Container**.

15. Select **Sequence Container** and go to the **Properties** window. In the **Properties** window, set **TransactionOption** as *Required*.

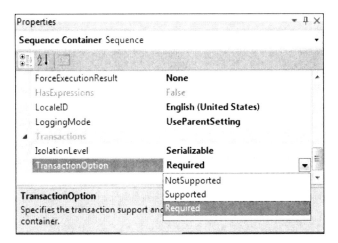

16. Run the package again. You will see that **SQL – Start Log** and **DFT – Transfer Data** finished successfully. And, if you double-click on Data Flow Task, you will see that it shows three rows transferred successfully. However, **SQL – Error Task** and **SQL – Finish Log** failed.

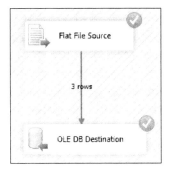

17. Go to SSMS and check both tables, you will see that both tables are empty. Even though **SQL – Start Log** and **DFT – Transfer** finished successfully in SSDT execution result, nothing happened in database tables! The main reason is that the whole operation rolled back when **SQL – Error Task** failed.

18. Now click on the **SQL – Start Log** and **SQL – End Log** tasks and change their **TransactionOption** property to *NotSupported*.

19. Run the package again. You will see that was successful except the **SQL – Error Task** which failed. And when you check database tables, you will see that the `Person` table is empty because the transaction rolled back, but the `OperationLog` table logged start and finish messages. We will discuss how this happened in the *How it works* section.

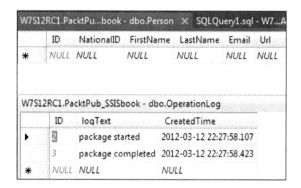

How it works...

Transactions can be implemented in SSIS packages with the `TransactionOption` property. Each task, container, and also package has a `TransactionOption` property. This property has three different options.

Required

The container, task, or package will be run under its own transaction. So at the start of executable object the transaction will begin, and at the end it will be committed or rolled back.

Supported

The executable object doesn't have its own transaction, but it uses its container's transaction, and will be a part of its container's transaction. This is the default value for `TransactionOption`.

NotSupported

Executable object doesn't use any transaction, even doesn't take part in its container's transaction. This option is very useful when you want to have tasks that don't need to be part of the transaction, like logging tasks. Note that logging operations typically shouldn't take part in transactions, they should log everything and if they are part of transaction the log entries will be rolled back! Steps 18 and 19 show a sample of working with logging tasks with `TransactionOption` as `NotSupported`. This is one of the most useful scenarios of using sequence container which we referred from the previous chapters.

Based on the preceding description, If we want to do some operations as a transaction we can gather them in a Sequence Container and then set `TransactionOption` of sequence container as *Required*, and leave `TransactionOption` of content executables as *Supported*. With this setting, transaction will begin at the start of Sequence Container and will commit if all executable were successful, or rolled back if an error occurs. Steps 14 and 15 show a sample of such scenario.

Note that for using transactions in SSIS you need to have MS DTC service running as we described in the first step of this recipe.

Configuration of transactions in loop structures is a bit tricky. If we set `TransactionOption` of Foreach Loop Container to *Required*, then a new transaction will start on each iteration of the loop. So if you want to put all loop iterations together in one transaction then you can put the Foreach Loop Container inside a Sequence Container and set `TransactionOption` of sequence container as *Required*.

Checkpoints: The power of restartability

Data transfer packages may transfer millions of rows every night and if one or more tasks fail during execution this may cause the package to fail. If we re-run a failed package then it will start from the first executable object in control flow, and this will be a problem because maybe a Data Flow Task which transferred 10 million records last night re-executed and got a lot of resource again; that doesn't sound worthy.

SSIS packages can be restartable, they can store the status of execution and start execution from the previous status, these are all supported by checkpoints. One of the most understandable definitions for checkpoint can be found in video games; Checkpoint will save the status of the game, and if the player failed, then the game will restart from the last status which was stored by the checkpoint.

SSIS Checkpoint provides a way to re-run package from the failed executable. In this recipe, we will take a look at how to use checkpoint.

Getting ready

Our sample in this recipe is very similar to the previous recipe sample (*Transaction*), just with a few changes, so we will use those materials again;

1. Copy the `source.txt` file from book materials from this recipe's folder into this address: `C:\SSIS\Ch13_Restartability and Robustness\R03_Transaction\Files`. Content of `source.txt` is as follows:

    ```
    ID,FirstName,LastName
    1,Reza,Rad
    2,Pedro,Perfeito
    3,Phil,Brammer
    ```

2. We use the same `Person` table which we used in our earlier recipes in `PacktPub_SSISbook`. If you have this table already, just run a simple `truncate table person` statement and if you don't, created it. Run the following statements to create the `Person` table:

```
CREATE TABLE [dbo].[Person](
 [BusinessEntityID] [int] NULL,
 [FirstName] [nvarchar](50) NULL,
 [LastName] [nvarchar](50) NULL
) ON [PRIMARY]
```

3. If you have the `OperationLog` table, just run the `truncate table OperationLog` statement. If you don't have it, create a table for log operations in `PacktPub_SSISbook` with the following script:

```
CREATE TABLE [dbo].[OperationLog](
  [ID] [int] IDENTITY(1,1) NOT NULL,
  [logText] [varchar](500) NULL,
  [CreatedTime] [datetime] NULL,
 CONSTRAINT [PK_OperationLog] PRIMARY KEY CLUSTERED
(
  [ID] ASC
)WITH (PAD_INDEX = OFF, STATISTICS_NORECOMPUTE = OFF, IGNORE_
DUP_KEY = OFF, ALLOW_ROW_LOCKS = ON, ALLOW_PAGE_LOCKS = ON) ON
[PRIMARY]
) ON [PRIMARY]
```

How to do it...

1. Create an SSIS project and name it as `R04_Checkpoint`.

2. Add an Execute SQL Task, name it as `SQL - Start Log`, connect it to `PacktPub_SSISbook`, and write the following statement in the `SQLStatement` property:

   ```
   insert into OperationLog (logtext,createdtime) values ('package
   started',getdate())
   ```

3. Add a Data Flow Task after the first task and name it as `DFT - Transfer Data`.

4. In the Data Flow Task, create a Flat File Source and Flat File Connection Manager, connect it to `source.txt` in OLE DB Source and connect it to this file: `C:\SSIS\ Ch13_Restartability and Robustness\R03_Transaction\Files \ source.txt`. Check the **Column names in the first data row** check box. In the **Advanced** tab of Flat File Connection Manager, change data type of the `FirstName` and `LastName` columns to `Unicode string [DT_WSTR]`.

5. After the Flat File Source add an OLE DB Destination, connect it to the `PacktPub_SSISbook` database, and choose the `Person` table as destination table and accept mappings as default.

6. Go back to Control Flow, add another Execute SQL Task after the File System Task, and name it as `SQL - Error Task`. Create a connection to the `PacktPub_SSISbook` database and write the following statement in the `SQLStatement` property:

    `Select 1/0`

    Note that this statement will raise an error at runtime.

7. Add another Execute SQL Task after `SQL - Error Task` and name it as `SQL - End Log`. Connect it to `PacktPub_SSISbook`, and write the following statement in the `SQLStatement` property:

    `insert into OperationLog (logtext,createdtime) values ('package completed',getdate())`

8. Till now, we created the package with tasks, and now we want to use checkpoint. So to use checkpoints do the following:

    ❑ Click on an empty area in Control Flow and then go to the **Properties** window. You will see three properties in the **Checkpoints** category in the **Properties** window.

    ❑ Set **SaveCheckpoints** as *True*, **CheckpointUsage** as *IfExists*, and finally set **CheckpointFileName** as *C:\SSIS\Ch13_Restartability and Robustness\ R04_Checkpoint\Files\checkpoint.xml*. Note that this file shouldn't exist already, but its container folder should exist. (We will discuss these properties in the *How it works* section later)

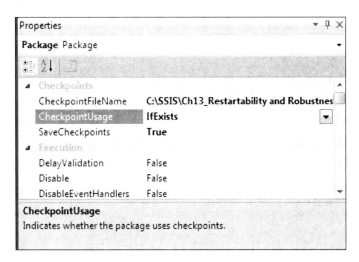

9. Click on the **SQL – Start Log** task and then go to the **Properties** window. Change the **FailPackageOnFailure** property to **True**. (the default value is **False** for this property)

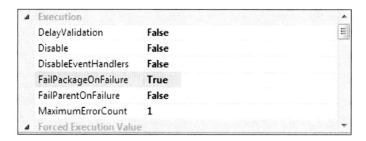

10. Do the previous step for all tasks in the control flow.

11. Run the package, execution will stop at `SQL - Error Task` and the package will fail. This sounds to be typical, but when you check this address: `C:\SSIS\Ch13_ Restartability and Robustness\R04_Checkpoint\Files`, you will see that the `checkpoint.xml` file is created there.

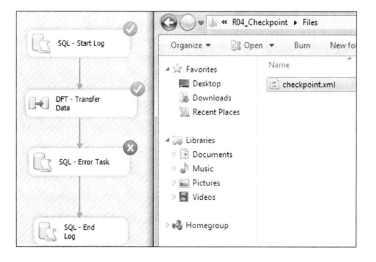

12. Run the package for one more time and you will see that package only starts at `SQL - Error Task` and it will fail again, because this task has error statement in it.

13. Change the `SQLStatement` property of `SQL - Error Task` to the following statement (we change this to don't raise error on this task again):

```
Select 1/1
```

14. Run the package again, this time package will start from `SQL – Error Task` and will finish successfully.

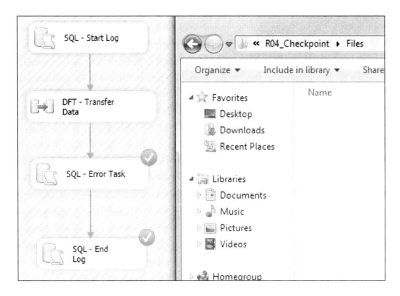

15. Note that `SQL – Start Log` and `DFT – Transfer Data` didn't execute this time; you can check it looking at the `OperationLog` table which has only one start log entry and also the `Person` table that has only one set of records from flat file.

16. Go to the `C:\SSIS\Ch13_Restartability and Robustness\R04_ Checkpoint\Files` address and this time you will see that checkpoint file disappeared. This is because the execution of package was successful. We will get into more details in the *How it works* section about this behavior.

17. Run package just for one more time, you will see that all tasks will finish successfully from `SQL – Start Log` to `SQL – End Log`. The reason is that last time the package was executed successfully.

How it works...

In this recipe, you saw how to create a restartable SSIS package with checkpoint. Checkpoints are XML files which store package state.

Checkpoints act in this way: on successful execution of each task an entry will be written in the checkpoint file. Whenever a task fails, the checkpoint file will have entries from all previous successful tasks, and when the package re-starts it will start from the next task after the last entry in the checkpoint file. If package finished successfully then the checkpoint file will be deleted automatically.

CheckpointFileName

Full path of checkpoint file will be set here. There is no need to create a checkpoint file because SSIS will create one if it does not exist.

These files will be updated after successful execution of each Control Flow Task, so after successful execution of `SQL - Start Log` an entry will be written in the checkpoint file, after successful execution of `DFT - Transfer Data` another entry will be written in checkpoint file. However, when execution fails at `SQL - Error Task` then nothing will append to the checkpoint file.

FailPackageOnFailure

For using checkpoints we need to change all Control Flow Task's `FailPackageOnFailure` property to `True`, this is because when the task fails then the package should stop working for the checkpoints to work properly.

CheckpointUsage

This property defines how package should deal with checkpoint files when it starts execution. This property can have three values:

- `Always`: means that package needs checkpoint file at the start of execution, so if there will be no checkpoint then package won't execute. This will cause a big problem, because checkpoint files will be deleted after a successful execution.
- `Never`: means that package never uses checkpoints.
- `IfExists`: means that package checks for the existence of checkpoints at the start of execution. If there be a checkpoint file then the package will start execution from the last state which was stored in checkpoint file, otherwise it will start from the first task. The best practice for `CheckpointUsage` is to use `IfExists`.

SaveCheckpoints

If you want to make a package restartable then you need to set this property to `true`, this will cause package to save checkpoints.

SSIS reports and catalog views

SQL Server 2012 comes with extensive integration with SSRS reports in different locations to support useful information for SQL server users. Some of these reports relate to Integration Service Catalog.

Integration Service Catalog reports are some standard reports which show execution status of packages, their validation status, connection manager's status and every operation done under the Catalog. These reports are useful for SSIS administrators who are responsible for maintaining SSIS packages, and also useful for SSIS developers who are responsible for part of deployment and execution for troubleshooting.

In this recipe, we take a quick look at SSIS Catalog reports and see their information provided.

Getting ready

For this recipe, we need to complete *Chapter 9, Deployment* and *Chapter 12, Execution* and practice some deployment and execution on SSIS Catalog.

How to do it...

1. Open SSMS and connect to the database engine.

2. Expand server node in **Object Explorer**, and then under **Integration Services Catalogs**, right-click on **SSISDB** and in the pop-up menu, under **Reports**, select **Integration Services Dashboard**.

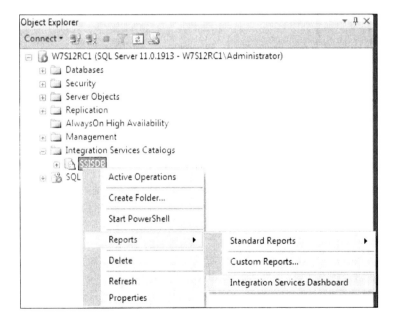

3. **Integration Services Dashboard** comes up and you can see an overview of execution information, how many packages failed, how many currently are running, and how many succeeded. Also, you will see in the middle of the page two tables, one of them is **Packages Detailed Information** (the one which is expanded in table level), which has information of last two packages detailed by some columns such as **Start Time** and **End Time** of execution of package, duration of execution, average of duration, status of package (failed or succeeded), and error message if applicable. First table in this dashboard is showing connection information (the one which is collapsed in the following screenshot) which is related to failed execution.

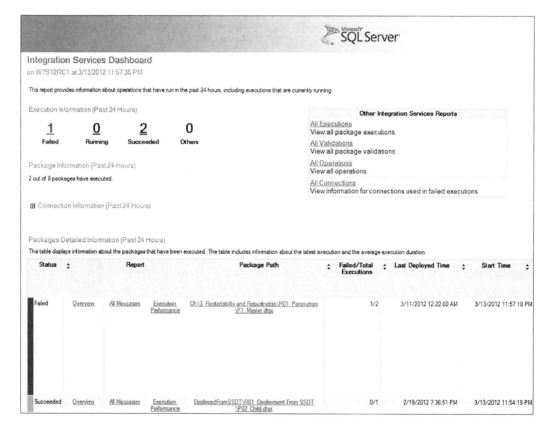

4. Now click on the **All Executions** link in the top-right corner, and you will see the **All Executions** report coming up. This report has the execution information of all packages and their details.

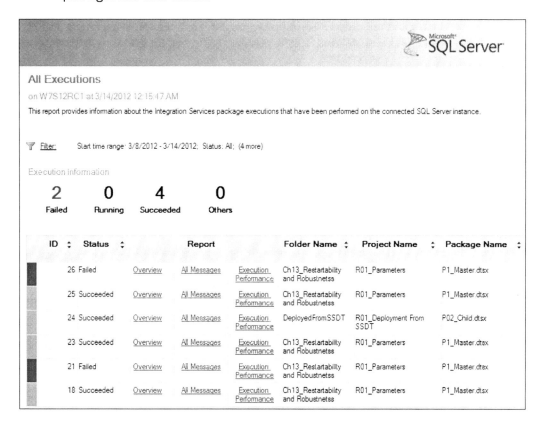

5. You can click on the **Overview** link on each row to see the overview of the package execution information with more details for the package on its own report. **All Messages** will show logging information which can be different based on the logging level at execution time.

6. Now click on **Execution Performance** on one of the rows. You will be redirected to the **Execute Performance** report. This report shows the execution duration on different executions of the package and also has a chart to compare performance. At the bottom of this report, there is a table which shows Data Flow Components information with their durations. Note that you can right-click on every report and export it to PDF, Excel, or Word. This is very handy method for gathering and delivering documents from SSIS reports.

7. Note that on the top of every table you will see a **Filter** link that provides a way to filter table's rows based on column values.

How it works...

SSIS Catalog reports provide a bunch of useful information for each package, task, and data flow component. They can show log messages, some performance reports, and also execution and validation details.

There are some SSIS Catalog views which are source of reports information. We will take a look at some of them in this section.

SSIS Catalog views

▸ **[catalog].[execution]**: Provides information about execution of packages such as `execution_id`, start and end time, status, system metrics at the time of execution such as total physical memory, available physical memory, and other details.

▸ **[catalog].[execution_parameter_values]**: Provides parameter information at the time of execution. It contains information such as parameter names, data types, values, and `execution_id`.

▸ **[catalog].[execution_property_override_values]**: Provides information of properties that has been overridden at the time of execution with their corresponding values and their related `execution_id`.

▸ **[catalog].[executables]**: Provides information of all executable objects in the package with their `executable_guid` and name and their related `execution_id`.

executable_id	execution_id	executable_name	executable_guid	package_name	package_path
1	4	DFT - Export Sales Order Headers to CSV	{06322C42-9821-4924-8A8C-942934F99136}	P02_Child.dtsx	\Package\DFT - Export Sales Order Headers to CSV
2	4	P01_Master	{D835B287-576D-4D22-81E8-BC7F9FB18C36}	P01_Master.dtsx	\Package
3	4	P02_Child	{BF595424-1B68-4B02-A863-01952636EA8A}	P02_Child.dtsx	\Package
4	4	EPT - Transfer Sales Order Header	{56546F52-CBBA-4CC6-A0A4-7D5DDCEA27F6}	P01_Master.dtsx	\Package\EPT - Transfer Sales Order Header
5	4	SQL - Log into TransferLog Table	{577FF09E-0F48-45EF-A03A-D7E4BCD97BFC}	P02_Child.dtsx	\Package\SQL - Log into TransferLog Table
1	5	DFT - Export Sales Order Headers to CSV	{06322C42-9821-4924-8A8C-942934F99136}	P02_Child.dtsx	\Package\DFT - Export Sales Order Headers to CSV
3	5	P02_Child	{BF595424-1B68-4B02-A863-01952636EA8A}	P02_Child.dtsx	\Package
5	5	SQL - Log into TransferLog Table	{577FF09E-0F48-45EF-A03A-D7E4BCD97BFC}	P02_Child.dtsx	\Package\SQL - Log into TransferLog Table

▸ **[catalog].[executable_statistics]**: Provides information about each executable's statistics like start time, end time, duration.

▸ **[catalog].[execution_component_phases]**: Provides information of different phases of components in data flow.

phase_s...	executio...	package_name	task_name	subcomponent_name	phase	start_time	end_time
1	10	P02_Child.dtsx	DFT - Export Sales Order Headers to CSV	Flat File Destination	AcquireConnections	2012-03-06 00:02:17.7648420 +13:00	2012-03-06 00:0...
3	10	P02_Child.dtsx	DFT - Export Sales Order Headers to CSV	Flat File Destination	Validate	2012-03-06 00:02:17.7668421 +13:00	2012-03-06 00:0...
5	10	P02_Child.dtsx	DFT - Export Sales Order Headers to CSV	Flat File Destination	ReleaseConnections	2012-03-06 00:02:17.7698423 +13:00	2012-03-06 00:0...
7	10	P02_Child.dtsx	DFT - Export Sales Order Headers to CSV	OLE DB Source	AcquireConnections	2012-03-06 00:02:17.7708423 +13:00	2012-03-06 00:0...

▸ **[catalog].[operations]**: Provides information about each different operation such as execution, deployment, validation with their detailed information like user who ran this operation, time of operation, and other details.

- ▸ **[catalog].[event_messages] and [catalog].[event_message_context]**: Provides information about events in package executions based on logging level at the time of execution.

- ▸ **[catalog].[environments] and [catalog].[environment_variables]**: Environment information and their variables will be provided by these catalog views.

Simple catalog views

There are other catalog views which are simple to understand such as `[catalog].[packages]` which has information of all packages, `[catalog].[folders]` which lists all folders in the SSIS catalog.

Knowing catalog views will be helpful when you want to write your own reporting system with a language like C# or VB.NET. They will help you to fetch information about packages, executions, and validations. Fortunately, SSIS 2012 provides this information in very good detail which will help troubleshooting and performance tuning in future development of packages.

14

Programming SSIS

by Reza Rad

In this chapter, we will cover the following topics:

- ▸ Creating and configuring Control Flow Tasks programmatically
- ▸ Working with Data Flow components programmatically
- ▸ Executing and managing packages programmatically
- ▸ Creating and using Custom Tasks

Introduction

SSIS is a Rapid Application Development tool. This means that SSIS developers won't need to write any code to do operations. On the other hand, we saw in *Chapter 8, Scripting*, that there are two script components that help developers to write their own customized .NET code to do any specific operation which is not listed in SSIS built-in components. All of these features are not enough for calling an ETL tool as an enterprise, because enterprise environment needs extreme dynamism and open-handed environment for developers. And fortunately, SSIS can be done from development to execution with .NET programming. You can create a package with some lines of .NET code, develop control flow and data flow all in code, and finally deploy and execute it with programming. Let's call this great feature SSIS programming.

SSIS programming means doing everything with code. You don't need to do anything with SSDT, but you need Visual Studio. .NET framework and obviously SSIS engine have to be installed. We believe that this feature will satisfy C# and VB.NET developers, who are much more comfortable with writing code to create an application without any limitation.

In this chapter, we'll illustrate how to use .NET code to create an SSIS package, create and manage Connection Managers, create and edit Control Flow Tasks, create and manage Data Flow components, deploy and finally execute a package.

This chapter is not mandatory for SSIS developers, but will bring a lot of flexibility for SSIS developers. Not all SSIS developers have .NET programming background, so if you are not familiar with .NET programming, it will be better to read some materials of C# or VB.NET programming first. However, don't worry, a basic knowledge of programming and .NET is adequate for this chapter, you don't need to be a C# or VB.NET expert to understand and execute recipes in this chapter.

SSIS provides a way to write your own tasks and components and add them to SSIS Toolbox for use in packages. We will see samples of creating SSIS tasks and components and how to use them in this chapter.

Creating and configuring Control Flow Tasks programmatically

Control Flow Tasks are executable objects in an SSIS package. Creating those objects programmatically and configuring them are the first steps of SSIS programming. In other words, you cannot create a package without any task!

Package is the main object which is needed in order to do SSIS Programming . SSIS Package is under the `Microsoft.SqlServer.Dts.Runtime` namespace. In this recipe, we will create a package and add a File System Task to it to copy a file to a destination folder.

Getting ready

Microsoft Visual Studio 2010 is needed to do this recipe.

How to do it...

1. Open SSDT or Visual Studio. Under Visual C#, create a **Console Application** project and name it as `R01_Creating and Configuring Control Flow Task Programmatically`.

2. In the Solution Explorer, right-click on the **References** folder and click on **Add reference**.

3. In the **Add Reference** window, go to the **.NET** tab and select **Microsoft.SQLServer. ManagedDTS** and then click **OK**.

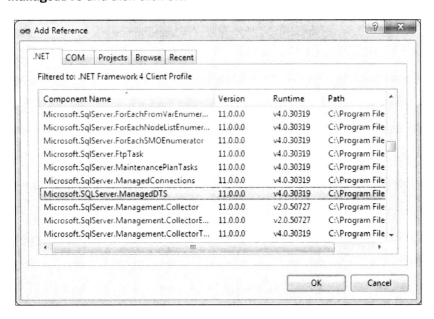

4. Right-click on the **Reference** folder and add another reference from the same location (**.NET** tab) with name **Microsoft.SQLServer.FileSystemTask**.

5. Go to the `Program.cs` file and add these `using` statements at the header part of file:

```
using Microsoft.SqlServer.Dts.Runtime;
using Microsoft.SqlServer.Dts.Tasks.FileSystemTask;
```

6. First of all, we'll create the package instance, so in the `Main` method write the following lines of script:

```
Console.WriteLine("Creating the package");
Package pkg = new Package();
```

7. Then we add the **File System Task** to package and get an instance of it:

```
//Add File system Task to package
Executable exe = pkg.Executables.Add(
typeof(FileSystemTask).AssemblyQualifiedName);

//Get an instance of File System Task
FileSystemTask fst =
  ((FileSystemTask)((TaskHost)exe).InnerObject);
```

8. Then we start configuring the File System Task, first of all set the `Operation` property with the following line of code:

```
//Set File System Task's properties
fst.Operation = DTSFileSystemOperation.CopyFile;
```

9. Then we need to set source file's address. For addressing the source file, we need to create a file connection to specified path. These lines will create the file connection for specified path and then set it as source address in File System Task:

```
ConnectionManager cnmgrSourceFile = pkg.Connections.Add("FILE");
cnmgrSourceFile.ConnectionString =
@"C:\Users\Public\Pictures\Sample Pictures\Penguins.jpg";
cnmgrSourceFile.Name = "Source File Connection";

fst.IsSourcePathVariable = false;
fst.Source = @"Source File Connection";
```

10. As in step 9, we need to create a connection for the destination folder and assign it to the destination address of File System Task with the following script:

```
ConnectionManager cnmgrDestinationFolder = pkg.Connections.
Add("FILE");
cnmgrDestinationFolder.ConnectionString = @"C:\SSIS";
cnmgrDestinationFolder.Name = "Destination Folder Connection";

fst.IsDestinationPathVariable = false;
fst.Destination = @"Destination Folder Connection";
```

11. After creating and configuring the Task, we can add code for executing the package and see the result with the following script:

```
//Execute package
Console.WriteLine("Executing the package");
DTSExecResult result = pkg.Execute();

Console.WriteLine(result.ToString());
```

12. We can run the application to see result, but before that just verify the whole script with the following code:

```
using System;
using System.Collections.Generic;
using System.Linq;
using System.Text;
using Microsoft.SqlServer.Dts.Runtime;
using Microsoft.SqlServer.Dts.Tasks.FileSystemTask;

namespace R01_Creating_and_Configuring_Control_Flow_Task_
Programmatically
```

```
{
    class Program
    {
        static void Main(string[] args)
        {
            Console.WriteLine("Creating the package");
            Package pkg = new Package();

            //Executable exec = pkg.Executables.
Add("STOCK:ScriptTask");

            //Add File system Task to package
            Executable exe = pkg.Executables.Add(
                typeof(FileSystemTask).AssemblyQualifiedName);

            //Get an instance of File System Task
            FileSystemTask fst =
            ((FileSystemTask)((TaskHost)exe).InnerObject);

            //Set File System Task's properties
            fst.Operation = DTSFileSystemOperation.CopyFile;

            ConnectionManager cnmgrSourceFile = pkg.Connections.
Add("FILE");
            cnmgrSourceFile.ConnectionString =
                @"C:\Users\Public\Pictures\Sample Pictures\
Penguins.jpg";
            cnmgrSourceFile.Name = "Source File Connection";

            fst.IsSourcePathVariable = false;
            fst.Source = @"Source File Connection";

            ConnectionManager cnmgrDestinationFolder = pkg.
Connections.Add("FILE");
            cnmgrDestinationFolder.ConnectionString = @"C:\SSIS";
            cnmgrDestinationFolder.Name = "Destination Folder
Connection";

            fst.IsDestinationPathVariable = false;
            fst.Destination = @"Destination Folder Connection";

            //Execute package
            Console.WriteLine("Executing the package");
            DTSExecResult result = pkg.Execute();

            Console.WriteLine(result.ToString());
        }
    }
}
```

13. Run the application with *Ctrl+F5*. You will see a command prompt window which shows result of the operation. Then you can go to the `C:\SSIS` folder to see that the `Penguins.jpg` file is copied there successfully.

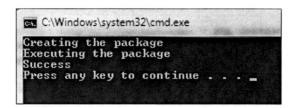

How it works...

For SSIS programming, the SSIS engine needs to be installed on computer (which can be selected from the list of options when you install SQL Server). Visual Studio also needs to be installed. Note that for working with SSIS you don't need to purchase Visual Studio usually, but if you want to use programming aspects of SSIS you need to write .NET applications, in C# or VB.NET languages. (You can write your code in other text editors and compile it manually, but working with Visual Studio brings a lot of features in scripting, compiling, and debugging .NET code).

The SSIS package is an object under `Microsoft.SqlServer.Dts.Runtime` which can be added as a reference to C# or VB.NET application. For creating a new SSIS package, we just need to get an instance of this object, as we did in step 6.

Control Flow Tasks can be added to a package in multiple ways. One of them which is used in this recipe needs the task's DLL to be added as reference. That is why we added `Microsoft.SqlServer.FileSystemTask` as a reference to the package. To add this task to the package, we just need to add it to `Package.Executables` which is a list of executable objects in the package.

Another way to add Control Flow Tasks to package is using the STOCK moniker. Most of the tasks in SSIS have STOCK moniker which is a specific identifier for them. For adding a task with STOCK moniker, you can use the following script:

```
Executable exec = pkg.Executables.Add("STOCK:ScriptTask");
```

Using STOCK moniker has this pro that you don't need to add reference for each task which you want to use. However, it also has some cons—first, all tasks don't have STOCK moniker and second, if you use it in this way you cannot set properties of each task with support of intellisense.

For the STOCK moniker's list go to the following URL:

`http://msdn.microsoft.com/en-us/library/ms135956.aspx.`

ActiveXScriptTask	PipelineTask	TransferObjectsTask
BulkInsertTask	ScriptTask	TransferDatabaseTask
ExecuteProcessTask	SendMailTask	WebServiceTask
ExecutePackageTask	SQLTask	WmiDataReaderTask
Exec80PackageTask	TransferStoredProceduresTask	WmiEventWatcherTask
FileSystemTask	TransferLoginsTask	XMLTask
FTPTask	TransferErrorMessagesTask	
MSMQTask	TransferJobsTask	

After adding the task to the package's executable objects' list, we need to configure it. Each executable is an instance of `TaskHost`. So first we need to convert the executable to `TaskHost` and then convert the `InnerObject` of `TaskHost` to the `FileSystemTask` object. This was what we did in step 7. `TaskHost` has some general properties for all executable objects like `DelayValidation` and other general properties.

After getting instance of specific Control Flow Task, it is very easy to set properties, as you saw we can simply set the `Operation` property of File System Task (step 8). However, for some properties which need another type of object, we should be careful. File System Task has a property named `Source` and `Destination` which accepts string name of the connection manager, not the connection string.

Creating connection managers in script can be simply done by adding them to `Package.Connections`. Each connection manager is an instance of the `ConnectionManager` class, in which its type can be defined with a string. For example, in this recipe, we used *FILE* which is an indicator of file connection. A list of all connection type strings are available here which is taken from the following URL: `http://msdn.microsoft.com/en-us/library/ms136093.aspx.`

String	Connection manager
"OLEDB"	Connection manager for OLE DB connections.
"ODBC"	Connection manager for ODBC connections.
"ADO"	Connection manager for ADO connections.
"ADO.NET:SQL"	Connection manager for ADO.NET (SQL data provider) connections.
"ADO.NET:OLEDB"	Connection manager for ADO.NET (OLE DB data provider) connections.

String	Connection manager
"FLATFILE"	Connection manager for flat file connections.
"FILE"	Connection manager for file connections.
"MULTIFLATFILE"	Connection manager for multiple flat file connections.
"MULTIFILE"	Connection manager for multiple file connections.
"SQLMOBILE"	Connection manager for SQL Server Compact connections.
"MSOLAP100"	Connection manager for Analysis Services connections.
"FTP"	Connection manager for FTP connections.
"HTTP"	Connection manager for HTTP connections.
"MSMQ"	Connection manager for Message Queuing (also known as MSMQ) connections.
"SMTP"	Connection manager for SMTP connections.
"WMI"	Connection manager for Microsoft Windows Management Instrumentation (WMI) connections.

Steps 9 and 10 showed how to create a file connection and set connection string property of the file connection manager, and finally set the `Source` and `Destination` properties of File System Task with file connection accordingly.

We will read more about how to execute the package and get results, so don't worry about what we did in step 11, we will discuss execution and deployment in a separate recipe in this chapter.

Working with Data Flow components programmatically

In this recipe, we will see how to deal with Data Flow components, create source component, destination component, initialize them, assigning connection managers to components, and map input and output columns.

Getting ready

We need an empty copy of the `HumanResources.Department` table in the `PacktPub_SSISbook` database, so simply just run the following statement:

```
USE [PacktPub_SSISbook]
GO

CREATE SCHEMA [HumanResources]
GO


CREATE TABLE [HumanResources].[Department](
      [DepartmentID] [smallint] NOT NULL,
      [Name] [nvarchar](50) NOT NULL,
      [GroupName] [nvarchar](50) NOT NULL,
      [ModifiedDate] [datetime] NOT NULL
) ON [PRIMARY]
```

How to do it...

1. Create a C# Console Application and name it as `R02_Working with Data Flow Components Programmatically`.

2. In the Solution Explorer, right-click on the **References** folder, and from the **Add Reference** window under the **.NET** tab add the following references:

    ❑ `Microsoft.SqlServer.ManagedDTS`

    ❑ `Microsoft.SqlServer.DTSPipelineWrap`

    `Microsoft.SqlServer.DTSRuntimeWrap`

3. In `Program.cs`, add the following `using` statements to the header of file:

    ```
    using Microsoft.SqlServer.Dts.Runtime;
    using Microsoft.SqlServer.Dts.Pipeline.Wrapper;
    ```

4. In the `Main` method, add the following line of code to create the package:

    ```
    Package pkg = new Package();
    ```

5. Now we want to add a Data Flow Task, so write the following statements after the statement from step 4:

    ```
    Executable exe = pkg.Executables.Add("STOCK:PipelineTask");
    TaskHost hostDft=(TaskHost)exe;
    hostDft.Name = "DFT - Transfer Departments";
    MainPipe dft = (hostDft).InnerObject as MainPipe;
    ```

6. We want to create a Data Flow that transfers data from `AdventureWorks2012` to the `PacktPub_SSISbook` database, so we need to create two different connections from OLE DB type, write the following statements to implement it:

```
//Create Source OLE DB Connection Manager
ConnectionManager cnSource = pkg.Connections.Add("OLEDB");
cnSource.Name = "OLE DB Source ConnectionManager";
cnSource.ConnectionString = string.Format(
            "Provider=SQLOLEDB.1;Data Source={0};Initial
Catalog={1};Integrated Security=SSPI;",
            ".",
            "AdventureWorks2012");


//Create Destination OLE DB Connection Manager
ConnectionManager cnDestination = pkg.Connections.Add("OLEDB");
cnDestination.Name = "OLEDB Destination ConnectionManager";
cnDestination.ConnectionString = string.Format(
            "Provider=SQLOLEDB.1;Data Source={0};Initial
Catalog={1};Integrated Security=SSPI;",
            ".",
            "PacktPub_SSISbook");
```

7. Now to create an OLE DB data source write the following statements:

```
IDTSComponentMetaData100 component =
dft.ComponentMetaDataCollection.New();
component.Name = "OLEDBSource";
component.ComponentClassID = "DTSAdapter.OleDbSource.3";
```

8. After creating the component, we need to instantiate it and initialize it with these lines of code:

```
CManagedComponentWrapper instance = component.Instantiate();
instance.ProvideComponentProperties();
```

9. Then assign connection manager to the OLE DB Source component:

```
component.RuntimeConnectionCollection[0].ConnectionManager =
DtsConvert.GetExtendedInterface(pkg.Connections[0]);
component.RuntimeConnectionCollection[0].ConnectionManagerID =
            pkg.Connections[0].ID;
```

10. To specify the source table and data access method on the OLE DB Source write the following lines of code:

```
instance.SetComponentProperty("AccessMode", 2);
instance.SetComponentProperty("SqlCommand",
"SELECT * FROM HumanResources.Department");
```

11. After assigning the connection manager and specifying source query, it's time to fetch metadata with these lines of code:

```
instance.AcquireConnections(null);
instance.ReinitializeMetaData();
instance.ReleaseConnections();
```

12. Till now we created and configured OLE DB Source. Now we are going to create and instantiate an OLE DB Destination as follows:

```
//Add OLE DB Destination
IDTSComponentMetaData100 destination =
            dft.ComponentMetaDataCollection.New();
destination.ComponentClassID = "DTSAdapter.OleDbDestination";
destination.Name = "OLEDBDestination";

//Instantiate Destination Component
CManagedComponentWrapper destInstance = destination.Instantiate();
            destInstance.ProvideComponentProperties();
```

13. Then we assign the connection manager to the destination component:

```
destination.RuntimeConnectionCollection[0].ConnectionManager =
DtsConvert.GetExtendedInterface(pkg.Connections[1]);
destination.RuntimeConnectionCollection[0].ConnectionManagerID
=pkg.Connections[1].ID;
```

14. Now we set OLE DB Destination properties to set destination table and data access mode:

```
destInstance.SetComponentProperty("OpenRowset", "HumanResources.
Department");
destInstance.SetComponentProperty("AccessMode", 3);
destInstance.SetComponentProperty("FastLoadOptions",
"TABLOCK,CHECK_CONSTRAINTS");
```

15. We need to connect the Source component to Destination with the following code:

```
dft.PathCollection.New().AttachPathAndPropagateNotifications(compo
nent.OutputCollection[0],
            destination.InputCollection[0]);
```

16. Now it's time to fetch metadata for OLE DB Destination:

```
destInstance.AcquireConnections(null);
destInstance.ReinitializeMetaData();
destInstance.ReleaseConnections();
```

17. We need to map input columns with external columns in the Destination component with the following lines of code:

```
IDTSInput100 input = destination.InputCollection[0];
IDTSVirtualInput100 vInput = input.GetVirtualInput();

foreach (IDTSVirtualInputColumn100 vColumn in vInput.
VirtualInputColumnCollection)
            {
                // Select column, and retain new input column
                IDTSInputColumn100 inputColumn = destInstance.
SetUsageType(input.ID,
                vInput, vColumn.LineageID, DTSUsageType.UT_
READONLY);
                // Find external column by name
                IDTSExternalMetadataColumn100 externalColumn =
                input.ExternalMetadataColumnCollection[inputColu
mn.Name];
                // Map input column to external column
                destInstance.MapInputColumn(input.ID, inputColumn.
ID, externalColumn.ID);
            }
```

18. Finally, add a code to execute the package:

```
DTSExecResult result = pkg.Execute();
Console.WriteLine(result.ToString());
```

19. You can verify the whole code with following:

```
using System;
using System.Collections.Generic;
using System.Linq;
using System.Text;

using Microsoft.SqlServer.Dts.Runtime;
using Microsoft.SqlServer.Dts.Pipeline.Wrapper;

namespace R02_Working_with_Data_Flow_Components_Programmatically
{
    class Program
    {
        static void Main(string[] args)
        {
            //Creating the package
            Package pkg = new Package();

            //Add a Data Flow Task
```

```
            Executable exe = pkg.Executables.
Add("STOCK:PipelineTask");
            TaskHost hostDft = (TaskHost)exe;
            hostDft.Name = "DFT - Transfer Departments";
            MainPipe dft = (hostDft).InnerObject as MainPipe;

            //Create Source OLE DB Connection Manager
            ConnectionManager cnSource = pkg.Connections.
Add("OLEDB");
            cnSource.Name = "OLE DB Source ConnectionManager";
            cnSource.ConnectionString = string.Format(
                "Provider=SQLOLEDB.1;Data Source={0};Initial
Catalog={1};Integrated Security=SSPI;",
                ".",
                "AdventureWorks2012");

            //Create Destination OLE DB Connection Manager
            ConnectionManager cnDestination = pkg.Connections.
Add("OLEDB");
            cnDestination.Name = "OLEDB Destination
ConnectionManager";
            cnDestination.ConnectionString = string.Format(
                "Provider=SQLOLEDB.1;Data Source={0};Initial
Catalog={1};Integrated Security=SSPI;",
                ".",
                "PacktPub_SSISbook");

            //Add OLE DB Source
            IDTSComponentMetaData100 component =
            dft.ComponentMetaDataCollection.New();
            component.Name = "OLEDBSource";
            component.ComponentClassID = "DTSAdapter.
OleDbSource.3";

            //Instanciate and Initialize
            CManagedComponentWrapper instance = component.
Instantiate();
            instance.ProvideComponentProperties();

            //Assign Connection Manager to Component
            component.RuntimeConnectionCollection[0].
ConnectionManager =
            DtsConvert.GetExtendedInterface(pkg.Connections[0]);
            component.RuntimeConnectionCollection[0].
ConnectionManagerID =
            pkg.Connections[0].ID;
```

```
            //Set other properties
            instance.SetComponentProperty("AccessMode", 2);
            instance.SetComponentProperty("SqlCommand",
            "SELECT * FROM HumanResources.Department");

            //Reinitialize source
            instance.AcquireConnections(null);
            instance.ReinitializeMetaData();
            instance.ReleaseConnections();

            //Add OLE DB Destination
            IDTSComponentMetaData100 destination =
            dft.ComponentMetaDataCollection.New();
            destination.ComponentClassID = "DTSAdapter.
OleDbDestination";
            destination.Name = "OLEDBDestination";

            //Instantiate Destination Component
            CManagedComponentWrapper destInstance = destination.
Instantiate();
            destInstance.ProvideComponentProperties();

            //Assign Destination Connection
            destination.RuntimeConnectionCollection[0].
ConnectionManager =
                  DtsConvert.GetExtendedInterface(pkg.
Connections[1]);
            destination.RuntimeConnectionCollection[0].
ConnectionManagerID =
                  pkg.Connections[1].ID;

            //Set destination properties
            destInstance.SetComponentProperty("OpenRowset",
"HumanResources.Department");
            destInstance.SetComponentProperty("AccessMode", 3);
            destInstance.SetComponentProperty("FastLoadOptions",
"TABLOCK,CHECK_CONSTRAINTS");

            //Connect source to destination
            dft.PathCollection.New().AttachPathAndPropagateNotific
ations(component.OutputCollection[0],
            destination.InputCollection[0]);

            //Reinitialize destination
            destInstance.AcquireConnections(null);
            destInstance.ReinitializeMetaData();
            destInstance.ReleaseConnections();
```

```
            //Map input columns with virtual input columns
            IDTSInput100 input = destination.InputCollection[0];
            IDTSVirtualInput100 vInput = input.GetVirtualInput();

            foreach (IDTSVirtualInputColumn100 vColumn in vInput.
    VirtualInputColumnCollection)
            {
                // Select column, and retain new input column
                IDTSInputColumn100 inputColumn = destInstance.
    SetUsageType(input.ID,
                    vInput, vColumn.LineageID, DTSUsageType.UT_
    READONLY);
                // Find external column by name
                IDTSExternalMetadataColumn100 externalColumn =
                input.ExternalMetadataColumnCollection[inputColu
    mn.Name];
                // Map input column to external column
                destInstance.MapInputColumn(input.ID, inputColumn.
    ID, externalColumn.ID);
            }

            //Execute Package
            DTSExecResult result = pkg.Execute();
            Console.WriteLine(result.ToString());
        }
    }
}
```

20. Run the package with *Ctrl+F5*. **Success** message will show up after a few seconds in the command prompt window. You can also check the content of the `Department` table in `PacktPub_SSISbook` and verify that all data rows are copied there successfully.

How it works...

Data Flow Task can be added to package with **PipelineTask** STOCK moniker. Step 5 shows how to add a Data Flow Task and name it and get an instance of it with the `TaskHost` object. And instance of Data Flow Task is an object of the `MainPipe` class type, which is in the `Microsoft.SqlServer.Dts.Pipeline.Wrapper` namespace.

Adding a component to Data Flow Task can be done with adding an instance of the
`IDTSComponentMetaData100` class to `ComponentMetaDataCollection` of the
Data Flow Task (Step 7). To specify the exact component in Data Flow, we need to set the
`ComponentClassID` property, for example in step 7 we used `DTSAdapter.OleDbSource.3`
to specify OLE DB Source component. To fetch a list of all `ComponentClassIDs` you can simply
run the following code:

```
Application app = new Application();
foreach (PipelineComponentInfo item in app.PipelineComponentInfos)
        {
                Console.WriteLine(item.CreationName);
        }
```

List of all `ComponentClassIDs` will be shown as follows:

If component needs to work with a connection manager, then the connection manager should be assigned to it, this is what we did in step 9 and created `RuntimeConnectionCollection` from package's connection manager.

Each component has properties which can be set simply using the `SetComponentProperty` method, which gets only two arguments—name of the property and its value. Step 10 showed a sample of this case.

As Data Flow components need to fetch their metadata, we can use the `ReinitializeMetaData` method to fetch their metadata to do this. If the component needs connection manager to fetch metadata, we need to open the connection with the `AcquireConnections` method and then close it with the `ReleaseConnections` method. This was what we did in step 11.

Steps 12 to 14 showed how to create an OLE DB Destination and set its properties. In Step 15, we created a data path from the Source component to the Destination component of type `IDTSPath100`. We created a new path in the `PathCollection` property of Data Flow Task, specifying the input and output columns. Calling the `AttachPathAndPropagateNotifications` method will attach the path to components and notify them of new changes. Step 16 fetched metadata of the Destination component after creating data path.

Mapping between input columns and external columns can be done with the `MapInputColumn` method for each separate column (Step 17).

Executing and managing packages programmatically

One of the most useful aspects of SSIS programming is executing and managing packages. We can load a package from DTSX file or SQL Server, add or configure logging parameters and other configuration, and execute it. This is a very useful ability because you may want to create a .NET application for managing packages, so you will need to run and manage packages programmatically.

In this recipe, we will save the package from the _Working with Data Flow components programmatically_ recipe and then add logging to it and execute it.

Getting ready

As this recipe is a complement to the previous recipe, just do steps 1 to 17 from previous recipe.

How to do it...

1. Write the following statements after step 17 of the previous recipe to save the package as a DTSX file:

```
Application app = new Application();
app.SaveToXml(@"C:\SSIS\Ch14_Programming SSIS\Files\R03_Package.
dtsx", pkg, null);
```

2. Create an SSIS project and right-click on the SSIS `Packages` folder and add the existing package. Add the **R03_Package.dtsx** which is saved in the previous step. Open the package, you will see that the Data Flow Task and its components are there as we created them in the previous recipe.

3. Create a C# **Console Application** project and name it as `R03_Executing and Managing Packages Programmatically`.

4. Add `Microsoft.SqlServer.ManagedDTS` as reference. (Right-click on the `Reference` folder and in the **Add Reference** window, go to the **.NET** tab and add a specific reference)

5. Load the package from file location with the following code:

```
Application app = new Application();
Package pkg=app.LoadPackage(@"C:\SSIS\Ch14_Programming SSIS\Files\
R03_Package.dtsx", null);
```

6. Create a connection manager for log provider:

```
ConnectionManager loggingConnection = pkg.Connections.Add("FILE");
loggingConnection.ConnectionString =
@"C:\SSIS\Ch14_Programming SSIS\Files\Ch14_R03_Log.txt";
```

7. Add the log provider to the package and set its properties as follows:

```
LogProvider provider = pkg.LogProviders.Add("DTS.
LogProviderTextFile.3");
provider.ConfigString = loggingConnection.Name;
          pkg.LoggingOptions.SelectedLogProviders.Add(provider);
pkg.LoggingOptions.EventFilterKind = DTSEventFilterKind.Inclusion;
pkg.LoggingOptions.EventFilter = new String[] { "OnPreExecute",
"OnPostExecute", "OnError", "OnWarning", "OnInformation" };
pkg.LoggingMode = DTSLoggingMode.Enabled;
```

8. Write the following statement to execute the package:

```
pkg.Execute();
```

9. Run the package and check the `Ch14_R03_Log.txt` file in this address: `C:\SSIS\Ch14_Programming SSIS\Files`. You will see the execution log stored there.

How it works...

In this recipe, we saw how to save a package, load it, configure it, and execute it.

Saving packages

Packages can be stored in three different locations—file system, SQL Server, and SSIS server. There are four methods in the `Application` class for saving packages and they are as follows:

Method	Location
SaveToXML	File system
SaveToSqlServer	SQL Server
SaveToSqlServerAs	SQL Server
SaveToDtsServer	SSIS Package Store

In this recipe, we used `SaveToXML` to save the package to a DTSX file. (Step 1)

Loading packages

Packages based on their storage locations can be loaded with different methods of the `Application` class as follows:

Method	Location
LoadPackage	File system
LoadFromSqlServer	SQL Server
LoadFromDtsServer	SSIS Package Store

In step 5, we loaded a package from the file system.

Steps 7 and 8 show how to add a log provider to the package and how to define logging options.

There's more...

The `Application` class has some methods to manage packages which are useful. We'll now take a quick look at name and usages of the most common methods of the `Application` class. Setting the value of parameters from outside the package is another topic which we will deal with in the following section.

Methods of the Application class

Here you will see a list of the most useful methods in the `Application` class and their descriptions.

- ▸ `CreateFolderOnSqlServer` and `CreateFolderOnDtsServer`: These methods create a folder with specified name in the specific address in SQL Server or SSIS Package Store locations.

- ▸ `ExistsOnSqlServer` and `ExistsOnDtsServer`: Check existence of a package in SQL Server or SSIS Package Store. Note that to check the existence of a package on the file system, we can use the `System.IO.File.Exists` method.

- ▸ `FolderExistsOnSqlServer` and `FolderExistsOnDtsServer`: Check the existence of a folder in SQL Server or SSIS Package Store. Note that to check the existence of a folder in the file system, we can use the `System.IO.Directory.Exists` method.

- ▸ `RenameFolderOnSqlServer` and `RenameFolderOnDtsServer`: Rename folders on SQL Server or SSIS Package Store.

- ▸ `RemoveFromSqlServer` and `RemoveFromDtsServer`: Remove the packages from SQL Server or SSIS Package Store

- ▸ `GetPackageInfos` and `GetDtsPackageInfos`: Return a list of packages in SQL Server or SSIS Package Store.

To see a list of all methods and their signatures browse to the following URL: `http://technet.microsoft.com/en-us/library/bb523941(v=sql.110).aspx`.

Set parameter's value programmatically

We can set value of parameters and variables from outside the package programmatically. Each package has a `Parameters` property which contains a list of package's parameters. With the following statement we can set the value of the parameter:

```
pkg.Parameters["ParameterName"].Value = "something";
```

List of variables is also accessible with the `Variables` property and can be set with the following statement:

```
pkg.Variables["VariableName"].Value = "something";
```

Creating and using Custom Tasks

SSIS has many Control Flow Tasks to help you in ETL development, but in real-world scenarios, you may need to write code to create something special. For example, suppose that you want to create a delay task which causes Control Flow to wait for some seconds. You can do it within a script task simply using .NET library, but what happens if you want to do the same thing in another package and probably in other projects? You can create your custom task and add it to SSIS toolbox simply, and then whenever you need it, you just need a drag-and-drop.

In this recipe, we will create a simple delay task and add it to SSIS toolbox.

How to do it...

1. Open Visual Studio 2010 and create a C# **Class Library** project and name it as `R04_Custom Object`.

2. Add the following DLL as references:

   `Microsoft.SqlServer.ManagedDTS`

3. Delete the `Class1.cs` file from Solution Explorer and add a new class and name it as `DelayTask.cs`.

4. Add this `using` statement at the beginning of `DelayTask.cs`:

   `using Microsoft.SqlServer.Dts.Runtime;`

5. Right before the class declaration, add the following statements:

```
[DtsTask
(
    DisplayName = "Delay Task",
    Description = "Delay Task",
    IconResource = "Hourglass.ico",
    RequiredProductLevel = DTSProductLevel.None,
    TaskContact = "DelayTask"
)]
```

6. Inherit the class from the `Task` class as follows:

   `public class DelayTask : Task`

7. Add two variables in the class as follows:

```
#region Private Members
private int secondsToWait;
private string messageText;
#endregion
```

8. Add properties to the class as follows:

```
#region Properties
        public int SecondsToWait
        {
            get { return secondsToWait; }
            set { secondsToWait = value; }
        }

        public string MessageText
        {
            get { return messageText; }
            set { messageText = value; }
        }
#endregion
```

9. Now override the `Initialize` method of the `Task` class with the following code:

```
public override void InitializeTask(Connections connections,
VariableDispenser variableDispenser, IDTSInfoEvents events,
IDTSLogging log, EventInfos eventInfos, LogEntryInfos
logEntryInfos, ObjectReferenceTracker refTracker)
        {
                base.InitializeTask(connections, variableDispenser,
events, log, eventInfos, logEntryInfos, refTracker);
        }
```

10. Override the `Validate` method to check validation of property values with the following code:

```
public override DTSExecResult Validate(Connections connections,
VariableDispenser variableDispenser, IDTSComponentEvents
componentEvents, IDTSLogging log)
        {
                DTSExecResult execResult = base.Validate(connections,
variableDispenser, componentEvents, log);
                if (execResult == DTSExecResult.Success)
                {
                    if (string.IsNullOrEmpty(messageText))
                    {
                        componentEvents.FireWarning(1, this.GetType().
Name, "Value required for DisplayText", string.Empty, 0);
                    }
                    if (secondsToWait < 0 || secondsToWait > 10000)
                    {
                        componentEvents.FireWarning(1, this.GetType().
Name, "Seconds to wait should be between 0 and 10000", string.
Empty, 0);
```

```
                }
            }

            return execResult;
        }
```

11. And then override the `Execute` method to implement the main scenario:

```
public override DTSExecResult Execute(Connections connections,
VariableDispenser variableDispenser, IDTSComponentEvents
componentEvents, IDTSLogging log, object transaction)
        {
                try
                {
                    System.Threading.Thread.
Sleep(secondsToWait*1000);
                    System.Windows.Forms.MessageBox.
Show(messageText);
                    return DTSExecResult.Success;
                }
                catch (Exception ex)
                {
                    componentEvents.FireError(0, "MessageBoxTask",
ex.Message, "", 0);
                    return DTSExecResult.Failure;
                }
        }
```

12. Till now we create the `DelayTask` class, verify the whole script of `DelayTask.cs` with the following code:

```
using System;
using System.Collections.Generic;
using System.Text;

using Microsoft.SqlServer.Dts.Runtime;

namespace R04_Custom_Object
{
    [DtsTask
    (
        DisplayName = "Delay Task",
        Description = "Delay Task",
        IconResource = "Hourglass.ico",
        RequiredProductLevel = DTSProductLevel.None,
        TaskContact = "DelayTask"
    )]
```

```
public class DelayTask : Task
{
    #region Private Members
    private int secondsToWait;
    private string messageText;
    #endregion

    #region Properties
    public int SecondsToWait
    {
        get { return secondsToWait; }
        set { secondsToWait = value; }
    }

    public string MessageText
    {
        get { return messageText; }
        set { messageText = value; }
    }
    #endregion

    #region Task overrides
    public override void InitializeTask(Connections
connections, VariableDispenser variableDispenser, IDTSInfoEvents
events, IDTSLogging log, EventInfos eventInfos, LogEntryInfos
logEntryInfos, ObjectReferenceTracker refTracker)
    {
        base.InitializeTask(connections, variableDispenser,
events, log, eventInfos, logEntryInfos, refTracker);
    }


    public override DTSExecResult Validate(Connections
connections, VariableDispenser variableDispenser,
IDTSComponentEvents componentEvents, IDTSLogging log)
    {
        DTSExecResult execResult = base.Validate(connections,
variableDispenser, componentEvents, log);
        if (execResult == DTSExecResult.Success)
        {
            if (string.IsNullOrEmpty(messageText))
            {
                componentEvents.FireWarning(1, this.GetType().
Name, "Value required for DisplayText", string.Empty, 0);
            }
```

```
            if (secondsToWait < 0 || secondsToWait > 10000)
            {
                    componentEvents.FireWarning(1, this.GetType().
Name, "Seconds to wait should be between 0 and 10000", string.
Empty, 0);
            }
        }

        return execResult;
    }

    public override DTSExecResult Execute(Connections
connections, VariableDispenser variableDispenser,
IDTSComponentEvents componentEvents, IDTSLogging log, object
transaction)
    {
            try
            {
                System.Threading.Thread.
Sleep(secondsToWait*1000);
                System.Windows.Forms.MessageBox.
Show(messageText);
                return DTSExecResult.Success;
            }
            catch (Exception ex)
            {
                componentEvents.FireError(0, "MessageBoxTask",
ex.Message, "", 0);
                return DTSExecResult.Failure;
            }
        }
        #endregion
    }
}
```

13. Now we need to build and deploy it. Right-click on the project name in the Solution Explorer and select **Properties**.

14. In the **Project Property** page, go to the **Signing** tab, and in the **Choose a strong name key file** drop-down menu, select **New**. In the **Create Strong Name Key** window, enter name as **CustomObjectKey** and also enter a password.

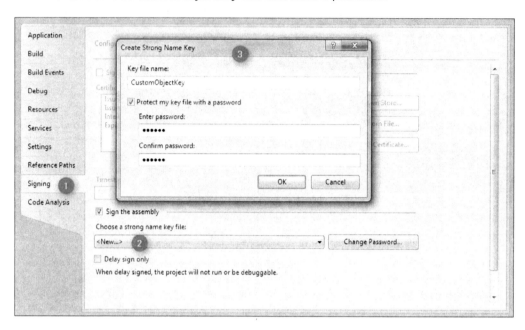

15. Go to the **Build** tab, click on **Edit Post-build**. In **Post-build Event Command Line** write the following statements:

```
"C:\Program Files\Microsoft SDKs\Windows\v7.0A\bin\NETFX 4.0
Tools\gacutil.exe" /u "$(TargetName)"
"C:\Program Files\Microsoft SDKs\Windows\v7.0A\bin\NETFX 4.0
Tools\gacutil.exe" /if "$(TargetPath)"
copy "$(TargetPath)" "C:\Program Files\Microsoft SQL Server\110\
DTS\Tasks" /Y
```

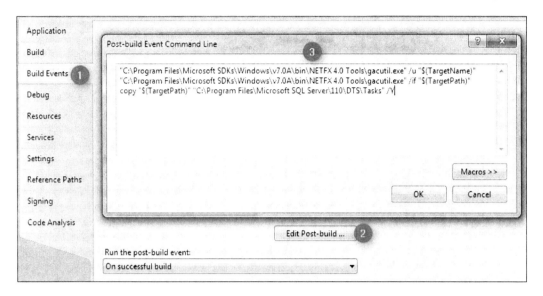

16. Now close the **Project Property** page, right-click on the project name in Solution Explorer, and select **Build**.

17. After successful building of project, close the Visual Studio and open it again.

18. Add a new SSIS project and name it as `R04_Using Custom Object`.

19. Go to Control Flow of `Package.dtsx` in the **SSIS Toolbox**, you will find the **Delay Task**.

20. Drag-and-drop the **Delay Task** onto the Control Flow. You will see a warning icon which shows that you need to enter display text.

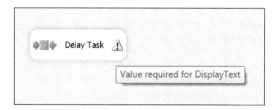

21. Click on the task in Control Flow and go to the **Properties** window, you can set the **MessageText** and **SecondsToWait** properties there as shown in the following screenshot:

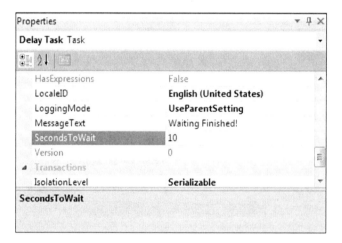

22. Now run the package and you will see that packages will wait for 10 seconds and then the **Waiting Finished!** message will show up.

How it works...

In this recipe, we created a simple task to wait for some seconds and finally showed a message. Note that in real-world scenarios you shouldn't raise message boxes in ETL packages because ETL packages are not designed to interact with user, we just used message box here to show a sample.

First thing which should be considered is that you should create a class for each task and that class should be inherited from the `Task` class in `Microsoft.SqlServer.Dts.Runtime`, this was what we did in step 6.

Control Flow Tasks have some properties such as `DisplayName` and `Description` which can be set with the `DtsTask` class attribute at the beginning of class (Step 5).

In this Task, we tried to get seconds to wait and message text as input properties of the Task, so in steps 7 and 8 we created private variables and their corresponding properties.

As this class is inherited from the `Task` class, we can override methods from the base class. There are three important methods which should override:

- ▶ InitializeTask: This method will be called at runtime. In this recipe, we just called `InitializeTask` from the base class (step 9).

- ▶ Validate: The `Validate` method will be applied when SSIS checks validation of this task, so we just checked the value of two properties to be valid and if not raise a warning (step 10).

- ▶ Execute: This method is the actual work which the Task will do. In this recipe, we used the `System.Threading.Thread.Sleep` method to wait for specified seconds and after that we displayed a message box (step 11).

Signing the project

First step in the deployment of Task we need to sign the application with a key file. Signing the application will assign a globally unique key to the application. Step 14 described how to sign the application.

Adding assembly to GAC

Building the package is the next step after signing. After that we need to register the assembly of application in Global Assembly Cache (GAC). After adding the assembly to GAC we can use it in SSDT. To register an assembly in GAC we can use the `gacutil.exe` command-line utility, `/u` switch will uninstall an assembly from GAC and `/if` will install an assembly into GAC.

After adding the assembly into GAC it's time to copy it to the specified directory. For Tasks in SSIS 2012, we probably need to copy Tasks into this folder: `C:\Program Files\ Microsoft SQL Server\110\DTS\Tasks`. If we want to create custom Log Provider or Foreach Loop Enumerator then we need to put assembly in their folders such as `LogProviders` or `ForeachEnumerators` under `C:\Program Files\Microsoft SQL Server\110\DTS`. In some cases, address of SQL Server installed folder may differ from the preceding default address, you can find the exact address by browsing the following registry address:

```
HKEY_LOCAL_MACHINE | SOFTWARE | Microsoft | Microsoft SQL Server | 110
| SSIS | Setup | DTSPath
```

There is an alternative way to do building and adding assembly to GAC and copying it to the specified directory all together. Visual Studio supports post-build commands, which will be executed after building the project. In step 15 we wrote a post-build command to add assembly to GAC and then copy it to the `Tasks` directory. This is a convenient method in creating custom objects in SSIS.

After registering assembly in GAC and copying it in the `Tasks` folder, SSDT will pick custom task and add it to SSIS Toolbox, but if Visual Studio or SSDT is already open, you need to close it and open it again, which we did in step 17.

One of the big advantages of creating custom objects is that you can create a custom object for specific case and use it everywhere. This will help you to create an ETL framework with SSIS in the enterprise environment.

For more samples on custom tasks use BOL: `http://msdn.microsoft.com/en-us/library/ms135965.aspx`.

There's more...

There are different types of custom tasks which can be created such as log providers and connection managers, but some of them need specific development tips, for example if you want to create Data Flow component, you may need to write more code and override more methods. Custom objects can have user interface to deal with developer in graphical interactive mode. You can create custom user interface and use it as UI editor of custom object.

Creating custom Data Flow component

Creating Data Flow component is like creating Control Flow Task with few changes. To create a Data Flow component, you need to inherit from the `PipelineComponent` base class and in the `DtsPipelineComponent` attribute you can set the `ComponentType` property to transform, source, or destination.

You can override the `Validate` method to check all connections, settings, and properties. Overriding `PreExecute` will help you in acquiring connections and in the `ProcessInput` method you can write code to run per data rows, finally the `PostExecute` method will help you to release the external resources.

As we discussed all of these methods and their usages in different recipes in *Chapter 8, Scripting* for source, destination, and transformation components, there is no need for more samples of custom Data Flow component here.

You can deploy Data Flow components such as custom tasks, just note that you need to copy assembly into the `PipelineComponents` folder.

Creating UI Editor for custom object

Custom UI Editor will help SSIS developer to configure the custom object much more easily. To create a custom UI Editor, you can create Windows forms or user controls as you want in C# or VB.NET projects. You just need to create a class to implement the IDtsTaskUI base interface. And in implementation of the GetView method you can return a new instance of GUI form or control you created.

Finally, you can assign the UI Editor to the custom object by adding UITypeName in the DtsTask attribute properties in custom object code class.

15

Performance Boost in SSIS

by Pedro Perfeito

In this chapter, we will cover:

- ▶ Control Flow Task and variables considerations for boosting performance
- ▶ Data Flow best practices in Extract and Load
- ▶ Data Flow best practices in Transformations
- ▶ Working with buffer size
- ▶ Working with performance counters

Introduction

When developing an integration SSIS project the most common concern is to guarantee that the data extracted from the source will be available to the end users as fast as possible. But if the scenario that lies ahead has huge data volumes moving from one source to some destination, performance concerns arise. What worked in a small data set will not work on big data sets.

If you keep in mind from an initial stage which tasks and which components should be used or avoided, and have a clear idea about when you should or shouldn't use the SSIS, it will help you to be more prepared for these scenarios. For this you need to understand the SSIS tool and the techniques that enable you to optimize the tool's utilization of system resources such as memory and CPU.

Control Flow Task and variables considerations for boosting performance

Several considerations can be applied to get even more performance from SSIS packages. To take control and make it possible, firstly you need to know the present performance in order to monitor and evaluate every step for boosting the performance. One important consideration when implementing SSIS projects is to avoid doing all the work in just one or a few packages. Splitting the work into several packages gives more flexibility for future troubleshooting and reduces risk when a change must be applied. Other considerations can be:

▶ Design the Control Flow in order to have tasks executing in parallel. If some of the tasks have precedent constraints and you cannot execute in parallel, make use of the the **Sequence Container**. In this way it is possible to execute some tasks in parallel (inside the container) and have others executed after the container's execution (the container status can be **Completed**, **Success,** or **Failure**).

▶ Reduce or remove SSIS transactions in the project.

▶ Reduce the amount of logging information saved on each execution.

Avoid using checkpoints. Create your own checkpoint without creating files on the file system. Use a database table to store information about all the packages and each status execution. For monitoring the performance of the Data Flow engine several methods can be used. Some of those are described during this recipe:

▶ Standard reports or SQL views from the `SSISDB` database (Project Deployment Model)

▶ SSIS logging provider to capture events that help calculate execution times and identify performance issues in your packages (both deployment models)

▶ Windows Performance Monitor with performance counters that measure multiple items related to the Data Flow performance

▶ Third-party add-ins or tools, for example BIDS Helper. BIDS Helper has a feature called **SSIS Performance Visualization** that shows you a graphical Gantt chart view of the execution durations and dependencies for your package to help you visualize performance

How to do it...

If the SSIS project uses the Project Deployment Model, then several queries can be made to the SSISDB that has the entire logging information automatically collected by the SSIS engine.

Using SSISDB Catalog

1. Open SQL Server Management Studio (SSMS) and connect to the `SSISDB` database.

2. Click on **New Query**.

3. Add the following SQL statement to get the list of all the past executions:

```sql
SELECT execution_id, folder_name, project_name
FROM [SSISDB].[catalog].[executions]
ORDER BY execution_id DESC
```

4. From the previous query result, choose an execution to monitor the performance.

5. Add the following statement to get the execution time for each subcomponent under a specific task and package. Include in the `Where` condition the **execution_id** chosen previously:

```sql
SELECT execution_id, package_name, task_name, subcomponent_name,
    SUM(DATEDIFF(ms,start_time,end_time)) AS TimeExecution
FROM [catalog].execution_component_phases
WHERE execution_id=150 -- Relace for a valid executionID
GROUP BY execution_id, package_name, task_name, subcomponent_name
```

6. Execute the query and verify the result.

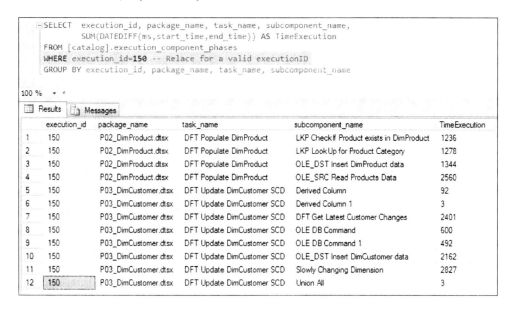

If the SSIS project uses the Legacy Deployment Model, then the performance information will be more limited. Nevertheless, the SSIS logging provider and also the system variables under SSIS can be useful to get interesting information about performance.

Progress Bar

While the package is running on SSDT, it's possible to monitor through the **Progress** tab when each task started, ended, and how long it took to finish. This information is very important to identify which tasks are pulling the performance down. The progress tab also displays information about package warnings, progress notifications, the success or failure of the package, and any error messages that are generated during package execution.

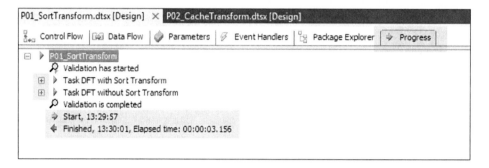

Windows Performance Monitor

The Windows performance monitor has several performance counters that allow measuring the Data Flow engine performance. More details about this method can be found in the *Working with performance counters* recipe of this chapter.

BIDS Helper

Another method to monitor performance has gained increasing importance through the years is BIDS Helper. This tool can be found in **CodePlex** and is available at `http://bidshelper.codeplex.com`.

1. Download and open an SSIS project.

2. The BIDS Helper add-in is now visible in the Solution Explorer.

3. To execute the package and get all the performance information, execute the package through **Solution Explorer**.

4. Select the package to execute and then select **Execute and Visualize Performance** instead of the normal option **Execute Package** as shown in the following screenshot:

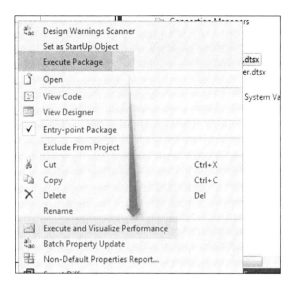

During and after package execution, the performance information will be displayed in the **Performance** tab:

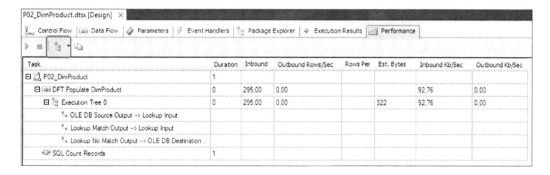

The information can be displayed in a **Gantt Chart**, **Statistics grid,** or **Statistic Trend**. To understand each option better and to go into deep detail on other BIDS Helper features, it's recommended to visit the official website in the CodePlex community.

How it works...

The previous steps explain in detail some of the basic steps that are usually followed by SSIS developers in their daily tasks on developing and testing SSIS projects. If you know what is going on with each package execution it is easier to understand and apply the best practices enumerated during the next recipes.

Data Flow best practices in Extract and Load

When we extract data from sources, the main focus is on getting just the changed data (inserts, updates, and deletes) since our last extraction. Reading all data (that could be millions of rows) from sources and then making a comparison row-by-row could cause a bottleneck in the system.

To get just the required data, several techniques can be applied:

▸ **Audit columns**: Having a date and time column for changes or even having two columns, one for insert and another for the update of a specific record.

▸ **Checksums**: Using an algorithm to create a unique identifier for a column set. Microsoft included in SQL 2008 a new SQL function that enables this technique to be applied faster and more easily.

▸ **Change Data Capture (CDC)**: Save logs from changes in a specific table using a higher performance approach than using triggers. This is a new functionality included in the SQL 2008 engine and now included in SSIS 2012 with a new task and two components.

Several other techniques can be implemented. Each one has advantages and disadvantages that should be analyzed.

When we load data into destinations, the main goal is to insert or update data as fast as possible. But the ability to do it fast will depend on several factors, for example data volume, CPU, and hardware characteristics.

Getting ready

To get ready for this recipe, use the following steps:

1. Open **SQL Server Data Tools (SSDT)**.
2. Open an existing solution located at `C:\SSIS\Ch15_Performance Boost in SSIS\Ch15_Performance Boost in SSIS.sln`.

How to do it...

Some of the best practices that should be considered in any SSIS implementation when extracting and loading data are highlighted as follows:

Optimize Queries

To optimize queries, the first step is to do it directly in the source database (for example, use the query plan provided by SQL Server). The second step is to use the appropriate **Data Access Mode** property, which controls how data is retrieved from the source.

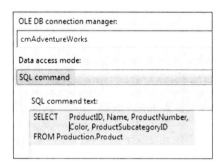

The **SQL Command** or **SQL command from variable** modes are the best but the use of **SELECT * FROM TableName** should be avoided in most cases. This statement is correct when all the columns will be considered, but is a bad practice if even one column is not used, because it will add unused columns to the pipeline. The **Table or view** and **Table or view name variable** should be avoided because they call the **OpenRowset** function where the data returned includes more than just the column metadata. Naturally, if the number of records is small, the differences between each approach will be unnoticeable.

The OPENROWSET method is a onetime ad hoc method to connect and access the remote data from an OLEDB data source. The syntax for OPENROWSET contains all information required to access remote data from an OLEDB data source. Further information is available at http://msdn.microsoft.com/en-us/library/ms190312.aspx.

OLE DB Destination

Wherever OLEDB destination is used, some of the properties can be changed to insert data into the SQL database table faster.

1. In the **Solution Explorer**, locate the project **R02_Data Flow Best Practices in Extract and Load**.

2. Open the package **P01_DimProduct.dtsx**.

3. Open the Data Flow **DFT Populate DimProduct**.

4. Edit the OLEDB Destination **OLE_DST Insert DimProduct data**.

5. Select the connection to the database.

6. In the **Data access mode** property, select *Table or view – fast load*.

7. In the **Name of the table or the view** property select the *[DimProduct]* table.

8. Set the **Table lock** property to *true*. By default this property is checked and it's recommended to leave it checked unless the same table is being used by some other process at the same time. The performance will increase because the destination table is exclusively locked to the current SSIS package.

9. Uncheck the **Check constraints** property checkbox. By default this property is also checked, but uncheck it if incoming data is not going to violate constraints of the destination table.

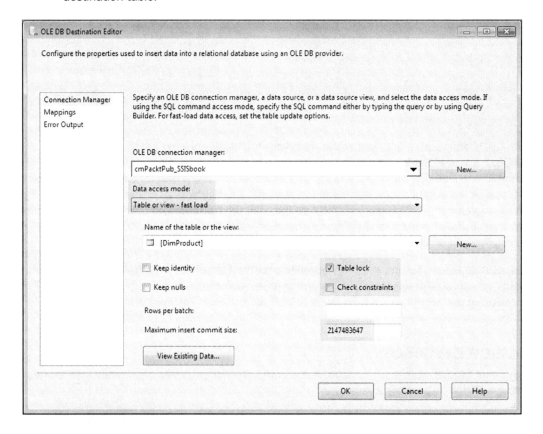

Data conversions

If during the Data Flow execution it is required to convert some of the source columns, it will be better if this conversion is made directly in the source component to avoid including extra columns in the pipeline. The conversion in the OLE DB Source component can be configured to use resources from the source system.

1. Edit the OLEDB Source **OLE_SRC Read Products Data**.

2. In the **SQL Command test**, apply the conversion SQL function into the SQL source statement:

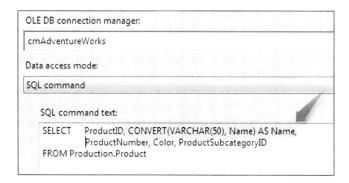

```
OLE DB connection manager:

cmAdventureWorks

Data access mode:

SQL command

   SQL command text:

   SELECT    ProductID, CONVERT(VARCHAR(50), Name) AS Name,
             ProductNumber, Color, ProductSubcategoryID
   FROM Production.Product
```

Or it can be configured to use the resources of the SSIS Server (that in some cases can even be the same).

3. Select the OLEDB Source **OLE_SRC Read Products Data**.

4. Right-click and select **Show Advanced Editor...**.

5. In the **Input and Output Variables Properties tab**, select **ProductID** and convert to **two-byte signed** integer as shown in the following screenshot:

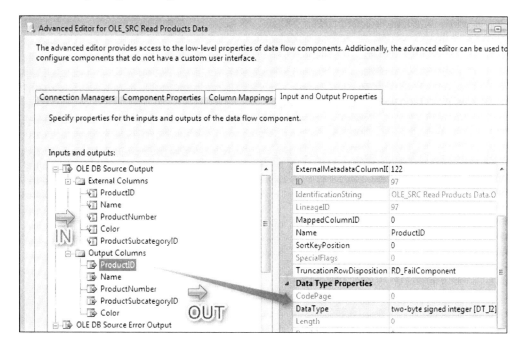

Update data into destination

Although the inserted data can be loaded through a bulk insert method (Fast Load), the update data could be a barrier and decrease performance significantly because the update is executed for each row on the Data Flow.

One practice that will improve performance when updating data is to split the data and update it in parallel to make use of the server's several CPUs. It's possible to split data for example based on the odd and even values of a specific column in the pipeline creating two different flows.

How it works...

The previous steps explain in detail some best practices to apply when data is being extracted from a source and/or loaded into some destination. Several others can also be considered based on the requirements of each project.

There's more...

Several more practices can also be considered if the scenario you have is even more complex. Some of these practices are as follows:

▶ Create indexes in your database tables and update the statistics regularly.

▶ If the volume is high, consider dropping indexes before the Data Flow execution and recreating them after completion. This can be done using a SQL statement under SQL tasks in the Control Flow design area.

▶ Use partitioning when dealing with large amounts of data.

Data Flow best practices in Transformations

One of the main goals of transforming data is to do all those transformations in memory to achieve the best performance possible in spite of saving data temporarily to disk. For that reason, if the transform uses some type of component that forces any delay, its use should be reduced or even avoided. The SSIS components could be one of the following three types:

▶ **Row Transformations**: This type of transformation does not block data in the pipeline. While new columns could be added, row transformations do not create any additional records and data is not blocked in the pipeline. Row transformations are also known as synchronous transformations because they reuse existing buffers and do not require data to be copied to a new buffer to complete the transformation. Some examples of this type of transformations are the **Derived Column, Multicast, Lookup, Copy Column, Conditional Split, OLE DB Command,** and several others that do not block Data Flow in the pipeline.

- **Partially blocking transformations**: Partially blocking transformations are often used to combine datasets. For that reason the input data (columns and rows) could have a different number from the transformation output. Partially blocking transformations are also known as asynchronous transformations because transformed data is copied into new buffers and they do not use the same buffers as the previous type. Some examples of this type of transformation are the **Merge Join**, **Term Lookup**, **Union All**, and others.

- **Blocking transformations**: Blocking transformations must read and process all input records before creating any output records. Blocking transformations are also known as asynchronous but this type have an even worse performance than partially blocking transformations, because they need all rows to apply the transformation, and for that reason should be avoided. A way to avoid them is by performing sorting and aggregation directly in the source when possible. As can be imagined, some examples of this type of transformation are the **Sort**, **Aggregate**, **Fuzzy lookup**, and others.

Getting ready

To get ready with this recipe, follow the given steps:

1. Open **SQL Server Data Tools (SSDT)**.

2. Open the existing solution located at `C:\SSIS\Ch15_Performance Boost in SSIS\Ch15_Performance Boost in SSIS.sln`.

How to do it...

We will look at the four important best practices that should be applied when you have too many columns in the pipeline and the data volume in source and destination is higher.

Remove unused columns from the pipeline

Removing unused columns can increase the pipeline performance. Although this can be achieved through setting the **RunInOptimzedMode** to *True*, a good practice is to remove the columns manually:

The unused columns can be identified through the SSIS event warning messages (available through the progress bar (from SSDT) or through SSIS logging created in the Legacy or Project Deployment Models) or with **Data Flow** column mapper directly in the Data Flow designer.

1. To identify the warning messages related to unsused columns in the pipeline, go to **Execution Results** and look up to the respective messages:

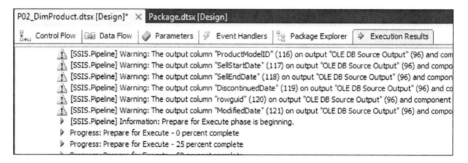

2. To identify the warning messages related to unsused columns through **data flow column mapper**, select an arrow that links two components, right-click and select **Resolve References** as shown in the following screenshot:

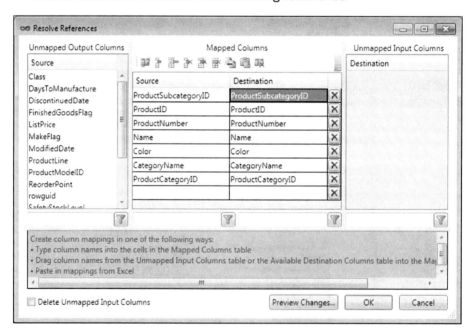

3. After identifying each unsused column, go to the preceding component (for example, a source component, a Derived Column, Copy Column, Data Conversion component, and so on) responsible for adding it to the pipeline and simply remove each column from it.

Avoid unnecessary sorting in the pipeline

The Sort transformation is one of the blocking components that should be avoided wherever possible. The Sort transformation forces the pipeline to "wait" for all the data and then sorts the respective dataset in the pipeline. The following example explains how to avoid using the Sort transformation in the pipeline. (Naturally there are several cases where this approach cannot be implemented, for example, when the source component cannot sort data or when data must be sorted during the pipeline to apply some business rules.)

1. In the **Solution Explorer**, locate the project **R03_Data Flow Best Practices in Transformations**.

2. Open the package **P01_SortTransform.dtsx**.

3. Open the Data Flow **DFT with Sort Transform** and execute it to see how Data Flow merges customer data using two Sort transformations.

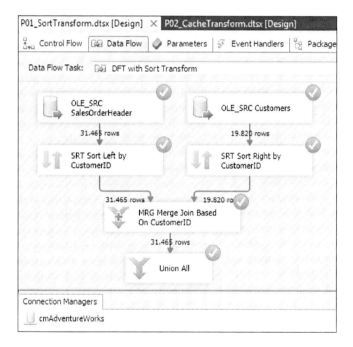

4. Copy and paste the existing Data Flow and rename it to **DFT without Sort Transform**.

5. Remove all the component from the new Data Flow except the two OLE DB Source components.

6. Right-click in the OLEDB Source component and select **Show Advanced Editor...**.

7. Go to the **Input and Output Properties** tab and in the **OLE DB Source Output** set the **IsSorted** property value to *True*. (You need to make sure that the input data is truly sorted though.)

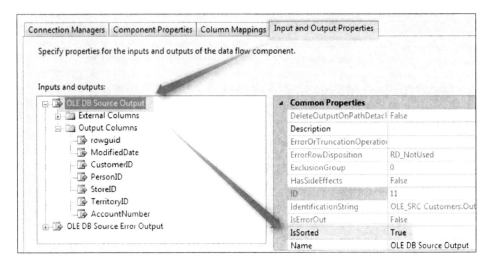

8. Set the **CustomerID** column with **SortKeyPosition** property value as *1*.

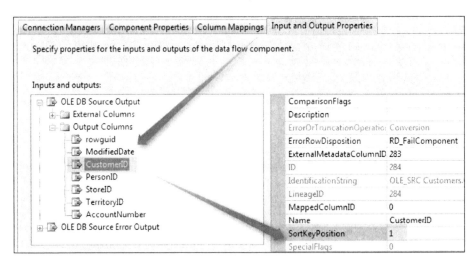

9. Execute the package and see how Data Flow merges customer data without the need to use Sort transformations as shown in the following screenshot

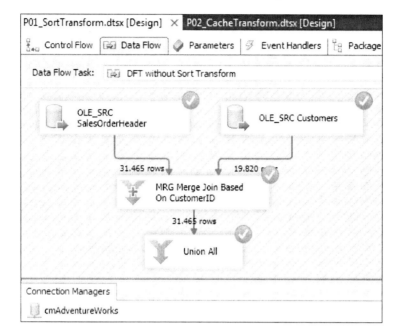

Lookup reference data

Minimize the size of the reference data in memory by entering a SELECT statement that looks up only the columns that are needed. This option performs better than selecting an entire table or view, which returns a large amount of unnecessary data. In some cases, a more complete and more thorough SELECT statement can be created to avoid the use of other lookups. (An example of a normalized table structure is **Product | Subcategory | category**.)

Make use of the Cache Transformation to store data in memory

Consider using the Cache Transformation to store a dataset in memory to be reused in several lookup components, instead of creating the dataset in memory repetitively. In the first step the cache will be created and then can be reused through the cache connection created.

1. Open the package **P02_CacheTransform**.
2. Open the empty Data Flow **DFT Populate DimProduct Cache**.
3. Add an **OLEDB Source** to the Data Flow and rename it to **OLE_SRC Read DimProduct data**.
4. Open the source component for editing.
5. Set the connection to the existing **cmPacktPub_SSISbook.**

6. Set the **Data acess mode** property to **SQL Command**.

7. Add the following statement to the **SQL Command text** property:

```
SELECT ProductSK, ProductID, ProductCategoryID
FROM DimProduct
```

8. Add a Cache Transformation to the Data Flow and rename it to **CACHE Inserts DimProduct data into cache**.

9. Link both the components and open the **Cache Transformation** for editing.

10. Create a new cache connection by clicking on the **New...** button. In the new pop-up menu, under the **columns** tab, set the **index position** to *ProductID*, which is the key that will be used in the several lookups in the Data Flows.

    Now that the cache is ready to be populated, it is just required to configure the existing or new Lookup transformations to point to this cache memory.

11. Open the Data Flow **DFT Populate FactInternerSales** and open the existing **Lookup Transformation** named **LKP For SubCategoryID**.

12. In the **General** tab, set the **Cache mode** property to *Full cache* and the **Connection type** to *Cache connection manager*.

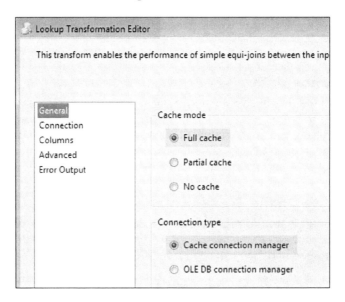

13. A final example would be the following, where lookup data is first populated into the memory and then reused in several Data Flows:

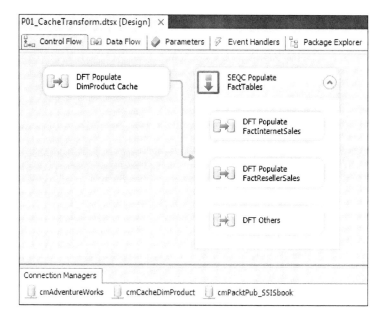

How it works...

The previous steps explain in detail some best practices that should be considered for transformations along the pipeline. Several transformations are associated with this transformation step, such as applying cleaning tasks and also business rules.

The most critical point is when blocking and partially blocking transformations are used. These transformations should be avoided if possible or at least reduced in the pipeline. Another critical point is the use of the lookup component when source and/or reference data volume is high.

There's more...

There are more suggestions in order to achieve the best performance under SSIS packages. One of these is described in this section and it is an example showing that SSIS is not always the best solution for a specific issue. Making use of TSQL statements can significantly improve performance.

Replace lookup by changing SQL statement at the source

When the reference dataset in a lookup component is very big (relative to the specific scenario), replacing the lookup by a condition split can make a huge improvement in the Data Flow. The logic inherent to this suggestion uses a LEFT JOIN SQL function to the reference data in the source component, then uses the condition split component to identify the match and no match cases based on whether the reference columns (from the LEFT JOIN SQL statement) are null or not null. Naturally this approach is only possible if the Data Flow source component uses a database as the source, a SQL statement can be applied, and both the datasets are in the same database (in a data warehousing scenario, this database can be a staging area that already integrates data from multiple and heterogeneous source systems).

Working with buffer size

SSIS processes data in the pipeline within memory buffers to efficiently load and manipulate datasets in memory. The main advantage of managing data in memory is that it is faster than storing data physically on the disk.

In most packages, changing the SSIS buffer properties is not required, because SSIS does a very good job optimizing it. But even so, it would be possible to tune the Data Flow performance manually to change the values of the SSIS buffer properties. The size of each buffer is determined at runtime and buffers will be created as required in order to process all the data.

The number of buffer created is dependent on how many rows fit into a buffer and the number of rows fitting into a buffer depends on defined data types and the length of each column. There are three internal parameters used to calculated the number of buffers:

- **Estimated Row Size:** This is the sum of the maximum sizes of all the columns from the incoming records
- **MinBufferSize**: This is an SSIS internal parameter, which cannot be changed; it sets the lower limit for the **DefaultBufferSize** property
- **MaxBufferSize**: This is an SSIS internal parameter, which cannot be changed; it sets the upper limit for the **DefaultBufferSize** property to, 100 MB

The two most important variables, and those that could be configured, are **DefaultBufferSize** and **DefaultBufferMaxRows**. They should be considered together.

- **DefaultBufferMaxRows**: This specifies a maximum number of rows that can be held in an individual buffer.
- **DefaultBufferSize**: This specifies the maximum size for an individual buffer in bytes

The **DefaultBufferSize** variable has a default value of 10 MB (10,485,760 bytes) and could grow to a maximum of 100 MB. The **DefaultBufferMaxRows** variable has the default value of 10,000 rows and could be increased up to the capacity of your available memory.

The main objective is to reduce the width of your rows in order to fit in as many rows as possible into each buffer. This means you must choose the correct data types and respective lengths and also reduce the number of columns if some are not needed in the pipeline.

How to do it...

To change the buffer configuration on each Data Flow, it is just required to open the respective Data Flow and both the buffer variables will be displayed in the properties as shown in the following screenhsot:

How it works...

SSIS calculates an **Estimated Row Size** per row, and then an **estimated buffer size** is calculated based on the estimated row size multiplied by the total number of records in the pipeline. Based on the total memory calculation, SSIS will create the respective buffers. If the size is smaller than the **DefaultMaxBufferSize** then just one buffer is created; if not, SSIS will create buffers until the total memory estimation is achieved. To improve the performance of the Data Flow, two variables referred to previously can be changed: **DefaultBufferSize** and **DefaultBufferMaxRows**. It's possible to increase both the variables but don't forget these variables are linked together. It's possible to increase the number of rows on each pipeline, but the buffer size should have available memory to store those rows and also the SSIS server must have the required memory for the buffers created.

Working with performance counters

Windows Performance Counter enables us to monitor in real-time multiple items that can measure the performance of the Data Flow engine. For example, you can watch the "Buffers spooled" counter to determine whether data buffers are being written to disk temporarily while a package is running. This swapping reduces performance and indicates that the computer has insufficient memory.

The performance counters are as follows:

- **BLOB bytes read**: The number of bytes of binary large object (BLOB) data that the Data Flow engine has read from all sources.

- **BLOB bytes written:** The number of bytes of BLOB data that the Data Flow engine has written to all destinations.

- **BLOB files in use**: The number of BLOB files that the Data Flow engine currently is using for spooling.

- **Buffer memory:** The amount of memory that is in use. This may include both physical and virtual memory. When this number is larger than the amount of physical memory, the Buffers Spooled count rises as an indication that memory swapping is increasing. Increased memory swapping slows performance of the Data Flow engine.

- **Buffers in use**: The number of buffer objects, of all types, that all Data Flow components and the Data Flow engine are currently using.

- **Buffers spooled**: The number of buffers currently written to the disk. If the Data Flow engine runs low on physical memory, buffers not currently used are written to disk and then reloaded when needed.

- **Flat buffer memory**: The total amount of memory, in bytes, that all flat buffers use. Flat buffers are blocks of memory that a component uses to store data.

- **Flat buffers in use**: The number of flat buffers that the Data Flow engine uses. All flat buffers are private buffers.

- **Private buffer memory**: The total amount of memory used by all private buffers. A buffer is not private if the Data Flow engine creates it to support Data Flow. A private buffer is a buffer that a transformation uses for temporary work only. For example, the Aggregation transformation uses private buffers to do its work.

- **Private buffers in use**: The number of buffers that transformations use.

- **Rows read**: The number of rows that a source produces. The number does not include rows read from reference tables by the Lookup transformation.

- **Rows written**: The number of rows offered to a destination. The number does not reflect rows written to the destination data store.

More information is available at `http://msdn.microsoft.com/en-us/library/ms137622.aspx`.

How to do it...

1. Open **Windows Performance Monitor** through the control panel or by adding the `perfmon` statement in the **Run** start menu.

2. Select **Performance Monitor** under the **Monitoring Tools** folder.

3. Create a new **Data Collector Set**.

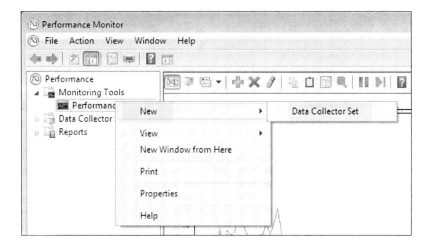

4. Add a name to the collector and click on the **Next** button:

5. Select the physical location for the log data and press the **Next** button:

6. Select the user that will be monitoring the performance log and start collecting the performance information about SSIS packages:

7. The performance monitoring is now collecting data but it is necessary to add the SSIS counters that will display the required performance information. Click on the add button as shown in the following screenshot:

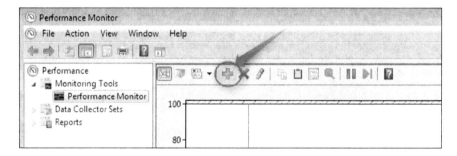

8. Select the SSIS server and then search for the SSIS counters.

9. Select **SSIS Pipeline 11.0** and click on the **Add >>** button as shown in the following screenshot to add the counters to Performance Monitoring:

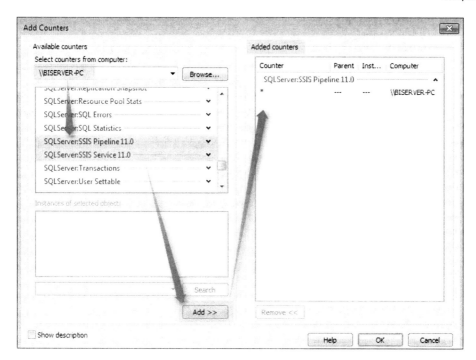

10. Repeat the previous step for **SSIS Service 11.0** and click on the **OK** button:

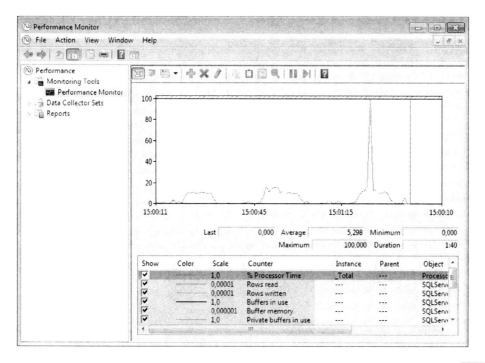

How it works...

The previous steps explain how Windows Performance Monitor could be used to monitor the performance of an SSIS package. The reality is that in almost cases SSIS developers don't use this tool too much, just in cases where a bottleneck persists. But it is a very good practice to follow the performance counters in the Windows Performance Monitor even if the package apparently works fine.

Index

Symbols

Thank you for buying
Microsoft SQL Server 2012 Integration Services:
An Expert Cookbook

About Packt Publishing

Packt, pronounced 'packed', published its first book "*Mastering phpMyAdmin for Effective MySQL Management*" in April 2004 and subsequently continued to specialize in publishing highly focused books on specific technologies and solutions.

Our books and publications share the experiences of your fellow IT professionals in adapting and customizing today's systems, applications, and frameworks. Our solution-based books give you the knowledge and power to customize the software and technologies you're using to get the job done. Packt books are more specific and less general than the IT books you have seen in the past. Our unique business model allows us to bring you more focused information, giving you more of what you need to know, and less of what you don't.

Packt is a modern, yet unique publishing company, which focuses on producing quality, cutting-edge books for communities of developers, administrators, and newbies alike. For more information, please visit our website: www.PacktPub.com.

About Packt Enterprise

In 2010, Packt launched two new brands, Packt Enterprise and Packt Open Source, in order to continue its focus on specialization. This book is part of the Packt Enterprise brand, home to books published on enterprise software – software created by major vendors, including (but not limited to) IBM, Microsoft and Oracle, often for use in other corporations. Its titles will offer information relevant to a range of users of this software, including administrators, developers, architects, and end users.

Writing for Packt

We welcome all inquiries from people who are interested in authoring. Book proposals should be sent to author@packtpub.com. If your book idea is still at an early stage and you would like to discuss it first before writing a formal book proposal, contact us; one of our commissioning editors will get in touch with you.

We're not just looking for published authors; if you have strong technical skills but no writing experience, our experienced editors can help you develop a writing career, or simply get some additional reward for your expertise.

Microsoft SQL Server 2008 R2 Administration Cookbook

ISBN: 978-1-84968-144-5   Paperback: 468 pages

Over 70 practical recipes for administering a
high-preformance SQL Server 2008 R2 system

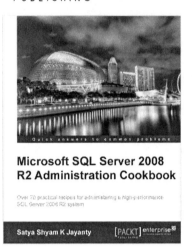

**Microsoft SQL Server 2008
R2 Administration Cookbook**

Over 70 practical recipes for administering a high-performance
SQL Server 2008 R2 system

Satya Shyam K Jayanty

1. Provides Advanced Administration techniques for
    SQL Server 2008 R2 as a book or eBook

2. Covers the essential Manageability,
    Programmability, and Security features

3. Emphasizes important High Availability features
    and implementation

4. Explains how to maintain and manage the SQL
    Server data platform effectively

Microsoft SQL Server 2008 R2 Master Data Services

ISBN: 978-1-84968-050-9   Paperback: 360 pages

Manage and maintain your organization 's master data
effectively with Microsoft SQL Server 2008 R2 Master
Data Services

**Microsoft SQL Server 2008 R2
Master Data Services**

Manage and maintain your organization's master data effectively
with Microsoft SQL Server 2008 R2 Master Data Services

Foreword by Ian Ahern, CEO of Profisee

Jeremy Kashel
Tim Kent   Martyn Bullerwell

1. Gain a comprehensive guide to Microsoft SQL
    Server R2 Master Data Services (MDS) with this
    book and eBook

2. Explains the background to the practice of
    Master Data Management and how it can help
    organizations

3. Introduces Master Data Services, and provides a
    step-by-step installation guide

4. Covers all features of Master Data Services,
    including hierarchy management, importing/
    exporting data, the MDS API, and business rules

Please check **www.PacktPub.com** for information on our titles

MDX with Microsoft SQL Server 2008 R2 Analysis Services: Cookbook

80 recipes for enriching your Business intelligence solutions with high-performance MDX calculations and flexible MDX queries

Tomislav Piasevoli

[PACKT] enterprise

MDX with Microsoft SQL Server 2008 R2 Analysis Services Cookbook

ISBN: 978-1-84968-130-8   Paperback: 480 pages

80 recipes for enriching your Business intelligence solutions with high-performance MDX calculation and flexible MDX queries

1. Enrich your BI solutions by implementing best practice MDX calculations

2. Master a wide range of time-related, context-aware, and business-related calculations

3. Enhance your solutions by combining MDX with utility dimensions

4. Become skilled in making reports concise

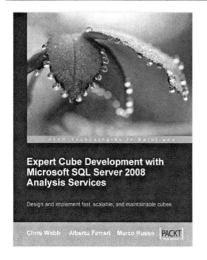

Expert Cube Development with Microsoft SQL Server 2008 Analysis Services

Design and implement fast, scalable, and maintainable cubes

Chris Webb   Alberto Ferrari   Marco Russo   PACKT

Expert Cube Development with Microsoft SQL Server 2008 Analysis Services

ISBN: 978-1-847197-22-1   Paperback: 360 pages

Design and implement fast scalable, and maintainable cubes

1. A real-world guide to designing cubes with Analysis Services 2008

2. Model dimensions and measure groups in BI Development Studio

3. Implement security, drill-through, and MDX calculations

4. Learn how to deploy, monitor, and performance-tune your cube

5. Filled with best practices and useful hints and tips

Please check **www.PacktPub.com** for information on our titles

CPSIA information can be obtained at www.ICGtesting.com
Printed in the USA
LVOW122237290512

283748LV00001B/1/P

9 781849 685245